STAR WISDOM & RUDOLF STEINER

STAR WISDOM & RUDOLF STEINER

A Life Seen through the Oracle of the Solar Cross

DAVID TRESEMER

WITH ROBERT SCHIAPPACASSE

STEINERBOOKS

2007

SteinerBooks
www.steinerbooks.org
AN IMPRINT OF ANTHROPOSOPHIC PRESS, INC.
610 MAIN STREET, SUITE I
GREAT BARRINGTON, MA, 01230

COVER AND BOOK DESIGN: WILLIAM (JENS) JENSEN

LIBRARY OF CONGRESS CATALOGING-IN-PUBLICATION DATA

Tresemer, David Ward.
  Star wisdom and Rudolf Steiner : a life seen through the oracle of the
solar cross / David Tresemer with Robert Schiappacasse.
    p. cm.
  Includes bibliographical references (p. 352).
  ISBN-13: 978-0-88010-574-3
  ISBN-10: 0-88010-574-7
  1. Steiner, Rudolf, 1861–1925. 2. Anthroposophists—Biography.
3. Astrosophy. I. Schiappacasse, Robert. II. Title.

BP595.S894T74 2006
299'.935092—dc^{22}
[B]

                                                    2006033123

CONTENTS

THE STORY OF THIS BOOK

FOR MANY YEARS, a small group of astrosophers—from *astro* (star) and *Sophia* (wisdom)—has worked to explore how heaven comes to earth, and how the earth responds. This "StarFire Research Group" includes Robert Powell, co-founder of the Sophia Foundation of North America and author of several books on this topic, Brian Gray at Rudolf Steiner College in Fair Oaks, California, William Bento at Gradalis Institute, Robert Schiappacasse at Sunbridge College, and myself. We have met annually for many years, sometimes to make presentations to the public, and always to spend some days together talking about the star research that we have pursued in the previous year. We continue to rely on the earlier work of Willi Sucher and Elizabeth Vreede, both inspired by the many hints given by Rudolf Steiner, whom Vreede knew personally.

For some of those years, Bento, Schiappacasse, and I met weekly to discuss star matters, focusing on the intersection of the comets Hyakutake and Hale-Bopp. They had passed through the same portion of the sky on the same day, April 11, one year apart, their two trajectories making a perfect cross. An astonishing coincidence? What was at that intersection point? The star Algol, the Eye of Medusa, reputed since ancient times as the most malefic of the stars. From our conversations about this event arose the book *Signs in the Heavens: A Message for Our Time.**

In subsequent meetings we found ourselves drawn to test our ideas on the life of Rudolf Steiner. With Brian Gray, who has been on the faculty of Rudolf Steiner College for many years, we gave two lectures at a large conference at Rudolf Steiner College in Fair Oaks, California, in June 2000. Since that time, we have discussed this material repeatedly, and it is now in preparation as a book tentatively titled *Life Star, Death Star, and the Life of an Initiate.* That approach will explore the life of Rudolf Steiner from a different point of view than the present study. Other works, such as a comprehensive astro-biography by Brian Gray, are in preparation.

---

* Please see the reference section at the end of the book for bibliographic information.

The present book introduces the Oracle of the Solar Cross and the techniques of interpretation that have grown around this resource, then applies these techniques to the six major Solar Cross Images for Rudolf Steiner.

The conversations at the core of our understanding of these Images and resonant moments in Steiner's life have occurred over the last several years, primarily between Robert Schiappacasse and myself—either sitting at lunch together, surrounded by charts and books, animatedly discussing world politics and star positions between pad thai and mint tea, or talking long-distance between Tasmania and Boulder. We look forward to these conversations. Something occurs in a good conversation where I realize that I as an individual am present and awake, and, at the same time, speaking insights that I didn't know were in me. I ride high on spiritual fire forming into ideas right before my eyes; brilliant ideas flash, then effervesce and disappear—and later wonder where it had all come from. Some insights remain as precious pearls that continue, with hard work, to grow. In the end, we both realize that we have received gifts of luminous revelations, and feel a deep gratitude for the blessing of true conversation.

As I researched and wrote this book, Robert not only translated many German passages, which has been essential in researching fine points of Steiner's biography, but through his continued participation in our conversations has created light-filled gifts from realms beyond the normal everyday.

Others, including William Bento, Brian Gray, Ginny Jordan, Robert Powell, Claudia McLaren-Lainson, Merlyn Querido, and, most especially, Lila Tresemer, have looked at the manuscript at various stages and to them, my deepest thanks. I appreciate also my editor, Sarah Gallogly, who worked this manuscript with expertise, helping me find better ways to express the intricate interface between mythos and real lives.

David Tresemer
StarHouse, Boulder, Colorado

PART I
PREPARING TO
USE STAR WISDOM

1. THE IMAGINATION OF A LIFE

As DEATH DREW near, the great painter Raphael asked that his last painting be placed at the head of his bed. It was the scene of the Transfiguration on which he had worked for many months. Art historians consider that perhaps Raphael's students under his supervision painted the lower scenes, where the disciples of Christ Jesus try to cure a mad boy, while the crowd surges around the boy and those trying to contain him in the darkness of the earthly realm. Raphael himself completed the upper portion, where Christ Jesus reveals his true nature as a being of intense light, still in human form but buoyed up into the air by his spirit nature. Clouds float behind, so white in their brilliance that they stun the eyes. Moses and Elijah attend him on either side, also floating. The three disciples who climbed up Mount Tabor with him cower, face down, before this revelation of searing light. Christianity calls this event the Transfiguration.

Raphael wished to permeate his own passage into spirit realms with this image of Christ-light as forerunner and guide, leading him out of the physical realm of this earth into heavenly realms, where he would discover or rediscover his essential nature of light and air, and would meet others who had gone before. He used an Image that he himself had imagined and manifested to propel him into realization of his own spirit.

We are each meant to discover the connection from our individual soul to spiritual realities not encompassed by the normal senses, requiring *supersensible* perception. Images can offer powerful assistance. When gazing upon the work of the great painters—the Sistine Chapel or Monet's water lilies or even Jackson Pollock's paint dribbles—we can feel something call to us from an undeveloped side of our own sensory apparatus. When hearing the poets and traveling with them into their image worlds, or standing before a Brancusi sculpture, or participating in fine live theater—all these can take us outside of our mundane concerns. Sometimes this feels like lifting up and out, and sometimes like penetrating deeper in. We stretch beyond the hegemony of our day-surviving personality into a meeting with our own greater nature. The art work becomes a springboard for our odyssey into our personal image world, where we, like Raphael, craft the images that speak most strongly to what comes from our inside to our outside as guidance and inspiration.

In our time, images are ubiquitous and rampant. We could quote statistics about how many images an average human being sees in a day, or how many images of violence a child sees before age sixteen. You may have seen such studies. You know it's a large number. The point is, *you are overwhelmed daily with other people's images.* Therein lies a problem. Knowing other people's images may assist us in establishing relationships with those people. That is a fine goal. However, we have forgotten about our own imagination, the creation of our own images. What was meant to be a balance between self-created imaginations and the enjoyment of others' imaginations has become seriously lopsided. There is no longer any balance. People are so overwhelmed with others' images that they reel, drunk with overconsumption.

The soul requires balanced nutrition. When experts refer to a "glut" of images, they are using a word that relates to consumption and overconsumption. We have become gluttons, even if unwilling gluttons, of images. The energetic body becomes fat while the soul starves. We are meant to feed the soul with our own realizations of its gifts. The personality and the soul feed each other, constantly.

Consider the possibility of following Raphael's example and creating your own images—images that may be there for your death, but also much sooner, images that will meet your soul at all the steps and major turning points of your life. In this study we will train the imagination, beginning from a seed Image and finding a way to make this seed grow in each of us. We will use the biography of Rudolf Steiner as a guide. By the end you will know more about Rudolf Steiner, more about Star Wisdom, more about life cycles in relation to the stars, and, most importantly, more about the tool of imagination that can assist you to become more intimate with your own soul life.

Forces are moving to alienate you from your own soul life. This approach will help you find it again.

2. RUDOLF STEINER AS OUR GUIDE

I PROPOSE A TECHNIQUE to understand the life of a human being in terms of the Images that were present at the person's birth, and at the person's death. These form the bookends of a life. When the birth time is known, I can add the Image that came at the person's conception. A thorough study of an individual can then become a gateway to the stars.

We will explore this with the example of Rudolf Steiner, the Austrian philosopher who lived from 1861 to 1925.

Here is a man of astonishing creativity and output who lectured to tens of thousands of people and whose ideas continue to affect our lives. He wrote forty-two books; over six thousand lectures have been transcribed. Most people know him best through Waldorf schools, which he founded, and for which he developed the pedagogy, meaning the theory of child development and the kind of education that best meets the needs of the child. Today there are over nine hundred of these schools worldwide.

Steiner also inspired the practice of biodynamic farming, which like Waldorf education has spread worldwide and is practiced in nearly every country. Though sometimes lumped together with organic farming, biodynamics takes a very different approach. Organic farming emphasizes the life of the soil, and rightly criticizes the dangerous chemicals used by modern agriculture. Organic farmers "feed the soil" instead with "natural" substances such as composted animal manures, bat guano (droppings of bats accumulated over centuries in bat caves), bacterial stews, and extracts from noxious flowers used against insect pests. A healthy soil replete with quadrillions of diverse microorganisms makes for robust and flavorful plants.

Biodynamics also seeks to feed the soil, but not by adding alternative chemicals. Biodynamics seeks to feed the spirit of the soil by spraying small quantities of specially prepared substances that have been stirred into water in a particular way, stirring vigorously one way until a vortex is created, then immediately changing direction and stirring the other way. This collapses the vortices one upon the other, and the substance is taken up into the water. To some the activities of biodynamics sound like hocus-pocus, yet the long-term studies of yield, flavor, and financial return give biodynamics high marks in comparison to other methods. Farmers have been forced to change the way they think about the soil and the earth, and to consider how spirit works into such mundane matters as growing food. How can a fraction of an ounce of special substance, no matter how special, stirred into water and then flicked out onto the soil, have any effect on an acre of vegetables? Steiner emphasized communication with the elemental spirits that make things grow and pioneered a way of thinking that today we might call homeopathy. Indeed, he warned about the effects of small quantities of substances, as in a few parts per million (ppm). Scoffed at then, ppm and ppb (parts per billion) are widely accepted by science today, both as positive influences in nutrition and as negative influences with pollutants.

Steiner also developed a new form of movement called eurythmy, a discipline of dance, gesture, movement, or, as he termed it, Greek temple dancing transformed for the modern age. He initiated a new form of medicine, which has come to be called anthroposophical medicine, after the Anthroposophical Society, which Steiner began under the tutelage of a divine being named Anthroposophia, from the Greek words for potential human being (*anthropos*) and the feminine principle of divine wisdom (*Sophia*). Steiner also founded a new approach to religious observation, the Christian Community, with its own liturgy and practices. He wrote four long "mystery" dramas, relating to the mystery traditions and mystery schools of ancient cultures brought into the present. The ancient mysteries confronted such topics as the purpose of life, the origin of consciousness, and the riddle of death. Though derived from this tradition, the "mystery novel" took a superficial track. Each of Steiner's mystery plays required eight hours to perform. They covered topics of reincarnation, magic, mysticism, destiny, and the dangerous road of self-development within the context of human lives, people we get to know and love as we follow them from one drama to the next.

To do all this and more, Steiner wrote books and delivered hundreds of lectures, traveling to many countries to share his wisdom. As Steiner's way of speaking and writing can be challenging, a host of books about Steiner have also appeared to explain his work.

We sometimes see Steiner referred to as "an initiate," meaning that he was extraordinarily developed in his faculties and in his power of soul. Great waves of energy and knowledge came through his person. Some call this stage of human development "enlightenment." Others differentiate between seven stages of initiation.[1] When we use the term we are not referring to the many "rites of initiation" that may accompany entry into special clubs or positions, ranging from the Lions Club to a public office in the government. By initiate, we mean someone who has realized his or her soul in its full potential through deeds on the earth.

A Brief Timeline of Steiner's Life

Steiner was born on February 25, 1861, in the village of Kraljevic, then part of the Austro-Hungarian Empire, in present-day Croatia.[2] His father was employed by the local railroad company. Steiner began as a serious young man who pursued his studies diligently. As a youngster, he thirsted for knowledge. He bought one of Kant's books, actually tearing the book into pieces and smuggling small parts of it into the elementary school, so that he could set it inside a textbook and thus appear to read the lesson for the day as he forged through Kant.

The family moved from the country to the city. In 1872 Steiner entered a Gymnasium just outside of Vienna, where he received the fine education that central Europe was known for offering at that time. After graduating in 1879, he enrolled in the Technische Hochschule (polytechnic college) in Vienna, where he studied natural sciences, mathematics, and chemistry. He was one of the few science students to study with the German language and literature professor Karl Julius Schröer. Steiner excelled in all the sciences and read widely in philosophy. One biographer makes the poignant observation: "If he had been born in America, he might well have become another Edison rather than a 'spiritual teacher.' "[3]

Just before his twenty-first year, he met Felix Koguzki, an herb gatherer who brought his product to town on the same train that Steiner rode to school daily. Koguzki had many philosophical insights to share from his experiences, and introduced Steiner to a mysterious man who, on Steiner's twenty-first birthday, gave him a powerful inspiration, energetically and in an epigram. Steiner had asked this man, whom he later called the Master, "How do I work constructively with the bull of public opinion and the dragon of scientific method that denies anything that cannot be perceived with the senses?" The Master replied, "Take the bull by the horns and put on the dragon skin to understand it from the inside." Steiner got inside the dragon skin of the natural sciences in his studies, and later was able to take the bull by the horns.

Schröer recommended the young Steiner as a collaborating editor of Goethe's scientific works under the supervision of Joseph Kürschner, who was editing the complete works. Johann Wolfgang von Goethe was the most prominent writer, statesman, dramatist, and scientist of the previous century, the center of the culture of middle Europe. The others working on Goethe's papers were humanists, not scientists. They did not understand Goethe's writings on science, from which Steiner teased very important insights into the life processes in nature within plants, animals, and human beings. Steiner began this work in 1883, at the age of twenty-two, eventually moving in 1890 to Weimar to work in the Goethe-Schiller Archive.

Steiner received a doctorate in 1891 from the University of Rostock in northern Germany; his thesis was later published as *Truth and Science*. His foundation work on philosophy—*The Philosophy of Freedom*, sometimes titled *The Philosophy of Spiritual Activity*, and recently retitled *Intuitive Thinking as a Spiritual Path*[4]—was published in November 1893. His work began to wind down at the Goethe-Schiller Archive, and he entertained for two years the possibility of taking on the editing of the Nietzsche papers, but this did not work out. In 1897, he moved to Berlin with Anna Eunicke, for whose children he had acted as tutor since 1892. They married in 1899.

A hinge point took place in Steiner's life in the final days of the old century, on or about December 2, 1899, wherein a meeting took place between Steiner and what he would later call the Greater Guardian of the Threshold—the threshold that separates everyday consciousness from spirit realms.

In 1888 he had discovered theosophy through the writings of Helena Petrovna Blavatsky, with titles such as *Isis Unveiled* and *The Secret Doctrine*. He gave his first talk to the Theosophical Society on September 29, 1900, the first time he spoke in public about his "spiritual researches." In a talk in November of 1900, Marie von Sivers was in the audience, who after the death of Anna Eunicke (1909) would become his wife (1914), and before that supported him financially and in other ways as he continued to give lectures and to publish.

He rose in the ranks of theosophy, becoming the Secretary of the Theosophical Society in Germany in 1902. Then, rather than speak from Blavatsky's books, Steiner insisted on speaking only from his own experience. The Theosophical Society at first accepted this, but later relations became strained. Steiner took his students in a new direction, to "anthroposophy," the wisdom of the possible human being, more literally translated the human-being-becoming-in-wisdom. Steiner and his students indicated this new direction in the Munich Congress in the summer of 1907, decorating the large hall with the artistic outpourings of those inspired to work with Steiner. In addition to the usual lectures on various topics, there was art and theater and music. The split with the Theosophical Society began then, and was complete in a few years. The Anthroposophical Society was born.

From there Steiner built a large movement that is very active today in many countries. He lectured widely on many topics and wrote plays that demonstrated how spiritual truths impact people's lives. These four mystery plays, one written each year from 1910 to 1913, provoked the most varied reactions, from complete adoration to complete rejection. They cannot be evaluated as theater. Their length of eight hours each, their stilted style, and the complexity of their content make them encyclopedias for researchers of esotericism rather than entertainment for theatergoers.

Steiner set the center of the Anthroposophical Society at Dornach, Switzerland, near Basel. Steiner named the first building constructed there the Goetheanum, after his spiritual mentor. The foundation stone of the building was laid on September 20, 1913. Even through World War I, with large artillery rumbling in the distance, Steiner supervised artisans from many countries, even countries at war with one another, as they constructed this great building from the woods of every continent. People from many countries simply showed up to help and were drawn into this great project of sacred architecture.[5] On the night of December 31, 1922, a fire started in the Goetheanum, perhaps by arson, and it burned to the ground. A newer version was constructed that still stands today. A year later, in a makeshift amphitheater, Steiner delivered a new Foundation Stone made not of mineral substance but of soul substance to knit together those who had come to anthroposophy.

Toward the end of Steiner's life, he delivered four to five lectures each day to different groups: to medical professionals on the new medicine, to priests in the new Christian Community, to actors and artists, to the workmen on the buildings, to the members of the Anthroposophical Society, and to those accepted for enrollment into the First Spiritual Class that he set up to hear his advanced teachings.

He passed over the threshold into spiritual worlds on March 30, 1925. Some say that this was too soon, that he should have lived longer. They suspected foul play. Certainly he left many groups and initiatives in their infancy, thirsting for more guidance from this amazing human being. So many things seemed begun but not fully developed.

We will learn more about Steiner's life in the coming study via vignettes related to important star events. I intend this brief chronology only as a frame within which we can understand those vignettes. Our main sources are biographies about him by those who worked closely with him, especially the biographies by Christoph Lindenberg and by Guenther Wachsmuth, Steiner's personal secretary. We also cite Friedrich Rittelmeyer (the first head priest in the Christian Community), Andrei Belyi, and others.[6]

Even with all this wonderful information, sometimes including daily registers of the deeds of Steiner's life, we often lack insight into his personal life: what he felt, what he struggled with, what took place in his heart. We would greatly appreciate the insights of a George Eliot or a Barbara Kingsolver into his inner world. To find the feeling realm of Steiner's life, we have to infer from what Steiner said in public to audiences of various sizes, from a few dozen to a thousand or more. We have to read between the lines of his autobiography and the letters that he penned to old friends. We will do this, and recognize that we would greatly benefit from knowing the more intimate unrecorded parts of Steiner's life. I say this because the technique of the Oracle of the Solar Cross can be more powerful in a person's life when the feelings are known.

The vignettes that follow are chosen in a unique way, not by my evaluation of what was important in Steiner's life, and not by a chronological plodding from one happening to the next, but rather by celestial events. We will seek in the heavens for signs about where to look in the life, and search through the doorways that are opened. Thus heaven and earth working together will reveal the major aspects of Rudolf Steiner's life.

ANTHROPOSOPHICAL CONCEPTS THAT WE WILL NEED

From Rudolf Steiner's anthroposophy, we will need certain concepts to understand this conversation between heaven and earth.

The Meaning of Anthroposphy

Let us begin with "anthroposophy," a term whose parts mean wisdom, indeed the feminine wisdom (from *Sophia*), of the possible human being (*anthropos*). More important, Steiner identified a spiritual being with the name Anthroposophia, that is, one who oversees the development of human beings into wisdom. Sometimes a translation will give this as "wisdom of Man," which is always meant to include both genders. It also refers to the vital role of *manas*, or imaginative thinking, in our development. Usually I will change Man to "human being" to avoid confusion.

Angels

Some years ago, I gave a talk in Crete wherein I spoke about spiritual beings responsible for various aspects of creation. A psychologist with whom I was staying asked afterward, "'Beings?!' What is all this talk about beings?!" She understood the supernatural entirely in terms of disturbances of the psychic structures of the human being—the only "being" she was sure about—projected outward into the world. In graduate school, ideas about other kinds of "beings" had been labeled superstitions and nearly completely drummed out of me. Nonetheless, urged on by friends, I had accepted as a hypothesis to test in my own experience the notion of divine beings of many types and kinds interpenetrating all existence, creating and sustaining, working behind and through what we call the "laws of nature." Having tested that hypothesis, I now accept these influences as fact. Of course, everyone must test such ideas for him- or herself. Let these thoughts then be guides of where to look, and not new dogmas.

Anthroposophy recognizes angels in nine ranks, with many qualitative differences between them. Those closest to humanity are named the angels—in which rank each of us has a personal angel. With the archangels, or spirits of fire, and archai, or spirits of time, angels constitute the third hierarchy. The word "hierarchy" has gotten a bad reputation. It originally meant sacred (*hier*) beginnings (*arche*), or the beings who go back closer and closer to the origins of creation, and care for what has come after. Its bad reputation comes from those who misuse their power.

The second hierarchy has a home in the sphere of the Sun, hence its members are Sun-Beings. They include exusiae (or elohim), or the spirits of form and creation of form; dynamoi, or the spirits of movement; and kyriotetes, or spirits of wisdom.

The first hierarchy of very powerful spirits includes the thrones or spirits of will, cherubim or spirits of harmony, and seraphim or spirits of love.

For this study we will not need to differentiate between these nine different kinds of "beings," yet it's helpful to know that some people can perceive the different qualities and kinds of beings working to hold this creation together and make it function. Perception of supersensible realities becomes helpful in understanding how creation occurred and continues to occur, and your own part in it. You can learn more about these divine beings through reading in anthroposophy and through personal inquiry.

Retarding Spirits

> Spirits who among us mingle,
> And who good and evil acts,
> Evil thoughts, suggest and whisper.[7]

Unfortunately, all is not rosy in heaven, as some spirits have regressed. Anthroposophy recommends very highly that one become familiar with the retarding spirits and how they insinuate themselves into one's thoughts, feelings, and actions. There are two major groups, under the supervision of what we call here the Illusionist and the Hardener, the beings often named by anthroposophy as Lucifer and Ahriman. We have renamed them so that people will understand their function more readily.

In the word illusion, *il* indicates a negative, and *-lusion*, from *ludera*, means "play," so the word means "bad play" or "foul play." The Illusionist takes us down false paths and frustrates our desire to see the truth of things. Given voice in a play by Pedro Calderón de la Barca, the Illusionist gloats behind the human scientist, Cyprian:

> Though thou givest
> All thy thoughts to the research,
> Cyprian, thou must ever miss it,
> Since I'll hide it from thy mind.[8]

The Illusionist is one who, using trickery and deception, likes to play with our thoughts, with our fantasies, by coaxing us up and out into floating realms of imaginations that are divorced from reality. Once out too far on too thin a branch, a branch made of inflated concepts and deceptions, we fall. The Illusionist laughs and mocks. We may for a moment feel consternation, and the betrayal of this alluring spirit. Then, realizing that we chose the deception, we feel self-blame. Most often the painful learning doesn't hold. The siren's song of temptation is so dreamy that, still in the thrall of enchantment, we ignore our injuries and begin to climb out on another limb, following yet again the Illusionist's promise to give us all that we desire. Because of the sacrifice of Christ through Jesus, now the Illusionist uses the tools of deception in service of divinity, rather than against it. Though the Illusionist may lure us out onto thin limbs of the tree of life, through service to humanity each of us becomes acquainted with the consequences of our actions over and over again. From this we mature and meet the Illusionist as mentor.

The word Hardener derives from a Greek word beginning with the cross- or X-shaped "chi," which has a harsh, throaty "k" sound—and indeed this word gives us a hard and heavy cross to bear. "Hardener" also has the same proto-Indo-European root as "cancer," which is a kind of hardening, and the same root as the suffix -cracy, meaning power, as in theocracy or plutocracy. In the name "Hardener," we find a sense of power and rigidification. The Hardener connives that humans will find truth only in material realities, so that they will deny the existence of spirit or meaning. The theory and application of neo-Darwinism gives a good example. Life and human beings are conceived as the chance outcomes of random and therefore meaningless events in a context of vicious and amoral competition for scarce resources. In a world of scarce resources, people fear for survival. Fear, struggle, and scarcity typify the Hardener's world.

The Illusionist tends toward warmth, moisture, elevation, and sweetness. Its gift is the empathy and aesthetic sensitivity that a poet would find useful. From this spiritual being, we have received the ability to think, to perceive that we perceive, to say, "I AM." This Prometheus has brought us the fire of mind—but too much influence of the Illusionist can bring the mists of deception.

The Hardener tends toward cold, dryness, heaviness and bitterness. A scientist would align with the Hardener, who fosters clear practical thinking. From the Hardener we receive the ability to stand and act in physical matter on the earth. Too much of the Hardener cultivates the negative qualities of cold rigidity, lack of feeling, and ruthlessness.

These two characters work together often. It's a real Mutt and Jeff team, and we can laugh at the contrast until we feel their grip on our lives. We can perceive the activity of the Hardener behind many wrong turns and many rigid beliefs in life. We can sometimes distinguish between them, but practically speaking they work together. For example, fear of delusion causes people to reject all non-sensory experience and fall into the grip of the Hardener. Those who reject materialism too strongly can often float into saccharine realms of New Age superstition, the trap of the Illusionist.

One can further imagine the Hardener and his servants as archangels who ceased to evolve and fell behind in their development on Old Sun, and the Illusionist and his servants as angels who fell behind on Old Moon. These are names of periods of world existence that preceded our Earth stage long, long ago.

Do these spiritual beings—the servants of the Hardener and Illusionist—actually exist? Are they more than a helpful way to organize one's confused thoughts? One can only become more attentive to one's experience in the world to see if one can notice their effects.

How do we deal with these two? I have a friend who makes seashell jewelry. She collects large numbers of a particular tiny shell on the beach. They look dun and boring, coated with hardened sea-bottom muck. She knows that beneath the brownness there lurks a shimmering, gem-like green-blue. To reveal that beauty, she puts the shells in water to which she adds a few drops of hydrochloric acid. Too little acid and the brown stubbornly adheres. Too much acid and the shell itself is dissolved. She has to watch carefully for progress, to make sure she doesn't dissolve too much. In this way, we have to work with the Illusionist and the Hardener. When I read a critique of Steiner, I have to ask how strong the acid is. Is it not strong enough to dissolve the vague and fuzzy feelings of adoration that obscure the truth? Is it too strong, destroying what I know to be the virtues of the man and the teaching? Can we cut through just enough of the projections to get to some truths?

Energy Bodies

The physical body has several sheaths of energy interpenetrating it and extending from it. We begin with the physical body itself, the substance that you can pinch.

The sensation of that pinch is registered by the etheric body, known also as the vital body or life-body. The etheric body organizes the energy of life-force that animates the physical substance of our material body. It governs the senses, sensation, and memory. The etheric body desires to fill the spaces we enter with its sensing. When overlooking the Grand Canyon, for example, we can feel its pull outward, trying to fill these spaces and giving us the feeling of falling into them.

The astral body, the body from starry worlds, extends outward from the physical body by eighteen inches in most people, what they call their "personal space," and much further in a few. It governs the soul functions of thinking, feeling, and willing. It gives meaning to the sensations reported from the senses and to memory traces stored in the etheric body. The pinch of the physical body becomes sensation in the etheric body, and that sensation is given meaning in the astral body. All enthusiasm, music, and geometry, all tenderness and compassion, dwell in the astral body. The higher or more refined astral body gives a home to the soul. The soul and astral body together leave the physical body at sleep to travel into other realms. The astral body forgets most of its experiences upon waking. When people speak of developing the heart, they mean the whole astral body, the body of love and compassion, made into action of the vital body moving the physical substance.

Crowning these sheaths is the soul, the "I AM," the sense of oneself as individuality, the spark of spirit that matures from lifetime to lifetime, the essence of what I call "myself."[9]

To review, the physical structure for the senses exists in the physical body, for example, actual nerve fibers. They are enlivened by the etheric body—sensory data flows through those pathways. The sensations are then given meaning by and within the astral body. The soul interpenetrates these bodies, giving overall direction and acting into the world through these sheaths. The personal angel, vanguard of the unseen realms, stands behind and lends support.

Cravings exist in the etheric body. Sometimes these are best observed in another person because the etheric body is not a wordy body and has little self-awareness. The craving of a pregnant woman for strawberries or ice cream shows the power of the etheric body. Often it doesn't register in the astral body, and weeks later she may deny that her night of craving for strawberries even happened. So too we have impulses and addictions coming from the etheric body that we don't recall.

To feel a simple example of the etheric body, close your eyes and touch your nose. You know where your parts are through your etheric sensing. It's amazing how the etheric body can find a light switch in a darkened room.

Marcel Proust found a smell that reminded him of his father's leather jacket. That smell was stored in the etheric body and reactivated there. The thousands of pages in *Remembrance of Things Past* then came from his associations in the astral body to this smell.

Our destiny as human beings is first to purify the astral body. Then we will experience the state of virginity of Mother Mary, as virginity means purity in the astral body. After that, the etheric body and finally the oldest of the bodies—the physical, created in the long-ago time of Old Saturn—will be purified. For this we look to the distant future.

If this quick review of concepts has seemed inadequate, there are Rudolf Steiner's forty-two published books and over three hundred collections of lectures, as well as many books about Steiner that you can find to help you. We make every attempt to speak plainly in this study, and these concepts may be helpful but are not necessary to understand the import of the stars and earth interweaving in the human life of Rudolf Steiner.

3. The Stars as Our Guide

A consummate human heart is a prerequisite to the right to an opinion in the social realm, but this no human being can possess without finding his or her relation with the cosmos, in particular, with the spiritual substance of the cosmos. —Rudolf Steiner[10]

STEINER'S LIFE IS our guide from the earthly realms. His philosophy points to the heavens. We call our approach Star Wisdom, which is a new and intelligent form of astrology. Actually, we will soon see that Star Wisdom has very ancient roots, which those who practice this science and art have brought up to the present.

Biographers seem only to look down at the earth, indeed often into the dirt of a life, without ever casting their eyes heavenward. They seldom ask what events took place "up there" that may have had something to do with the lives that they study. How can a life be understood when the whole heavens are left out of the picture?

The approach of Star Wisdom has certain features in common with modern astrology, and certain features that are completely distinct. First, it should be said that we often use the term "star" to include the fixed stars, such as the Pleiades or the Big Dipper, as well as the Sun, our local star, and the planets—from the Greek word meaning "wandering stars"—adding also the Moon.

Using the beautiful and perhaps unfamiliar term "astrosophy"—from *astro-* (star) and *Sophia* (wisdom)—those who study life in this way assess how human beings and the stars interact. Astrosophers observe the actual heavens, and thus agree with astronomers about the location of planets in the constellations. We say this because conventional Western astrologers do not agree with astronomers, a point of great contention.

I won't explain everything about Star Wisdom here, but will leave it to other works on astrosophy. Several astrosophers are preparing a primer on Star Wisdom that will present the basic approaches in a very readable way. Finally, a more formal presentation of the Star Wisdom of Rudolf Steiner's life is in preparation.[11]

Speaking to the Stars

Rudolf Steiner gave us many lectures and initiatives. In addition to the wise words, we also have the deeds of the life. Are these deeds a teaching in and of themselves? That is, beyond what was said and what was demonstrated, is there a discernible pattern that tells us something also? Steiner spoke often of the "starry script," that is, patterns written in the heavens that can influence a person's life. He hinted that human beings could also, by their deeds, influence the "starry script," altering it in service of the continued development of humanity. Here is how Steiner saw it:

> The stars once spoke to humanity.
> It is world destiny that they are silent now.
> To be aware of this silence
> Can bring pain to earthly humanity.
> But in the deepening silence
> There grows and ripens
> What humanity speaks to the stars.
> To be aware of this speaking
> Can become strength
> To spirit humanity.[12]

From other talks by Steiner, it's clear that this verse overstates the notion that the stars are silent in their speaking to humanity. They spoke much more clearly and loudly in times past, when human beings had a natural clairvoyance that opened them to ongoing conversations with spiritual beings in the heavens. But they have not ceased speaking altogether. New in this verse is the notion that human beings can speak back; indeed, we can all develop to the point that terrifically great beings can hear what we say through our words and our deeds.

How does this operate in a life? How do we listen and speak to the stars? We will see how Rudolf Steiner demonstrates this by looking at Steiner's life through the lens of his Solar Cross Images.

The School of Zarathustra (or Zoroaster)

When you were born—or at some specific day that you are investigating—the Sun lay in a particular part of its annual cycle, against the backdrop of a particular zodiacal being. In the school of Zarathustra, thousands of years ago, one could still experience these zodiacal beings as living cosmic beings. One could still see them. Since then we have lost that capacity for clairvoyance. Was that development good or bad? Should we mourn the loss of that capacity? One notion is that humans had to develop individuality and the ability to think in isolation, in the darkness of a room closed to spiritual realms, in order to develop a sense of individuality, then return to the spirit as individuals empowered and awake. A very few individuals could do this even in ancient times. We begin to see more and more children with these capacities, and soon we will see many people able to speak to the stars.

The title Zarathustra, meaning "golden star," may have been a ceremonial title given to advanced seers. It is also the name used to refer to a series of lives of a great individuality who touched into the world through incarnations into a human body, to lead humanity through its development of consciousness.

At the time of the school of Zarathustra (known to the Greeks as Zoroaster), in Babylon in the sixth century b.c.e., the stargazing magi (magicians, or priest-kings) experienced directly the zodiacal belt as twelve distinct beings to whom they gave the names Ram, Bull, Twins, Crab, Lion, Virgin, Scales, Scorpion, Archer, Goat, Waterbearer, and Fishes. Now we know them by their Latin names: Aries, Taurus, Gemini, Cancer, Leo, Virgo, Libra, Scorpio, Sagittarius, Capricorn, Aquarius, and Pisces. Why twelve? As John Michell, author of *Twelve-Tribe Nations*, said, "The fundamental character of nature is duodecimal."[13] As we see from the Revelation of John, the last book of the Christian Bible, which speaks about the distant past and the distant future, the Tree of Life has twelve kinds of fruit, producing its fruit each month. There are twelve forms of basic nourishment and healing, now and into the future.[14]

THE PICTURE FROM SLEEPING BEAUTY

From the tale of Sleeping Beauty, we have a very good picture of what the magi saw. Recall that in the tale an extraordinary young princess is born and the king and queen decide to celebrate. They invite the twelve known fairies. Each brings important gifts. Then a thirteenth comes and makes trouble. She complains that she was not invited, and the King and Queen fret because they had no place for her. Indeed, there is no seat for her, nor plate, nor cup, nor utensils. How is that?

These twelve picture for us what we all receive at birth, the twelve great beings of the zodiac poised around our infant selves. The twelve bring many fine qualities. Imagine them surrounding the little infant, giving and giving, blessing and blessing, perhaps entrancing everyone in a kind of blissful stupor of abundance. The entrance of the thirteenth is jarring. She puts it all into the context of time. She puts everyone to sleep for a hundred years, because this much grace would otherwise be premature. The youngster would not know what to do with it. The thirteenth fairy knows that, when the time is right, the young prince will come and awaken the princess and the whole kingdom. Thus the thirteenth fairy is Time itself. There is no one place for her at the table of the twelve because Time is everywhere.

THE SCIENCE OF THE SCHOOL OF ZARATHUSTRA

The Zoroastrians identified the twelve great beings of the zodiac. They then divided each of these twelve regions into thirty steps or degrees, for a total of 360 degrees in the full circle: 360 different qualities, 360 different gates to the heavens.

From the School of Zarathustra we have the way of measuring a circle into 360 degrees. We also have our modern clock going from one to twelve. Every time we look at a clock, we are looking at Zarathustra's reminder from many centuries ago that a fundamental order exists in the heavens in twelve divisions. And look, the thirteenth fairy is there in the movement of the hands, never resting in one place, as she moves around the other twelve.

Why measure the heavens via the course of a day? Because we live punctuated discontinuous lives completely conditioned by the Sun's light—awake, asleep, awake, asleep.... The pulse of sunlight forms the foundation of consciousness. As Rudolf Steiner said, "The truth is that the Sun is a meeting-place for hierarchies of spiritual beings, whose deeds come to expression in the warmth and the light streaming from the Sun."[15]

360 degrees and 365.25 days in a year—where do the other five and a quarter fit into the circle? These extra days were considered especially sacred and were inserted or, as they say, intercalated through the course of the year. Sometimes these extra days were observed as holy days; sometimes they were simply slipped into the regular calendar. Tucked in here and there we see the ceaseless activity of the thirteenth fairy.

Modern Western astrology orients not to the zodiac but to the seasons. What is the difference? As this is important for our study, we shall take a side trip into the comparison of tropical and sidereal astrology.

What Month Is It?

In ancient days, stargazers were not laughed at. Indeed, they were the priest-kings who knew intimately the night and its secrets. We could better understand these priest-kings—the members of the School of Zarathustra—if we imitated one thing that we know they did. Take a few minutes to gaze at a single star, just one, using your physical eyes and the eyes of your heart. Don't use a telescope—we'll explain why later. The mind gets restless to move on very quickly to the next thing and the next, but stay with one star. Holding our concentration quiets the labeling mind. Then something begins to stir in us. Feelings begin to move, perhaps as inchoate swirls of mist, unidentifiable at first, then hinting at forms, and not only superficial forms, but forms with depth, with a history, and finally with meaning. The star becomes an oracle with a message.

The priest-kings practiced this nightly. Theirs was not the day world of our brightest star—the Sun—but rather the night of a billion stars. Slowly they became intimate with them, creating a lore based on their own experience. From their intimate knowledge of the lawful rhythms and events of the heavens, they were able to tell the people about the seasons, about the weather, and about what the guiding spirits of the zodiac told them. Thus they earned the greatest respect from the general populace.

So what turned popular respect for the priest-kings to derision? The main reason that astronomers laugh at conventional Western astrologers is that the two groups don't agree about the night sky. An astronomer sees, for example, Venus in front of the fixed star Spica, in the stalk of wheat held aloft by the Virgin, at the end of the constellation Virgo. The astronomer can demonstrate it with photographs taken by high-resolution telescopes. The conventional astrologer says, "Actually, Venus is near the end of Libra and went through Virgo a month ago." Hence the title of this section: What month is it? Usually we ask, "What time is it?," meaning we already know it's morning, but need to know the minute. Sometimes we say, when signing a check, for example, "What day is it?," meaning is it the sixteenth or the seventeenth? But does anyone really not know what month it is? Well, as it takes the Sun one day to go one degree in the sky, a difference of twenty-five degrees—the disagreement between the astronomer and the conventional astrologer—puts them most often in different months from each other.

How can we explain such a discrepancy? The science of the stars, including the movements of the planets, Sun, and Moon, was well known thousands of years ago. Thus Stonehenge and other monuments mark moon cycles and even complicated eclipse cycles. In the second century c.e. the Greek scientist Ptolemy wrote down the knowledge of the day. Then a series of wars destroyed most of the texts. Ptolemy's work was lost in the original Greek but was preserved in its Arabic translation for centuries. These writings found their way into Europe much later, in the Middle Ages, where they were translated into Latin. Why are we following this thin thread of knowledge written down by Ptolemy? Because he wrote that the vernal point—the position of the Sun on the first day of spring, equal day and equal night, what we call the spring equinox on March 21 every year—occurred at the beginning of Aries. That was true when Ptolemy wrote about it. However, the very slow wobble of the precession of the equinoxes has moved the spring equinox point to five degrees of Pisces in our time. Ptolemy's writings show that he knew about this movement of the equinoxes—it had been written about since the fourth century b.c.e.—though he doesn't mention it in that particular passage. Readers of Ptolemy's recovered works in the Middle Ages accepted that the spring equinox was always at zero degrees Aries, hence the growing split since the second century. The astrology that went directly from Babylon to India, without going through Arabic, then Latin, then English, did not suffer from this confusion, and uses actual astronomical positions for the planets.

Conventional Western or tropical astrology uses a seasonal calendar, beginning every year with March 21 as the first day of spring, no matter what lies behind in the starry heavens. Tropical astrologers have found this seasonal calendar approach very helpful in understanding a client, and work mostly with planets in relation to each other. Sidereal (from *sidus*, "star") astrology looks at the placement of the Sun, Moon, and planets in relation to the constellations of the stars. East Indian astrology, also called Vedic or Jyotish astrology, is sidereal in its approach.

Tropical astrologers unfortunately use names of actual star constellations for their twelve seasonal divisions—Aries/Ram, Taurus/Bull, Gemini/Twins, etc. These are the names of actual star groupings and, as we know from astrosophy (Star Wisdom), the locations of living divine beings. The problem is that the season of spring, which follows the spring equinox, does not occur in Aries anymore, and won't until the precession of the equinoxes has taken us back to that point again, a bit more than twenty thousand years from now.

What if tropical astrologers changed their naming to reflect the seasons to which they refer? Instead of Taurus, they could use something that evokes the feeling of the season. Here is a short collection for the month of May collected from North American Indian tribes: Blossom Month, When the Ponies Shed their Shaggy Hair Month, Geese Go North Month, Season When the Leaves Are Green Month, The Strong Month When the Trees Begin to Bloom, Frogs Return Month, Month When the Horses Get Fat. Aren't those better choices than using a name of something that isn't there?

Our month names have come through a long history of abuse. The month of November comes from the Latin root meaning the ninth month, and December from the Latin meaning the tenth month. What happened?! Politics interfered with the accurate measure of time, as when it was decided that Caesar Augustus was so important that he rated his own month, August, and the other months were pushed later.

Let's sample the American Indian seasonal names for the time we call November: Freezing River Maker Month, White Frost on Grass and Ground Month, Deer Rutting Month, Month When the Water Is Black with Leaves, Time of Much Poverty Month, Month of the Turkey and Feast, Snowy Mountains in the Morning Month, Turkey Month.

Now let's look at seasonal names for the time of December: Ice Lasts All Day Month, Buffalo Cow's Fetus Is Getting Large Month, Big Winter Month, Eccentric Month, Month When the Wolves Run Together, Popping Trees Month, Respect Month, Obsidian Month, The Sun Has Traveled South to His Home to Rest Before He Starts Back on His Journey North Month, Full Long Nights Month, The Full Cold Month.

These seasonal names evoke the feeling of a living world. Consulting our feelings is the best way to relate to the change of light and temperature, the bursting of life force in the spring, the decay in the autumn, and the challenge in the winter.

Despite the delicious feeling tones of the seasonal approach that would come from these very dynamic new names for the months, we will not use tropical astrology here. In this study we use a star-based or sidereal approach, orienting to the actual locations of the 360 degrees in the starry heavens. We focus on zodiacal memory, on what lies constant beyond the vagaries of changes in the seasons or in the weather.[16]

In this study, we like to know where the sun really stood in relation to the stars when historical personalities were born. If I read that Rudyard Kipling was born on the same day of the same month that I was, that doesn't mean we share a star-date. We have to recalculate the star-dates for birthdates of historical personalities. In Jesus's time, the part of the zodiac that lay behind the Sun on the first day of spring (March 21) was three degrees Aries. Today the degree that lies behind the Sun on the first day of spring is five degrees Pisces, a movement of twenty-eight degrees, or one degree every seventy-two years. If someone shares a calendar birthday with you, but was born more than seventy-two years before you were, he or she is not in the same sidereal degree and has a different star-date. To find your Star Brothers and Star Sisters, look to the previous calendar day for those born 72 to 144 years before you, the day before that for those born 144 to 216 years before you, etc.[17]

THE ROYAL PERSIAN STARS

When we know we are looking for star dates rather than seasonal dates, we begin again to notice the stars. We can say "again" because we can reconnect to the magi of the School of Zarathustra communing with the night sky. In that tradition, gaze upon a single star or a group of stars—a "stellium" or a "constellation"—and "consider," recalling that this word "consider" comes from being-with (con) the stars (sidus). With the stars, we ponder. Perhaps we converse, either in words or in feeling. It opens an entirely new avenue of relationship. Perhaps you feel an affinity with a particular star—"Oh, there's Regulus!"—that you may experience as childlike wonder or as the warmth of adult companionship, as in seeing a friend after a separation.

We highly recommend that you develop this friendship through simply looking, what we might call naked-eye astronomy. Some people say, "I can get closer and see more detail by looking through a telescope." Yes, but looking through a telescope focuses and restricts your sensory experience to the visual, and at the same time separates you from your star with several pieces of rounded glass. If you were going out on a date with a boyfriend or girlfriend, would you prefer to see him or her through several lenses and mirrors? Here we're speaking about relationship, which uses the eyes of the heart. We even recommend that people who wear eyeglasses take them off when viewing the heavens. Visual accuracy and detail is less important than how you experience these beings in your etheric and astral bodies.

In the School of Zarathustra, five stars earned the rank of the Royal Stars of Persia. Two of these, Aldebaran and Antares, form the main axis of the heavens. Aldebaran lies at 15 degrees of Taurus, at the very center of this sign, the Eye of the Bull. Its opposite point, Antares, lies exactly half the circle or 180 degrees away. Aldebaran and Antares were used by the ancient Babylonians to measure out the whole map of the heavens.[18]

The exactness of the opposition and the closeness of these bright stars to the ecliptic—the apparent path of the Sun and planets—gave them special importance to the stargazing priest-kings. The other Royal Stars are not so perfectly placed, though two come at nearly right angles to the Aldebaran-Antares axis, namely Regulus in Leo (at 5 degrees, not 15), and Fomalhaut in Aquarius (at 9 degrees, not 15). The fifth star, Spica, lies at the very end of Virgo, at 29 Virgo, and forms the bright star of the stalk of wheat held aloft by the Virgin Mother of the Universe.

We pay special attention to the Aldebaran-Antares axis because it lies at exact right angles to Rudolf Steiner's Sun and Saturn at birth. Thus the main axis of the heavens lies in Rudolf Steiner's Solar Cross.

In the StarFire Research Group, we have begun to perceive *Aldebaran as a giver of life, and Antares as a bringer of death.* Here are to be found beings whose activities create a tremendous polarity, sustaining the deepest mystery of earthly existence. One can experience Aldebaran as a cosmic source of divine life—the Life Star—from which flows to us great blessings of growth, abundance, and self-awareness. Anthroposophy understands the region of Taurus (the Bull), with Aldebaran at its center, as the giver of the "I AM" to humanity—the ability to say and understand "I," the ability to perceive and know that we perceive, rather than act only unconsciously out of instinct.[19] This is the route of consciousness expanding out to the cosmos. Here lives the soul-sense of the existence of individuality, the gift of selfhood that can lead to selfish egotism or mature into the flower of spirit-infused Freedom, awake and aware.

Across the heavens, Antares stands at the heart of the Scorpion. Its effect can be found in nearby degrees and even throughout the entire sign of the Scorpion. Antares can be viewed as the Threshold Star, or the Star of Death and Rebirth. From its region comes the sting of the Scorpion that diminishes and kills.[20] Here also live influences—symbolized and experienced by those of an earlier time as the Eagle—that call on us to confront what we shall take with us over the threshold of death into spiritual realms and back again. In an important way, Antares can bring an encounter with death that embraces the spiritual realities on the other side, evoking a kind of selflessness as a complement to the self-sense found streaming from Aldebaran—selflessness that matures into love. Thus the lower expression of Scorpion transforms into the Eagle soaring above, and even into the purity of the Dove. Scorpio is unique among zodiacal beings in having three transformational forms.

The effect of Antares can appear to us in earthly life as the threat and terror of death and annihilation. In its right time, this kind of transformation marks development of the human being, on his or her path of dying and becoming, as suggested by Goethe and by Buddhist and Christian teachers through the ages. Out of its time, such transformation can create the crisis of terror for an individual and for society.

The Aldebaran-Antares axis is complemented by the two signs directly perpendicular: Leo, the Lion, and Aquarius, the Waterbearer. With Taurus and Scorpio, these are called in astrology the "fixed signs," as opposed to the "cardinal signs" (Aries, Cancer, Libra, Capricorn) and the "mutable signs" (Gemini, Virgo, Sagittarius, Pisces). They have been observed since ancient times, for example, the four beings of the four directions as described by Ezekiel. Each being, surrounded with whirling fire, has four wings and four faces—one a bull, one a lion, one an eagle, and one a radiant human being. In the Revelation of John, these same cherubim appear around the center-piece of the throne of the Divine Presence.[21]

POLARITY

We live in a world betwixt polarities in the heavens, set there so that our consciousness can grow. How do we depict polarity? Imagine two objects at a distance from each other with something in the middle that connects them, often shown simply as a line:

The one notices the other from afar and, though they don't interact in their essence, they have a thread of a relationship. Perhaps they send post-cards from their respective extremes. When the relationship grows, the circulation of a lemniscate begins:

You can imagine that influences from both sides begin to flow in movement with each other, setting up a rhythmic pulsation. As the movement becomes more dynamic, one can picture the relationship in another form, as overlapping realms of influence:

Two realms, Aldebaran and Antares, life-force and death-force, emanate, interact, and overlap. When the perimeter of one circle includes the center of its neighbor circle, then the area of overlap has, since ancient times, been known as a *vesica piscis* or *mandorla*. One can see Christ in this almond-shaped form, without the circles to the sides, carved in stone above the door of Chartres Cathedral. One can see in various places Mother Mary, Buddha, various saints, and many Islamic designs, all appearing inside the lens-shaped vesica piscis form. However, not always do the circles overlap in exactly that way. Not always are the two circles the same size. The circles are meant to suggest dynamic forces emanating from their respective centers. The place of overlap suggests the realm where both worlds are true, in this case, where life forces and death forces interact, namely our earthly existence.

This way of understanding polarity is very important to our study of Rudolf Steiner. He taught that all spiritual impulses come in opposites, that when something exquisitely light-filled happens, then some greater challenge of the dark also shows itself. The challenge of finding balance between extremes will come up over and over again in the episodes of his biography.

The Stars and the Sun at Our Birth

From the only world we remember knowing—warm, wet, dark, and quiet—we pop into another world—cold, dry, bright, and noisy. Inside we were protected. Outside, we're not. Birth marks the greatest life change we have experienced. On this ride of life, the next biggest change we can look forward to is our transition at death. In between, despite the dramas that we experience in our lives, nothing matches the first big step of birth. At that moment, in the midst of what we could rightly call a trauma, we are so impressionable. At our first breath, our astral body—the word *astral* comes from the Latin word *aster*, for star—entered the physical much more deeply. The astral body is that patterned structure of energy wherein our thinking, feeling, and willing will grow, until, maturing at age twenty-one, we receive our soul firmly into our being. Before this, the soul is present but not firmly seated.

Rudolf Steiner suggested that the impressions we take in at our birth moment go very deep, not just in the form of emotional reactions to the bright lights, which psychologists write about, but deeper into the psyche. Steiner suggested that the pattern of the planets and stars of the heavenly sphere imprints itself into the sphere of our cranium and every cell of our bodies.[22]

The impressions burn more intensely from the location of the Sun. The Sun acts as the focalizer, the laser beam that amplifies what lives behind that small portion of the heavens, the one degree of the 360 that belongs to us, with which we are so intimate, and around which we create a series of celebrations called "birthdays" when the Sun comes back to that same place in the sky.[23]

Is the Sun just a large ball of hot gas, nuclear explosions creating heat and light? Is it just a mechanical process on which we depend? No. The Sun is much more than that. Let us give a flavor of the Sun by talking of Ra, who imparted these words to ancient seers in Egypt, who in turn wrote them down as the Egyptian Book of the Dead:

> Ra rises. He goes out into the world, a passion, a fire burning up night, making day. ... He warms the belly of the sky. ... He walks the upper regions, his heart inflamed with love. ... He fears no living thing. He made them, what is known and not known. ... His words are smelted into gold. With a kiss, Ra turns poison into magic.[24]

We take in from that heavenly location whatever lives there, whatever is stored there. It comes in more strongly because the power of the Sun, the source of light and warmth, sears this pattern into our being—whether we were born at midnight, noon, or anywhere in between. That is the main hypothesis of the approach of the Oracle of the Solar Cross.

Starfire, focused through the Sun, enlivens, illuminates, warms, and sometimes burns. An imprint from the heavens can feel like a branding iron, searing and scarring. It also can feel like the fire that incinerates the dross of life. The ten thousand distracting inconsequentials are burned away, leaving only the essentials.

Over long stretches of time, the imprints of the great deeds of great human beings work on that spirit realm, changing its nature. Thus the Sun works in both directions as an amplifier—not only as a focusing lens for the heavens' imprint onto the new human being, especially at birth, but also as a lens focusing the mighty deeds of human beings into the stars, slowly to *humanize the face of the zodiac.* This is humanity speaking to the stars— behold, the stars themselves are changed by the conversation!

LIFE STAGES

In anthroposophy, the timeline of a life is often painted in terms of the planetary forces or beings that oversee the different phases of the life. We will be brief here. If you're interested, you can find good studies of the life cycle to take you further.[25] For our purposes, we can look at the life in three main periods, with different seven-year periods overseen by different beings:

PERIODS SUPERVISED BY BEINGS OF MOON, VENUS, AND MERCURY SPHERES	PERIODS SUPERVISED BY BEINGS OF THE SUN	PERIODS SUPERVISED BY BEINGS OF MARS, JUPITER, AND SATURN SPHERES
0–7, 7–14, 14–21	21–28, 28–35, 35–42	42–49, 49–56, 56–63

The early part of the life is devoted to preparation for receiving the soul or "I AM" into one's being at the age of twenty-one. The "I AM" doesn't drop in fully formed, like Athena from the head of Zeus, at age twenty-one. It takes some time to seat the soul and the soul's work in the world into one's life. During the "Sun" years, in Steiner's terminology, one moves from realization of the *sentient soul*—the soul function that orients to sensory information, thus the kinesthetic and aesthetic person—to the *mind* or *intellectual soul*—where the cognitive powers attain their full development—to the *consciousness* or *spiritually aware soul*—which has the greatest capacity of heart in relation to spirit. More could be said in a treatise on development, the point being that the soul isn't outside, then suddenly inside the human being. Ensoulment, as with enlightenment, is a gradual process with many qualitative differences along the way.

We will speak about the importance of the age of twenty-one in Rudolf Steiner's life. We will also speak about the importance of the Sun years whose correspondence to Steiner's dates is as follows:

Age 21–28: 1882–1889, realization of the sentient soul
Age 28–35: 1889–1896, realization of the intellectual or mind soul
Age 35–42: 1896–1903, realization of the consciousness soul or spirit-
    soul

The course of a life can look like this:[26]

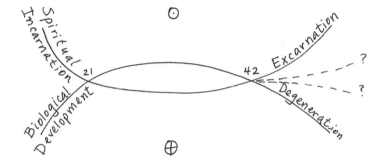

Biological development rises up from the Earth toward the Sun and then sinks back to Earth again. Spirit bends down from the heavenly spheres of the Sun, grounding into the biology most strongly at age twenty-one. Actually, what happens after forty-two years depends very much on what the person has done with him- or herself in the earlier part of the life. The soul moving through the middle of these two forces can actually expand at the end, and embrace Earth and heaven alike.

As we move from age to age in Steiner's life, backward and forward, we must keep in mind the different developmental issues that face the human being in these different phases of a life.

The Points of Entry and Departure

Birth is followed by the life, which prepares for the death. Our whole life prepares us to enter a gate into spirit realms whose crossing point is as abrupt as our birth, one moment on one side, the next moment on the other.

Rudolf Steiner spoke many times about the nature of this crossing that we call "death," and even wrote long plays about it.

The influences of birth coming into the life, and leading up to death, can look like a crescendo and decrescendo. The Image given at the gate of entry through the stars—i.e., the Birth Image at the position of the Sun (what I usually call the Gate Image) along with the three other Images received in a Solar Cross at birth—has a slowly diminishing effect over the course of the life.

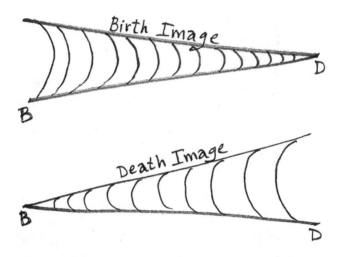

Meanwhile, the gate of exit at death, into which one delivers his or her life's harvest, exerts a stronger force as the life grows longer. We can look at the lives of people who have passed the threshold into spirit worlds to see how the Birth Image and the Death Image have interacted.

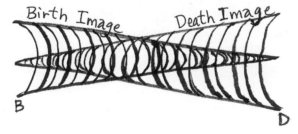

In general, the two Images interact something like this, in a pattern that bears a strong resemblance to the diagram of the curves of the life stages, just above.

The Beginning Before the Beginning: Conception

Birth is preceded by conception, the moment when the spirit first comes into the matter that will form our vehicle for learning in this earth realm. What comes as spirit spark at *conception* brings the strongest sense of pre-earthly intention directly from realms of spirit. If we can find that moment, then we discern what pattern lay in the heavens, impressing itself upon the whole will of the life. We can discern an intention and a goal for the life.

At birth, a flowering takes place. The time of gestation has developed the spark of spirit to the place where it is ready to make the transition into the earth plane as an aware being, slowly developing this awareness to the point where a full sense of "I AM"—of ensoulment—can occur at age twenty-one. Birth indicates the way or the path by which we unfold our destiny.

At death, we realize the harvest of our life, uniting this harvest into a particular place in the heavens, where our gifts are received as nutrition by divine beings. We lift up the fruits of our life's tree and then move into the future.

The following diagram can be helpful in our work with biography. Conception (C) gathers influences from spiritual worlds, focusing into the moment of birth (B). From that point on, deeds on earth begin to emanate in all directions, affecting others and speaking with the stars. These deeds become more focused as the life progresses. Toward the end of the life, they all begin to point to the passageway of death (D), bringing one's life harvest to that particular place in the starry worlds.

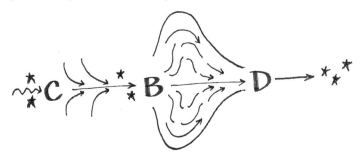

Our whole life focuses on delivery of this gift into a particular place in the heavens. We exit bearing the gifts of what we have accomplished in our relationships to other people and to the world.

THE TIME OF CONCEPTION

How do we know the time of conception? If we know the date and time of the birth, we can use the Rule of Hermes to determine the time of conception. The exact time of birth shows us the location of the rising sign, the exact degree that lay on the eastern horizon when the birth took place. Then we look back ten lunations (lunar months), that is, about 273 days, to a time when the rising sign (that degree of the zodiac that lay at the horizon at the minute of our birth) was at the same place as the Moon at birth, and the Moon at the same place as the rising sign at birth. In other words, these two positions switch places. This "Rule of Hermes" comes in ancient Egyptian lore from Hermes Trismegistus, student of Zarathustra. It gives a time that accords with studies of human gestation periods, but cannot be proven. Thus we may think of it as the "spiritual conception" time.

In astrosophy, we make much use of the conception time. From it we have another theory, suggested by Steiner and put into practice by Willi Sucher, that the events occurring in the sky during gestation are part of the pre-earthly intention of the soul readying for birth, what we call prenatal anticipations. Thus we can map those celestial events that occur during gestation onto the actual life after birth as one lunation to one seven-year period of the life. We will make use of this mapping later in this biographical study. [27]

The dynamics in utero thus become a patterning of the rhythms of the life. Of course, the context of a life is unique—King Louis XIV will play out a particular prenatal dynamic in a different way from the German poet Edouard Moricke, born on the same Solar Day with the same Gate Image. Louis had a great deal more resources than the poor Lutheran minister and poet. The contexts of their lives differed completely. However, we aren't interested in fame and fortune, or whatever is determined by the constraints and possibilities of the social milieu and how much money someone was born into. We discipline ourselves to look for soul gestures. In their soul gestures, Moricke and Louis had a great deal in common, something it takes time to discover, as we cannot get stuck in the outer clothing of the life, but must penetrate to its core.

Four Kinds of Celestial Resonant Moments during the Life

In the work with Solar Crosses, we pay attention primarily to the position of the Sun at conception, birth, and, for historical personalities, at death. In astrosophy, we also look at the positions of the planets at the time of these events, which we can simply consider as points of sensitivity. Then we look at how the moving planets interact with these points of sensitivity. If a moving or transiting planet crosses over the position where the Sun or a planet lay at the moment of birth, we consider that the movement plucks a string that re-arouses all the dynamics having to do with that point of sensitivity. This can be disturbing, coalescing, resolving, or arousing of many other dynamics. It is not still. We call these transits to the birth chart.

The moving planets—now I include the Sun and Moon in this term—can interact with the soul's sojourn on earth in various ways. We will look at each one in turn.

1. *Prenatal anticipations.* To review what we said above, during the time between conception and birth, the planets move in the sky and interact with each other. We look for celestial events during the prenatal period. As we hypothesize that the incarnating soul knowingly chose this time period, we understand these events to constitute Moon Karma. That is, the planetary interactions demonstrate something about what the incarnating soul is ready to confront in the upcoming life. These map onto the life lived and can be seen many years later in the circumstances of the life after birth. Thus the celestial events during gestation can be understood as "prenatal anticipations" of periods of importance in the life, very much part of the soul's pre-earthly intentions for this incarnation. In this study, we don't look at the slow-moving planets outside of Saturn, or at the Moon, which moves too fast, crossing the Sun position nine times during gestation; we look at the whole life; and, in Solar Cross work, we look only at conjunctions to the Sun positions.

2. *Transits to the birth chart.* At the moment of birth, a celestial pattern of planets (again, including the Sun and Moon) impresses itself into every cell of the body. The positions of the planets at that time become

points of sensitivity. Planets moving through the heavens may, during the life, interact with those positions, plucking the strings over and over again until we retune those strings from something disharmonious into something harmonious. A well-known example is the "Saturn return," when Saturn moving through the sky comes back to the same place that it occupied at the moment of birth. This occurs approximately twenty-nine and a half years after the birth, then at fifty-nine years old, etc. Transits are understood as Sun Karma, that is, opportunities placed before the individual by fate that can be taken up or not. In Solar Cross work we emphasize transits of other planets to the location of the Sun—either the Conception Sun, the Birth Sun, or the Death Sun position. We leave the study of other transits to a full astrological study. In this study, we don't look at fast-moving planets, anything closer than Jupiter; we look only at conjunctions to the Sun position; and we concentrate only on the latter part of the life, gathering only three to five major transits for discussion. Otherwise, we would be overwhelmed with information.

3. *Transits to transits.* Occasionally events occur in the heavens that are unrelated to the birth chart and are interesting in and of themselves. You can find out about these from astronomers. They are mentioned in easily accessible places such as *Sky and Telescope* magazine. Venus crossing in front of the Sun, for example, is a rare celestial event, occurring for us in 2004 and 2012, and also in Rudolf Steiner's time (1874 and 1882). We understand these events as Saturn Karma, that is, linked with the cosmic memory of the Earth's purpose, but not linked with an individual. Here a person is free to interact with the energy patterns created by such an event or not. We mention these to complete the picture, though we will not go into them in detail, as we are concentrating on the Sun positions in Rudolf Steiner's life.

4. *Saturn crossing the planetary positions at death.* After death, we can look back to see events in the life that prefigured the death and tell us something about the planetary spheres crossed by the spirit released. We will describe this technique in the chapters on the death chart. Again, we will use only a portion of the information that can be gleaned from this approach, as we concentrate on the Sun position at death, and not the other planets.

In each of these views of the heavens, we have mentioned that we will look only at a portion of all the possible interesting celestial dynamics. We are interested in finding the purer and stronger tones of celestial resonance, not every note of the symphony. Astrologers can deluge themselves with information, looking at planets, asteroids, and many different angles (aspects) between them. Such studies can be interesting as long as you don't lose the main chords of the heavenly music. In this book, we will focus on the main chords, where there is much to hear.

ECLIPSES

When the Sun, Moon, and Earth are very closely aligned, one can shade the other from the Sun's light, and we see an eclipse of light, either a lunar eclipse of the Moon's reflected light, or a solar eclipse of the source, the Sun. Steiner spoke of these eclipses as times of letting off pressure in the emotional realm of humanity:

> When there is an eclipse of the Sun, then the opportunity is present for that which is negative upon the Earth to spread itself out in heavenly regions.... at a solar eclipse that which spreads out as negativity upon the Earth can be borne up [in a delusional or luciferic way—from the Illusionist] into cosmic space where it can bring about further damage; and the lunar eclipses are such that evil thoughts from cosmic space can come to those human beings who quite especially want to be possessed by evil thoughts.[28]

This is strong talk, and a warning to be prepared for these events. For this reason we will look at eclipses also, as they relate to the specific locations of the Sun at conception, birth, and death. This is strictly speaking an instance of a transit to the birth chart (no. 2 in our list), but deserves its own mention and explanation.

RETROGRADE MOTION

Often the slower-moving outer planets will cross a position in the sky, then appear to stand still, then move backward, then stop, then move forward again, thus crossing one point three times. This phenomenon of reversal is known as "retrograde motion," and occurs not from the Sun's point of view, but from the Earth's point of view. Sometimes an outer planet will pass over the same point five or seven times. Astrologers make much of Mercury retrograde, seeing in it reasons for backwards thinking and miscommunication. Star Wisdom approaches "retrograde" as a time of emphasis and increased intensity of that planet's activity.

With multiple crossings, each passing has a different flavor. The first crossing initiates the issues that require resolution. The second retrograde crossing deepens the issues, and can often be the most challenging. The third and final pass shows how the resolution has been achieved over the issue at hand.

ASPECTS, ORBS, AND FAVORED PLANETS

For my analyses, I limit myself to the most potent interrelations between celestial bodies—conjunctions where the planets occupy the same position in the heavens and oppositions where the planets are directly across from each other, with Earth in the very center. Of the many aspects or angular relationships between planets, conjunction and opposition are the most simple and straightforward. In Star Wisdom we often look at the "square" aspect where two bodies appear at right angles from the vantage of the Earth. In this study, I will use this aspect only once.

The "orb" in astrology refers to how close two planets are. An orb of zero degrees means that two planets appear directly on top of each other. A chosen orb of ten degrees means that the researcher thinks two planets are close enough to warrant attention if they are within ten degrees of each other. Adding both sides to a ten-degree orb means a twenty-degree zone where a researcher might consider two planets in vibrational relationship to each other. Some astrologers use orbs this wide (and some use wider), with the explanation that a more sensitive human being can feel planets in relationship to each other when they are farther apart. These orbs are appropriate for reading someone's personal chart. In Solar Cross work and in this study, we are much more conservative, and use much tighter orbs.

The orb that we use in the Oracle of the Solar Cross is very small, one half of one degree. We differentiate between one degree and its neighbor. In comparison to conventional astrology, these standards are extremely tight.

Again, we are interested in the pure chords of the celestial symphony, not in every possible thing we can find. Exceptions in this study are explained when we get there.

In our look at transits, we restrict ourselves to the slower-moving planets. A connection between them—a conjunction or opposition—gains importance by its rarity. Mercury and Venus, in contrast, move quickly, and connect frequently with birth positions of planets or with each other. Again, we are interested in the larger cosmic communications, not so much in the chatter.

The Outer Planets

Steiner spoke about the outer planets—Uranus, discovered in 1781, Neptune, discovered in 1846, and by inference Pluto, discovered in 1930, after Steiner's lifetime—as visitors to the Sun's realm, and not as essential elements of our celestial experience. They have also been understood as off-shoots of the development of our solar system over vast ages of time, a period astronomy would describe as the slow creation of a star, and that in Steiner's terms would be differentiated into four ages: the age of Old Saturn, which became Old Sun, then Old Moon, and finally our Earth age. Modern conventional astrology pays a great deal of attention to these outer planets, finding in them a huge power. We also have found correspondences of these planets to the events of Steiner's life that cannot be dismissed.

What are these planets all about? Over the years we have been impressed by their power. Yet their nature remains elusive. Willi Sucher saw two sequences: one of distance—Uranus, then Neptune, then Pluto—and one of types of retarding spirits—Illusionist (Lucifer), Hardener (Ahriman), and Asuras (beings who attack the human physical body and desire to consume the "I AM" of the soul). He thought the two series might be related, and hypothesized that activities of the planet Uranus might have to do with activities of the Illusionist, Neptune with the Hardener, and Pluto with the Asuras.

To begin to test this hypothesis, the StarFire Research Group brought out the charts of a handful of villains and scoundrels, people whose lives we could agree were fraught with retarding spirits, affecting themselves as well as others. We could see that the outer planets played a prominent role at their births, but it was not always the same planet. There is not a consistent signature for these planets' effects in people's lives. Now that the International Astronomical Union has demoted Pluto to the status of "dwarf planet,"[29] it begs the question even more of how that particular rock with an erratic orbit affects human lives. We are actively engaged in further research on these questions.

Just as we can't say that the archangel Michael works here and not there, or that Divinity is more here than there, we also can't say that the retarding spirits of the Illusionist or Hardener or Asuras are exclusively here and not there. Actually, this is a famous conclusion reached long ago by the Neoplatonist philosopher Iamblichus: To the wise, the Gods are everywhere, but dull people may need to find them in dedicated temples and at particular springs and groves.[30]

Let us review descriptions of these planets, sourcing from conventional astrology as well as our tentative ideas here.

Uranus

In conventional astrology Uranus has the reputation of the locus of the unexpected, of shocks, including electrical shocks and lightning, also rebellions and anything upsetting the normal order. In the easy association between planetary distance and the retarding spirits that we have described above, Uranus can be seen as the home to spirits who serve the Illusionist and who intend to deceive humanity with illusions of all sorts. This can serve as a trial for humanity—how do you realize an illusion, face it, and overcome it? What makes an imagination "genuine"? Though we will find corroboration for this association, we have to hold it very loosely because it is not exclusive. The Illusionist's creation of distracting belief patterns occurs whenever the opportunity arises. Let us see what the life events tell us about Uranus's effects.

Neptune

To conventional astrology, Neptune is understood as a source of spiritual inspiration, the ability to soar beyond the limits of physical realities. It is possible that Neptune acts as a focal point for spirits who intend to bring humanity down to the level of simple material existence, rejecting all spirituality, rejecting the soul, and slowly becoming robotic and mechanical servants of the Hardener. In contrast, conventional astrology pictures Neptune as a locus of illusion and thus a home for the Illusionist's minions. The Hardener's attempt to capture the soul in a prison of anti-spiritual materialism can be seen as the worst illusion of all. To confront the beings of the Hardener who cling to Neptune, one must develop the capacity for warmth, for love.

Pluto

Even though Pluto has recently been reclassified as a "dwarf planet," astrologers of all kinds have found that its position has potent effects. From its action in the birth charts of thousands of people, Pluto has gained a reputation for transformation, for opening up the depths and darkness of hell, for connections with death, for anything to do with the underworld. The one enduring these trials, and coming out the other end, emerges a new person. Perhaps Pluto has some special relationship with Asuric spirits who intend to eat away the "I AM" or ego or soul of humanity, to cut humanity off from any experience of the spirit. Perhaps not. The association shows up in the present study, but cannot be taken as exclusive of other effects. Pluto is sometimes thought of as the "Christ planet," but this association stems more from the fact that, to overcome the challenges pressed into one's life by a Pluto connection, one has to find the Christ light within to make it through.

This approach to the outer planets may be seen as a set of hypotheses, ideas that can be tried out in relation to the facts of experience. From this point of view, each of these concentrations of physical substance can have a dramatically negative impact that, when weathered and mastered, creates opportunities not otherwise available. We know enough to be very interested when these planets are prominent in an astrological chart. We would be wise to listen to the evidence rather than be too free with assigning labels of meaning.

4. CONNECTING HEAVEN AND EARTH: THE ORACLE OF THE SOLAR CROSS

Cross pattern in pottery from the time and place of the School of Zarathustra: Eridu, the earliest settlement of Sumer, 6300 B.C.E.[31]

WE HAVE THE polarity of the stars in the heavens and the human life lived on earth. What links them? Astrology and astrosophy study all the many ways in which the events in the stars and the events on earth interrelate. The Oracle of the Solar Cross forges the bridge in a unique way, by revealing messages from the starry worlds as word-images that are formulated in terms of earthly realities. These hints can become guides, constraints, or aids, as the person works with them in his or her life.

The Basic Picture

Imagine yourself standing on the earth, outside at noon, on your birthday. You can choose any birthday, even your first birthday, though you must imagine yourself as standing. Above you, at the midheaven lies the Sun. Behind the Sun lies the exact degree—just one out of the 360 of the zodiacal circle—with which you are familiar. It's the Solar Gate for your birth. Something of you came through the Sun from that one place. In that Solar Gate you may recognize a living spiritual essence. We can observe that essence in those who were born with the Sun at this degree, taking with them the strengths and qualities of that heavenly location. We can also perceive this essence in those who died with the Sun at this degree, lifting up their life's harvest into that place. We can learn something about that celestial address from deeds performed with the Sun at that degree. We can learn something about it from studying you.

Something has come with you into this life, and we access this something through a cross-shaped set of Images.

The essence that came through the Solar Gate for your birth—depicted below using an ancient symbol of the sun streaming down the gifts of the heavens—we call your Gate Image. Something about it should feel familiar to you, somewhere in your being.

Directly below you lies the Earth, symbolized as a circle with a cross in the center, very like the ancient plate that began this chapter. Even if you were born at night, this exercise summarizes the archetypal relationship of Sun and Earth: the Sun above, commanding the day-consciousness of the heavens, and Earth beneath your feet, offering you the substance to create your body. The Earth draws us down with its love for our being —which we call "gravity." Drawing us upward is the love of the heavens so that we may stand upright. A straight line drawn from the Sun above at noon down through the Earth will come to the opposite place in the zodiac. In astrology, we have found that these places of opposition are related to each other. From the location opposite the Sun came—and still comes—your Earth Image.

Lift your arms to either side. One will face east and one will face west, depending on which hemisphere of our globe you're standing on.[32] From these horizons came at your birth the Horizon Images. For example, let us say you were born with the Sun at 5 degrees Leo, the Sun conjunct the Heart of the Lion, Regulus. With the Sun high above at 5 degrees Leo, your Gate Image (or Solar Image) would come from 5 Leo, your Earth Image would come from 5 Aquarius, your Eastern Horizon Image would come from 5 Scorpio, and your Western Horizon Image would come from 5 Taurus. This is true for everyone born during the twenty-four hour period that the Sun lay in the fifth degree of Leo, no matter where on Earth, no matter whether night or day. You share these Images with many people. How you as an individual work with the impulses from those four quarters will vary depending on your culture, family constellation, and the development of your soul.

In astrology, the degree at the eastern horizon at the moment of your birth is termed your "rising sign," and the degree opposite, at the western horizon, your "setting." As the world turns or rotates, a new degree arises every four minutes. The symbols for the horizons in these drawings suggest the phenomenon of sunrise and sunset. In the Solar Cross view, we relate entirely to the Sun, in the archetypal picture that we have developed—Sun above, Earth below, horizons to the right and left—all related to the Sun's position. Thus our "horizon" comes from this relation to the great being of Sun, the source, and not from the "rising sign" in your birth chart.

Here is a picture of the archetypal Solar Cross:

Gate
Image

Eastern Horizon Image

Western Horizon Image

Earth Image

The Earth below pulls you down with its love for you, gravity. The Sun above pulls you upright. The Earth is a little more powerful; otherwise we would float above its surface. To the east and west are the stimulating contents of what is at the edge, what is hidden one moment and is revealed the next.

Make this more than an imagination. Stand up and take the position shown in the diagram, feet together, feeling the pull of gravity down and the pull of the heavens skyward, and your arms outstretched to the horizons. You have defined a cross, the verticality down through the Earth and up through the Sun, and the horizontality through the horizons.

The form of the cross predated Christianity in the traditions of all indigenous peoples. The cross has achieved special meaning, and also grave misunderstanding, in Christianity. It is not an instrument of torture but a tool for development. From Valentin Tomberg:

> The Cross was given to Mankind just as it was given to the Angels—that is the great revelation that Jacob received. And moreover he became aware that an exalted spiritual Being must come down, so that the Cross may be given to human beings on Earth; but a long preparation is necessary throughout generations, so that a suitable body may be prepared.[33]

Thus, in recognition of the ancient power of this symbol, it could be said of Jesus: He always blessed in the form of a cross.[34]

The great astrologer Marc Edmund Jones understood part of this principle. In his assignment of imaginations to each degree of the zodiac, the Sabian Symbols, he said:

> The degrees which lie face to face across the circle will be found to complement each other in a fashion that is mutually illuminating, and this fact has been of the greatest assistance in working out the detailed symbolism.... In nearly every instance the interpretations are keyed through this sort of diametrical relationship... Many of the symbols are wholly ambiguous if taken by themselves.[35]

The Solar Crosses include two oppositions at right angles to each other. The foursome becomes a whole, much like the separate notes of a chord.

ORIGIN OF THE IMAGES

And the human being then sees the image of Divinity.

So spoke Divinity to Moses and his sister Miriam.[36] It is a promise that human beings can penetrate into unusual realms, places that many teachers claim to be our birthright. The Images of the Solar Crosses are intended to assist in this penetration. Where do these Images come from? The full story has more details than are appropriate to this chapter, so I have given it in Appendix A. In brief, after the research detailed in Appendix A, and the gathering and study of all the different materials related to a particular gate, the Images came through me, through my own inspiration and imagination. In the next chapter we'll share techniques that can assist readers to participate in this creative act, as that is essential to continue in this work. "Active imagination," "moral fantasy," or "lightning gift of insight"—whatever you call the process, it's essential to develop these capacities to meet the future.

RIDDLES AND TREASURE

The process of the Oracle of the Solar Cross is a treasure hunt, with riddles along the way. When you come upon a riddle, at first some parts may make no sense at all. Then you ponder it, and perhaps you find that it becomes like a long-lost piece of a jigsaw puzzle. Then, lo and behold, another piece fits in perfectly!

From doing Solar Cross readings, I have observed many people working their riddles and making their way through to deeper and deeper levels. Images are a bit like magic dust—you sprinkle it around and nothing happens, and you go to sleep thinking that there wasn't much of anything after all. Then the next morning you wake up and there are giant beanstalks growing, or the fruit on the tree is large and ripe, or you have a new passageway opened up to you.

These riddles lead to a treasure. What is the treasure? For what kind of treasure would you have received a clue at your birth? Is it the location of large crates of gold coins? Is it a fast car or a big house? Is it the man or woman you've been waiting for? You know the answer. At the end of the journey, the completed puzzle, you find that treasure is yourself. It is written in every tradition, even over the entry to the Temple of Delphi in ancient Greece: "Oh, human being, know yourself!" The old prophet Samuel said, "Divinity looks not at outward appearance but looks at the heart."[37] The treasure lies so close yet so far away. You have developed in this general direction for years. Perhaps many choices of path in your exploration have led to distractions or dead ends. Perhaps this approach holds an important clue to the riddle.

Here is the fundamental thesis of the Solar Cross work: Great deeds, great feelings, and great thoughts by human beings on Earth shine out and impress their patterns into the cosmos. Indeed, all deeds, feelings, and thoughts are impressed there. Even in the ancient Book of Enoch, we find the statement "And now know ye, that the angels shall inquire into your conduct in heaven, of the sun, the moon, and the stars, shall they inquire respecting your deeds."[38] That is, the Sun, Moon, and stars know your deeds! All really great deeds, feelings, and thoughts are stored in the stars, a repository that ancient philosophers call the akashic record. Today, scientists have renamed this impressionable matrix of universal energy "the field" or the "zero-point field."[39] Where is this akashic record? It lives in the zodiac, the belt of constellations that lies behind the Sun in its annual journey through the sky. As the Sun moves in its journey through the sky, these resources become available, from the cosmos through the Sun back to the Earth, to human beings who can receive them. The most potent time of reception comes at your first breath in this world, at your birth. The heavenly truths to which the Images refer were impressed into you at that time. They can serve as your routes to find what lives in those places in the zodiac, which are most powerful when applied to your particular life.

The treasure becomes a resource meant for you, held for you since your birth, indeed a birthright to assist you to advance, to avoid obstacles, overcome difficulties, and realize the best that waits in you as potential. The Images can be challenging and that is because, as I have understood in my readings with people, we come into this world with challenges, right from the very beginning.

STAR BROTHERS, STAR SISTERS, AND BODES

After the Images were created (in the manner described in Appendix A), my research took me to historical personalities, meaning anyone for whom I found enough of a biography that I could see the themes of the Images at work in the life story.

It soon became apparent that those who share your star-birthday are Star Brothers and Star Sisters. They breathed in the same Image as you when they were born. Thus their life can show a way to deal with the challenges and opportunities implicit in your Birth Images.

We should note immediately that calendars that have the birthdates of "famous people" on them all use a seasonal calendar and not a star calendar. Thus someone born on March 22, 1854, was born one day after the spring equinox. Someone born this year on March 22 would also be born one day after the spring equinox. The star positions of the two people would not be the same, however, as the seasons move one degree every seventy-two years in relation to the starry heavens, thus separating the star locations of the births of these two.

Furthermore, a birthdate of March 22, 1700, might have been in the Julian calendar, with the same names of months and the same number of days in each month, but, because of a miscalculation in assigning leap years, very much in error by the time it was changed. The switch from the Julian to the Gregorian calendar took place in different countries at different times, beginning in 1582, Russia being among the very last in 1918. You have to know these things in order to find the proper star-dates and thus your real Star Brothers and Star Sisters.

Astrosophers are also very interested in the dates and times of death of historical personalities, because here you see the imprint upon the soul as it exits "this mortal coil." We have come to realize that those who have died into the place where you were born have a conditioning effect on your Birth Images and how they become available to you.

Imagine a hallway that is the passageway of your birth. Your Star Brothers and Star Sisters are those whom you can see traveling before you. As elder brothers or sisters, they hold your hand and go before you, gently pulling you along. Or they go further ahead and you observe them from afar, to see how they fared with the challenges that life brought them. They breathed in the very same Images from the Solar Cross that you did, and you can learn from them how they integrated that into their lives. When you learn who your Star Brothers and Star Sisters are, you then know the names and details of those to whom you have felt related all along. It can bring a sense of warmth, as for an elder sibling, long lost and now found.

There are others who stand along the sides of the hallway, whose imprint at death has gone into that degree. They condition or qualify your experience of passage into this life. Sometimes this assists you as you feel the bright light of their life further illuminating this passageway. Sometimes you encounter those who have been troubled. The soul of the being has moved on, leaving behind a fragment of patterned energy that may be positive or not so positive. We call such an impression from fragments from someone dying into that gate of the heavens a Bode, as when something bodes well or bodes ill. These are the people whose legacy at death is something that you have dealt with since you were born, perhaps without knowing about it.

Thus your passage is marked by those who go before you, as in a Star Brother or Star Sister, and by the Bodes who color your experience in passing through that way, who stand at the side of the hallway either helping or hindering you. We can imagine that the Star Brother or Star Sister has said, "I'm ready to experience this quality of existence now, and that's why I'm coming through this particular hallway."

Bodes are more complicated. They may say, "I offer to this particular spirit container all of what I bring from my life—this is my contribution." You may find such a person helpful, even if distant in time, as a mentor. A Bode might also say, "I want what I sense is in this place in the heavens; I thrash about for a life raft; I cling to this place." A troubled Bode might even create a difficulty in your finding the essence of the Image and its blessings.

Thus a Bode might be seen as a blessing, a companion, an irritant, or even a danger to watch out for. The Australian aborigines, among others, see personality fragments as lurking energy packets that can stick to you, draining your energy. The good fragments have more consciousness, are cleaner, and can truly guide you through difficulties. The cultures that hold these beliefs can cite many experiences to prove them.[40]

Such thinking brings up the question of whether the time of death is known by the soul, and we leave this discussion to the last part of this book, where we can investigate it for the being of Rudolf Steiner.

Why does one choose the degree of birth? Perhaps because the soul intends to encounter this group of individuals. We already know that we have parents and siblings in the stream of physical heredity. Star Brothers and Star Sisters form another group in which we have membership. Crossing over centuries, combining rich and poor, in every geography—these form a group with whom we share a kind of destiny. Seeing them in terms of the Images of one's birth Solar Cross helps find the commonality of soul gesture, hardly ever a similar physical or cultural circumstance.

Of course, there are millions of people who have been born out of and died into any one gate. We only look at those who have been strong enough in their life force to leave an imprint, and at those we know something about. We have to have a biography of some kind. There are certainly some highly developed human beings whose birthdays and death days we don't know who condition your passage in a positive way. We don't know the death dates or degrees of Padmasambhava or Mirabai or Moses or other beings full of light and love. We wish we did, but we don't, and we might imagine that they make themselves available all of the time.

In our study of historical personalities, we have included the best … and we have also included the worst—villains, scoundrels, criminals, and eccentrics. Why? Because it's important for the individual to know what fragments of personality he or she has had to pass through in that hallway into birth if that person died into that gate. It's important to see how a Star Brother or Star Sister came into a life and was unable to overcome the challenges implicit in the Images of the Solar Cross. The Russian composer Modest Mussorgsky, for example, born into a Gate Image that was full of tempestuous storms and near drowning, tried mightily to lift himself up through music, but did indeed drown in alcohol. One can hear in his music the struggle with the tempest—*Night on Bald Mountain* and parts of *Pictures at an Exhibition*. He didn't have the strength to come through the storm.

We always cite composers first, because then you can listen to their music—early compositions if they were born into that degree or late compositions if they died into that degree—as you reflect on the other historical personalities involved. Listen to the music within the context of the Image, as if the Image were being expressed in some way in the nuances of the music. Let the music lead you to the essence of the Image. As Nietzsche said,

> Has one noticed that music frees the spirit, gives wings to the thoughts, that one becomes more of a philosopher, the more one becomes a musician, that the grey heavens of abstraction are lighted by flashes of lightning, that the light is strong enough for all the tracery of things, the large problems near enough for grasping, and the world is seen as from a mountain?[41]

Imagine that the composers would like you to hear their music left behind as a guide to navigation of that Image.

Remember when we go through the historical personalities in the Solar Cross of Steiner's birth that all of them share the entire Solar Cross with him. The Images may come in different locations. For one who was born six months apart from Steiner, his or her Sun Image would be Steiner's Earth Image. The Gate Image, Earth Image, and Horizon Images may differ, but they each share all four Images. These historical personalities do not, however, share Steiner's Conception and Death Images. They also do not share the particular circumstances of Steiner's birth, that is, the planetary configurations that give Steiner's life a qualitative difference, as well as the karmic or hereditary streams leading up to Steiner's life, or the particular circumstances of geography and culture in which Steiner found himself. Individualities find a way of using the same hallways as others, yet remaining unique in their soul's expression in the world. Due to the different circumstances of their births, they have different resonant moments in their lives.

5. How Images Can Fire Your Imagination

Imagination as a Gateway to Development

Steiner spoke many times about the importance of Image, for example:

> Many secrets of the spiritual world must first be explained symbolically or
> partly symbolically, although the images are real and should be taken as
> realities. It is necessary to use an imaginative language … it is necessary to
> speak in the form of images, which you can meditate in your soul.[42]

In Steiner's philosophy, *Imagination*, "what can be called the soul world,"
precedes Inspiration and Intuition, though "Inspiration speaks through the
Imagination."[43] In other words, all three stages of development interact and
interlace with one another, but Imagination develops first.

How can we develop Imagination? First, we can "take a fast from unlawful images."[44] That is, we can stop overstuffing ourselves with images that we
don't have time to digest before we take in even more. If we were to do to
our body what we do to our mind, it would rebel and throw up the excess.
Our technologies have found a way to overstuff our minds beyond the limits
that nature has put there, by convincing us that movies and magazines and
television are all real. When you set a two-year old in front of a television
because it's the most convenient babysitter, and then try an hour later to
take the youngster away, you have an opportunity to understand the allure
of this medium. The child kicks and screams and, even as you drag her away
from the machine, she cannot avert her eyes from the source of its hypno-
tism. Then you see the power you're dealing with.

Why are these "unlawful" images? Because lawful images come from
our actual perceptions of real life-processes in front of us, and their inner
manipulation under our care into imaginations that are created and transformed by us.

A "fast from unlawful images" means setting out on your own for a while. Popular books on the creative process, such as *The Artist's Way* and *Writing Down the Bones*, suggest that we cease reading or even writing for a whole week before beginning the practice of finding out what words can arise within our own being.[45] A more thorough fast may take much longer than this.

Once you have begun your fast, you come very quickly to the stage of withdrawal symptoms, and you simply have to get through it. Nature helps here. Nature gives you the encounter with life-force that your eyes have been seeking all along. You may not "see" the streams of life-force in a plant or an animal. You may not "see" what have been called the elemental beings at work and play—the gnomes in the mineral kingdom, the undines in the water, the sylphs in the air, and the fire elementals in warmth phenomena. But you can feel them. Even the gruffest naysayer has moments of happy contemplation of nature.

Then you become increasingly ready to develop your own imaginations. We find that this works best with a little seed—just as a crystal grows best in a supersaturated solution when a tiny crystal can act as a seed for it to expand upon in its own way.

One technique that we find very helpful, known as mind-mapping, has been designed around how the mind actually works. By "mind," we mean the mechanical brain functions plus feelings plus ideas plus passions, not just a dry intellectual process.

Take a concept, an idea, the seed of an image. Write it in the center of a piece of paper. Then begin writing associations, moving out from the center, as swiftly as possible, making major branches from the core concept, then minor branches that relate to the secondary concepts. Do it for a full three minutes.

Take the idea of "Sun," for example. Starting from the center, here is one view of all the implications of "Sun" (next page). You can scan this mind-map much more quickly than you can skim this paragraph, and get the essential meaning from it in a way that "fits" better with how your brain works. Mind-mapping uses space better as far as the mind is concerned. Some mind-mappers insist on using many different-colored pens, not really to keep track of themes by color-coding them, but simply to keep the mind interested.

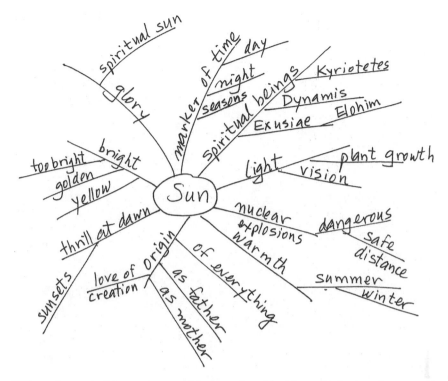

When they mind-map onto a whiteboard or blackboard, the hand not used for writing bristles with pens of many different colors.

Soon we will make a mind-map for a written image. In a few pages, you will pause and ready your paper and pen (or pens). We will turn the page, read an Image, then close the book and begin writing a mind-map of that Image.

This is not a dictation exercise to see how much you remember of the Image you just read. In this activity, we encourage you to let your imagination add things. Yes, it's helpful to write down what you do recall, the actual nouns, verbs, adjectives, and adverbs that are in the original. However, the point is to let the Image live in your being, unlocking other aspects of that Image that aren't on the page. New words and phrases will come out. We feel that those new parts also relate to what lives in the zodiacal degree in the heavens. Thus your mind becomes your resource to find out what lives there.

PART II
STAR WISDOM IN THE LIFE OF RUDOLF STEINER

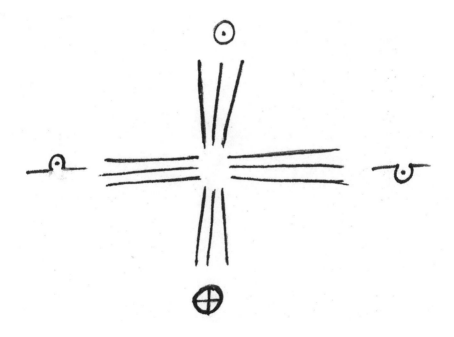

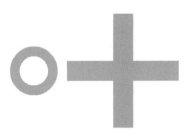

6. THE GATE IMAGE
AT STEINER'S CONCEPTION

A T THE MOMENT of conception, a spirit spark enters into physical matter. It carries with it the soul's intention for the life, what we call pre-earthly intentions. For Rudolf Steiner, this occurred on June 1, 1860, when the Sun lay between 18 and 19 degrees in the sign of Taurus (to be exact, at 18 degrees and 19 minutes of Taurus).[1] What lived in that degree to condition his spirit spark?

Do not turn the page until you have blank paper and a writing implement. When you do turn the page, read the Image, then close the book and make a mind-map of what you remember as well as what adds itself to this material. Choose a central focus, and then build a mind-map from what you've read, and what begins to come as extended imagination. That is, amplify the Image into something that you can relate to personally because you created it—you imagined it!

Conception

Accompanied by stern professors of theology, a wise man passes through a group of children who sing, play musical instruments, and hold palm branches. The professors prefer to speak of texts and traditions. The wise man pauses to greet the children. He bends down to teach them a new prayer: "Sun brilliance, come to Earth. Sun brilliance, come to Earth."

Working the Image

As soon as you have read the Image, take the time to make a mind-map of it, described just before this chapter. It really is worth the three minutes that this takes. Perhaps you think that you can skip this part, and that you only want to get the essence of Rudolf Steiner's life. You will access that better by going through this process. It will awaken your imaginative meeting with the essence of Rudolf Steiner, which will feel much more genuine and real.

For example, here is a possible mind-map of this Image:

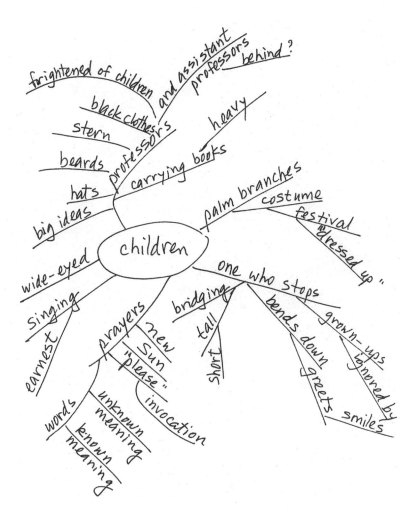

Note that the central concept is not given ahead of time. It could have been another aspect of the Image. Instead of "children," it might have been "professors" or "the one who pauses" or something not even in the Image, such as "soul between thinking and feeling" or "festival day."

Note also that we find a combination of specific words from the Image as well as words that suggested themselves as related. It is best to have a balance of these two sources—at least some of the words of the Image and at least some words that rise up spontaneously in you as you create the mind-map.

If you were to make a second mind-map of this Image, it might be very different. If this were an Image to which you were connected by birth (or by conception), then a Reader in Star Wisdom would encourage you to ponder it for a day or so and make another mind-map as a way of expressing and organizing your thoughts and feelings about it. New feelings emerge, and the Image slowly begins to transform in your being. We encourage clients to use the written or spoken Images as springboards to their own imagination, and not be bound by the original wording. You are meant to be the engineers and construction workers of your own soul images.

Let's try a second mind-map of this Conception Image:

A new center has come forth. New observations have arisen. In this way, one grows and metamorphoses a living imagination.

Now we have the Image as printed, and two mind-maps of it. From this foundation work we can work this Image in more detail.

COMMENTARIES ON THE IMAGE

Can you see the children's smiles and bright eyes, looking up to the newcomer in awe and expectation? They are already full of Sun-brilliance. The new song that they learn focuses their attention on the appeal to the soul to come into their bodies, for the Sun-brilliance to make itself known on earth.

What do their musical instruments look like? How many are there? What are the colors and the smells of these children in this festival? Can you imagine the song? At first it may sound far off, high-pitched echoes of a song. Let your imagination grow so that you hear actual notes, tones that you could sing or sound out on a piano. Compose the song, and add more lyrics as necessary.

The Professors

> Far too little attention is paid in the Anthroposophical Society to the fact that Anthroposophy should not be abstract theory but real life.... It becomes theory only when it is made such—i.e., when one kills it.[2]

Though it is not stated in the Image, the stern professors seem to the imagination of most people to appear tall and dressed in black, with dour faces. Many people imagine the professors carrying books, heavy tomes. Learned, certainly, *very* learned in many languages, arts, traditions, books; so learned that they can argue the fine points of many texts. As we look at Rudolf Steiner's life, we can see him as belonging partly to this group, yet having the interest and the time to attend to the children.

At first glance, many perceive that the upright thinkers—the professors—do not care for the things of the earth. They spurn or simply fail to notice the ignorant children and the simple pageant. Their lofty thoughts soar upward, especially with the inducements of the Illusionist. Grand ideas take them into intellectual discussions, and away from the messiness of life. These philosophers might tend toward what Freud called "intellectualization as a defense," a helpful psychological term that describes those who avoid the messy feelings of being human by becoming all head, hiding behind their books.

Often in this polarity we see that the pure intellect looks upward and the earthly children tend downward, in the opposite direction. But here we see the children lifting upward too with their palm branches and song. They just don't lift high enough to catch the interest of the professors. The one in the middle, whom we can easily identify as Rudolf Steiner, forges a bridge. He becomes the soul linking the lofty spirit and the willing but ignorant body. That is a first impression.

One thinks of Steiner's differentiation between the Shepherd Stream and the King Stream (see Appendix B). He spoke in terms of the events of Christ Jesus's birth, of kings bearing gifts coming from afar and shepherds seeing angels in the heavens. Steiner understood the simple, childlike shepherds to have a more developed heart and the learned kings to have a more developed intellect. In the Image we see the active person bridging these two worlds.

Steiner related later in his life that "the Christian revelation as a whole is actually a Sun revelation, ... Christ is the Being who comes from the Sun."[3] Perhaps he was led to this realization by his own spirit living into this Conception Image.

Let us turn to the historical background of this Image.

BACKGROUND OF THE CONCEPTION IMAGE

On this Solar Day, the Teacher visits a new community and is greeted by representatives of the Shepherd Stream and representatives of the King Stream in the community.[4] The Shepherd stream includes people adorned as if for a feast, children singing and carrying palm branches. The King Stream includes the doctors of theology escorting him into a reception hall where a washing of the feet is performed for the Teacher and his thirty followers.

The Teacher speaks from the new prayer that he is building. Though conventionally named "The Lord's Prayer," in Aramaic its first words are "Abwoon d'bwash maya," meaning, "Father-Mother birther of worlds," so we leave aside the patriarchal name of this prayer and simply call it the Abwoon Prayer.[5]

The Teacher delivers the second petition, what has come to us in Aramaic as "Teytey malkuthakh." The compressed and thus inadequate translation is "Thy Kingdom come." A more complete translation finds in "Teytey" the sense of "come" as in "come here!" and also the sense of mutual desire, even a relationship to a nuptial chamber where a marriage is consummated. If you ask Divinity to "come" to you with this word, it is from a desire to create something living together.

"Malkuthakh" means either kingdom or queendom, and has a close relationship to the sphere of the Kabbalistic Tree of Life named Malkuth, meaning Divinity firmly seated in matter on the Earth. Thus we find in this petition to Divinity an appeal that the realized truth, brilliant light, and effulgent love of the divine Sun realm be brought into the relative darkness of earthly existence, emerging from the inside of every particle.[6]

This can be an individual request, but the Teacher frames the Abwoon Prayer always as a collective appeal. "Give *us* this day *our* daily bread." It's not just about me. We participate as a community in our request. The events of the Revealing and the Sacrifice are the actions of one individual supported by a community to bring the Sun brilliance to Earth.[7] As it takes a village to raise a child, it takes a community to invoke and manifest Divinity.

What does it mean that heaven manifest on Earth? For those who can experience something that is *becoming*, can experience the shimmering of the almost-physical, that is, the etheric existence of a living process, heaven on earth may come in a sense of the aliveness of life, of etheric vitality. For others the Divine presence may be experienced as glory everywhere and always. Those waiting for physical signs—and what would those be?—may be asking for something that will come in a far distant future time, when the physical is consumed back again into the primal creative fire.

For now, can you see the light streaming from the faces of these children? How does their light meet the light of the one who teaches them this new song? Are the lights of the wise and lights of the innocent different or the same?

THE IMAGE IN RELATION TO STEINER'S LIFE

From the point of conception, Steiner was placed into the context in which he would work his entire life—amongst the learned philosophers and theologians. The son of a minor railroad employee who lived in the country, Steiner could have worked for the railroad, too, or he could have become a carpenter, or many other things. But his Conception Image put him in the world of the professors, the People of the Book. From the country boy, he rose to become editor of the scientific works of Johann Wolfgang Goethe, the king of European culture. There was the possibility that he might do the same for the great author Nietzsche. Certainly Steiner could have aimed for and settled down as a learned professor at some German university. The German universities formed the pinnacle of education in the world at that time. Promising young lads were sent from the United States and England to obtain this superior education. Was it stiff and stern? Yes. Was it dry and technical? Yes. However, Steiner excelled here, and could have had a brilliant academic career as one of the professors in his Conception Image.

In your imagination, do these professors have a particular gender? So far, I haven't indicated one. In the imagination of most people, this Image has no women in it. From the beginning, Steiner enters a man's world. How he works with this will be discussed with his four Birth Images. For now, we notice their absence. Maybe there are females among the children. But where will they go when they grow up?

In Images of the Solar Crosses, we often see a challenge and a hint or path to its resolution. In this Image the challenge is membership in the guild of stern professors. In his play *The Wonder-Working Magician*, Calderón gives voice to the Hardener in the case of professors:

> By your dress and by these books
> Round you, like a learned circle
> Of wise friends, I see you are
> A great student, and the instinct

Of my soul doth ever draw me
Unto men to books addicted.[8]

The quote itself works like an academic lecture. It lures you on from phrase to phrase, everything sounds right, then the punch line comes and you realize that you're stuck inside the system. The last word summarizes the entire situation in the Image.

We see the after-effects of the Germanic style of thinking and speaking in Steiner's more philosophical works. He embraced the philosophers of Middle Europe in the nineteenth century, and spoke frequently about the intricacies of their ideas. His summation came in a book originally titled *The Philosophy of Freedom*. It has since been republished under the title *The Philosophy of Spiritual Activity*, and more recently *Intuitive Thinking as a Spiritual Path*, but the new titles do not make the content any easier to comprehend. This book, which at one time Steiner said was his finest work, seats him firmly in the professor's chair, in the world of the stern philosophers. It speaks in the language of philosophy, painstakingly moving step by step from the classical structures of philosophy to the world of spiritual realization. Many people simply cannot get through this book, preferring not to step onto a bridge to philosophy at all. They prefer the talk of angels and elementals, of the arts and drama, that dominated the latter part of Steiner's life work. However, we must see this bridge in the context of the Conception Image, as meeting a heavenly impression formed at the first moment of entry into the physical. *The Philosophy of Freedom* bears marks of the stern professors, as well as marks of the childlike appreciation of the wonder of creation. Steiner returned to this book again and again, bringing it out in many editions.

In Solar Cross Images, the challenge is often set, as well as a path to resolution. One of Steiner's students summarized the trap as follows: "The thought that comes to a standstill is a habit; a habit that stagnates is an instinct; the firmly rooted instinct is death."[9] Here "instinct" is associated with unconsciousness and death, whereas later, in the discussion of Steiner's views of Nietzsche, it becomes a synonym for "intuited direction." The point is that thinking that is not living can retreat into the basest of habits—unconscious instincts—even though they have thoughts attached and are named "thinking." I have had professors who were not living, and their habits killed off the entire field to my interest; they were incapable of doing something new. Steiner's student continued: "Deterioration begins with the feeling of self-satisfaction in traditional virtues," exactly the temptation that the philosophers feel with their texts and systems. Rittelmeyer's account of his relationship with Steiner documents his struggle as a successful pastor, with a large following and a preset intellectual tradition, to open enough to Steiner's ideas that he might test them through personal experience.

What is the resolution that the Image—and Steiner—set for us? To "bend down" to the children and affirm their childlike wonder. To the upright professor struggling to uphold his reputation, what is the cost of bending down? Do the other professors look on in admiration or horror at their colleague bending down? Do their eyebrows rise? Do they imitate or repudiate?

One often feels that Steiner brought out a childlike quality in his audience, not patronizing but respectfully leading them. He affirmed the importance of festivals for the human soul, and certainly valued singing, music, and the waving of palm branches. Indeed, watch for the term "festival" later in this book, and recall how it came at his conception. He sought to take these ancient urges of the human soul, often connected to seasonal celebrations that had lost their purpose, and revivify them. Thus Christmas, the Holy Nights, Easter, St. John's Day, and Michaelmas all became important for him, as well as the celebration of each and every day. They all made sense within the context of the heaven come to earth by way of the Sun-Being.

He bends down to teach the children about the Sun-Being. In one of the last lectures of his life, Steiner says it clearly: "The Christian revelation as a whole is actually a Sun revelation, that Christ is the Being who comes from the Sun and who sends Michael with his hosts on ahead."[10] In the course of his life, Steiner found the Christ in a personal and powerful way. Can we overcome the arguments about doctrinal differentiations that consume the attention of the stern professors, and say that this Sun-Being belongs to all humanity, despite the prejudices for and against the name Jesus Christ? Just as the Sun belongs to all, the Christ that Rudolf Steiner found had come for everyone in every religion and social group. The children can feel this, and Steiner encouraged them to maintain their innocence.

At the end of 1923, Steiner gave a Foundation Stone Meditation to revivify the Anthroposophical Society. The final panel of the Meditation sums up his views of "Sun-brilliance." After a prologue, we come to the forceful invocation, very similar to what the wise man bending down taught the children: "Sun-Being—come to earth!"

> At the turning-point of Time,
> The Spirit-Light of the World
> Entered the stream of Earthly Evolution.
> Darkness of night
> Had held its sway;
> Day-radiant Light
> Poured into the souls of Men:
> Light that gave warmth
> To simple shepherds' hearts,
> Light that enlightened
> The wise heads of kings.
> O Light Divine!
> O Sun of Christ!
> Warm thou our hearts,
> Enlighten thou our heads,
> That good may become
> What from our hearts we would found
> And from our heads direct
> With single purpose.[11]

Can we hear this as a new song that Steiner teaches others?

The children who receive these new songs are grateful. One student, Andrei Belyi, the most expressive chronicler of meetings with Steiner, wrote it thusly: "Thanks, thanks, thanks—thanks to you for every-, every-, every-, everything! And most of all for being what you are!"[12] This childlike exuberance is becoming increasingly rare among children today. At all times plugged in to several electronic gadgets, having difficulty going to sleep unless the television is on, lost in personality cults of rock stars and movie stars (the least accurate use of the term "star"), restlessly puffing up their personalities long before a personality deserves to be formed from an understanding of oneself, our children are losing their ability to notice a man of power and wisdom bending down to them with a gift. That even the most lost of children have moments of openness to loving wisdom reaffirms our faith in basic human nature, though it ought not relax our vigilance to the forces that would steal the childlike from the child.

Steiner warned about the relation of the intellect—the philosophers—to the childlike:

> The expression of spiritual force … should not be entangled in abstract, theoretical ideas if the child's soul is not to become dry and disturbed, instead of remaining linked to the deep roots of human life.… Even we adults, given to reason and intelligence, can never be torn away from these roots of existence.[13]

Like Thomas Aquinas, to whom he was spiritually related, Rudolf Steiner could have spent his energy in formulations of whole systems of philosophy, even Germanic theological philosophy. However, he chose to meet the children, to find ways to lead them forth to the brilliance of the Sun. Not only did he formulate a soul-affirming curriculum in Waldorf schools, but he emphasized the childlike with everyone. Even the "advanced" group of the First Spiritual Class is centered on beautiful verses whose every word has special meaning, creating a feeling of awe and wonder.

In an Image such as this, we have to place Steiner in every position. We have considered Steiner as the standoffish philosopher and as the mediator who knows both groups. We must also imagine Steiner as the child, or as the children. Whom do we imagine might have been the one bending down to Steiner-as-child and teaching him to invoke the Sun-brilliance? Pause to consider this, as we have to answer it. Who taught Steiner to sing to the Sun-Being, to address the festival of life to spiritual foundations? Several persons may suggest themselves during the course of this book, ending with a particular figure in the last chapter of Part II.

A good way to learn about an Image is to physicalize it, to go through the motions, setting it up with oneself in all parts, or with helpful friends. You can learn so much this way, for in the gestures of the body enacted, one finds great wisdom.

When working with the Oracle of the Solar Cross, we always query whether the person succeeded in meeting the challenge and bringing it to resolution. Our answer for Rudolf Steiner would be yes. From the clients we have worked with on their Solar Crosses, and from the study of historical personalities, we realize that some people are not capable of coming to resolutions. In this case, others with the same Conception Image might not be able to move out of the self-important club of experts. As we shall see later, this question comes up again in Steiner's birth Solar Cross. Steiner was able to remove himself from the professors. He succeeded at mastering the gift of the spiritual beings living at the degree of his Conception Sun.

SOUNDING THE GONG OF THE IMAGE THROUGHOUT THE LIFE

In the course of this study, I will, after each Image or each polarity of Images, present related material in lives and in time. For the four Birth Images, I will do this through looking at historical personalities who have the same Image in their lives. This includes the Star Brothers, Star Sisters, and Bodes to whom Rudolf Steiner is related. For the Conception Image, I will not look at historical personalities because I do not wish to overwhelm the reader with this approach.

For each Image, we will look at how the moving planets during the course of the life interact with points of sensitivity in the birth or conception moments. We can think of this as a moving striker hitting against the gong of a place in the heavens to which the individual is particularly sensitive. For these points, we will ask of the biography—"What happened at these times? What repercussion of the striker hitting the gong can we perceive in this life?"

We restrict ourselves in this study to the position of the Sun, which at conception was at 18 degrees 19 minutes of the Bull, Taurus. For the Conception Image we look at one aspect only, that of conjunction, that is, a planet crossing that very same position.

We begin with the projection of prenatal events into the life, then look at the actual or real-time crossings of the point of sensitivity.

PRENATAL ANTICIPATIONS IN RELATION TO THE CONCEPTION IMAGE

As explained in Part I, the planetary events of the time between conception and birth can be imagined to project out into the actual life. Thus events during gestation can be seen in the events of the life as lived. What planets interacted with the position of Steiner's Conception Sun during the time of gestation? We don't look at the slow planets past Saturn, because the projection of their conjunction into the life is not very accurate. We moreover restrict ourselves to conjunction with that one position only. We find that there is only one such conjunction with the Conception Sun position during the prenatal period.

Prenatal planet crossing the Sun position at conception	Corresponding date in Steiner's life	Steiner's age
Mercury in Taurus	December 15, 1861	0 years, 9 months

Prenatal Mercury conjunct the Conception Sun position, projected into the life to December 15, 1861, age nine months

In his lectures on education, Steiner made the point that the most prodigious feats that any human being accomplishes occur during the first two or three years of life, when the little human being lifts the body into an upright position and learns to move in space with balance, to form the capacity of speech in the mouth and thinking in the brain. But we forgot all those accomplishments. We can't say much about Mercury passing this place at so young an age, as we simply don't know the specific details of what happened then. It may interest you, however, to know that the extraordinary things that children do—"Isn't he amazing? I don't know where he got that!"—may have correlations in the heavens.

Uranus's long conjunction with the Conception Sun position

During gestation the planet Uranus moves over this point also, then moves back again, never getting very far from the Conception Sun position between the ages (projected into the life) of fifteen and thirty-nine years—far too much time to characterize in any particular way. This illustrates why slow-moving planets aren't very useful in prenatal anticipations beyond the prompting to say something like, "Temptations of the Illusionist and unexpected changes in terms of the Conception Image affected Rudolf Steiner from the ages of fifteen to thirty-nine." This sounds far too broad. But consider also that this marks the long period of preparation for a major event in Steiner's life at the end of 1899, at the end of his thirty-ninth year, a "festival" that we shall discuss in the four Birth Images. When Uranus passes by the Conception Sun, he is ready to receive a revelation from the Sun-Being.

Having just one conjunction during the prenatal period suggests that the pre-earthly intention was not to charge or encumber particular times in the life with the Conception Image. Relation to the send-off of the Conception Image was left more to the free deeds of the individual.

REAL-TIME CROSSINGS OF THE CONCEPTION SUN POSITION

These are transits in real time during the life. In contrast to our examination of the prenatal anticipations, in regarding the Conception Sun position we look less at the fast-moving planets that cross the point of sensitivity many times. We concentrate on the slower-moving planets, Jupiter and beyond. We will begin with the last transit of a major planet over the Conception Sun position, and then move about the latter part of the life. As the Conception Sun is very close to the Eastern Horizon Image of the birth, we may expect some similarities in some instances, and some surprises in others.[14]

TRANSITING PLANET CROSSING THE CONCEPTION SUN POSITION	CORRESPONDING DATE IN STEINER'S LIFE	STEINER'S AGE
Jupiter conjunct conception Sun (Taurus)	April 23, 1918	57 years, 2 months
Jupiter conjunct conception Sun (Taurus)	May 10, 1906	45 years, 2 months
Saturn conjunct conception Sun (Taurus)	July 2, 1913, January 17, 1914, and March 9, 1914	52 years, 4 months, to 53 years, 0 months
Pluto conjunct conception Sun (Taurus)	Five passes, from August 5, 1894 to May 14, 1896	33 years, 5 months, to 35 years, 2 months

Jupiter conjunct the Conception Sun position, April 23, 1918, age fifty-seven years, nearly two months

What would we expect when Jupiter transits over the Sun position at conception? We might expect an encounter with significant thoughts (Jupiter), indeed a life philosophy (Jupiter), powered by the primary metamorphic force (Sun) in relation to one's pre-earthly intentions (Conception).

In lectures around this date, Steiner spoke about the link between the dead and the living, and the communion with the dead. Indeed, at this time, at the end of World War I, many felt the "army of the dead" around them.[15] So many young people were killed before their time in World War I—can we see them as the youngsters of the Image, crowding into the dreams of the living, awaiting guidance from someone wise in matters of life and death?

Steiner recommended a link through ever-present spiritual beings to the dead and gave suggestions on how to use these paths of communication and exchange. He noted that spiritual help from the previous century had been ignored, causing great suffering all around him. He sought to reinvigorate the founts of life-force in order to counteract the despair prevalent at the time.

Significant in terms of the Image of conception in this month, Steiner was working diligently on preparing a new edition of his *Philosophy of Freedom*. He was also preparing a new version of his book about his mentor, *Goethe's World-View*. Both of these works had come out originally twenty years before, but he sought to make little changes to improve them, and to set himself in relation to the philosophers of his time, as well as the past. In terms of the Image, these books and these lectures made his relationship to the stern—and dead—philosophers much clearer, opening up the realm of thinking to new life force, that is, to the children. Steiner worked constructively with the opportunity given by the celestial event of Jupiter atop his Conception Sun position. He sought to perfect his articulation of the higher self working into life via the proposals of ethical individualism and true creative thinking, divorced from associationism.[16]

Through actual examples you will see how we can build up a picture of what was happening at the time of a transit. We don't expect that an activity by Steiner will conform exactly to our concepts, nor should it. The stars create opportunities in their dynamic movements, and each individual works with these in unique ways.

Jupiter conjunct the Conception Sun position, May 10, 1906, age forty-five years, two months

Jupiter again, twelve years earlier, awakening the issue of allegiances to this or that stream of philosophy and theosophy. On May 7, Steiner attended a commemoration of the death of Helena Petrovna Blavatsky, who had died fifteen years earlier (actually on May 8) in London. Born in Russia in 1831, she had studied in Tibet, started the Theosophical Society in 1875, published *Isis Unveiled* in 1877 and her grand work, *The Secret Doctrine*, in 1888. She passed over the threshold in 1891. In her will, Blavatsky suggested that her friends might gather together on the anniversary of her passing and read from Sir Edwin Arnold's *The Light of Asia* and from the essential treatise on Hindu philosophy, the Bhagavad-Gita. One year after her passing, lotuses grew in great quantities, earning May 8 the name White Lotus Day in theosophical circles.

Near the turn of the century, Steiner became interested in the Theosophical Society and rose quickly to the post of General Secretary of the German Theosophical Society. His contemporaries in the Society included Annie Besant and C. W. Leadbeater, with whom at first Steiner cooperated. By 1906, however, his relationship with the Theosophical Society had become conspicuously strained.

Just at this time, C. W. Leadbeater was ejected from the Theosophical Society. This gave Steiner an opportunity to write to the German members of the Society about Leadbeater's particular type of spiritual inquiry. "I have to reject the methods by which he arrives at his occult knowledge and what he recommends to others as a useful method of working....the methods employed are dangerous and apt to mislead."[17] Here Steiner makes clear with whom he is aligned, and with whom not.

Steiner spoke at a Congress of the Federation of European Sections in Paris, on the great personalities who had fostered the spiritual traditions into the nineteenth century, including Paracelsus, Jacob Boehme, Lessing, Herder, Goethe, Schiller, Novalis, Fichte, and others. In terms of the Image, Steiner was setting up the facts about anthroposophy in relation to these giants of philosophy, including Blavatsky herself. That is, he was negotiating his relationship with the philosophers in the Image. He had gone beyond the philosophers that the academics accepted as their colleagues—Fichte, Lessing, etc.—to include the theosophists—Blavatsky, Olcott—and others outside of the halls of academia—Novalis, for example. He saw philosophy—*philia* (collegial love or the love of friendship) for *Sophia* (wisdom, the feminine divine principle)—in the broadest terms, and was making his position clear.

At this Paris conference, he met for the first time Edouard Schuré, with whom he would collaborate especially on dramatic presentations of esoteric material. Schuré wrote later that this meeting with Steiner was pivotal: "For the very first time, I was certain of having before me an initiate."[18] Schuré could perceive the Sun-Being light streaming from Steiner.

Steiner's lectures constituted the basis of what later was printed as his book *Occult Science*, since retitled *An Outline of Esoteric Science*, dealing with the "Sun-brilliance" at the foundation of all existence. Notes the host of Steiner's additional lectures, "We began at our residence with only fourteen—Russians and Germans—and soon we were over sixty. Then we were able to have the Branch hall after the Congress, and the number of listeners from all countries continued to grow."[19] This is the way that children spread the word. (You see how we can be instructed about aspects of the Image not explicit in the Image, but implied there.) The audience came from here and there to hear significant thoughts such as the origins of the Earth, Sun, and stars.[20]

Saturn conjunct the Conception Sun position, three passes, July 2, 1913, January 17, 1914, and March 9, 1914, age from fifty-two years, four months, to fifty-three years

Saturn passed over the Conception Sun position, then appeared to go backwards over it again (moving in retrograde motion), then passed it going forward again, a third and final time, before moving on. What would we expect of Saturn here? We would expect these events to stimulate one's pre-earthly intentions through the metamorphic force of the Sun in order to awaken cosmic memory and assert the essential truth (Saturn) of one's personal life and of all life.

At the first pass, Steiner was preparing his last two mystery dramas, *The Soul's Awakening* and *The Guardian of the Threshold*, for performance. He was working with Edouard Schuré again. All his efforts went into these very comprehensive and lengthy dramas, each one taking about eight hours to perform. He gave no lectures during these weeks, pouring all of his attention into the plays.[21]

This is the first time that the final play, *The Soul's Awakening*, was performed. Its most astonishing action occurs in the eighth scene. In previous scenes, we have been in homes, in offices, and in the countryside. Suddenly we are in a grand temple of Egypt with great statues about us, many priests dressed in ornate costume preparing for a grand ceremony. Our heroine of these plays, Maria, in a previous incarnation as a young man in ancient Egypt, undergoes an initiation ceremony in the temple. There arrayed are all the various notables of the temple, what we could understand as the philosophers in the Image. When the young man (Maria) undergoes the initiation, he experiences himself as an individual embraced and empowered by spiritual beings, and centrally by fire and light. As the young man reports to the priests gathered in the temple: "I felt the loving tide of cosmic fire receiving me as flowing spirit waves.... Spirits rayed light on [my body that I had departed as in a sleep] from lofty worlds; like shining butterflies there hovered near the beings tending, quickening its life."[22]

The assembled priests in the Egyptian temple are dismayed. From their point of view, initiation is not about bringing brilliance to Earth, to one's physical body—it's about getting away from Earth. They shout, "Sacrilege! Punish!" Yet the youth has experienced a Sun-brilliance that has come to Earth, precisely the Conception Image. Thus is born something new, the human individuality. Steiner remarked later: "This scene is a quite decisive, concrete picture that is written into the Akasha chronicle. It is that moment in which, for the first time, an initial sign lights up of the approaching Greek culture."[23]

"Akasha" is the ancient Sanskrit name for the impressionable substrate of energy that scientists now call "the field."[24] In the Greeks we see the celebration of the "sense of joy in warmth of life," in the body on the Earth, exactly what the children in the Image value.

Steiner had a particular love for the sphere and influence of Saturn. Here at the crossing of Saturn over his Conception Sun, he worked very constructively with the opportunity.

At the second pass, January 17, 1914, Steiner gave a lecture on the origin of evil (January 15). He said that evil came not from the nature of matter itself, but from something that humans have brought from spiritual worlds and inappropriately placed into the physical world. A modern illustration would be the development of the atomic bomb—what ought to have been left to spirit realms as spirit power was brought into the Earth realm, and from this an evil has been created that is barely under control. One can see the conflict between the wide-eyed children in the Image and the philosophers, the latter bringing down these dangerous secrets into the world, which affects everyone.[25]

During these days, the artists were arriving from everywhere to participate in the construction of the Goetheanum, the great building made of the woods of every part of the globe, as a sanctuary of the spiritual life. The Goetheanum was located on a hill in Dornach, Switzerland, which Steiner identified as an important location in the ninth-century epic of Parzival.[26] Parzival, also Parsifal or Perceval, means "pierce the veil," or reveal the truth of the situation. The tale involves King Arthur, the Round Table of Knights, and the search for the Grail Castle.

At the final pass of Saturn over the Conception Sun position, on March 9, 1914, we learn that, on March 11, Rudolf Steiner began to carve the Saturn capital that would crown the mammoth Saturn pillar in the Goetheanum.[27] A Saturn transit finds Steiner artistically related to the essence of Saturn. These carvings were based on the most comprehensive understanding of sacred geometry, the wisdom used in the construction of the cathedrals.

To get a little of the flavor of this carving, let's listen to one of the artists in the carving shop. Nathalie Turgenieff-Pozzo, sister-in-law of Andrei Belyi, describes Steiner hurrying from one workshop to another, sketchbook in hand—recalling the professors in the Image with their books:

> We have before us a row of wooden blocks more than a yard each in height and width.... We take chisels and mallets. A great effort is needed to cut even a splinter out of the block. We take counsel, we pull on the wood, we are already tired. Our arms are sore, yet one sees no result of the effort. Dr. Steiner ... takes a mallet and a chisel, climbs on a wooden crate and begins to work. He too has never done such work before, but after a few blows with the mallet he appears to be quite familiar with it and cuts one furrow after another. We see him hammer for ten minutes, one hour, two hours, without stopping. We stand at a distance, pale with exhaustion, and look at him in awed silence. We knew by experience how hard the work was.[28]

We would say that Steiner derived his extraordinary energy for this particular task from the play of Saturn on his Conception Sun position! He was seizing an opportunity to work with his own spiritual destiny.

Steiner essentialized the tradition of the search for the Grail Castle in five steps, first in the location of the Goetheanum in this sacred landscape of Parzival, then in the design of the building as a whole, and even further in the designs of the major pillars holding up the building. The most essential capital of all was Saturn, the holder of cosmic memory and the origin, in the period of Old Saturn, of all existence. We could therefore say that this experience is the fifth essence—or quintessence—of the teachings of the cosmos. The rendezvous with this artistic outpouring was set as a pre-earthly intention, that is, from Steiner's spirit at conception, to be unlocked at this moment. Here we see Steiner speaking to the stars.

He said, "The plastic forms of the capitals are what the 'seer' hears."[29] We must imagine Steiner with hammer and chisel pounding into the wood—and listening.

Astrologers feel affirmed when connections such as this—Saturn transit and Saturn pillar—are revealed. However, we cannot expect, nor should we hope for, this kind of strong connection with every transit and every prenatal anticipation. That would give us a picture of a mechanical existence, everything that happens on earth being in reaction to some planetary movement or other. We are more interested in the *quality* of these meetings, and in what else we can learn from them. Look at this series with Saturn—in every case, Steiner works with his relationship to the philosophers of all kinds, from mainstream thinkers to theosophists. One can imagine that the work on the Saturn capital distills entire lectures and writings into their most profound essentials. The man of many words finds expression for his philosophy in the proportions of the shapes in that sculpture. We can say this with greater certainty because the modern sculptor Frank Chester has explored the fundamental curvatures and proportions of the Saturn capital for a decade with mathematical exactitude, finding there the seeds of design ideas for water purification, for new cathedrals, for a model of the human heart, and even for the energy patterns of the interior of the Earth.

A small part of a fantasy play written by Steiner's student and later colleague Albert Steffen shows the importance of these capitals. The play sets up a meeting at the end of the workday, when the workmen can no longer see well enough to chisel the wood, between the workmen, the overseer of the building, and Steiner, who visits them in their studio. War is still raging not far away. The little play includes this exchange:[30]

OVERSEER

When will peace come?

RUDOLF STEINER

Only when the dead
can be included in our conferences.

OVERSEER

But how?

RUDOLF STEINER

Why, in the language of these forms.
Would that the living too might listen to them.
Then they would know themselves to be immortal,
while still encumbered with an earthly frame,
and cease to harbour hate in scornful hearts.

This insight from a poetical workman writing about his teacher, poised on high scaffolds day after day, indicates that there may be another group in the Conception Image. Behind the whole scene of stern philosophers and cherubic children, we can imagine that the group of the dead watches and listens. We can all listen, even to a mute sculpture. As the central figure of the Image teaches a song to the children, so he supervises the sculpting of hardwood to sing out, that others may hear and the hate in their scornful hearts be healed. The dead watch and learn.

On March 7, Steiner spoke on the fivefold gestalt of the primal first word—the archetypal original word, the Logos word—from the beginning of the Gospel of John. Here too he took many words back to one word, essentializing to the first word, then back through that to the spirit beings behind the word and words. He traced, in other words, the path of Sun-brilliance to the Earth and back again, back and forth. We can imagine that the first word, and the first words, were sung, and that some have the ability to teach this song to us, a song of our own inner nature.

In astrology, we would call this brief series a successful negotiation of a Saturn transit. Saturn poses a certain kind of challenge. In three crossings, the human being either succeeds in finding something new or transforming in some way, or fails, allowing this focus on the important question of a lifetime to sink back into the complexities of everyday affairs, to arise again at the next Saturn passage.

As we shall see later, the activity of building things has more to do with his Gate Image. In this interplay with Saturn over his Conception Sun, we can see the particular activity of the one who goes back and forth from the stern professors to the bright-eyed children, consulting the knowledge of the first group and using the boundless energy of the second group to make things happen, from drama to the carvings in the Goetheanum. Certain details arise that relate particularly to the Image and the amplifications of the Image through mind-mapping. In these Saturn transits, we see how creativity becomes grounded in actual creations. The formative forces depicted in the seals and column designs, culminating in the Saturn seal, the Saturn column, and finally the Saturn capital, are brought into the hardwood, into actual physical substance. Children mature in the process. Here is an account of one who worked on carving these capitals: "He turned us from impractical, dreamy eccentrics who often ran away from life into workmen who used their bodies in the service of the spirit."[31]

Pluto conjunct the Conception Sun position, five passes, from August 5, 1894 to May 14, 1896, age thirty-three years, five months, to thirty-five years, two months

Pluto moves slowly, taking just over 247 years to pass through the entire zodiac. Because it is so small and distant, many would like to ignore Pluto, and today its status as a planet is being challenged. In our other work in Star Wisdom, we have been forced to recognize Pluto's power, so we do include it. Can we really look at five different conjunctions during the life? For most lives, we would not be able to do this. For Steiner's, however, we have a more thorough chronicle than for most lives, and we can see what part Pluto played.

This period of time, in sum, had all to do with Steiner's relationship with one major philosopher, Friedrich Nietzsche, from its beginning to its end, all within this Pluto transit. Having successfully worked in the Goethe-Schiller Archive, Steiner was the "wonder-working magician," arranging, editing, and commenting upon Goethe's works while publishing his own works. Nietzsche's sister, Elisabeth Förster-Nietzsche, began to woo Steiner over to tackle Nietzsche's stacks of notes and unfinished bits and pieces. The correspondence commenced at the beginning of the Pluto period and the whole relationship ended as Pluto passed on its way.[32]

Friedrich Nietzsche was born in the autumn of 1844 and rose quickly to professor of philosophy by 1869, when Steiner turned eight years old.

Nietzsche worked in the university for ten years. From 1870 his health began a long, slow decline. His final lucid year was 1888, and in January 1889 he collapsed and had to be taken care of from that moment on. Later physicians diagnosed his illness as the madness that comes from delayed syphilis, a particularly painful way to die. Steiner had another diagnosis, which we will discuss later.

Steiner first read Nietzsche in 1889, beginning with *Beyond Good and Evil*: "I was fascinated ... yet repelled at the same time.... I loved his style, I loved his daring.... I felt myself near to his struggle."[33] By then it was too late to meet the author himself.

Meanwhile, Nietzsche's sister, younger than her brother by two years, had married an anti-Semitic agitator, Bernhard Förster, and the two of them had gone to Paraguay to found a Christian Aryan colony. The community failed, and Bernhard killed himself. Just then Friedrich's needs were very great, and Elisabeth returned to Germany to care for him, eventually becoming executor of his personal and literary estate. She began by visiting the Goethe-Schiller Archive in the spring of 1894 to find out how it functioned, so she could set up something similar for her brother. There she encountered the impressive young Dr. Rudolf Steiner, the master at organizing messes of notes, one who understood philosophical concepts and was a philosopher in his own right. He had just published his *Philosophy of Freedom* in November of 1893. We have records of letters from Elisabeth to Steiner, the first visit to the Nietzsche Archive (in Elisabeth's house), then a closer look at the papers, more letters back and forth, the publication of Steiner's book on Nietzsche in May of 1895, then the first and only meeting with Nietzsche himself, languishing ill and mad on a couch in Elisabeth's house in Naumberg.

Friedrich Rittelmeyer, Steiner's lifelong friend and head of the Christian Community movement, made much of this one and only encounter between Nietzsche and Steiner on January 22, 1896. He suggested that before Nietzsche's blank gaze stood the true realization of Nietzsche's highest ideal, the "superman."[34] This visit to Nietzsche will come up again in a later chapter.

Let's look at Steiner's appraisal of Nietzsche, helpfully summarized by Steiner himself in his book *Friedrich Nietzsche: A Fighter Against His Time*, written in this Pluto crossing of the Conception Sun position and published at its center, in May 1895. The admiration in these pages—evident in statements such as "This is a thought of a boldness hardly to be surpassed"[35]—was to change later when, beyond the influence of Pluto, Steiner seemed to discover Nietzsche's pathology. We shall look into that part in a moment. For now, let's examine how Nietzsche appeared to Steiner from inside this turbulence from Pluto.

When Nietzsche blasts modern culture as enslaving, Steiner agrees. When Nietzsche says that the fundamental urge of the human being is an instinct for life, instinct meant in the most primal and positive sense, Steiner agrees. Steiner agrees also when Nietzsche, trained in the classical Greek authors, contrasts the Apollonian mode of thought—cold, controlling, intellectual, and life-hating—with the Dionysian—life-affirming, freedom-loving, passionate, dancing, and liberated. Dionysos is primal ecstasy. Occasional mentions of Dionysos in Steiner's life all refer back to this dichotomy constructed by Nietzsche. When Steiner sponsored Edouard Schuré's *Sacred Drama of Eleusis* at the 1907 Munich Congress of the Theosophical Society, he had his future wife, Marie von Sivers, play Persephone, who at her rescue rebirths her brother, Dionysos.

In *Christianity as Mystical Fact*, Steiner extols Dionysos:

> As soon as this divine element, Dionysos, comes to life, the soul experiences a great longing for its true spiritual status.... As in Demeter was worshiped the divine creatrix of the eternal in man, so in Dionysos was worshiped the divine element, ever changing in the whole world.[36]

Later on, Rittelmeyer notes the way in which freedom can express itself, in the being of Rudolf Steiner as lecturer: "At one moment he looked quite young, the next sallow with age; one moment he had the virility of a man, the next the fragile delicacy of a woman; one moment he was the dry teacher, the next an inspired Dionysos."[37] Freedom means you can be all these people in one. You don't become a certain Thing, you become capable of many enactments.

Steiner rejoices in repeatedly quoting a certain passage from Nietzsche's *Thus Spake Zarathustra*:

> You say you believe in Zarathustra, but of what account is Zarathustra? You are my believer, but of what account are believers? You have not

searched for yourselves yet.... Now I advise you to forsake me and to find *yourselves*; and only when all of you have denied me will I return to you.[38]

Nietzsche sees "believers" not only in the students of the stern professors of the Conception Image but in the professors themselves. He pours derision upon them, beginning with simple personal dislikes—"There is mistrust in me for dialectic, even for proofs"[39]—then becoming more severe. Steiner quotes him, describing the "dissatisfied, proud, disagreeable creatures who cannot free themselves from a deep dissatisfaction with themselves, with the earth, and with all life.... clever, secretive, invisible anemic vampires."[40] Nietzsche's words are a powerful addition for this Image: "When I beheld my devil, I found him serious, thorough, profound, solemn: it was the spirit of Gravity."[41] Gravity as excessive seriousness and as dead weight lived in the Image in the form of the stern professors. Steiner adds his own bit about the philosophers: "animated textbooks of logic" who try to prove their position with "legal artifices."[42] With Steiner's agreement, Nietzsche sees in philosophers and priests, critics and politicians, a fundamental *ascetic nihilism*. The asceticism comes from the denial of the life force naturally arising in the human being. The nihilism comes from serving not a changeable and shifting life force, but an unseen god, fixed, stable, and dead. Alignment with "divine will" or a "categorical imperative" or a patriotic ideal or any grand concept, when not actually experienced and especially when defined as unknowable, is allegiance to a Nothing.[43] Allegiance to a Nothing annihilates life, exactly Pluto's reputation.

Steiner notes the way Nietzsche contrasts the strong-willed individual with the weak-willed follower: the latter tries to parasitize the former. He admires the strong-willed individual, who has the courage to find what lives in him- or herself. Rather than blind obedience to concepts beyond experience, the strong individual faces life as it actually presents itself. He or she allows the natural "will to power," by which Nietzsche means the instinct to become empowered as an individual, to develop. Thereby the strong-willed individual comes to know freedom.

Steiner reports and supports Nietzsche's theory that people like to affiliate with something bigger because of their self-hatred. Rejection of the puny self looks like asceticism and can be fashioned into something virtuous. If I deny my unworthy self and affiliate with something truly grand, even though I don't know what it is, the exhilaration of power rushes in. Later Steiner would speak of this phenomenon in terms of vacuums—when we create a vacuum, either physically or, in this instance, energetically and spiritually, spirits rush in. If we are unconscious of the dynamics here, we may easily let in demonic and dark spirits.

The strong-willed individual, Nietzsche declared, becomes a "superman" in relation to the timid many. For Steiner, this completely affirmed his ideas about freedom, and he added: "The strong, truly free human being will not receive truth, he will create it."[44] People tend to erect altars to false gods. Steiner saw Nietzsche as willing to topple them all.

In line with Steiner's Conception Sun Image, Nietzsche's ideal became the child: "I named for you three metamorphoses of the spirit: How the spirit became a camel, the camel a lion, and the lion at last, a child. Thus spake Zarathustra."[45] The child is supported by music—Dionysian dancing music, festival music, just as in the Image.[46] Also, "the child is innocence and forgetfulness, a new beginning, a sport, a self-propelling wheel, a first motion, a sacred Yes."[47]

In Nietzsche, Steiner found a fellow fighter against the ravages of time on the human spirit. But what seemed destined for a union of ideas began to fall apart. The conflict with Elisabeth became too great. As Steiner expressed it, "This woman plays frivolous games with other people's lives. She turns the words around in her mouth, speaks in one sentence five lies, injures other people, and masks her own intentions."[48] Her intentions become clear in the years after Steiner's death. She published notes that Nietzsche never intended to be published, and edited to the point of interference, even forging and then publishing letters to and from Nietzsche. She had an agenda: to link up Nietzsche's brilliant ideas to the aspirations of German nationalism—aims that Nietzsche himself would have repudiated. She became so successful at this that there were two books put into the rucksack of every German solider in World War I—*The Gospel of John* and Elisabeth's version of Nietzsche's *Thus Spake Zarathustra*. She died in 1935 before she could see the full use that the Nazi party made of selections of Nietzsche's writings. The "will to power" concept, for example, intended to reveal the essence of life force, was corrupted to become a justification for the strong suppressing the weak.

Coming out of the period where Pluto was ruffling his Conception Sun Image, Steiner began to see Nietzsche in a new light. He spoke and wrote about Nietzsche's "psychopathology," the case of "a critic made ill by his own criticism."[49] He saw Nietzsche's frequent antipathy and antagonism, as displayed in passages such as this one: "These alone are my readers, my true readers, my readers intended for me; what does the *rest* matter? The rest are mere humanity. One must surpass humanity in strength, in elevation of soul—through contempt."[50] Indeed, Nietzsche concluded that "sympathy humiliates."[51] Steiner saw that antipathy was Nietzsche's rule: "I walk among this people and I let many a word drop; but they know neither how to accept nor how to retain... And when I shout, 'Curse all cowardly devils in you who like to whine and fold their hands and pray,' they shout, 'Zarathustra is godless.' ... I am Zarathustra the godless."[52] We have spoken of Zarathustra and we will see Zarathustra's mighty role in Steiner's life. Quite unaware of this connection, Nietzsche was luring Steiner with potent bait with his invocation and identification with Zarathustra. But it was bitter when it should have been sweet, and Steiner awoke to that fact after a few years in the thrall of Nietzsche's version of Zarathustra.

It was an act of humiliation not of a human but of an animal that aroused Nietzsche's sympathy just at the end. In early January 1889, he wrote wild letters to people, signed "The Crucified One." Several were sent to Cosima Wagner, one that included, "But this time I come as the victorious Dionysos, who will make a festival of the earth ... the heavens rejoice that I am here ... I have also hung on the Cross..." Just after this, Nietzsche passed by an old horse being whipped on the street by its owner. He ran for the horse, flung his hands around its neck, and prevented the owner from whipping it again. A crowd gathered, a scuffle, shouting. A few days later he was taken by a friend to an asylum and committed.[53] A drawing of him from this time appears later in the book.

Steiner observed that Nietzsche leaned toward an "intellectual lust for destruction," often rampant and unconcerned with the facts, indeed, incoherent.[54] Destruction and annihilation come up often when there are strong angular relations with the Pluto sphere. At the latter end of the Pluto transits, Steiner became increasingly aware of this. Much later, Steiner said that Nietzsche was absent from himself prior to his collapse and confinement, indeed that he had been possessed by the Hardener.[55]

Steiner began to feel that Nietzsche had gone too far. The extreme of independence is unrelatedness. As Steiner was beginning to understand that the true aim of soul growth is relationship with other human beings, a middle ground had to be found, not an extreme position. Steiner envisaged "sovereign individualities" in relation to each other. Unrelatedness becomes feelings without thought. From observation, one might assume the opposite—that those who are unrelated to others have no feeling, and are caught up in the ivory tower of their thought process. But Steiner meant something very special by "thought." He focused on true thought, the kind of thought that connects us to spirit and to earth. Through language, thought's child, we find a universal heart that connects us with every other human being.

Steiner criticizes Nietzsche for not emphasizing that the instinct that guides the free individual should be conscious, and thereby can be a source of "moral fantasy"—by which Steiner means motivations for action in the world that are derived from pure thought and are consciously experienced.[56] This is very important. Unconscious instinct will not really make someone free. The liberty to let any impulse express itself may look like freedom, but actually it is not. The compulsive anarchist becomes the most unfree.

To Nietzsche was ascribed the sound bite "God is dead," a topic that he wrote about in *Antichrist* and other books. From the perspective of a hundred years later, we can see that Nietzsche was reacting to the vise grip of the church on the imaginations of human beings. In what the churches presented as "God," Nietzsche saw only a grand Nothing. He was happy for the death, for it was the death of an illusion. Steiner went along with Nietzsche to a great extent because of his identification with the "fighter against his time." Though Steiner agreed that "all ideals stem from natural instincts,"[57] he saw in this a cause for optimism about humanity. Given what was coming soon in Steiner's life at the very end of the century, this disavowal of the being of Christ appears like a complete cleansing of all preconceptions.

Fundamentalists see life in black-and-white terms. One simply is either in or out, and there's no avoiding judgment for those who don't make it. The black-white system doesn't move; it is static and unchanging. Contrast the path of Dionysos, which we here recall with a quote from Steiner: "In Dionysos was worshiped the divine element, ever changing in the whole world."[58] "Ever changing"—never still, always in development. True Christianity can be seen in these terms, as assisting others in their development. Indeed, the spiritual beings at the core of Christianity—Christ consciousness, the vessel of Jesus, and the others involved (and named in Appendix B)—continue to develop in relation to world evolution. Heaven isn't a dead place, but living and everywhere—"in the whole world"—not only in a few special places.

The churches' hold on society relaxed in the hundred years after Nietzsche, whose bombastic contempt did its part to trigger that change. Some of the severe criticism of Nietzsche can be understood when the cultural milieu of the critic is freethinking and tolerant. Today the vise grip of religion has returned. Does it help us to understand modern fundamentalism as ascetic nihilism? Can we better shake off the hair shirts and find our freedom from within?

In hindsight, we can see that Steiner was preparing for his initiation on or about December 2, 1899. On the road to this initiation, he had climbed to the castle of the philosopher-king of the day, Nietzsche, to meet the man and his work. Who else was talking about freedom of the essential human being? Who else was working with Zarathustra? During his time with Nietzsche and the Nietzsche material, Steiner had to discern what was worthy, what was corrupt, when one is right in rejecting the weak-willed humans, and when one must cultivate a relationship with the developing souls in all human beings. Elisabeth's disdain and manipulations alerted him to the contempt and caricature in Nietzsche's writings, signs of the Hardener. He felt the fundamental comradeship with the philosopher-king, but the man before him was mad, possessed. Steiner backed away. It made him the more pure, the more cleaned out of preconceptions, ready for an important encounter at the end of 1899 with the Sun-Being itself, just at the turn into a new century.

During this Pluto transit, Steiner had to confront his affiliations with philosophy. This was a test, one might say, set in place at his conception, that is, guided from spiritual worlds. One commentator has stated that this trial with Nietzsche and Nietzsche's sister marked the completion of the purification of his astral body, and now Steiner moved to purify his etheric body.

Eclipses at the Conception Sun Position

There were no solar eclipses within two degrees of the Conception Sun position during Steiner's life, another indication of the lack of encumbrance of the Conception Image.

There were two lunar eclipses at the Conception Sun degree in Steiner's life, one on June 1, 1863, too early to have anything recorded, and on June 4, 1909. Let's look at this latter one briefly.

On May 30, 1909, the Budapest Congress began, a gathering of theosophists from all over the world. The previous one, in May of 1907, had been in Munich. There Steiner had had a strong hand in its design, and the arts flourished—dramas were presented, and the decorations of the hall were extensive. One could say that the festival of the children of the Image was shown in full maturity at the Munich conference of 1907. We will see this event highlighted later in relation to the four Birth Images.

The 1909 conference had reverted to speakers delivering papers, the talking heads of stern philosophers. Steiner and his students commented on the lack of the "harmonizing principle," that is, theater, music, color—in short, the beauty that appeals to the children. In terms of the Image, the philosophers had taken over again. The other presenters, led by Annie Besant, gave talks on various theosophical topics. Steiner gave his, "From Buddha to Christ," on the second day, linking the oriental wisdom traditions with the deeds of Christ-light. There was tension between the different streams within the Theosophical Society. As Marie Steiner later summarized the conference: "Annie Besant became the tool of an anti-Christian movement. In the summer of 1909, in Budapest, Rudolf Steiner had to tell her that their paths inwardly parted. This conversation was the point at which their outward separation began."[59] Annie Besant, then leader of the Theosophical Society, and Rudolf Steiner never saw each other again. The severance of the connection to the Theosophical Society, after growing up within its ranks, was a momentous event in Steiner's life.

As we explained in Part I, a lunar eclipse is more personal than transpersonal. This was a personal crisis for Steiner. Throughout, he smoothed out the differences, saying that many different views are acceptable. Marie Steiner's extreme picture may have shown what was going on in the background. The split was complete by the end of this eclipse. In terms of the Image, Steiner demanded that the festival orientation of the children, their bright sun-like faces, the light of Christ, be given prominence in the world of the philosophers. To do that, he had to leave to form his own group.[60]

SUMMARY OF PLANETARY DYNAMICS FOR THE CONCEPTION SUN

From these transits, we can bring worldly activities to the Image and deepen our relationship to it. We find that the Image blossoms. We can, for example, imagine Rudolf Steiner as teaching the children to call for the visitation of their own soul. "Sun-brilliance! My own soul! Come to Earth! Come into my body and my mind!"

The children look up to the tall, wise philosophers as to the gods, and we are reminded of a scene from the Parzival legend. The young Parzival, reared in the forest and protected from the modern world, one day sees three knights riding on horses through the trees, the Sun streaming through the leaves onto their rich clothing and weaponry. He has never seen anything like it. In the middle of their path he falls down onto his knees in complete awe, asking, "Are you gods?" Similarly, the children in the Image might perceive with awe that one of the tall philosophers comes to visit them. They wonder if they have been visited by one of the gods, who teaches them about the Sun-brilliance, which they will remember forever.

We can also understand the children themselves as the sun-like souls. Steiner, on behalf of the tall human philosophers, holding their books as their guides through life, appeals directly to the angelic souls to come to Earth. Rather than *teaching* the children the song, he *sings* to them the song: "Sun-brilliance—come to earth! Souls—awaken—come into these bodies!" Steiner was very concerned that modern conditions would make it such that souls would have a much more difficult time coming into human beings. On behalf of the over-intellectualized philosophers, he cajoles the souls to come down into human bodies.

FROM THOSE WHO KNEW HIM

Those who knew Steiner speak in the terms of this Conception Image. From a woman recalling her first meeting with Steiner when she was five years old: "Even today I can feel the kindness that flowed from him to me as he took my hand and put his other hand on my head."[61] Another woman recalled a meeting: "In that one handclasp and the warm directness of his gaze I felt recognized in my deepest strivings, and yet in a quite impersonal way that left me so free that it almost took my breath."[62]

A woman describes the first Waldorf School in Stuttgart:

> Dr. Steiner had directed that on every first Thursday [Jupiter's day] of the month there should take place a so-called Monatsfeier [monthly festival], in which the whole school gathered in the assembly hall, and the various grades showed what they had learned in foreign languages, recitation, eurythmy, singing, and so forth. Very often Dr. Steiner was present at these festivals and addressed, first, the younger pupils, then us older ones, and finally the teachers.[63]

Another student offers a picture right out of the Image: "Rudolf Steiner walking across the schoolyard, surrounded by countless children, the little ones literally hanging on his arms and legs like grapes on a vine, he struggling to get his arms free to be able to shake hands with us older students."[64]

The children feel, "How can a man say such amazing things, one after the other, unendingly new, and make such astounding statements?" And they feel *seen*: "I have never seen anyone who could look at another so attentively."[65] At the first Steiner lecture that he attended, Rittelmeyer said, "What pleased me was the evidence of a mood of festive devotion," just what the children in the Image experience.[66] Many people in an audience had the experience of Steiner speaking directly and personally to them alone.[67]

Steiner himself was observed to be the child at times: "laughing with all his heart like a child" or having "the eyes of a child," a "childlike clarity," or creating "childish designs" in the carved windows for the Goetheanum, summing to a picture of Steiner as a "pure-white little child"—"he himself was like a child, that in its utter openness and vulnerability is immune to all temptations."[68]

Andrei Belyi observed Steiner become most like a child when he spoke about the young Jesus.[69] Then Steiner would move from head to heart, and his words became "heart-thoughts that transformed hearts more than the heads."[70] As Steiner could become a child, so could other adults around him, and we see the important verb of the Image—"bends down"—when, after a Herr Werbeck had risen to thank Steiner for his gift of the Foundation Stone Meditation, "the frail but majestic figure of Rudolf Steiner bent down—and kissed him."[71]

When working with an Image, you can nurture different versions simultaneously, Steiner as philosopher, Steiner as child. There need not be one right answer. The process of working with an Image arouses the soul to activity and many things are discovered. We already see the themes of the Image flowing into Steiner's life at various points. Conception has set him on his road in many respects. Now we will find out how this plays out at his first breath.

7. THE GATE IMAGE AT STEINER'S BIRTH

RUDOLF STEINER BREATHED his first breath when the Sun was between 14 and 15 degrees in the sign of Aquarius.[72] The first breath charged the astral body, his body of feeling and thought. Into his physical and etheric bodies were imprinted the patterns of the heavens, into his brain and into his every cell. What was an intention at conception has now matured to possibility, the functioning organism ready to make its way through the world.

We will look at the entire Solar Cross at the moment of birth, all four Images, each one in turn. After each Image, we will look at the historical personalities to whom he was related through that degree. After each of the two polarities we will look at celestial events that relate to the birth in terms of the Images.

We begin with the Gate Image: what streamed through the Sun directly into Steiner's being.

Do not turn the page until you have blank paper and a writing implement. When you do turn the page, read the Image, then close the book and make a mind-map of what you remember as well as what adds itself to this material. Amplify the Image into something to which you can relate personally.

Gate Image at Birth

People rebuild the stone chairs on hills and in natural amphitheaters where wise men and women once spoke true words. The formulas they give are gems for the future that you can eat, from which you may find nourishment. Without these gems, the people have been starving.

WORKING THE IMAGE

As soon as you have read the Image, take the time to make a mind-map of it. We recommend that you let this Image work in your own imagination for a short while before going on. Read it again, and let it begin to expand for you. Make another mind-map of it before you go on. This will be worth your while.

COMMENTARIES ON THE GATE IMAGE

First we shall look at the meaning of some aspects of the Image. Stacks of stones in prominent places, on hills commanding a view of the surrounding countryside, or in an amphitheater where the acoustics are good and the natural folds in the land embrace the listeners, gave places for teachers to instruct, entertain, and guide. Elijah and Elisha had traveled from place to place, speaking from such meeting spots. Politicians in all ages have created "platforms," meaning a list of their main points of view and also literally meaning raised-up places from which to speak.

The stakes are high; the people are starving. Is this soul starvation or bodily starvation? Are the two related? Wise words feed the whole person, and are a necessary part of a healthy diet.

We expect the stakes to be high, poised as we are in the perpendicular to the important Aldebaran-Antares axis, the axis of life and death forces, the fundamental axis upon which the School of Zarathustra built its understanding of the zodiac. We shall explain that axis when we come to the Horizon Images. This serves as notice that we are in celestially important territory.

To whom does the pronoun "they" in the second sentence refer? Does it refer to the "people" or to the "wise men and women"? Indeed, all can speak, if not from wisdom welling up from within, then from memory of wise words that you have heard elsewhere and can pass on to others, thus knitting the community together more strongly.

Contemplating this Image, we can begin to feel the sorrow of separation in our modern world. We no longer use these teacher's chairs in open-air locations where the community can gather to hear wise words and discuss them. Now we live in separate caves, where our most intimate community consists of television personalities.

Gems

> I drained [the manuscript] in a single draught. Just as a precious drink that suits our nature slips down willingly and shows its health-bringing effect already upon the tongue, putting our nervous system into a good mode, these Letters were pleasing and beneficial to me.
> —Johann Wolfgang von Goethe [73]

When people are forced by circumstances to flee their homes, they take with them only the most precious objects they own. Light weight and small size are virtues when you're on the run. Gemstones are perfect. Refugees swallow them and that keeps the gems safe for a few days. Gem-like words are the lightest weight and the most precious. They too can be eaten or taken in, and provide nourishment for a good long time. Goethe describes exactly this process in the quote above.

Those held in captivity have expressed afterward the importance of the spiritual gems that they had with them, words of great teachers and traditions that helped them through the lonely hours.

How are gems made? From the concentration under heat and pressure of the best that the mineral world has to offer, clarity comes from opaqueness, and the materials are refined. Some of these refined minerals have been pressed to service so that in the ancient mysteries, the priest could see the holy quartz-crystal vessels sending forth sun-radiance.[74] The colors of the gems likewise come from the Sun—"the green of the emerald, the wine-yellow of the topaz, the red of corundum"—these all come from the different qualities of the Sun through the zodiacal ages, that is, during the long passage of the Vernal Point through the signs, taking 25,920 years to cycle through all the signs and come to the starting point.[75]

Gems are new and not new. The base material from which they are fashioned has survived the erosions of time because of the purity and concentration of substance. Sometimes they are found as river-rolled lumps that can be recognized by the experienced eye, then polished or cracked open and faceted to sparkle. Sometimes gems are found closer to their source, before they tumble into the river, as crystals fully formed in a matrix of concentrated substance. I have had the privilege of going to one of the mines open to the public. Large bulldozers pull out sections of the hillside, and people can then dig through the heaps, looking for quartz crystals. Short crystals abound. People seek the large ones. What impressed me most was the quality of the area immediately around the crystals, the matrix from which they were generated. Even though the prize was the completed crystal, the context that reared it became much more interesting to me. Here was the place, chaotic in itself, in which something hard, enduring, and extraordinary was made. It was gritty, layered in colors as the silicone-dioxide concentrated toward the center and the impurities were drawn away. It had the feeling of a factory of light, where cosmic light was concentrated into physical substance. I felt the presence of many hands, or many forces, working to make something beautiful and light-filled.

How are gems made in the social-spiritual world? They don't just appear, fully formed. There is a matrix and there is polishing. Once polished, gems emanate particular qualities of power and have been used for ages to heal many different maladies. But before that, they are made. The teacher's chair has to be used by those who have not yet polished their gems. As the lecturer René Querido said, "You throw away the first hundred lectures." By this he meant that the gem isn't there yet. It has to be polished. You can't avoid the fact that these first hundred lectures are not what they could be, and you have to go through it. Medical students are taught that, before they become doctors, they will be directly responsible for the deaths of ten patients. The matrix that polishes is the combined souls of others—patients for doctors, and hearers for lecturers. The practice of any trade includes the mistakes that are made along the way, and the realization that only by grace are such mistakes forgiven.

Contrast the process of digestion from all directions with the linear and unidirectional stream of words in the books of the stern philosophers. These are two very different ways of accessing knowledge.

Background

By the time of the Teacher, the stone chairs had fallen into disuse. The Teacher caused them to be rebuilt so that true words could again be shared between people.

On this Solar Day, the Teacher imparted the formulas of the nine Beatitudes and the seven petitions of the Abwoon Prayer. Note the connection with the background of Steiner's Conception Image, where formulas were also spoken.

Each of these statements—the Beatitudes, the Abwoon Prayer, all the statements we see in the Christian and Hebrew Bibles—is vastly compressed. In a sense, each statement is hard like a gemstone. In order to understand a statement and get its benefit, you have to open it up. You can do this for each statement, on its own, through contemplation. Then you can make use of the virtues of that gem. The gem turns from a pretty rock to a feast for the soul. You can also relate the statement to other statements made by the Teacher, in a mutually fructifying matrix of meaning that comes about from study and contemplation.

The first line of the Beatitudes is often translated, "Blessed are the poor in spirit," which more properly understood translates as, "Blessed are those who admit that they are undeveloped in matters of the spirit." Or, as Aramaic is a metaphoric language with many possibilities, the translation might best read: "Happy and aligned with the One are those who find their home in the breathing; to them belong the inner kingdom and queendom of heaven."[76]

The first line of what we call the Abwoon Prayer is given by King James as "Our Father who art in heaven." As we mentioned in our discussion of the Conception Image, in Aramaic the first line reads, "Abwoon d'bwash maya." As the elements of Abwoon include references to the archetypal father and mother, the more thorough translation could be, "Father/Mother, Creator of all creation and Birther of worlds." Or it could be, "Wordless Action, Silent Potency—where ears and eyes awaken, there heaven comes."[77] The short form is acceptable to use if one understands that it has been compacted. The short form reminds; it is not the teaching itself.

The Teacher also makes it very clear on this Solar Day who he is: "My flesh is true food and my blood is true drink."[78] You cannot understand such a "gem" on its own, or as referring to the speaker in human terms. He does not recommend cannibalism here, but identifies himself with the living presence of Creation, permeating all living things. To drink and know that all liquid is filled with Spirit, to eat and know that all substance is filled with Spirit—and to participate in this knowing consciously—makes the world and oneself sacred. To eat "true food" and "true drink," which are eternal, means that you have fed your soul.   *the true gem of all*

Formulaic thinking thus has a benefit—the formulas are lightweight and easy to carry—and a danger—that of holding on to the formula in its compressed form without unpacking it. Like dehydrated food eaten without water, the formula can be indigestible. It has to be unpacked, soaked, and then eaten. Then you have the gem's brilliance.[79]

The counter-image from our time: As individuals identify television personalities as their community, they also receive "sound bites" as gems, a dangerous fallacy. Visit a school for youngsters and you realize the number of witty phrases and clever bits that have come from television, false gems that cannot be unpacked; that is, they have nothing stored inside. Empty nutrition for the soul distracts us from the places where true word-gems are given. Those who have a relationship to this Image help to rebuild the places where true word-gems can be imparted.

Anne Catherine Emmerich related how the Teacher built up the Abwoon Prayer. Each line was given, one at a time, and he spent days explaining one line. Can you imagine a whole day spent on "Give us today our daily bread," a discourse so powerful that people stayed, perched on a hillside, to listen to every word? How it would shine differently then! That day is the matrix in the crystal-forming process, the product at the end being the compacted and glimmering gem. Gems in physical or social-spiritual form become more precious when you realize what has gone into their making. Their light and healing come from hard work.

Rudolf Steiner's Life in Relation to the Solar Gate Image

We begin with the realization that Stein in German means stone. Once upon a time, the surname Carpenter meant that you came from a family that worked with wood and constructions. In that tradition, the surname Steiner means the family that works with stone.

Stones and Gems

Steiner dedicated his life to rebuilding the stone chairs of the ancient wisdom traditions. However, he didn't give us museum pieces to contemplate, or piles of rough-hewn rocks, but platforms for new and living wisdom transformed for a new time. He knew that the letters of the alphabet and the words formed from them are, as Hebrew wisdom tells us, "stones quarried from the great Name of Divinity."[80] These he revealed, polished, and presented to others. He has left us many gems and unpacked many obscure formulas. He brought us the fruits of the zodiacal being of this Image, Aquarius, the sign of the Waterbearer, the future of humanity. Anyone who has studied the work of Steiner can recall those times when a statement was received as a precious gem. Then the concentrated statement had to be worked with, dissolved slowly, to become food for the soul, for the entire life. Steiner has, indeed, provided gems for the future.

In anthroposophy, one hears about the "indications" of Rudolf Steiner, implying that the statements are gems, not immediately digestible, but to be mixed with the personal experience of the hearer, decompressed, and made useful. An "indication" is not a directive or a command. It cannot tell you what to do next, though some people would like that very much. An "indication" can only offer itself for this process of digestion. Steiner didn't hand out baby food, but something that you had to work on to receive its nutrition. "He spoke as an educator, never as a mere revealer." He became very upset when the most precious gems—the revealing of one's previous lifetimes and thus the key to one's soul mission—were used flippantly or egocentrically, that is, without first being digested.[81] The gems that he gave had to be continually polished by one's life experience.

Steiner's most beautiful gems are the verses that he gave, some for children, some for weekly contemplations in the Calendar of the Soul, some reserved for the serious students of esotericism (the First Spiritual Class), and some for everyone. We have given other examples elsewhere. Here is a special example:[82]

> Asleep is the soul of Earth
> In Summer's heat,
> While the Sun's outward Glory
> Rays through the realms of Space.

> Awake is the soul of Earth
> In Winter's cold,
> While the Sun's inmost Being
> Lightens in Spirit.

> Summer's day of joy
> For Earth is sleep.
> Winter's holy night
> For Earth is day.

This is the kind of thing that must be pondered for a while. Straight up, it may not digest easily. It may even seem simplistic. Keep at it. When it begins to digest, it opens an entirely new relationship to the seasons as revelation of the secrets of Earth and heaven.

Class Readers for the nineteen lessons in the First Spiritual Class spend years studying the nineteen verses in those lessons and learning to help others digest the concentrated substance therein. The sessions in which those gems are given out are only for those who have become members of that class by application and acceptance, because they need to be pre-qualified as to their ability to digest very hard gems. The hour of presentation that builds up the gem, sometimes read from Steiner and sometimes "freely rendered" from the inner knowing of the Class Reader, comprises a strong concentration of digestive juices, so to speak. When you hear a particular lesson several times, you get the feeling that it always has nourishment. Something new arises on each hearing, meaning that the digestion process continues its opening up of the precious gem.

Emil Bock, a priest in the Movement for Religious Renewal and an author of many books about anthroposophy, recounted how the precious gems were delivered:

> Through this period, above all, ran the golden chain of moments, when he transmitted to us as a gift of the spiritual world the words which completed our sacraments.... When, early in 1923, I received from him in this way the Burial Service for children, he was himself radiant with thankfulness for this special form of creativity, which was at the same time the highest art of receiving. Twice he came to me on that day—it was during a conference—with the words: "Is not the text beautiful!"[83]

Bock goes on to describe another in the "golden chain of moments" when he received other precious gems.

Rittelmeyer speaks about the difficulty in digesting Steiner's words—"If I read for any length of time a feeling of nausea came over me. All this mass of knowledge weighed like undigested food." Later he learned how to take in the gems. He learned to read *freely*, "with much more open-mindedness" than the usual, to read *with inner activity*, testing each statement in the arena of his own life, and to read *meditatively*, "with constant and fairly long pauses." Thus he describes digestion of gems.[84]

Steiner's own digestion of gems is evident in his practice of reciting in his private rooms, each afternoon around 3:00 P.M., the Abwoon Prayer, loudly enough that those in adjoining rooms heard his recitation.[85] He had changed the words to reflect his understanding of the truths therein. Changed the words? Of the Holy Bible? Yes, that's the whole point—*he had eaten the gems of the sacred texts, and digested them*. They had become part of his own body.

Some of Steiner's students have been unable to digest what he said, and resort to long quotations from the original lectures and books. Others, however, took what he said, digested it, and came up with gems of their own. In his very poetical memoir, Albert Steffen gives many, including:[86]

> The joy of knowing the world must not become submerged in the
>   afflictions of the body.
> Rise up against nightmares, despair, and death.
> Pain must never be the victory of matter, but always its defeat.

When people in the audience ask someone speaking about their researches into Steiner's philosophy, "Where did you get that? What is the lecture, please, with date and page reference?" they undermine the process that Steiner worked so diligently to establish: one that attends to the livingness of the moment. Some of what these listeners request is understandable. It says, "Tell me where to find the gem that you ate, digested, and made into something concordant with your own spirit." It can also say, "I don't trust anything but the original gems themselves, certainly not yours—I want to sit among Steiner's gems, though I will not dare to eat and digest them, even though my spirit cries out in hunger." Strong words, but when you've experienced the preference for footnotes of the past rather than the transmission of the present, you will see what I mean.

Stones

Though Steiner worked as an artist mostly in wood, he had a very special relationship with stone, most especially the foundation stone that he set under the site of the Goetheanum, orienting it along an east-west axis. One can imagine that the builders of the stone chairs for teachers were very aware of the directions and intentionally oriented their work in a specific direction. This is one of those insights that you can arrive at by studying a life related to an Image—that directionality, and the specific directions of east, west, north, and south, are a fundamental part of this Image. Directionality is not specifically mentioned, but is an obvious and important aspect of the Image. Steiner invoked the specific directions in his great Foundation Stone Meditation, which I quote here and there in this book, especially at the introductions to the Eastern and Western Horizon Images.

Steiner knew about the stone monuments left from long ago, pointing out to his secretary, Guenther Wachsmuth, how the stone circles of Penmaenmawr, Wales, were aligned to the surrounding peaks, to the directions, and to celestial events—long before these alignments of stone circles were revealed by archaeo-astronomers.[87]

Steiner's whole life was dedicated to building, literally to the building of two Goetheanums, with which he was intimately involved, assisting the stacking of stone upon stone. He approached architecture in a completely organic way:

> We are trying to develop a total style in building, which originates neither from some abstract purpose nor from a—perhaps very profound—allegorical consideration. Instead, we stew this style in the juices of its own depth, as it were, where the intellect is silent and the creative lives.[88]

His designs baffled engineers, some of whom said that Steiner's constructions would collapse, which they did not. "There they were, firm as rocks."[89] He did not wish to build on old foundations, least of all on the cultural foundations of medieval times, but to construct something completely new and relevant to the world of today.[90]

Steiner—"with a face that seemed carved out of stone"[91]—was also a builder of the stones of individuals. Helena Petrovna Blavatsky had said: "You must become a living stone," meaning the vivifying through spirit of the dense matter of our incarnation. Those who joined the fellowship of the Rosy Cross (*rosen-kreutz*) earned the title Knight of the Golden Stone. Unaware, perhaps, of this history, one student remarked that Steiner "made those dance who had become lifeless as stones," making them into living stones.[92] Steiner himself wrote, anticipating our work with the axis of life and death, Aldebaran-Antares:[93]

> Through the perception of quite distinct processes in what is dead, serious alchemists would grasp traces of nature's creative activity and, with it, the presence of the spirit ruling in the phenomena. The symbol for what is "dead" but is recognized as the revelation of the spirit is "The Golden Stone."

Dead stones and living stones. Another student had the feeling that Steiner realized the promise from the Revelation of John that "To everyone who conquers I will give some of the hidden manna, and I will give a white stone, and on the white stone is written a new name that no one knows except the one who receives it."[94] When you contribute your stone to a chair from which wise teachings will come, then the teachings are strengthened by the combined power of those stones.

At the StarHouse in Boulder, Colorado, we have a sevenfold Cretan-style labyrinth whose paths were originally defined by stacked sod taken from the path and put at its edges. We invited people to take a stone from a stack that we had made, and for each time that they walked this meditative path, they could put a stone on either side of the path. We began with large stones that clarified the pathway, and now use primarily small milky white quartz stones found on the property around the StarHouse. Over time, the number of stones has grown to thousands, and this gives the walking of that form a special meaning. This is a small example of how sacred places have in their stones an imprint of the power of the words spoken there as well as the sincerity of those who have built those places yearning to hear those words.

Teacher's Chair

Let's begin with a seemingly minor custom peculiar to Steiner and anthroposophy. After his lectures, Steiner would often come to sit in the audience. Everyone would sit together quietly for a couple of minutes. Then Steiner would get up and exit back through the stage.[95] This still happens at anthroposophical lectures even without Steiner. It cultivates a sense that we all sit in chairs admiring the spiritual beings left on stage who are responsible for the wise words just given. It also gives a couple of minutes to begin the digestive process.

Note that building a teacher's chair on a hilltop implies that there is a teacher, a teaching, and a community to hear the teaching. Steiner had all three, the teacher—himself and the ones whom he was introducing—the teaching of anthroposophy, and a community that was growing with people from all over the world. Steiner's teachings have gone out to thousands of people, and have had a very large impact. Though many people in the general public do not recognize the name of Rudolf Steiner, and very often don't recognize the word "anthroposophy," nonetheless they recognize the effects of this work in Waldorf schools, biodynamics, and other initiatives.

Steiner wished for these teachings to reach out to everyone. When he heard that some of his students were objecting to the construction of a house near the Goetheanum because clothes drying on a laundry line would be unsightly so near to this temple, he countered that true anthroposophy must exist side by side with all aspects of life, adding, "Here particularly, diapers should flap on the wash line in the wind."[96] Rather than the multicolored prayer banners near a Buddhist temple, Steiner wanted banners of family life, evidence that people were here fully living their lives.

But we encounter a problem here. The Image depicts one building a chair, but does not suggest that the builder ought to be the one who sits in it. Steiner first built a chair in the world of philosophy—he created a way of speaking about the accomplishments of others. For many years, he set Goethe in the chair that he had built, and then others, including Nietzsche. He did not speak from his own understanding for a long time. When he moved to Berlin to edit a literary magazine, writing reviews of plays and social commentaries, he couldn't make it on his own. Then he aligned with the Theosophical Society, first putting theosophy in the chair, then speaking more and more from his own discoveries and inner knowledge. The audiences swelled. He built the chair up further, and sat in its center. People began to flock around him, and the whole enterprise seemed to make terrific sense. In one short decade, Steiner went from the editor of a failing literary magazine to an internationally known "spiritual teacher." Around that chair were always dozens of people. Those who knew him reported that after every lecture Steiner would be mobbed by appreciative listeners, and that his waiting room would be full at all hours of the day and night. Even when he had given four lectures during the course of the day, he came back to a waiting room full of people. Increasingly, the questions that they brought were personal, because Steiner gave everyone the impression—it comes out in every account about him—that he "knew the answer." It was demonstrated repeatedly, with individual prescriptions for healing physical ailments, fine-tuning one's diet, increasing memory, etc. This could only increase the clamor to see him, despite appeals from those around him to please stop, as Herr Doctor was becoming exhausted. Hundreds of people had the conviction that Steiner knew about their soul's journey, their previous lifetimes, and what they needed right now, and they meant to find out what it was. Several commentators blamed Steiner's death on the petty and personal demands of his admirers. How frustrating—to preach from the chair about freedom, independence, the "I AM" in personal relation with the gods, and be surrounded by those who persisted in their dependence.

Whose fault was that? Steiner built a chair, then sat in it. As time went on, the stones supporting that chair became monumentally tall. Could he have cultivated successors, trained students who could take on the work? Yes, he did this to some extent. He didn't teach every class at the Waldorf schools, nor see every client seeking anthroposophical medical advice. Yet his central role in the teacher's chair was so much higher than the others. It demanded of him more than he had, and there was no one to replace him.

In some fairy tales, a young princess speaks and gems come out of her mouth. The counterpoint, such as an ugly stepsister, speaks and toads and dark insects come out. Steiner's "problem" was that the gems came out, and wouldn't stop coming out—great quantities of gems, a kind of Midas curse. It attracted scores of adherents—when do we see today a speaker attracting an audience of two thousand to whom he or she speaks without amplification?—all eagerly awaiting a gem, almost like souvenir hunters at sacred sites, with the added conviction in all that the gems he dropped were personal, for them alone. It also attracted scores of critics. "His single greatest mistake"[97] may have been making public his most precious gems, the most esoteric, because the critics went wild in their mockery. In the end, though the teaching ought to have created successors of everyone who heard him, and did so in a myriad of directions, Steiner did not cultivate a successor who could take the Teacher's place in the Great Chair.

HISTORICAL PERSONALITIES

Let us look at some historical personalities born at this same time to see if we can learn some more about Steiner's Gate Image, and about Steiner himself. We can begin with the lives of others born on this day, who are Rudolf Steiner's Star Brothers and Star Sisters, so to speak, as they breathed in this very same Image. We have the benefit of being able to look at their lives, to see how they expressed this Image. We will have to be brief, giving a little background and then seeking soul gestures. Of course, we recommend a more thorough study of the biographies of these individualities to those who are drawn there.

Star Brother: Honoré Daumier

Born on February 26, 1808, Daumier began his training for art at a young age. Very early he was attracted to lithography, meaning rock-drawing. He became famous for his caricatures of the vices of his day, in astonishingly expressive depictions of the faces of businessmen, lawyers, doctors, professors, merchants—everyone he met. In the year 1832, at the age of twenty-four, Daumier was imprisoned for six months by King Louis-Philippe for artwork showing his scorn of the political regime. Here we see a little of the political anarchism that Steiner was also drawn to. Indeed, one interesting implication of the Image is that when you are building stone chairs in the country for a teacher, it means you have turned away from a fancier throne in the center of the city. You are interested in more than the official party line. Likewise, Steiner parted company with the official doctrines of the day and found gems in unexpected places.

Many of his lithographs show people in high standing in the chairs of authority who abuse their power. In this one, titled *The Legislative Belly*, many teachers sit in the main "chairs" of the land, the seats of the lawmakers. But they are bloated, unhealthy, and inattentive. They are trying to digest the words in the legislative belly, but are unable to do so.

Lesser known are Daumier's stone sculptures of the politicians of the day, including the King, a sculpture that the artist hid from public view because he knew it would get him in trouble. Above all else, he valued painting, though the demands of making a living brought him back to his popular cartoons.

Le ventre législatif: Aspect des bancs ministériels de la chambre improstituée de 1834
(The Legislative Belly: View of the Ministerial Benches in the Prostituted Chamber of 1834)
The Metropolitan Museum of Art, Rogers Fund, 1920 (20.60.5)
Image © The Metropolitan Museum of Art, New York City

Here we have a man who worked intimately with stones, the foundation of the technique of lithography. Pressing paper to prepared stone surfaces, he created over four thousand finished pieces and left many more unfinished. We can imagine him caressing each and every stone, preparing their surfaces to express the subtlest features. We can add his stone sculptures here, too. From this foundation in stone, he actively fought for social justice. The tearing down of many of his subjects was the destruction that necessarily preceded the construction: He was able to overcome his cynicism and embraced the revolution of 1848. He was chosen to replace the King's portrait with a portrait of the ideals of the Republic. However, he had begun to turn at this time to a new technique of representation, for which some later called him the first Impressionist, in which the "faces and bodies are devoured by the surrounding light and becoming one with the atmosphere."[98]

Investigating darkness and light, learning to show the gems of light even with black ink, he entered what we would call the "gem" phase of his life.

In today's world, where the refined technique of Daumier is so rare as to be nearly extinct, each of his pieces has the quality of a gem that teaches through exposure of the details of constrained lives, in which the constraint has been made so clear, and the yearning to break free so potent. Remember this when we look at the Earth Image opposite to this one.

Daumier won the hearts of the people by emphasizing life's everyday challenges and the foibles of common people. In the same way, in the Image, the teaching chairs emphasize the needs of the common people, who come to hear wise words, and who, on occasion, may find a wisdom and vitality in themselves that causes them to take the chair and share what they know. Here is a little summary of Daumier, written by one whom we will see in the opposite or Earth Image, Charles Baudelaire, about a painting of Daumier:

> The man whose image this presents,
> In art more subtle than the rest,
> Teaches us sagely, as is best,
> To chuckle at our own expense.
>
> In mockery he stands apart.
> His energy defies an equal
> In painting Evil and its sequel—
> Which proves the beauty of his heart.[99]

Star Brother: Pierre-Auguste Renoir

Born on February 25, 1841, Renoir sought to reinvigorate the world of painting. The convention at the time was to paint landscapes in the painting studio. Renoir and his companions moved to the forest, to paint directly from nature.

> By using small, multicoloured strokes, he evoked the vibration of the atmosphere, the sparkling effect of foliage, and especially the luminosity of a young woman's skin in the outdoors. Renoir and his companions stubbornly strove to produce light-suffused paintings from which black was excluded.... Renoir, because of his fascination with the human figure, was distinctive among the others, who were more interested in landscape.[100]

Pierre-Auguste Renoir

Thus he moved from the stilted and stylized manner of painting popular in his day into something alive. Renoir was classically trained, however, and would visit the Louvre and gaze at the masterpieces of the past that he venerated. Even in the last days of his life he would visit the Louvre, in a wheelchair, to see these gems that had sustained him.

The people recreating the teacher's chairs strive in faith to emphasize light and wisdom, and the vitality described in the quote above about Renoir's work. This idealistic faith lost Renoir many commissions and placements in galleries, and yet he remained true to it. At the age of forty-two (end of the Sun years and entry into the Mars years) Renoir brought black into his paintings for the first time, and with a vengeance. With his new ability to incorporate the dark, he gave his gem-like coloration an even greater depth of meaning. Look at his voluptuous women, merging into the voluptuous landscape, and you can imagine that the Image takes place in these same settings of natural beauty, the revelation and gift of Sophia, the Divine Mother. Gazing upon Renoir's paintings, one experiences true soul nutrition.

When we view a life of a Star Brother or Star Sister, we don't expect that the details of the life will be identical to that of Rudolf Steiner, or that Steiner's house will be filled with the sensual paintings of naked women for which Renoir was known, or the caricatures of Daumier. What we look for is how Renoir and Daumier coped with the Gate Image that they shared with Steiner.

Star Brother: Wilhelm Grimm

Wilhelm Grimm, born on February 24, 1786, and his brother Jacob, older by one year—"the Brothers Grimm"—became famous for bringing a fascination for the word, the epigram, the fairy tale, and the folk tale into the modern world. Grimm's fairy tales, first published as *Children's and Household Tales* in 1812, have been translated into seventy languages. "Snow White and the Seven Dwarfs," "The Red Shoes," "Rumplestiltskin," "Iron John"—these are like stones stacked up as a foundation for our whole

culture. When Walt Disney made an animated film of "Snow White and the Seven
Dwarfs" in 1937, the tale—and subsequent
tales—found its way into every household in
every country.

Where did the tales come from? Scholars
argue about whether these are fundamentally Germanic tales from Eastern Europe,
or imports from Charles Perrault's *Mother
Goose* collections in France. In either case, the
Grimms were able to preserve something that

William and Jacob Grimm

Padraic Collum, in his introduction to these tales, makes poetically clear:
the storyteller seated on a roughly made chair on a clay floor, surrounded
by listeners.

We can, of course, savor this picture in relation to the Image—the
teacher's chair. Collum explains how this tradition came to an end, giving
us insight into the Image itself:

> [The storyteller] was ready to respond to and make articulate the rhythm
> of the night. When the distinction between day and night could be passed
> over as it could be in towns and in modern houses, the change of rhythm
> that came with the passing of day into night ceased to be marked. This
> happened when light was prolonged until it was time to turn to sleep. The
> prolongation of light meant the cessation of traditional stories in European
> cottages.... The tradition ceased to be appropriate because the rhythm
> that gave them meaning was weakened.[101]

When we move into the realm of artificial light—what Rudolf Steiner
would have termed "false light," that is, light based on subearthly forces—
we lose something of the secrets of the night. True light understands and
gives way to the dark, for discoveries are made in the dark that serve the
true light. The single light bulb hanging in the middle of the farmhouse
kitchen increased efficiency, and yet something was lost. The replace-
ment of cottage crafts with factory production also took away the reason
that these tales were told. Many indeed were spinning tales, told amongst
women spinning fibers into threads, gathered in a candlelit room after the
day's labors.

Something is growing here, the sub-theme of darkness. Note Daumier's work with black ink, using the black in such a way as to make light visible. Renoir feared black for many years, only introducing it in his forty-second year, the end of the Sun period. Now we see Grimm related to this tradition of darkness. Perhaps this shows us in the Image that behind the sparkle lies a darkness deep within the gem.

Storytellers were and are holders of memory. They know how to enchant and how to disenchant. They know about the deepest recesses of the human psyche and what lives there. Rudolf Steiner could speak about these tales in terms of the evolution of the human being—that giants, for example, came into the tales because giants were cast off as undeveloped parts of the human being, long ago.[102] Bruno Bettelheim could speak about the essential work of the tale in bringing to the surface the primitive urges of the unconscious, and seeing the forces toward violence and incest played out.[103] Even though the Grimms sanitized the original tales somewhat by taking out much of the sexuality in them and adding in themes of morality, the core of fears, phobias, terrors, cruelty, and murder can still be found there.

Bettelheim says, and Steiner would agree, that it's best to speak the tales from memory rather than read them. In this way the tales become more alive. Not remembering all the details is less of a sacrifice than the loss of the living storyteller. Thus the tales as gems must be softened and digested before sharing with others. Parents reading these tales to little children, take note! Eat the gems and let them become part of you before sharing them.

Here's a quote from Wilhelm Grimm that relates to our Image: "The mythic element resembles small pieces of a shattered jewel which are lying strewn on the ground all overgrown with grass and flowers, and can only be discovered by the most far-seeing eye."[104] The teacher in the chair trains the eye to find the gems in the grass and flowers.

The Brothers Grimm also wished to know about the nature of the gems of words in and of themselves. With Wilhelm's consultation, brother Jacob published extensively about the natural laws of vowels and consonants, creating a method of scientific etymology, that is, research into relationships between languages and the development of meaning. Thus we see that they worked with the gems themselves, taking from the past the gems that had been left there, in a somewhat ruined state, and giving them a new framework—new chairs from which to speak to people.

In 1840 they accepted an invitation from the King of Prussia to go to Berlin, where they lectured at the university. There they began the *Deutsches Wörterbuch*, a comprehensive German etymological dictionary, that included every German word found in the literature of the three centuries "from Luther to Goethe," with historical variants, etymology, and semantic development, along with usages in proverbs and everyday language. It has taken until recently to finish this multivolume work. This was Jacob's main project, while Wilhelm took over the fairy tale work. Wilhelm helped also on the *Wörterbuch*, and died after finishing the letter D.[105]

Wilhelm could be considered, in the terms of the Image, as a connoisseur of gems of wisdom, those left behind by tradition—the many traditions that he sifted through in his hunt for gems.

We recommend reading the Brothers Grimm story called "The Queen Bee" for its multiple uses of stones, the moving of stones, the building with stones, and cryptic messages left on stones. The story itself is a kind of stone, one of the many stacked up by these preservers of the oral tradition of Europe.[106]

THE QUEEN BEE

by Jacob Ludwig Grimm and Wilhelm Carl Grimm

ONCE UPON A time it happened—where then was it? Where indeed was it not?—that two King's sons who sought adventures fell into a wild, reckless way of living, and gave up all thoughts of going home again. Their third and youngest brother, who was called Witling, and had remained behind, started off to seek them; and when at last he found them, they jeered at his simplicity in thinking that he could make his way in the world, while they who were so much cleverer were unsuccessful. But they all three went on together until they came to an anthill, which the two eldest brothers wished to stir up, that they might see the little ants hurry about in their fright and carry off their eggs, but Witling said, "Leave the little creatures alone, I will not suffer them to be disturbed."

And they went on farther until they came to a lake, where a number of ducks were swimming about. The two eldest brothers wanted to catch a couple and cook them, but Witling would not allow it, and said, "Leave the creatures alone, I will not suffer them to be killed."

And then they came to a bees' nest in a tree, and there was so much honey in it that it overflowed and ran down the trunk. The two eldest brothers then wanted to make a fire beneath the tree, that the bees might be stifled by the smoke, and then they could get at the honey. But Witling prevented them, saying, "Leave the little creatures alone, I will not suffer them to be stifled."

At last the three brothers came to a castle where there were in the stables many horses standing, all of stone, and the brothers went through all the rooms until they came to a door at the end secured with three locks, and in the middle of the door a small opening through which they could look into the room. And they saw a little gray-haired man sitting at a table. They called out to him one, twice, and he did not hear, but at the third time he got up, undid the locks, and came out. Without speaking a word he led them to a table loaded with all sorts of good things, and when they had eaten and drunk he showed to each his bedchamber. The next morning the little gray man came to the eldest brother, and beckoning him, brought him to a table of stone, on which were written three things directing by what means the castle could be delivered from its enchantment. The first thing was that in the wood under the moss lay the pearls belonging to the Princess—a thousand in number—and they were to be sought for and collected, and if he who should undertake the task had not finished it by sunset—if but one pearl were missing—he must be turned to stone. So the eldest brother went out, and searched all day, but at the end of it he had only found one hundred; what was said on the table of stone came to pass and he was turned into stone. The second brother undertook the adventure the next day, but it fared with him no better than with the first; he found two hundred pearls, and was turned into stone.

And so at last it was Witling's turn, and he began to search in the moss; but it was a very tedious business to find the pearls, and he grew so out of heart that he sat down on a stone and began to weep. As he was sitting thus, up came the Ant King with five thousand ants, whose lives had been saved through Witling's pity, and it was not very long before the little insects had collected all the pearls and put them in a heap.

Now the second thing ordered by the table of stone was to get the key of the Princess's sleeping-chamber out of the lake. And when Witling came to the lake, the ducks whose lives he had saved came swimming, and dived below, and brought up the key from the bottom.

The third thing that had to be done was the most difficult, and that was to choose the youngest and loveliest of the three Princesses as they lay sleeping. All bore a perfect resemblance each to the other, and only differed in this, that before they went to sleep each one had eaten a different sweetmeat—the eldest a piece of sugar, the second a little syrup, and the third a spoonful of honey. Now the Queen of those bees that Witling had protected from the fire came at this moment and, trying the lips of all three, settled on those of the one that had eaten honey, and so it was that the King's son knew which to choose. Then the spell was broken; every one awoke from stony sleep, and took his right form again.

And Witling married the youngest and loveliest Princess, and became King after her father's death.

I once saw this, and if what happened in the spiritual world did not perish, if it is not dead, it must still be alive today.

THE END

Star Brother: Camille Flammarion

We know little about this French astronomer, born on February 26, 1842. He was most interested in the starry heavens, life after death, and spiritism. He would have approved of the stone teacher's chairs being built in an outdoor setting, so that one could bathe in the light of the stars. One of the illustrations of his *L'Atmosphere: Météorologie Populaire* (Paris, 1888) is very well known. It shows an explorer—a philosopher?—on his hands and knees in a flowery meadow in a delightful world, having pierced through the surface of a dome of sky, and looking into the dynamics of the heavens. We can hardly make sense of the patterns and chaos that we see revealed there. Perhaps we see the mechanics of the heavens, how the stars and planets move. A closer look shows row upon row of spiritual realities.

Flammarion's caption reads, "What, then, is this blue [presumably, blue sky], which certainly does exist, and which veils from us the stars during the day?" Partly from this cue, fantastical colorized versions have been made after Flammarion's time. The figure in the illustration breaks through not only the "blue," but the firmament itself, revealing the hidden workings of creation.

Flammarion investigated the other realities behind the stars, and would have been a good candidate to speak from the teacher's chair. The woodcut that he brought to the world is often labeled medieval and alchemical, but it originated with Flammarion, and gives a vision with which Steiner would have agreed, that of the human being stretching past the limits of the senses into the supersensible world.

Star Brother: Valentin Tomberg

Valentin Tomberg

Another bearer of gems was also born this Solar Day, Valentin Tomberg.[107] He could be considered a younger Star Brother, as he was born in 1900. Tomberg has a complicated history with anthroposophy, one that is beyond the scope of this book. Whole books have been written about Tomberg, some praising and others rejecting, and then more books to rebut the others![108] I wonder if the passion of these discussions stems partly from Tomberg's intimate relation with Steiner through their shared Solar Cross.

Tomberg's connection with Rudolf Steiner is unmistakable in his works, which are devoted to making the gems of the past live anew into the present and future. We can note the *Anthroposophical Studies of the Old Testament*, followed by *Anthroposophical Studies of the New Testament*, based on talks he gave between 1933 and 1937, full of life-nourishing gems. An example of a gem from Tomberg may suffice to show his connection with this degree and with Rudolf Steiner's thought:

> The parable of Christ Jesus in which He tells us of joy over the lost sheep is an accurate expression of the cosmic fact that the Good of a sinner—that is, one who has absorbed Evil into his [psycho-spiritual] organization—is of more value than that of a saint—that is, one who has not thus absorbed Evil. The finest expression was given to this phenomenon by Rudolf Steiner in the words, "Man is the religion of the Gods."[109]

Chew on that for a while! The one who admits the existence of evil and overcomes it, rather than spurning or denying it, becomes a deeper human being, more capable of understanding and helping others. Isabel Allende said that those who deny that they could ever torture become the worst in the end. Those who admit that the possibility lives within them are able to resist it. The "Gods"—the various hierarchies of divine beings who create and maintain our physical-emotional existence—regard these dramas of conscience with awe. The parable referred to involves the hundredth sheep in the flock. About the ninety-nine who had all behaved themselves and followed the shepherd, there is no fuss. About the hundredth that was lost and then found, the shepherd is joyous.[110]

Here are other examples of gems from Tomberg:

> Life is space streamed through by time; death is time become rigid in space. When time becomes space, forfeiting its control over form, then it dies and becomes a corpse.

> It is when "forgiveness" lies on the one scale of human initiative, that "redemption" can be laid on the other scale of the balance by the Spiritual World.

> Only in the school of the physical body can be learnt such humility and courage as is required by the free man, the initiate, for the concluding and realizing of a free alliance with the Spiritual World.[111]

Each of these gems must be digested slowly to unlock its essential nutrition.

Tomberg wrote several of his major works anonymously, for, spending much of World War II in Nazi-occupied Holland, he had to make secret his efforts to counter the militaristic materialism of the occupiers through prayer. His notes have only recently come to light and now comprise meditation courses on each line of the Abwoon Prayer, and also on a prayer received directly by Tomberg in Amsterdam in 1942, which he called the Our Mother Prayer. Each line is meant to be savored as a gem.

> Our Mother, Thou who art in the darkness of the underworld,

This was appropriate at the time of the Second World War. Note the theme of darkness that we find in various Star Brothers in this degree. Since then, through intuitive work of Robert Powell, it has been changed to, "Our Mother, Thou who art in the heart of the earthly realm."

> May the holiness of Thy name shine anew in our remembering.

You can only name something if you have found it in yourself; hence this constitutes self-knowledge.

> May the breath of Thy awakening kingdom warm the hearts of all who wander homeless.

We are all homeless, especially in these modern times where there are so many wars and as our consciousness soul releases us from geographical attachment.

> May the resurrection of Thy will renew eternal faith
> even unto the depths of physical substance.

We are reminded that divine will works through personal will, that is, through our activities, all the way down into our physical bodies.

> Receive this day the living memory of Thee from human hearts,
> Who implore Thee to forgive us for forgetting Thee,
> And are ready to fight against temptation,
> Which has led Thee to withdraw into the heart of the Earth,

And now we enter the connection with the Teacher, called the Son, and the meaning of the Sacrifice.

> That through the Deed of the Son,
> The immeasurable pain of the Father be stilled,
> By the liberation of all beings from the tragedy of Thy withdrawal.

It ends with the affirmation that we live and move within the garment, body, and soul of the Divine Mother, Sophia.

> For Thine is the homeland and the boundless wisdom
> And the all-merciful grace.
> For all and everything in the Circle of All.
> Amen.[112]

Meditations on each word and line of the prayers evoke astonishment. Studies of the gems in these compressed sayings, of how to unfold them into useful nutrition for the soul, are extraordinary. They include many gems of Tomberg's own thinking.

What do we make of the sense of anonymity and secrecy in Tomberg's life? Is this another appearance of the theme of darkness that we have seen in other Star Brothers? Certainly we can understand how someone could develop a sense of secrecy who had lived through World War II, when the publication of a prayer such as the Our Mother Prayer might well have meant his death. Is there more to his secrecy?

Steiner was sometimes criticized for revealing what was meant to be secret—and criticized by others for keeping other secrets. His critics would have had him keep all the secrets secret, behind closed doors. In their view, these pearls were not meant to thrown in front of those unprepared to receive them. Steiner felt, however, that humanity was ready for the knowledge, and indeed needed the maturity locked in the secrets of the wise in order to negotiate the treacherous shoals that lay ahead.

Goethe called for "an open secret," that is, something precious—a gem—that is nonetheless made freely available. Revealing secrets can lead to problems in two ways. Sometimes the revealed teachings are far too complex. Many have had the experience of picking up a Steiner book, or a Tomberg book, and not being able to wade through what at first appears to be Germanic intellectualism and an overwhelming waterfall of concepts. Rather than climb the cliffs, the audience wanders away.

Then sometimes we see great teachings presented to us in a diluted form, that is, popularized.

One must strike a balance. These spiritual truths are meant to nourish, and are needed especially in challenging times such as those we face now. Perhaps the teachings that come from the stone teacher's chair must have in common a sense of sacredness, not related to a human personality. Steiner often mentioned that the teachings came *through* him. Tomberg tried to take himself out of the middle of the picture by claiming anonymity.

We recommend that anyone interested in the relationship between Valentin Tomberg and Rudolf Steiner evaluate Tomberg's writings on their own merit, rather than depending on the judgments of others. One recent critique, for example, concerns an unpublished and unsent letter by Tomberg written just before his death. This seems unfair. From the point of view of the Solar Crosses, something written late in life shows more the magnetic influence of the death degree than the birth degree. Typically, to see how one of the Birth Images works into the life, we look at the early and middle parts of the life. From those vantage points, we find Tomberg a master of gems—like the princess in the fairy tale, he opened his mouth and gems came out.

The Different Gesture of Death into a Degree

The death gesture differs from the gesture of birth. The birth shows an innocent coming into life, breathing in the challenges and opportunities of an Image. At death, we see Lady Jane Grey lifting up her life's harvest as a gift into this degree. Born in 1537, Lady Jane was manipulated by her relatives into taking the throne at the age of fifteen, that is, into taking the stone chair prematurely. She was queen for two weeks, then was deposed and put into prison. At trial she pleaded guilty to treason. Even at her young age, she knew it was wrong to sit where she had not the wisdom to sit. Thus we see a sense of the importance of the throne—the stone chair—lived out in a life.[113] And we sense the importance of acceding to a higher truth in political matters, something that was not referred to among the kings and queens in the Horizon Images. So little is known about her—what power does she wield as a Bode past whom Steiner came through the gate of birth? We will learn much more about Bodes in later Images, and may need to come back to this one.

Another Bode was Aloys Senefelder. Though we know little about this poet and playwright who died on February 26, 1834, we know one thing of importance. He invented the technique of lithography so effectively used by Daumier, the technique of drawing on stone with grease pencil, then etching the stone—all about working with quality of stone, so interesting in terms of the Image. Did Senefelder align with this Image at death for this very reason, this love of stone, and the stacking of stones in order to artistically express the truth?

This is the kind of connection that we discover in this kind of work over and over again, confirmation of an aspect of the Image without a clear and easy explanation.

Though we have in our database no Star Sisters for Steiner's Gate Image, ongoing research on the dates of birth and death of historical personalities will reveal some. At this point, we find human beings associated with Steiner's life who have taken up the tasks of the Image, to build with stones the places where true words would be said. How astonishing! They do this in so many different ways. Each one, however, pursues his work not as entertainment, but as a matter of life and death. Even Daumier's humorous caricatures had the intent of awakening the people to the basic principles of human justice. Likewise with Steiner, whose outpouring of formulas and gems of heartfelt thinking continue to nourish people to this day—and will do so into the future.

We often ask with Solar Cross Images if the person was able to understand the Image in his or her life and realize it, that is, manifest it as real. Rudolf Steiner certainly met the challenge of his Gate Image.

8. THE EARTH IMAGE AT STEINER'S BIRTH

IN THE SOLAR Cross work, the four Images go together, in the shape of a cross. If you imagine Rudolf Steiner standing upright at noon on his birthday (either the first one or any birthday afterwards), with the Sun directly overhead, it looks like this image:

Let us now look at the Image directly opposite to the Sun's Image, that is, the Earth Image, at 14–15 Leo.

Ready your blank paper and a writing implement. Turn the page, read the Image, then close the book and make a mind-map of what you remember as well as what adds itself to this material. Amplify the Image into something that you can relate to personally.

Earth Image at Birth

The living dead—lepers, simpletons, the incurably diseased, the miserable, and the lost—are locked up in a dark building separate from the town. Many have no clothes. The single caretaker provides barely enough food by sliding it through a hole in the door in such a way that he never touches or sees the inmates. Behold, a healer approaches, the healer's students holding back for fear. The healer calls out to those inside. The healer opens the gates and brings the living dead into the light of the Sun. They are renewed by voice, light, presence. What is the utterance—what is the song—of the incurable cured, of the living dead brought to life?

Make a mind-map of this Image. Take your time for this. Then read over the Image again and let it continue its chemistry in you. When we work with these Images in a counseling session for an individual, we encourage him or her to take a day or two with the Image alone before proceeding to commentaries and historical personalities. Take that day or two and come back to this study. Now, assuming that you have done this, we can move on.

Preliminary Commentaries on the Earth Image

"The living dead" are some of the most miserable people that we meet in all 360 Images of the Oracle of the Solar Cross. Are they here because of the extraordinary power available from the Life Star and Death Star, Aldebaran and Antares, at the centers of Taurus and Scorpio in this Solar Cross? They are barely alive, dead to the world, in a terrible limbo. One can hear the words of Paul here: "The whole creation has been groaning in labor pains.... We ourselves ... groan inwardly while we wait for adoption, the redemption of our bodies."[114]

These bodies are corrupt and in pain. Some of these pains are specified, so let's look at them.

A person with "leprosy" has one of various skin diseases—rashes and sores, psoriasis, vitiligo, wounds that won't heal, mildews and fungus, scale disease, etc.—that are so serious that, fearing infection, the populace has banished the person from the center. By Jewish law, lepers are supposed to advertise themselves by wearing ragged clothing, looking wild and unruly, and crying aloud to passersby, "Unclean! Unclean!"[115] They are the living dead. In an advanced stage, they are not even permitted to eke out a living by begging at the edge of civilization; they are locked up as they itch to death. Steiner speaks about leprosy as an illness caused by destruction of a part of the astral body from deeds in past lives.

What are here called simpletons include people with many dysfunctions, from hereditary deficits such as Down's Syndrome to concussions or strokes, Alzheimer's disease, severe autism or psychosis, anyone who cannot join in the activities of this town of tentmakers and blanket makers.

The medical profession separates different diseases by cause. When resources are few, these miserable people are bunched together. Those who are out of the reach of help are considered lost and are gathered up, away from society, to die. How are these decisions made? Are there mistakes made? Note the statement by American Supreme Court Judge Antonin Scalia:

> The very core of liberty secured by our Anglo-Saxon system of separated powers has been freedom from indefinite imprisonment at the will of the Executive. Blackstone [in 1765] stated this principle clearly: "Of great importance to the public is the preservation of this personal liberty: for if once it were left in the power of any, the highest, magistrate to imprison arbitrarily whomever he or his officers thought proper ... there would soon be an end of all other rights and immunities.... But confinement of the person, by secretly hurrying him to gaol [prison], where his sufferings are unknown or forgotten, is a less public, a less striking, and therefore a more dangerous engine of arbitrary government."[116]

These inmates enjoy not freedom, but the secret confinement where the "sufferings are unknown or forgotten."

Their complete isolation and the feeding through a small aperture in the door reminds one of Plato's cave, where the prisoners chained inside can only see the shadows of people moving around in the world, the shadows cast against the back wall of the cave. From these shadows a whole philosophy arises about the nature of reality. In the meantime, health is kept from them.

Imprisonment deepens the sub-theme of darkness, secrecy, and blackness that we saw in the Star Brothers of the Gate Image.

Plato's prisoners are miserable, just as these lepers and simpletons are miserable, but Plato makes a bridge to the rest of us. From his metaphor, we learn to understand that we are all those prisoners, seeing only a portion of reality, and that because of this limitation we are miserable too and had best acknowledge our fundamental condition.

The Healer—Jesus Christ in his heart function—makes the bridge too. He sees past the nasty afflictions to the souls within. Becoming Sun-like, he cures them and directs his students to give them clothing. The cure was thought impossible. For example, when a king of Israel was asked to heal a leper, he responded, "Am I Divinity, to kill and to make alive, that this man sends words to me to cure a man of his leprosy?"[117] Yet the Healer does cure these outcasts of their disease, their uncleanness, and their social ostracism. He sends them to the priests to confirm that they have been cleaned and renewed.[118]

The notion that one can "cure" a mentally retarded person changes our views of the permanency of that condition. Karma and heredity are overturned, and these people have a new chance to grow and develop. They come from the periphery back to the center, into the sunlight of the fiery sign of Leo, home of the King Star, Regulus.

Another consideration: Can we view the inmates of the prison as parts of ourselves? We begin as a rough stone, and we don't really know if something precious lives inside. It is often for others to tell us about the gem that they sense deep down in us. The polishing comes from life experience lived in awareness. We ought not look for magic but for the fruits of our labors in relationship to others. Steiner used to say, "Three steps in moral development to each step in occultism."[119] We make mistakes along the way, some with dire consequences for others. We can see those mistakes as hidden away from view in a windowless cell. When one has greeted the light of the Sun within one, then the mistakes can be brought out into the daylight for cure, a vigorous polishing that brings out the true gem that we recognize for the very reason that it sparkles in the sunlight.

We can add one more question. How does the Healer know to come to this remote place, far from the towns and the roads that connect the towns? There is a sense here that the Healer has developed a kind of clairvoyance that can sense the existence of such a place from afar, and can see past the walls of the prison to the souls within.

Steiner's Relation to His Earth Image

> The light of the Sun is flooding
> Through widths of space;
> The song of birds is ringing
> Through fields of air,
> The gracious plants
> Spring upward from the Earth,
> And people's souls
> Lift up their thanks
> To the spirits of the world.
>
> —Prelude to *The Portal of Initiation*,
> the first mystery play by Rudolf Steiner [120]

Rudolf Steiner was born in Kraljevic, which means King's Village, so right away there is a sense of the kingly that lives in the sign Leo. As a kind of good king, Steiner actively sought out those who had been imprisoned by their afflictions and sought to assist them. That is because he saw the soul in all. He could have walked right by the various places where human beings were suffering, but he chose to make his knowledge and power available to all, even those with afflictions of soul that parallel the descriptions of physical ailments in the Image. One can see in this Image a forerunner of the Camphill Movement, inspired by Steiner and manifested by Karl König, wherein emotionally and developmentally challenged youngsters are given a home in a farm setting, with adults who can do chores with them and celebrate the seasonal festivals.

One can also see in this Image Steiner's willingness to work with all of us. He didn't have to. He could have found a handful of people proficient in esoteric ceremonies and privately pursued his own spiritual growth with this select group. Rather, he chose to work with all human beings. He too had students hanging back for fear, and he patiently brought them forward, again and again leading them into difficult situations and instructing them on what to do with those in greater need. He understood that through service one grows more comprehensively and swiftly.

In Dornach during wartime, Steiner and his students learned to care for the wounded. He designed a badge that was given to the most ardent workers that read: "Hail to the helpers of healing." Helping hands were pictured receiving the rays of the Sun in order to send them to the dark places of the Earth.[121] As we quoted at the beginning of this section, "The light of the Sun is flooding through widths of space." The helper harnessed that light and put it to the service of healing.

Most of all, Steiner's philosophical work championed freedom. His great and complicated work *The Philosophy of Freedom* tells us of freedom's central role in human evolution. Today anthroposophists insist that all human beings should be able to make choices through a "free deed." Activities, writings, and people are evaluated by the extent to which they leave one free or unfree. Sometimes the anthroposophist's fear of treading on another's freedom can be taken to extremes. These concerns continue the theme of freedom into which, as we see here, Steiner was born.

How did he characterize freedom? In the first words of his mystery plays quoted at the beginning of this section, we see plants springing, birds singing, and people thanking. To translate, etheric body springing, astral body singing, and soul expressing gratitude.

He spoke in many places about the imprisonment that precedes true freedom: imprisonment in our intellectual thinking, imprisonment in cultural patterns, imprisonment in our nerve system.[122] And he took it further. Speaking about the elemental beings that have been bound into our physical, etheric, and astral bodies, we find that we have become the jail and jailer:

> Thus, through our own spiritual life, we can, without changing them, either imprison within us those spirits which are bewitched in air, water and earth, or else through our own increasing spirituality, free them and lead them back to their own element.[123]

How is this release from prison to be accomplished? By the light of our own being. Thus, in terms of the Earth Image that Steiner breathed in at birth, every human being can play the part and become the Healer.

Steiner himself struggled with imprisonments, too. When anthroposophists revere Steiner as "the Master"—a term that had a special meaning for Steiner, as we shall see—they sometimes forget that he dealt with challenges that placed him on the inside of the prison as well. Though he didn't smoke, he used snuff, a purified form of tobacco placed directly into the nose. Students noticed the white powder on his black coat. Sometimes he looked "as pale as death" from overwork. Steiner's eyesight was bad in the dark. He wore his hair in such a way that one stray bunch would come down across his forehead and into his eyes, which he would brush away with the hand holding his glasses—yes, he wore glasses—or flick "the stubborn strand of hair" back up atop his head, sometimes flicking repeatedly.[124] In other words, he shared humanity with human beings, with his own particular quirks and eccentricities.

Quirks and eccentricities are a natural part of human manifestation. When minor in scope, these differences make people interesting. Everyone becomes a character. When exaggerated, they become disease. Even anthroposophists are susceptible. In a retrospective, Gladys Mayer reported about the time after Steiner's death: "I saw enacted in Dornach during the next years in a small scale the tragic drama which was later enacted all over Europe. Doubts, confusion, recriminations and suspicions, one of another."[125] Freeing the prisoners in oneself and others is ongoing and continued work; Steiner didn't finish it.

Steiner was the first to say that those who wish to help humanity must understand humanity by living fully. "When one looks more deeply into one's inner being, one discovers things of which one does not like to speak." However, this speaking can be therapeutic, part of the cure, and he thanked people for the opportunity to help them. Indeed, he modeled a life of service: "The only love people can show me is to call me day and night when they need me."[126] His waiting room was famous for being crowded at all hours.

Steiner related freedom to the Sun, the true spiritual Sun: "Nothing would please the opponents of Christianity more than if human beings entirely lost their vision of the Sun as a spiritual being and retained only the view of the Sun as it is in physical existence."[127] He understood that people who may have been walking around in the daylight also lived inside a dark prison.

One student relates her experience of Steiner in ways that come right out of the Image: "The whole seemed steeped in the clarified sunlight of a super-awareness—a reality so immediate and instantaneous, so fresh and powerful, that the everyday seems shadowy in comparison."[128] Rittelmeyer likewise spoke of light: "It was as though [the spiritual insights from Steiner's teaching] came from a world of light, in which all fear ceased."[129]

We can hear Emil Bock also, on attending his first lecture as a narrative of a prisoner released:

> With eager expectation, but with a touch of skepticism, I went in too. I could have no idea that through what I was to hear a curtain would be lifted from me upon a new world. With amazement I looked into a realm which was at once very strange to me, and yet on a deeper level very familiar... One cramping limitation after another, in my thinking and in my soul, fell away... A comprehensive life of knowledge revealed itself in illumined clarity.[130]

Steiner spoke the word "leprosy" on a few occasions, at one time giving the term "the leprosy of materialism," which he linked with the Revelation of John, in which frightful pictures are given of the results of the working of materialism on the soul.[131]

The notion that the healer somehow knew about the plight of those in the remote prison and found its location in the countryside has parallels in Steiner's life. Steiner's assistant and housekeeper, Anna Samweber, relates a story in which she was "walking along a long, wooden blank wall when suddenly two human shapes appeared from the dark and attacked me." She called inwardly, "Doctor, help me!" The effect was immediate: "Both fellows fell back like lightning and were gone." The next morning, when she related the tale, Steiner wondered why she was anxious about the episode, pointing out, "But I did help you, didn't I?"[132] Likewise, Andrei Belyi tells several stories in which Steiner appeared at just the right time to liberate him from himself, noting also that when he wasn't ready, meaning he had not yet prepared himself sufficiently, Steiner seemed aloof and distant, appearing only at the critical time when Andrei had completed the inner work necessary for a new transformation.[133]

Demonstrating his clairvoyance and his capacity to deliver light through distance and through time, Steiner wrote an important verse, "To the Berlin Friends," at the end of 1923, prefiguring events that would not take place for twenty years:[134]

> For pain passes upon us
> From powers of material force,
> But hope illumines
> Even when darkness enshrouds us.
> And it will one day
> Emerge within our memory
> When at length, after the darkness,
> We may live again in light.

This sounds like a message to the inmates of the Earth Image of his birth. He also says in this verse:

So may the lightning shatter into dust
Our sense-built houses.

Light in all forms, the memory of light and the promise of light, can keep people going in a difficult, dark situation. This dark situation lay at the root of the Image into which Steiner chose to be born.

Helping others was thus natural to him. Learning of this Image at Steiner's birth, I realized why he wrote some of the books that he did, the ones wherein he delves into the work of nineteenth-century philosophers, some of whom were little known in his day—let alone today. What do we care for Fichte or Haeckel or Hartmann or ... ? Why not lay out the good news— the sunny revelation of spiritual truth—and forget the dusty philosophers? Because Steiner saw the errors in their thinking as illness and sought to bring them from prison into sunlight. In these writings, one can see Steiner leading these old philosophers, one by one, wounded and diseased, out into the light. In this way the Image wells up from earth and compels the one born into it to action.

Are We in Prison?

In order to understand Steiner's method for release from prison, we have to understand his realization of how the human psyche is constructed. For it is different from the common conception that spirit is good and Earth is bad, that on Earth we have only illusions that we have built up to get by, and that spirit is only accessible through meditation that turns off the senses. Listen to what Steiner says in his autobiography about *The Philosophy of Freedom*: "I tried to show in my book that nothing *unknowable* lies *behind* the sense-world, but that *within* it is the spiritual world." Already this is revolutionary, then and now too. We don't have to go elsewhere to get to the good truth. We can poke our head through the veil in just the way illustrated by his Star Brother Flammarion. He goes on: "And I tried to show that Man's idea-world has its existence within that spiritual world. Therefore the true reality of the sense-world remains hidden from human consciousness *only* for *as long as* Man is merely engaged in sense perception."[135] In other words, we think we are in prison—you can ask anyone on the street, and they would agree—but we actually aren't. Leading us into the sunlight does not mean taking us from one place to another, but realizing that the sunlight is already here, though appreciation of that fact may require disciplined cultivation of our senses, beyond the levels of perception at which we function most of the time.

Historical Personalities

Looking at those born into this degree, we will find the most astonishing connections.

Composers First: The Bode of Tomás Luis de Victoria (sometimes given as Vittoria)

The Spanish church composer died in 1611 into this degree. One can listen to Victoria's music—"O Sacrum Convivium" or "O Magnum Mysterium"—as gifts lifted up by the composer into this particular gate of the heavens. One can find in it the strength to enter prisons and feel compassion upwelling within oneself for the inmates. This is music of one who has sensed the best of his Death Image and made the most of it. Listen to "¡O Celestial Medicina!" or any of his settings of "Ave Maria" when you reread the Image or your mind-map of it, or anything about this Image. Imagine that this music sounds out from the very air when the inmates exit the prison into the light. Beautiful voices sing out so plainly in "Ave Regina Caelorum": "Hail, Queen of Heaven, Hail, mistress of the angels, hail, holy root from whence came the light of the world." Are these the prisoners singing out or the light itself?

Star Sister: Maria Montessori

A younger Star Sister by nine years, Maria Montessori was born on August 31, 1870. Whenever we hear these days about the vanguards of "alternative" education, we find Montessori and Steiner linked often in the same sentence.

Montessori was the first woman to earn a medical degree in Italy, in 1894. She was appointed assistant doctor at the psychiatric clinic of the University of Rome, where she became interested in the educational problems of mentally retarded children. She felt that most mental deficiency was a

pedagogical problem rather than a physical problem. After working with a group of "retarded" children for two years she administered a state exam
that the children passed ahead of "normal" children. At the turn of the century, a real estate devel-
oper, concerned that gangs of young children from
the slums would destroy his buildings under construction, asked Montessori's advice. Seeing that
the children needed a place of their own, she created a learning environment within the apartment
complex and called it "La Casa dei Bambini," The

Maria Montessori

Children's House. From observations of the learning styles of these children
arose the techniques now known as the Montessori Method.

How interesting that Montessori's original connection was to those
who had been shut away and named "retarded." The thrust of her work was
to bring these children out into the light. As a young man, Steiner also
worked as a tutor to a family with four boys, the youngest of whom was
"retarded." Steiner developed techniques for educating the "retarded" boy
that, in two years, graduated him from elementary school, whereupon he
entered the Gymnasium and then medical school, and became a physician.
These techniques later became the foundation for Steiner's curative education curriculum.

Star Brother: Johann Valentine Andreae

> The world moves towards a time of universal enlightenment
> before its ending.
> —FRANCES YATES, *The Rosicrucian Enlightenment* [136]

Born on August 17, 1586, which in the Julian calendar equates to this
same Solar Day, Johann Valentine Andreae began life as a sickly child and
could not stand unaided until the age of two. As one of the leaders of the
Rosicrucian movement, Andreae authored at the age of seventeen (in 1604)
The Chymical Wedding of Christian Rosenkreutz, which in a revised version
of 1616 became a well-loved book of initiation for anthroposophists. This
allegory, romance, and symbolical recipe book for chemical experiments
contains references to the spiritual-social movement of the rose cross.

Johann Valentine Andreae

The varied streams that assembled for this event deserve mention, as we will see many of the contributing factors later in this study.

The Setting. In the early part of the fourteenth century, King Edward III of England founded the Order of the Garter, which became a league of the powerful, devoted to chivalry, defense of morality, all the other character traits that we might associate with King Arthur's Round Table and the tale of Parzival. Indeed, Edward got the idea from the Knights who joined the Crusades with women's garters around their legs. After some decades the Order languished in importance, but Queen Elizabeth I revived it in the sixteenth century, using it to gather noblemen who gave their allegiance to the Crown of England. Upon Elizabeth's death, her successor, James I, kept up the Order of the Garter and its ornate ceremonies. One of those to whom he awarded this prize was Frederick V, the Elector Palatine, a Protestant from the area that we would today call Germany, to whom James I gave his daughter in marriage, Elizabeth Stuart.[137] Frederick and Elizabeth were married in London in February 1613, in a great celebration of what people called the meeting of the Thames and the Rhine. The couple soon moved to the city of Heidelberg. There they created a court that was open to many ideas and many religions. Theirs was a middle ground between the governments still aligned with the Catholic Church and the new orthodoxy of the Protestants, Calvinists and Lutherans who had rebelled against the Church of Rome but created rules and dogmas of their own. At this time, there was an uneasy truce between Protestants and Catholics.[138]

Just before this, in Prague, King Rudolf II, Holy Roman Emperor, had created another world between the strictures of Catholic and Protestant. From all over Europe to Prague came anyone interested in esoteric and scientific studies, for the two were closely linked then. The Jews pursued their studies of the Kabbalah there. Playwrights and symbolist painters had venues opened to them. Alchemists had laboratories. King Rudolf himself had many pieces of alchemical equipment. He listened to astrologers, psychics, physicians, and prognosticators, who visited one after another. "His Majesty is interested only in wizards, alchymists, kabbalists and the like, sparing no expense to find all kinds of treasures, learn secrets.... He also has a whole library of magic books."[139] It was a Renaissance city. Rudolf even tolerated the first alternative church, the Bohemian Church of Jan Hus, and the mystical Bohemian Brethren attached to that church. (I note this because Hus will come up again with a Star Brother at the Taurus Image.)

In their castle at Heidelberg the court of Frederick and Elizabeth built upon the accomplishments of Rudolf's cosmopolitan and liberal Prague. For the next seven years, there ensued a great outpouring of literature— symbolical, psychological, mythical, alchemical, allegorical, all intermixed. Buildings with special grottoes were built, as well as gardens with symbolical sculptures, some with moving parts. They created a fantastical landscape, precursors of Steiner's activity with sculpture and architecture. Alchemy as early chemistry and physics was indistinguishable from alchemy as magical pathway to spirits of the divine.

Chief among the works published at this time, the ones that created the "Rosicrucian furore," were three. In 1614 was published the *Fama* (an abbreviation for *Fama Fraternitatis, or a Discovery of the Fraternity of the Most Noble Order of the Rosy Cross*). In 1615 appeared the *Confessio* (abbreviation for *Confessio Fraternitatis, or The Confession of the Laudable Fraternity of the Most Honorable Order of the Rosy Cross, Written to All the Learned of Europe*). In 1616 appeared *The Chymical Wedding of Christian Rosenkreutz*.

These documents claimed to represent a secret brotherhood, called The Order of the Rose Cross, or Rosy Cross, which in German is Rosen-Kreutz. The books said that there would be great breakthroughs in thinking, in science, in all of culture. In the style of Andreae's Gate Image, the *Confessio* promised:

> God hath certainly and most assuredly concluded to send and grant to the World before her end ... such a Truth, Light, Life and Glory, as the first man Adam had ... wherefore there shall cease all servitude, falsehood, lyes, and darkness, which by little and little, with the great Worlds Revolution, was crept into all Arts, Works and Governments of Men, and have darkened the most part of them.[140]

From this point of view, nearly everyone was in the windowless prison, and the Order of the Rose Cross had come to liberate them.

The Rosicrucians invited to join all those who wished to unite themselves with this liberation in the most efficacious way, that is, through the magical arts of alchemy. Great numbers of people began to hunt for the secret order, to submit their application to join. They made public announcements of their intentions in the newspapers, on street corners, and in printed books, but the secret Order remained secret. Meanwhile, these books spawned an entire literature of symbolical alchemy, in which great claims were made of discoveries that would make life easy, turn dross into gold making everyone rich, curing all diseases, lifting anyone who knew the secrets into heaven... The fantasies knew no limit. In 1620 the outpouring suddenly stopped. Why?

Frederick and Elizabeth, celebrated as the sacred marriage, the "chymical wedding" of the highest order, had supported in Heidelberg a culture that accepted all the arts. Their twin towers were the setting of many dramatic presentations, including Shakespeare's *The Tempest*, known for its themes of magical power, which had been performed for them on their betrothal night, December 27, 1612, as well as after. When Rudolf II died, the successor began to suppress the Bohemians, who had grown used to their freedoms. The people appealed to Frederick V to become crowned as King of Bohemia, to take the seat of the Holy Roman Emperor and restore the golden age of Rudolf. The sense of promise of the magical kingdom led to fantasies of invincibility.

Frederick paused, then accepted in 1619, moving from Heidelberg to Prague. He was crowned by the brothers of the Bohemian Church of Moravia, the followers of Jan Hus. The Catholic forces resented this incursion. A combination of Austrian troops of the Hapsburgs and Spanish troops from the south met Frederick's army in early November 1620 and smashed them. The Catholic victors went on to destroy utterly the castle and its wonders at Heidelberg, as well as every trace of the previous liberal cultures. The books were burned, the equipment crushed, the people tortured and killed. Thus began the Thirty Years' War, which demolished central Europe, just where this cultural creativity had been the strongest.

Frederick and Elizabeth escaped to safety, leaving behind even the famous garter—for which loss Frederick was mocked by the victors from afar, with cartoons showing the deposed King with one leg of his pantaloons fallen down around his ankles.

Steiner's Star Brother Johann Valentine Andreae also escaped. He had enjoyed the core of this brief flowering of culture. He is known to be the author of the *Chymical Wedding*, and is quite likely the author of the *Fama* and the *Confessio* as well. For our study of him as a Star Brother, it doesn't matter whether or not he wrote these two earlier books, for he was imbued with their content.

We must realize how crucial was the period and place of the "Rosicrucian Enlightenment" to the development of modern science, exoteric and esoteric. Everything that modern astrologers, alchemists, symbolical psychologists, Kabbalists, and theologians now take for granted was informed by or wholly determined by the explorers in this period and place between stunting religious wars. This is also true for modern science, astronomy, and chemistry. Andreae, Steiner's Star Brother, was in the thick of it, helping bring the benighted into the light.

Christian Rosenkreutz

Frances Yates declares in her study of the "Rosicrucian Enlightenment" that "No serious person can now believe in the literal truth of the Rosenkreutz story."[141] But Rudolf Steiner did. Indeed, Christian Rosenkreutz as a guiding force for all of humanity stood close to Steiner in the unseen worlds. The teachings of the Rosy Cross, or Rosicrucianism, formed a pillar for all of anthroposophy.

If Rosenkreutz existed, he may have lived in the years inferred from the three documents by Andreae, from 1378 to 1484—106 years—and the vault of his grave was discovered 120 years after his purported death as predicted in the documents themselves. From the grave itself came the inspirations for Andreae's writings.[142] In this view, Andreae was reporting on events that occurred over a hundred years previously.

The name Christian Rosenkreutz is as much a title—the bearer of Christ in the form of the rose cross—as it is someone's name. It may have been a function in a mystical brotherhood that actually existed. Through Andreae's extension to the Red Cross of the Garter, it may have connected the tradition of the Order of the Garter to the Red and Rosy Cross.[143]

The Chymical Wedding. The beginning of the story of *The Chymical Wedding* involves people imprisoned together, completely miserable, suffering horribly. The author finds himself

> … in fetters chained,
> Within the darkness of a dungeon prison;
> And round were multitudes of men who strained
> To grab each neighbor who had slightly risen
> And push him down, so that the same low level be maintained.[144]

Every so often a window opens from above, and a shaft of light enters. Is it the little hatch in the doorway through which food was slid in the Image? Then the hatch closes again. Sometimes a rope ladder hangs down. The inmates in the miserable realm fight with each other to grasp the ladder so as to be lifted up and away from the torment below. Thus we find the terms of the Image of Andreae's birth. Later in his book, a few are released into the sunlight—taken up and up through various trials into the beauties and verities of heaven. To turn the pages of the original, and set it within the context of the many alchemical references that are made there, is to be astonished by the power of this fifteenth-century allegory.[145]

Steiner on Andreae

Steiner spoke about Christian Rosenkreutz and *The Chymical Wedding* on many occasions, and a few times spoke about Johann Valentine Andreae, his elder Star Brother.

> I wrote an article on *The Chymical Wedding of Christian Rosenkreutz* and I drew attention to the fact that it was written down by a boy of seventeen or eighteen. The boy himself understood not a word of it…. The boy … became a pastor, a good, honest pastor of the Württemberg-Swabian type, who wrote exhortations and theological treatises which are distinctly below the average, and very far indeed from having anything to do with the content of *The Chymical Wedding of Christian Rosenkreutz.* Life itself proves to us that it was not the Swabian pastor-to-be who wrote this *Chymical Wedding* out of his own soul. It is an inspired writing throughout.[146]

Steiner was referring to the earlier version of the *Chymical Wedding*, the one written in 1604, no copy of which has been found, though it is known that it was changed quite a bit for its 1616 publication, when Andreae was thirty years old.

Steiner's observation about inspiration of a young man raises the question—when are we ourselves and when are we not ourselves? What speaks "through" us and what "is" us? Look at the rescuer in the Image from this point of view—is this person "inspired" or acting on his or her own? Steiner spoke often of what came "through" him; for example, the first two mystery plays state the authorship as "Through Rudolf Steiner," most people presuming that Archangel Michael himself brought this work into existence.[147] Steiner, however, was conscious of this connection, as Andreae seems not to have been; Steiner seems to have succeeded in receiving inspiration and uniting this with his own being.

Though Andreae may not have been powerful enough to contain all of Christian Rosenkreutz, he made a good vehicle for this source of light, and he had his own strengths, too. At the age of thirty, he delivered a eulogy for a friend that shows how he thought. As he reports what the anatomists found in the body of his friend, we can imagine that this is the kind of diagnostics that served the healer in the Image:

> The heart was healthy and saturated with the clear red blood of Christ; a small trace of the contagious fluid of original sin was to be found only in the foremost chamber. His lungs had been filled to the full with the breath of God the Holy Spirit—the presence of only a few tiny ulcerations of academic science was detected. His Christian liver had so well distributed the finest virtues over his entire body that only a small number of weaknesses of corrupt human nature could be found. His spleen had cooked only the best blood of charity ... his kidneys ... had remained totally chaste.[148]

Imagine how Andreae looked at other human beings, and how he sought to help them, bringing them out into the sun brilliance for healing.

Andreae wrote another work, published in 1619, just before the end of the remarkable years under Frederick and Elizabeth. The *Reipublicae Christianopolitanae Descriptio* lays out a well-developed and detailed utopia of the divine city, one filled with light, where music, astronomy, astrology, and mathematics are studied. "Religious choral singing is taught and practiced.

They do this in imitation of the angelic choir whose services they value so highly. These choral performances are given in the Temple, where they also present sacred dramas."[149] Andreae loved dramas, having written several as a young man, and supported them, even after times turned hard.

Sometimes we find people who have felt warmly toward a Star Brother or Star Sister. Rudolf Steiner did that and more—he made much use of the work of his elder Star Brother. The previous paragraph shows how, point for point, Steiner realized his Star Brother's theoretical utopia. Perhaps the most important gift that Steiner received from his Star Brother was the verse or mantram or gem that was given at the end of the *Fama*:

> Ex Deo nascimur. (From out of Divinity we are born.)
> In Christo morimur. (In Christ consciousness we die.)
> Per Spiritum sanctum reviviscimus. (Through the Holy Spirit we will be reborn.)

This gem (Gate Image) to free our soul (Earth Image) is spoken at many anthroposophical gatherings. Steiner uses the initials for it – EXD, ICM, PSSR – to adorn various designs that he made. It is one of the most potent formulas I have ever used, and releases nourishment at every recitation. Andreae writes in the *Fama* that he found it at the end of the document *T*, grasped by the hand of the undecayed body of Christian Rosenkreutz, which he found when he opened the burial vault after 120 years.

Star Brother: Johann Wolfgang von Goethe

Steiner's mentor on earth, the brilliant life to whom Steiner was drawn by personal desire and circumstance, is also his elder brother in the stars. Goethe's Sun position at birth—on August 28, 1749—is directly opposite Steiner's; Earth and Sun exchange.[150] In this way we can understand Steiner's statement that Goethe was "the Copernicus and Kepler of the organic world."[151] Copernicus and Kepler replaced the Earth as center of the universe (the geocentric view) with the Sun as the center (the heliocentric view). Steiner realized that the Sun was in the Earth. Earth and Sun—which is the center? Goethe and Steiner –which is Earth and which is Sun? In Goethe, Steiner found both: an Earth to stand upon, in his fourteen years of work with Goethe's writings, and, in that process, a Sun to guide him.

As a young man Steiner became the editor of Goethe's scientific papers. Later on Steiner began to speak about Goethean thinking, a prelude to his own views about spirit-filled thinking, a method of hyper-sensible and supersensible thinking that overcame the prison of normal perception. Steiner also produced Goethe's play *Faust* and emulated Goethe in his own dramatic writings. Here we see how someone else born into one's Solar Cross as a forerunner can lead the way into meeting with life's demands. Steiner

Johann Wolfgang von Goethe (by Evert A. Duyckinick)

as a young man basked in the sunlight of Goethe's scientific observations and way of thinking, and then, maturing, brought that way of thinking to new levels of brilliance. Naming the building that housed his life's work the Goetheanum, Steiner acknowledged his mentor and elder Star Brother. Then Steiner brought Goethe's insights into modern times with greater understanding and applications.

How did Goethe live into the Image into which he was born? We will look at three areas of Goethe's life, choosing from many. Before we look at the book that Goethe published at the age of twenty-five that made him widely and quickly famous, let's visit a scene from Goethe's seventh year.

An Altar to the Creator

Goethe had suffered smallpox as a youngster, something that would give him compassion for those inside the prison of his Gate Image.

At the age of seven, he erected an altar to the forces of creation. Ponder this in terms of his Earth Image (Steiner's Gate Image). In an unused room, Goethe secretly chose the most beautiful of his father's collection of treasures taken from nature. As a foundation, he used a red-lacquered music stand, built as a four-sided pyramid for playing and singing in parts. "Upon this he reverently built up the objects whose tangible wonder and mystery revealed the powers of the unspeakable, intangible object of his devotion."[152] At the top, he placed a little dish with incense ready to go. In the morning, with sun streaming in the window, he used his magnifying glass to light the incense. "Sun-Being—come to earth!" He experienced a communion with the spirit world, the smoke swirling about his uplifted treasures. Later he wished to repeat the experience, but could not find the little dish. Setting the incense directly onto the music stand, he didn't notice that the burning embers were eating down through the stand's beautiful finish. His parents, however, did notice, and quickly put an end to this childish ritual.

The Sorrows of Young Werther

At the age of twenty-five, Goethe published *The Sorrows of Young Werther (Die Leiden des Jungen Werthers*, 1774). It tells the tale through letters of Werther's imprisonment in the madness of unrequited love for Lotte, to the point where he becomes insane and shoots himself. The book served to ease Goethe's own pain at a similar circumstance, a prison of mental torture wherein "waves of death" engulfed him. His adolescence was the epitome of *sturm und drang* (storm and stress). This type of experience was shared by many adolescents of that time. *Werther* was the most popular expression of the pains of growing up in an era of great culture-wide pain. Many young men imitated Werther, looked for the characters and geographical locations in the book, wore Werther's yellow pants, found their "Lotte," and tried to shoot themselves. It touched a nerve of a society imprisoned, and filled the newspapers with stories of madness. Early on in the book, we listen to Werther before he goes mad. In a section from the May 22 letter of Book I, Werther acknowledges that society is a prison: "...we amuse ourselves painting our prison-walls with bright figures and brilliant landscapes." Do you see how this takes the parable of Plato's cave a step further? Not only do we not see what is "real" and only see its shadows on the back wall of the cave, but we also paint over these shadows with concepts that further obscure the truth. Go back to Flammarion's woodcut to perceive that, though gay and beautiful, the landscape inside the sphere has an essential falseness to it. Werther was unable to penetrate the sphere. However, in this same letter, young Werther sees the light at the end of the tunnel:

> But the man who humbly acknowledges the vanity of all this, who observes with what pleasure the thriving citizen converts his little garden into a paradise, and how patiently even the poor man pursues his weary way under his burden, and how all wish equally to behold the light of the sun a little longer, — yes, such a man is at peace, and creates his own world within

himself; and he is also happy, because he is a man. And then, however limited his sphere, he still preserves in his bosom the sweet feeling of liberty,
and knows that he can quit his prison whenever he likes.

However, our young hero does not have the ability to choose to "quit his
prison." His madness deepens until finally he can take it no longer. He kills
himself. In terms of the Image, he lacks what can lead him outward, that
is, the light of Divinity. At this stage of his life, Goethe was struggling and
failing to meet his Gate Image.

Goethe's Flight to Italy

In September 1786, at the age of thirty-seven, Goethe left his bureaucratic post and traveled incognito to Rome. He spoke of his journey as a flight,
as if from prison. He had asked himself, "Is my eye clear, pure, and bright,
how much can I grasp in passing, can the creases be eradicated that have
formed and fixed themselves on my heart?"[153] Imprisoned within himself
and his role in the government, he had to escape into the light. He expressed
that whenever he thought of Italy or tried to read from the classics, he had
"the most dreadful pain." Just before leaving, he felt the imprisonment most
strongly: "for while the things stood there only a hand's breadth away, I was
separated from them by an impenetrable wall."[154] His life had closed in on
him as a prison.

The achievement of his journey? The light. "O my love," he wrote, "what
is the high point of all human activity? To me as an artist what is most precious is that it gives the artist a chance to show what is in him and to bring
unknown harmonies up from the depth of existence into the light of day."[155]

Along the way, in Padua, he devised the concept of the "primal ideal
plant" (Ur-Pflanze), the ideal that informs every individual plant but that
no individual plant can become—that is, a kind of guiding spirit of each
plant. From these observations, he was able to express the ideal growth of
the plant: the contraction of the seed, the expansion of the shoot and leaf,
the contraction of the flower bud, the expansion of the flower, the contraction of the sexual organs of the flower (the stamen and pistil), the expansion
of the fruit, and the contraction inward to the hard seed, which begins the
process all over again. In terms of Goethe's Gate Image, we can see this as
a coming in and out of prison, first constrained, then freed, back and forth,

a necessary dynamic balance that is fundamental to life in physical expression.[156]

Goethe was given *The Chymical Wedding of Christian Rosenkreutz* just before setting out on his Italian journey. At that time, he said he could see a fairy tale in it that would come out. Eight years later, *The Tale of the Green Snake and the Beautiful Lily* appeared.[157] We see here how Goethe takes the work of his own elder Star Brother, Andreae, to stand upon and surpass.

The Green Snake

Steiner attached great importance to this tale: "In his *Tale of the Green Snake and the Beautiful Lily*, Goethe tried to express in his own way the extraordinary soul experiences that Schiller brought forward in a more abstract, philosophical style in the *Aesthetic Education of Man*."[158]

One can imagine this last statement entirely in the terms of Steiner's Conception Image, the central figure bridging between the philosophers with their abstractions and the listeners who eat the gems that sparkle, the ones that come in fairy tales.

The conclusion of the *Green Snake* story is in fact the construction of a bridge, a bridge between this world and spirit worlds. It may risk oversimplification to say so, for with a snake that eats gold, will o' the wisps that make gold out of air, kings made of silver and gold, a ferryman who demands payment in artichokes, a dog that turns to onyx and then is revived, this story barely touches the reality of this world. Resembling opium-induced fantasies or paintings by Hieronymous Bosch, it nonetheless grows through repeated reading, telling, and retelling to an answer to the question: "How do I find exit from the insanities of the so-called real world?" For the oddest things occur in this magic-show of a story, and yet we can learn to take them for granted, and deal with whatever comes our way.[159]

An important exchange occurs between the Green Snake and the King made of gold.

No sooner had the Snake beheld this revered figure, than the King began to speak, and asked: "Whence comest thou?" "From the chasms where the gold dwells," said the Snake. "What is grander than gold?" inquired the King. "Light," replied the Snake. "What is more refreshing than light?" said he. "Conversation," answered she.[160]

From the caves wherein gold lives we move to light, paralleling Goethe's Gate Image. Between two sincerely listening individuals, a more refined light lives, the glowing and radiant energy engendered by exchange of soul-filled words. Here is an amendment to the Image, suggesting that releasing the prisoners and flooding them with light is not enough. One must engage them with the light of the heart, and listen in turn; then all may be freed.

What are the words that one should say to someone just coming out of their confinement in hell? The tale of Parzival in the ninth century as told by Wolfram von Eschenbach in the thirteenth century hinges on just this point: What is the question that the young Parzival needed to ask the Grail King to cure the King's painful ailment and rescue the entire kingdom? On his first visit to the Grail Castle, amid the wonders of knights and ladies, he neglects to ask this question. Kicked out in the morning, he wanders for years and endures many adventures. More mature, he returns to the Grail Castle, and asks the right question. Then the Grail King is cured, the people of the Grail are released of their sorrow, and the land is returned to productivity. What was the question? The common translation is, "Uncle, what ails thee?" The answer to such a question might look like a list of complaints. But the original words suggest a different emphasis. The old German begins, "*Oeheim*," which is a familiar term for a relation such as an uncle. It continues, "*was wirret dir?*" This can mean "What is confusing you? What is your error? What is going wrong? What is going astray?" That kind of warm interest activates a soul and begins a true conversation.[161]

Prelude to Faust

Goethe wrote his great masterpiece, *Faust,* over a period of decades, revising continually until shortly before his death. In the part begun in Goethe's twenties, we also see the theme of prison, especially at the very end of Book I, where Mephistopheles takes Faust to meet with Gretchen in her cell.

Even from the very beginning, we learn how Faust felt that his life was a prison from which he could find no escape: the prison of intellectual heights. The top philosopher in the world, he could still find no answer to life's questions. This might put one in mind of Hamlet, who conversed with his old schoolmates, Rosencrantz and Guildenstern, in the following way:[162]

HAMLET

Denmark's a prison.

ROSENCRANTZ

Then is the world one.

HAMLET

A goodly one; in which there are many confines, wards and dungeons, Denmark being one of the worst.

Why do we bring Hamlet in suddenly? Because Rudolf Steiner said that Hamlet was the perfect reflection of Faust, and could have been Faust's student. They had both been to Wittenberg and had very similar personalities. Speaking of the two of them, Steiner observes, "The pallor of thoughts makes him ill in his inner being.... Spiritual vision cannot tolerate intellectualism because the outcome of it is a mood of soul in which the human being is inwardly torn right away from any connection with the spirit."[163] Faust and Hamlet become inmates of the prison of the Image, suffering from "pallor," deprivation of the Sun.

Steiner understood Goethe's efforts through his work to exit his own prison. "When you understand what Goethe intended with his *Faust*, you sense that he was endeavoring to pass through a certain gateway."[164] As in Steiner's Gate Image, he awaits the Sun being.

More about the Legend of Doctor Faust

Many acknowledged *Faust* a masterpiece. It is still beloved in Germany, where it is read, taught, and performed. The Goetheanum has since Steiner's time held performances of scenes or even the entirety of *Faust*, which can last for many hours. Knowing this, if you have found help in the initiatives of Rudolf Steiner—if you are a biodynamic farmer or eat biodynamic food, or if you have a child in a Waldorf school—ought you to read *Faust*? If you wish to know more about Steiner, and his elder Star Brother, yes!

The story follows a professor skilled in many disciplines, who dabbles in alchemy and magic. He comes to the end of his powers, and finds at this dead end only despair, realizing that he doesn't really know anything. This despair is tempting territory for the Devil, Mephistopheles—more Illusionist but also combined with the Hardener—to enter, and offer him whatever experience he would like in exchange for ... a mere trifle, simply the man's soul, and the agreement to be signed, just a detail, in blood. Faust at first desires all knowledge, not just book knowledge, then all experience, beginning with a young woman, Gretchen, who lives in the village, whom he wishes to ravish and possess.

At first reading one can feel a kind of shock that there is not one likeable person in this tale. The closest to likeability is "dear Gretchen," the object of Faust's amorous desires. She is innocent and religiously faithful, but her innocence is exaggerated into ignorance and her faith into superficial repeated prayers. The townspeople are crude and drunken. The devil enjoys this: "Notice how delightfully their bestiality will be revealed."[165] Gretchen's friend Martha is ready to jump into bed with the devil, and her other friend, Lieschen, is petty and prejudiced. There's a hell scene with witches reveling in their perversities, and another that parades the roles that people play—including a Fiddler, a Dogmatist, an Inquisitive Traveler, a Theater Manager—all of them absolutely stuck in the absurdities and limitations of their roles. In short, we're inside a lunatic prison.

Faust, too, is among the inmates—"Alas, am I still stuck in this jail!"[166] Jail images abound. Everyone is stuck, some behind bars, and some within the senses:

> I curse, now, all that holds the soul
> In blandishments and treachery—
> That here in this sad cavern of the flesh
> Imprisons it in lies and flattery.[167]

Over time, however, we can nurture a sympathy for Faust despite the terrible things he does. We sympathize precisely because he has vowed to plunge himself into the human condition: "Let me suffer in my inmost being/ Whatever is the destiny of Man!"[168] Thus Faust is Everyman. What we see expressed through him are the trials of the other inmates of the prison of humankind. They are reflections of ourselves. We ask, "How much of what Faust says is true for me?":

> Am I not homeless? Fugitive? The monster
> Without aim, without peace, that like a cataract
> Plunges from rock to rock, in greedy rage,
> Down into the abyss? . . .
> Here within my bosom, all is night.[169]

How much of this have we too experienced? To understand our condition as human beings, must we experience it all? Gretchen adds her part:

> There isn't any hope for me.
> What good is it to flee? They'd catch me anyway.[170]

Life catches us no matter where we go. No matter what we do, we will find ourselves in the prison of the Image.

Even at the beginning, Faust sees where people, emerging from their private prisons, seek the cure, in the sunlight of Easter day.

> See, from the gateway's cavernous gloom
> There surges a many-colored throng.
> They're eager to sun themselves, today,
> To celebrate the Lord's resurrection,
> For they themselves are resurrected:
> From the mean houses' dingy rooms,
> From the manacles of craft and trade,
> From the burden of roof and gable,
> From the streets' suffocating narrowness,
> From the churches' venerable night,
> They are all brought forth into the light.[171]

All humanity seeks to emerge from prison into the light of the sun, just as in the Image. But there is a problem. As Goethe says in his *Prose Sayings*, "Everything that frees our spirit without giving us mastery over ourselves, is harmful."[172]

We can't be freed from the prison by someone else. Without a sense of mastery, we leave with our worst prison, ourselves. Thus Faust, plunged into the destiny of Man, must follow his desires and reap their consequences. For we are chained to our own lower natures. Toward the end of the play, Faust turns away from his captor, the Devil, and turns his face upward to ask: "Why have you chained me to this infamous being who gloats over suffering and delights in destruction?"[173] How close this is to Steiner's description of Johannes's agony in the first mystery play, *The Portal of Initiation*!

> There from the dark abyss,
> what being gloats on me?
> I feel the chains that hold me fettered fast to you.

Steiner makes a further step that Goethe only hinted at. When Johannes asks, "Who are you, horrifying being?," he discovers within himself the answer:

> Oh, now I recognize you.
> It is myself.
> So knowledge chains to you, pernicious monster,
> myself, pernicious monster.[174]

Faust has yet a few steps to travel before he gets the full truth of this. Steiner has brought Goethe's teaching across the decades and improved upon it.

Back to Gretchen's Cell

At the end of Book I, we see an actual prison with bars and locked door, from which Faust hopes to liberate his love. Faust has come for complicated reasons—because he is attracted to Gretchen sexually, because he feels guilty that he impregnated her, because he wishes to free her. Does he have the power of the Sun to do so? Gretchen has gone mad with her own guilt over murdering their illegitimate child—and, accidentally, her mother (by giving her a sleeping potion provided by Mephistopheles and delivered by Faust). She suffers from terrors about death. As Faust enters the prison, it is dark, and one cannot see well. At first, Gretchen thinks he is her executioner. Faust tries to reassure her, and must come to grips with her madness. Thus might one experience entry to the inner reaches of the prison of the retarded, the insane, and the diseased as pictured in the Image. Let us hear Gretchen at Faust's entry to her cell:

> **FAUST**
> Gretchen! Gretchen!
> **MARGARET** (*attentively*)
> That was my beloved's voice!
> (*She jumps up. The chains fall off.*)
> Where is he? I heard him call. I am free!
> . . .
> He called out: Gretchen! He stood on the threshold.
> Through all the howling and clanking of hell,
> Through all the devils' raging mockery
> I recognized his sweet and loving voice.
> . . .
> The death-bell tolls, the wand is broken.

> They seize me, they bind me fast!
> Already they lead me to the block,
> Already there flashes down to every neck
> The sharpness that flashes down to mine.
> The world lies there silent as the grave.
>
> **FAUST**
> I wish that I had never been born![175]

Thus Gretchen experiences a partial rescue—the chains drop off. Did Faust accomplish this? Are these the chains that bind her to her own lower self that now, near the end of her life, in the clairvoyance of heaven and hell that attends her madness, drop away? Is there a moment of hope in this for the hopeless? Gretchen's suffering has given her maturity, but it is not enough to save her. She falls again into madness and imaginations of her pending execution. At the end of the scene, as Mephistopheles takes a grieving Faust out of her prison, she dies. Gripped by the Image of his own first breath, Goethe made this into one of the most chilling scenes in all of drama and literature.

Wrestling with Creation

Does Faust, like Gretchen and Werther before her, succumb to despair, unfulfilled? No. Though suffering in the prison of his own tortured guilt, he doesn't collapse. He wrestles with his own inner motivations and past errors. He strives. And then he is redeemed, at the end of Part Two of the play. The point is that he strives, not that he succeeds—and thus Goethe discovers and affirms how humankind can find a doorway out of the prison of its existence. Human striving is noticed by divine beings, who dispense grace. At the very end, Goethe sees Gretchen among the angels coming to take him up into heaven. She speaks to him, all in an interplay of heavenly light and celestial sound:

> Incline, incline,
> That art divine,
> Thou that dost shine,
> Thy face in grace to my sweet ecstasy!
> He whom I loved in pain
> Now returns free from stain,
> Comes back to me.

And in a scene that could be right out of the Image, as if spoken by one of the Healer's students receiving those liberated from the institution:

> Grant that I teach him; he appears
> Still blinded by the new day's glare.

The new day's glare—the Christ light that comes in grace.

The Mater Gloriosa—Sophia or Divine Wisdom herself—instructs the one "formerly called Gretchen" on how to assist the person newly released from his prison:

> Come, raise yourself to higher spheres!
> When he feels you, he follows there. [176]

When the released prisoner feels the light and warmth of the guide, then he or she can follow. Thus Christ Jesus instructs his students to care for those who have suffered and now emerge, stumbling but cured, into the light.

When was this written? Very near the end of Goethe's life. Thus, Goethe worked his Gate Image for his whole life, and came at the end to overcome the tragedy of it.

Similarly, in his mystery plays, Steiner worked with imprisonment in challenging situations, and again and again showed that the way out could be won by earnest striving. Johannes—who follows the path of Faust, as Steiner follows the path of his elder Star Brother, Goethe—finds his way through adversities in earthly and in heavenly worlds. In both, we can begin to understand that the trials of the inmates are not for naught. For Goethe, color—practically, aesthetically, and morally—is "the deeds and sufferings of the light."[177] The rescue by pure light in the end does not negate the beauties of the colors produced by these sufferings.

Perception Itself as the Source

> Is there not for the human soul the possibility of freeing itself from the
> ideas which come only from the perceptions of the senses, and of
> grasping a supersensory world in a purely spiritual contemplation?
> —Rudolf Steiner, paraphrasing Goethe [178]

From historical personalities we can often learn about the Image itself. In emphasizing naturalistic observation and the method of permitting concepts to arise in speaking, what has been called Goethean conversation,

Goethe suggested a method for release of what is locked up inside. Rather than cover over the world with one's pre-existing concepts, one lets the perceptions of phenomena and concepts about how the world works intermingle without demanding a quick fix. This involves listening rather than labeling, patience rather than restlessness. Restlessness to "fix" a situation—to secure it, repair it, make it stable, render it changeless—quickly erects the walls of the prison. Openness to surprise and malleability lets in the sunlight of consciousness itself. This sunlight draws out the words that are most appropriate to speak and the actions most appropriate to make.

Goethe also hinted at the nature of the intervention by the one who gives freedom. He is widely quoted as saying:

> From every power that holds the world in chains,
> Man frees himself when self-control he gains.

Does this imply that the lack of self-control is the cause of the inmates' predicament? How does the healer teach them self-control? Let's try to imagine that. One of the most important features of all our organs is the capacity for self-regulation, the ability to curb excesses. We know that deficient organs of the brain can cause both decreases in activity and rampant increases in activity. The amygdala, for instance, when not kept in check by communication with other parts of the brain, can give rise to panic attacks at the slightest provocation (or at no provocation), or to raging, murderous aggression. The highest purpose of the amygdala is to facilitate patterns of love. When working cooperatively with other organs of the brain, especially the thalamus and hypothalamus in the limbic brain, as well as the masters of control of the frontal lobes, it enables control over the excesses of behavior. One could say that the organs are always involved in Goethean conversation with each other.

The Healer of the Image begins the process with a strong infusion of light, sunlight and holy light, that can reset the proper relations between all the organs, especially those of the brain. Rather than blame the victim for lack of self-control, we can assist him or her in finding self-regulation again. Are many diseases lacking a kind of healing in light from the outside that then resets the self-regulating mechanisms of the healthy human being?

Through his diligent observations of the world before him, Goethe found the liberator into the sunlight not in an outside source, but within:

> Sunlike itself the eye must be,
> else it no glint of sun could ever see.
> If, in us, there dwelt not God's own might,
> in things divine we could take no delight.[179]

"Sunlike itself the eye must be." Such a concept is truly a gem (Goethe's Earth Image) that has to be digested and expanded. The release of the diseased inmates of the prison into the healing light of the Sun occurs from within, by finding the light within the eye and all the other organs of the body. Goethe was fascinated by light, and had apparatuses to study it, among them a prism borrowed to study Newton's ideas about color. From his observations, he came up with a very different view of how light works, one more in accord with how healing can come from light itself.[180]

We must imagine that Goethe sought, through his work, to teach this way of being, and thus emulate the Healer of the Image into which he was born.

Star Brother: Jean-Auguste-Dominique Ingres

As with the other Star Brothers, we find the themes from the Earth Image in the life expressed in very different ways. Ingres, born August 29, 1780, was famous for his lifelike depiction in paintings of the skin of healthy nude females, especially in *The Grand Odalisque* (completed 1814, displayed at the Salon in Paris in 1819), the opposite of the leprous skin diseases of the Image.

For much of his early career Ingres was vilified by the critics, outcast over and over again, labeled a savage and a primitive. He knew about the sufferings of the rejected. His most famous early painting, *Oedipus and Sphinx* completed in 1808, shortly after the above portrait, was likewise rejected. He revised parts of it later in 1827, but the main parts of the painting remained the same, and he left the 1808 signature on the rock beneath Oedipus's foot.

In the background, all of Thebes is under quarantine because it has been taken over by plague. Here we find the cultural entity, not just a windowless building but a whole city, full of the diseased and dying, shut out from the rest of the world. Ingres knows this background material, in consonance with his Gate Image.

Ingres chooses as his subject matter the turning point of the story, the meeting between the cause of the plague—the Sphinx—and the Sun-hero

Oedipus. The Sphinx embodies nearly all the parts of the Solar Cross into which Ingres was born—the legs and feet of a lion (Leo), the torso and head of a female human being (Aquarius), and the tail and wings of a dragon (aspects of the scorpion and the eagle of Scorpio). In this Sphinx, there are no hints of a Bull quality. The juxtaposition of lion and human takes up the polarity of Leo and Aquarius that interests us for Ingres' Gate and Earth Images.

Jean-August-Dominique Ingres
Self-Portrait at Age 24

Because of some fault in the society of Thebes, the Sphinx has arrived as the righteous avenging angel. Many have died. She continues to ravage the town because no one can answer her riddle. Those who have tried beforehand are shown to the bottom left, bones and a foot of a dead man. Sun-hero Oedipus agrees to try. The riddle she asks is, "What being walks in the morning on four feet, in the daytime on two feet, and in the evening on three feet —and has only one voice?" Today we must imagine the tormented inner activity necessary to answer this question, as the stakes are very high, and because this riddle has become demeaned by frequent telling, as if the answer were simple.

In fact, it is a more complicated esoteric riddle than one might realize at first, as it involves the very important number series 4321, to which Blavatsky's theosophy, and later Rudolf Steiner in his own way, connected intimately. The 4321 relates to the true and esoteric development of the yugas or ages of time, including the passing of the Iron Age or Kali Yuga, to the evolution of worlds, to the origin of the human being, and to its future. It has been arranged as a *tetraktys* since very ancient times and used to explain many mysteries.[181]

$$+$$
$$+ \quad +$$
$$+ \quad + \quad +$$
$$+ \quad + \quad + \quad +$$

The only way to answer this riddle correctly is to be graced with knowledge from the beings of the Sun. Oedipus's head shines forth in the sunlight with sun-knowledge inspiring him.[182]

Steiner spoke of the Sphinx many times, finding in the riddle keys to the evolution of humanity. He included a painting of this encounter between Sphinx and Oedipus in the first Goetheanum. He termed the Sphinx a "Lion-Spirit," as distinguished from the Bull-Spirits, Eagle-Spirits, and the Man-Spirits,[183] thus making it an appropriate subject for someone born through a Leo gate.

Steiner also speaks about the Sphinx in terms of the important connection between the physical body and the etheric body or vital body that animates it. Some people, including actors, public speakers, and healers, attempt to expand the ether body beyond the physical. This calls in the Illusionist. Steiner explains,

> In its normal state, the ether body moulds and shapes the physical form of man. But as soon as the ether-body expands, as soon as it tries to create
> ✓ for itself greater space and an arena transcending the boundaries of the human skin, it tends to produce other forms. The human form cannot here be retained; the ether-body strives to grow out of and beyond the human form. In olden days men found the solution for this problem. When an extended ether-body—which is not suited to the nature of *man* but to the Luciferic nature—makes itself felt and takes shape before the eye of soul, what kind of form emerges? The Sphinx! Here we have a clue to the nature of the Sphinx. The Sphinx is really the being who has us by the throat, who strangles us. [184]

When Oedipus answers, "The human being—for we begin by crawling, we end with a cane, in the middle we walk on two feet, and we each have one voice," note how his right hand points to his own throat, his voice. He is able to overcome the sense of being strangled. He speaks with his "one voice."

He is able to answer this riddle, but we know the answer to another riddle that lives within him, about his true identity. Because he does not know who he came from in an earthly sense, he will unknowingly marry the queen of Thebes, his mother, have children with her, and then learn that he has killed his own father. When this secret comes out of its windowless cell, he will not have the resources of Sun to meet it, and will destroy the windows through

Jean-August-Dominique Ingres, Oedipus and Sphinx

which the Sun reaches into his own body by blinding himself. All this was known to Ingres' audience, and is thus implicit in the painting. These are the matters into which Ingres plunged himself as a young painter.

The Sphinx in this painting keeps to the shadows. After her riddle is answered, she will plunge herself deeper into the shadows, into "the abyss." Oedipus alone stands in the sunshine, in his glory. Yet the Sphinx's breasts shine naked and bright in the sunshine, very close to Oedipus's face. His left forefinger points to her womb. Not only is she the destroyer, but she is also Oedipus's origin, the nurturing mother, what in Indian lore would be called Kali Ma. Ingres understood this in a way that many other iconographers of this encounter did not, in a way that his Star Brother Rudolf Steiner also understood. Oddly, the Sphinx looks not at Oedipus but toward the audience, to us, the ones who must wrestle with the inside of the prison in the dark and the outside in the light, and with the questions put by the gatekeeper.

Another Theme from a Star Brother—The Inspiration of Ossian

> Let clouds rest on the hills: Spirits fly, and travelers fear. Let the winds of the woods arise, the sounding storms descend. Roar streams and windows flap, and green-winged meteors fly! —THE CHIEF, from *Fingal* [185]

We mention another early work by Ingres, *The Songs of Ossian*, completed in 1813, picturing the fantasies of the third-century Gaelic bard Ossian (originally Oisin), because Goethe's Werther is said to have moved, in his deepening madness, toward a preference for the poems of Ossian. This is one of those interesting connections—are these soul connections?—that we meet with in the work with Solar Crosses. The Scottish poet James Macpherson wrote between 1760 and 1763 three works that claimed to be the rediscovered writings of Ossian. [186] Though rejected by several critics, these *Songs* were embraced by the culture of the day, including many writers and artists—even Goethe, who translated some of the *Songs* into German, and Ingres. The hostile critics felt vindicated by Macpherson's inability to produce the originals from which he had made his translations. That would satisfy a philologist that the translations were fabrications. However, not all lineages have paper trails. There are other routes of connection, and Steiner embraced these poems also as genuine gifts to Macpherson from spiritual realms. Steiner lectured on one occasion about these poems and the Cave of Fingal (the father of Ossian), four days from his birthday, that is, the time when his whole Solar Cross would have been activated.[187]

Let us delve into this interesting piece a little more deeply. On March 3, 1911, in Berlin, the audience had heard Mendelssohn's *Hebridean Overture (Fingal's Cave)*.[188] Steiner rose to speak about it, beginning with the natural cathedral built of hexagonal basaltic pillars on the island of Staffa near Iona, Scotland.

> If we look back and see how deeply people were impressed by what they heard about Fingal's Cave, we shall be able to understand how it was that James MacPherson's revival of these ancient songs in the eighteenth century made such a mighty impression upon Europe. Nothing can be compared with this impression. Goethe, Herder, Napoleon, harkened to it, and all of them believed they discerned in its rhythms and sounds something of the magic of primeval days. Here we must understand that a spiritual world as it had existed during Fingal's time, arose within their hearts, and they felt themselves drawn to what sounded out of these songs! What was it that thus sounded forth?[189]

That is the question that brings us back to the Image. What were the words the Healer used to call forth the inmates into the sunlight? Let us hear from the poems of Ossian about the figure of his father, Fingal, who could be compared to the Healer at the entrance to the prison of the miserable:

> The King stood by the stone of Lubar. Thrice he reared his terrible voice. The deer started from the fountains of Cromla. The rocks shook on all the hills. Like the noise of a hundred mountain streams, that burst, and roar, and foam! Like the clouds, that gather to a tempest on the blue face of the sky![190]

Thus the "rhythms and sounds" are all important. This excerpt reminds one of the roar of Aslan that created all the worlds, in C. S. Lewis's *Chronicles of Narnia*. Let us complete the scene of our hero Fingal:

> So met the sons of the desert around the terrible voice of Fingal.... They bent their blushing faces to earth, ashamed at the presence of the King....

Fingal, like a beam from heaven, shone in the midst of his people. His heroes gather around him. He sends forth the voice of his power.... We reared the sunbeam of battle, the standard of the King! Each hero exulted with joy, as, waving, it flew in the wind. It was studded with gold above, as the blue wide shell of the mighty sky.[191]

Fingal becomes a being of the Sun, showing that Christ is meant to live in all of us, not just in an ancient character long ago and far away.

What has sounded forth to release and cure the miserable? What are the words of power? What do the inmates experience?—"And a voice calls to us on the wind. We have passed away like flames that have shone for a season. And another cries...."[192] What arouses them, and brings them out into the sun, and into the "blue wide shell of the mighty sky?"

Steiner emphasized that the dreams and actions of the Celts were intimately related, that they knew their deeds were registered in spirit realms, to be accessed and sung by bards in some future time. What were the inmates dreaming before the Healer rescued them? What would happen to their lives once they were released?

In the Cave of Fingal on the Isle of Staffa the Celts found a grand cathedral made by spirit hands, preparing them for a later embrace of Christianity. This dark place was not a prison, but a shrine. Listen to Mendelssohn's *Hebridean Overture (Fingal's Cave)*, and you can enter into this Image more deeply. Music and gems—what richness we have in this Solar Cross!

Back to Ingres

The vilified Ingres became the most celebrated painter in France in the 1824 Paris Salon, in which he exhibited *The Vow of Louis XIII*, depicting an almost exact copy of Raphael's Sistine Madonna and Child above, but instead of winged cherubim below, we find King Louis XIII, giving his crown and scepter, indeed, all of France to her. Louis had proclaimed: "We have declared and we declare that, taking the very holy and glorious Virgin Mary as special protectress of our kingdom, we particularly consecrate to her our own Self, the State, our Crown and our subjects." We recognize Raphael's Sistine Madonna and Child, in the same colors, but something has changed. The eyes of both do not look straight out, but down to the King, accepting the offering and vow of human beings, from their prison, so to speak—even from the ornate prison of a king.[193] They even accept all the gems (Sun Image for Steiner, Earth Image for Ingres) being offered up to them. Ingres' painting reinforces the sense in this Image that we stoop low to the lowest of humanity, and meet them there in their suffering, liberating them into the light of day and the warmth of care.

Thus at the age of forty-four Ingres moved from out of the confinement of his own rejection into the sunlight of the Virgin and Child. He wove into his work several themes important to Rudolf Steiner. Was Steiner's interest piqued by the example of the Star Brother that went before him? In this way we look at how Star Brothers and Star Sisters affect a life.

Star Brother: Saint Anthony of Padua

St. Anthony of Padua

Saint Anthony of Padua was born in this degree in 1195 (August 15 in the Julian calendar). Let us illustrate something about his life by one of the tales told about him. St. Anthony of Padua came to the town of Rimini to preach. Some ignored him and some were rude to him. After repeated efforts to find receptive ears were rebuffed, Anthony went to the river just where it entered the sea, and began to speak aloud to the fish, calling them from near and far to hear what he had to say.

> Suddenly there came toward him so great a multitude of fishes—great, small, and middle-sized—as had never been seen in that sea or in that stream, or of the people round about; and all [the fish] held their heads up out of the water, and all turned attentively toward the face of Anthony. And the greatest peace and meekness and order prevailed; insomuch that next the shore stood the lesser fish, and after them the middle-sized fish, and still after them, where the water was deepest, stood the larger fish. The fish being thus ranged in order, St. Anthony solemnly began to preach. Upon these and other familiar words and the teachings of St. Anthony, the fishes began to open their mouths and to bow their heads; and by these and other signs of reverence, according as it was possible to them, they praised Divinity.[194]

The whole populace then showed interest and crowded around, including the ones who had treated Anthony rudely. They asked him to teach them. Thus Anthony drew people—and fish—out of the prison of their narrow views into the sunlight of new ideas.

Even fish can be let out of the prison of their circumstances for a time!

The Bodes of the Leo Image

Who died into Steiner's Earth Image? How did they unite with this Image?

The Bode of Philippa of Hainault

Born in 1314, Philippa married Edward III of England in 1328, when she was fourteen and he fifteen. She died on August 15, 1369, and is buried in Westminster Abbey. She gave birth to fourteen children, who would later argue with each other over the throne in what has become known as the Wars of the Roses. The story for which she is best known has exactly to do with this Image, negotiating for the release of the imprisoned citizens of Calais after Edward's year-long siege. We shall discuss Queen Philippa's act of compassion further when we meet her husband in Chapter 10.

Queen Phillipa of Hainault

The Bode of Wilhelm Wundt

Wilhelm Maximilian Wundt was born in 1832, and died on August 31, 1920, into this Image. He is acknowledged as the founder of experimental psychology and cognitive psychology. It is most interesting to imagine Rudolf Steiner passing by this Bode on his way into birth, because Steiner spoke about Wundt. However, Wundt died nearly sixty years after Steiner's birth. So we can try playing loose with time, and hold it all lightly.

Wundt wrote thorough studies of human behavior, from *Principles of Physiological Psychology* (1874) to his ten-volume *Völkerpsychologie* (Social

Psychology, finished in 1920). Though Wundt's ideas were rejected by the Skinnerian behaviorists in the middle of the twentieth century, his ideas about inherent structures of mind have sparked renewed interest, both by those who seek a specific physiological location for these structures and by those who see the structures of mind existing outside of mechanical location. We can imagine the little prison of the Image as Wundt's version of the human brain, and wonder what he saw going on in that building.

Steiner spoke extensively about Wundt in *The Riddles of Philosophy*, summarizing: "Wundt does not observe a soul; he perceives only psychical activity."[195] He had to wrestle with Wundt's philosophy, which was quite popular in Steiner's time. This kind of wrestling is the kind of thing that one would expect to take place with a Bode, and is most often not so visible.

Wilhelm Wundt

Steiner read Wundt, including the early volumes of *Elements of Folk Psychology*, from which he obtained confirmation of something he had come to on his own: the story of the origin of the earth—cosmogony—that he wrote about in the astonishing fourth chapter of *An Outline of Esoteric Science*. He gives earnest thanks to Wundt in a lecture of 1913.[196]

Thus the very formal Professor Wundt knew about fairy tales, one of the sub-themes of this Image. His approach was to catalogue folk tales into categories of types. In *The Psychology of Peoples*, Wundt proposed the following division: (1) mythological tale-fables; (2) pure fairy tales; (3) biological tales and fables; (4) pure animal fables; (5) "genealogical" tales; (6) joke tales and fables; and (7) moral fables.[197] Some might say that thinking like this puts human creativity into the little prisons of categories. However, Wundt's gathering of these resources provided Steiner with what he needed even if Wundt did not have the temperament to use them himself.

The Bode of Charles Baudelaire

Baudelaire died on August 31, 1867, hailed the finest French poet of his time, primarily for his last book, *Les Fleurs du Mal*, or *The Flowers of*

Evil. Each poem is a gem that, however, presses the boundaries of acceptability. The French government took Baudelaire and his book to court in an attempt to ban it for obscenity, which of course ensured that the first printing sold out quickly. He knows the territory of those who are "damned, wandering, far from living people,"[198] and one can hear in the final two stanzas of the book (section VIII) an understanding of the wild madness of those in the prison of the Image.

*Charles Baudelaire
by Félix Nadar*

> Oh, Death, old captain, hoist the anchor! Come, cast off!
> We've seen this country, Death! We're sick of it! Let's go!
> The sky is black; black is the curling crest, the trough
> Of the deep wave; yet crowd the sail on, even so!
> Pour us your poison wine that makes us feel like gods!
> Our brains are burning up! — there's nothing left to do
> But plunge into the void! — hell? heaven? — what's the odds?
> We're bound for the Unknown, in search of something new![199]

Though Baudelaire died six years after Steiner's birth, we mention him because he tells us something about the Image. Since the unfinished business of those who die into an Image can affect how the Image may impact others, those born in this Solar Cross would be wise to study Baudelaire in order to understand what quirks they may recall passing on the way into this life.

The Bode of Lope de Vega

"The Phoenix of Spain," author of an astonishing eighteen hundred plays and hundreds of poems, died on August 27, 1635. He knew prison from the inside, as his passions led him to libel others, and this got him in trouble. Over and over again his plays use the formula of overcoming human emotions—passionate love, jealousy, revenge—that imprison everyone. Was Steiner inspired in his own playwriting by this Bode? Vega boasted that he composed at least twenty pages every single day of his life. Did this inspire Steiner to perform in an equally prolific way, if not with plays, then perhaps with spoken words that were then transcribed into hundreds of volumes?

Battles

We have begun to collect other kinds of information that pertain to specific days, including famous battles. We have included fifty-six such military encounters that occurred on a specific day, or began on a specific day, as opposed to beginning slowly and unfolding over some long period of time. For example, the American Revolution heated up over many days and months, but there was one day and one moment when the first shot was fired at Lexington, Massachusetts, "the shot heard round the world."

For only fifty-six battles in 360 degrees, we sit up and take notice when three of them show up on the same day, which makes their mention worthwhile.

Kublai Khan's Aborted Invasion of Japan

Kublai Khan sent 4,400 ships against Japan in 1281, focusing their attack on Hakata Bay. As the story goes, a Buddhist monk saw the invasion fleet spread out in a great net around the Bay. He began to chant. As he chanted, winds arose and grew in strength. As the ships retreated from the typhoon, many were lost—some say ten percent, and others say most of them. This gave rise to a new phrase in the Japanese language, "kami kaze," meaning "divine wind." Not only were the ships routed in their attack, but an epidemic spread among Kublai Khan's soldiers, killing thousands. When in World War II the term "kamikaze" was unearthed and dusted off, to motivate young men to die for the cause, it had this notion of "divine wind" behind it, something that the inmates of the prison in this Image may relate to—the divine and liberating wind that opens the prison of their life and releases them to a new freedom.

The Goths and the Romans at Adrianople

In the early centuries of the Common Era (meaning according to the dating system commonly used), the Huns harassed the Visigoths and Ostrogoths of the Balkans so much that they fled across the Rhine River into the Roman Empire. At first they were accepted by the Empire, then neglected. After many years they revolted and began traveling toward Rome. The Roman army under Emperor Valens met the Goths at Adrianople (or Hadrianopolis, in Thrace, on the Greek side of the Bosporus Straits, northwest of Constantinople, or present-day Istanbul). In 378, on this day, the Romans advanced in straight lines upon the Goths' circular encampment, wrapping around the camp, with plans to overrun and kill every man, woman, and child therein. The Goths' cavalry had been away and suddenly came onto the scene, wrapping around the Roman infantry. Pressed between the inner circle of the Goths' camp and the outer circle of the Goths' cavalry, the Roman army was crushed. Forty thousand soldiers were killed, including the Emperor. Many have seen this battle as the tipping point of power away from Rome, away from infantry warfare, and to the "barbarians" and to cavalry as the decisive tool. Did it mark the end of the Roman empire? Perhaps. The significance of this battle is still discussed after seventeen centuries.

The deaths of so many would lodge as Bodes into this solar degree. More than the many individuals who died, the event itself, its themes and its dynamics, becomes the Bode in the hallway through which one passes into birth. We can study events in this way, and note the effects they have on those being born at that same degree. In both instances, there is a sense of an entrapment, in Japan the encircling ships, in Thrace the encircling Roman army, further encircled by the Goth infantry. In the first case, calling on the divine brought a divine wind. In the second, the women and children in the camp were liberated by their men on horses. The sense of prison and the joy of liberation from it lives in these events. We have discussed these themes with the Star Brothers and Star Sisters, and a bit with Steiner, and will do so in greater detail below.

The Beginning of World War II

On this day, Germany invaded Poland, which it had agreed to divide with Russia; Britain and France declared war against Germany, and events rapidly followed that involved everyone on the planet. In terms of the Image, we can perceive that this event marked a reversal of the movement of the Image. The consequences of this day of eruption between men of zeal plunged everyone into darkness, into a prison in uncomfortably close proximity with many very disturbed, diseased, and crazy people.

Star Brothers and Fairy Tales

Look how many people in this Sun-Earth axis were attracted to fairy and folk tales. Wilhelm Grimm (Gate Image) and Wilhelm Wundt (Bode at Earth Image), two of the greatest chroniclers of the German and Eastern European folk tale, the most prolific playwright and fantasist of all time, Lope de Vega (Earth Image), also Baudelaire (Bode at Earth Image), Andreae (Earth Image), Goethe (Earth Image), and Tomberg (Gate Image). Let's look at this in terms of the polarity of Rudolf Steiner's Sun above and Earth below.

Wilhelm Grimm
Rudolf Steiner
Valentin Tomberg

+

Johann Valentine Andreae
Lope de Vega
Johann Wolfgang von Goethe
Wilhelm Wundt
Charles Baudelaire

Goethe was given Andreae's *The Chymical Wedding of Christian Rosenkreutz* just before setting out on his Italian journey, and it became the seed from which his *Fairy Tale of the Green Snake and the Beautiful Lily* appeared.[200] Steiner received *The Fairy Tale of the Green Snake and the Beautiful Lily* as a gift from his teacher, Karl Julius Schröer, on his twenty-first birthday, and it eventually gave rise to the mystery plays.[201] Steiner's epic-length mystery dramas have fairy-tale interludes, and they can be understood in their entirety as fairy tales of the soul's progress.

Steiner knew that fairy tales acted as spiritual food: "The nourishment that satisfies the hunger [of the soul] is just this conscious filling of the soul with fairy tale pictures.... The fairy tale becomes for the soul very much like nutritious food when it is put to use by the whole organism."[202] Fairy tales as nutrition, gems as nutrition. The people are starving and this is how we feed them.

What is nutritious? What really serves one? Is it saccharine? Or is it honest rough food, broccoli rather than sweet rolls? Fairy tales are famous for their subject matter, sometimes crude and sometimes refined, but always dealing with deep and difficult issues. A comment from Nietzsche seems appropriate: "War and courage have accomplished more great things than love for one's neighbor. Until now, not your sympathy but your courage has saved the unfortunate."[203] Steiner would add that there is also a time for sympathy.

Steiner understood that much of history, especially up to and including the lives of the Greeks, is really fairy tale in the way that we take it in.[204] Fairy tales are gems that are more easily digested than philosophical treatises that lay concept upon concept until one shouts out, "What on earth is he talking about?!" Goethe, Steiner, and Tomberg gave us both the philosophical works and the more easily digested fairy tales.

Joseph Campbell observed: "The folk tale is the primer of the picture language of the soul."[205] Steiner would have agreed with these exact words.

Steiner emphasized that fairy tales ought to have a proper beginning and ending. The Frog King in the Grimm collection begins: "In olden times, when wishing still helped one...."[206] Doesn't this take you immediately into a time out of time, returning you to the magical present? Steiner suggested that tales should begin like this: "Once upon a time it happened—where then was it? Where indeed was it not?" And it should end like this: "I once saw this, and if what happened in the spiritual world did not perish, if it is not dead, it must still be alive today."[207] These are gems of insight into how doors of our prisons are easily opened into soul-realms.

The Power of Darkness and Light

Various Star Brothers have called our attention to darkness and light. In Grimm's tales, so much happens in the dark of night or the dark of the forest. We noted the blackness of Daumier's ink, Renoir's trepidation about black until he was old enough to embrace it, the blackness of Gretchen's cell in *Faust*, the blackness of Young Werther's moods, and so on. Darkness is not dwelled upon in the Images—light shines, and we must infer the darkness that precedes it or lurks behind.

How does this relate to Rudolf Steiner's life? One could point to many times that he spoke about darkness and light, but we wish something more personal. One tale by his assistant and housekeeper, Anna Samweber, hints at a whole world of Steiner's inner life that we know little about:[208]

At the end of the lecture I went immediately with Rudolf Steiner to the artists' room. He shut the door behind me, turned the key and said: "Don't call anybody." Then he dropped to the floor like one dead. I got a deep shock and thought: "This is the end." His countenance seemed very old, as touched by death. He lay like that for some minutes, which seemed to me much longer. Suddenly he began to move, got up on his own and then said to me: "I have fought with demons but I have conquered them."

Steiner confronted the demons that had come from the people in the audience. We can understand how the students in the Earth Image stepped back anxiously as the healer opened the Pandora's box of the prison, releasing those possessed along with their demons. This act makes visible something that we do with others all the time, though we remain unaware of it. What if we were to become aware of the forces of the darkness, the power of the black, in our lives? Would it bring into relief all the more the powers necessary to encounter and fight with these dark forces? One of the strengths of anthroposophy is its demonology. The rationalists thought they had stamped out demonology, and had already celebrated its defeat. The notion of demons can be so completely misused, used to label others and then to reject them—anathematize was the old term. Steiner brings it back with notions of the legions of the Hardener and the Illusionist. Naming these beings can be extremely helpful in understanding one's experience. And one must always ask, how can this knowledge be misused?[209]

A person with a connection to this axis of Images knows the dark, even becomes familiar with those realms, and also knows the light. Apply now the story recorded by Anna Samweber to Goethe, Renoir, and the rest. Picture them having a private knowledge of demonic and retarding forces. They can see others in all the forms of disease revealed in the Image. How does this affect how they move in the world and in relationships with others? Such a comparison of Star Brothers and Star Sisters to each other can be very helpful in understanding the main themes that run with an Image.

Are those born in this Solar Cross more able to perceive the legions of the dead from the two great battles fought on this particular day? Can they perceive the diseases that plague others, that may be veiled with various disguises?

We can now comment on a particular way in which the notion of prison arises in Steiner's life. After he had separated from the Theosophical

Society, he said that Madame Blavatsky, its spiritual head and founder, had been "occultly imprisoned." We can translate this to mean that her efforts to reveal the secrets of the spiritual adepts who always work behind the scenes had met walls erected by some of those adepts using dark magic, that therefore what she revealed was tainted by her inability to see clearly into spiritual worlds and compounded by her unawareness of this inability. Others since Steiner in the anthroposophical movement have accused individuals of being "occultly imprisoned," which amounts to saying, "You are possessed by demons, and you don't know it, but I know it about you." These are serious charges, and not ones open to discussion or reply. In a Society that values freedom above all, and the enhancement of human senses to the point of being able to practice "spiritual science," this kind of charge should simply not be laid on anyone else. I bring it up because it shows the continuing susceptibility of the Society to aspects of an Image from Steiner's birth.

SUMMARY COMMENTS ON THE
IMAGES OF THE SUN-EARTH AXIS

Rudolf Steiner used the fructifying power of this Solar Cross to give us gems that we need to unpack. Seeing the gems in the souls of even the miserable and ugly, he released all of us into the sunlight. He implanted very potent seeds, some of which he kept secret—note the entry and secrecy requirements for membership in The First Spiritual Class—and some of which he freely shared, especially at the end of his life, as in *Anthroposophical Leading Thoughts*. He championed the resurrection of the old traditions and left us a legacy that also needs to be rebuilt, over and over again, stone upon stone, so that those who speak the words of spirit may be heard. While Aquinas's contemporaries said admiringly of him, "He led reason captive into the house of faith," we can say of Steiner, directly from his Earth Image, that "he led the irrational to freedom through the light of Sun-brilliant knowledge."

9. RESONANT MOMENTS IN THE SUN-EARTH IMAGES

WHEN A CELESTIAL event occurs, especially something dramatic such as two celestial bodies in the same place at the same time, or exactly opposite each other, or a lineup of several bodies over a great distance, then an astrologer asks how this event in the heavens might translate to an event on earth. Imagine that celestial concentrations of energy and matter (that is, stars and planets) might have a vibration. Bring those vibrations together and you have a superimposition, which makes for a greater intensity of the vibration. When we view moving bodies, they come into exact geometrical relation to each other, which increases the intensity of the vibration between them. As they move out of this geometrical relation, the intensity subsides. Hence the notion of a "moment," which may be fleeting or somewhat prolonged. In a still countryside, standing next to the tracks, you can hear a train coming from a long distance. When it passes you, the noise and rattle can be completely unnerving. Then it's gone, and recedes into the distance, though you can hear it for a long time. Thus resonant moments build up, have their climax, and then die away. It's never instantaneous.

We can look at resonant moments in two ways, as prenatal anticipations from the gestation period and as transits of planets in real time during the course of the life.

Prenatal Anticipations in Relation to Gate and Earth Images

We can look for several kinds of events in this prenatal period, the most dramatic being the crossing of planets, either as conjunctions or oppositions. These are rare, as we are looking only at nine months of physical time.

Here we are interested in the times when planets crossed the place of the Gate or Earth Images, the Gate Image at 14–15 Aquarius and the Earth Image at 14–15 Leo. To be accurate, we are looking for 14 degrees and 33 minutes of these signs.

We would expect that such a crossing would project out into the life as some kind of event related to these Images. We can look to either side of the exact crossing day by several days and remain in the same degree, even the same minute of a degree. For the movement of the Sun, for example, one day in the womb equals about one degree of actual time. Projected into the life, this maps out to about ninety days. Thus the effective interaction of the prenatal Sun and the Birth Sun positions is still very exact by looking in both directions by even a couple of weeks.

Here are the major crossings of the Gate Image–Earth Image axis during the period of gestation, and how they map out onto the life of Rudolf Steiner. We don't look at the Moon, as it moves so quickly, and crosses the Sun Image position nine times and the Earth Image position ten times.

Prenatal planet crossing the Sun–Earth axis	Corresponding date in Steiner's life	Steiner's age
Sun in Leo	March 25, 1884	23 years, 0 months
Mercury in Leo	October 20, 1886	25 years, 7 months
Venus in Leo	February 7, 1896	34 years, 11 months
Saturn in Leo	November 5, 1899	38 years, 8 months
Mars in Aquarius	February 15, 1908	46 years, 11 months

Prenatal Sun crossing the place opposite to the position of the Birth Sun, projected to March 25, 1884

What would we expect when we have the Sun crossing the Birth-Sun axis for the only time in gestation? Of course, the gestation is less than a year, so we don't expect the moving Sun to cross the actual Birth Sun position. Gestation would have to last three months longer for this to occur. The Sun crosses the Earth Image Sun position, in Leo, opposite to the Birth Sun position in Aquarius. A significant crossing by the Sun would relate to the soul purpose of Steiner's life, what exists at his foundations.

This period has to do with Steiner's activity as editor of Goethe's scientific writings. As a young man of great potential, he was led to boxes and cabinets of Goethe's papers, some important and some not, scribbled notes amongst published books, scientific equipment, some broken, and some in good repair. His job was to make sense of it all and organize it for publication. At the end of February, Kürschner wrote Steiner in appreciation of his masterful sorting process, finding the wheat in the chaff, so to speak. On March 8 the first volume of the natural scientific writings of Goethe appeared. Other volumes were in process. On March 28, Steiner was able to write Johannes Rehmke a long letter laying out Goethe's science of the organic world; that is, he was able to glean what underlay Goethe's contribution.

Here we have Steiner rebuilding the disheveled stones of the teacher's chair. He is enmeshed in the life of his elder Star Brother, Goethe, and taking guidance from him. One can see Steiner in the dusty, dark storage rooms, going through the old papers, taking the spiritual hand of Goethe to be led out into the light, uncovering the gems of Goethe's thought. The work of this time, illuminated in the crossing of Sun on Sun, makes the foundations for Steiner's further contributions to the science of nature, establishing the literary foundation for what he will teach.[210]

Prenatal Mercury crossing the place opposite to the position of the Birth Sun, projected to October 20, 1886

What would we expect when Mercury visits the Sun-Earth axis? We might expect to see the brilliance of communication, and anticipation of connections with the groups of importance to Steiner's life.

From the various biographies, we don't have much information about Steiner's twenty-fifth year, except the significant publication right at this time of *The Theory of Knowledge Implicit in Goethe's World Conception*. Steiner sent copies to Rehmke, to his teacher and mentor, Karl Julius Schröer, and to the philosopher Hammerling.[211]

Thus the young man emerged from the dusty halls with a true gem, which he promptly shared with others. He accomplished this in the same year of life that Goethe published his *Sorrows of Young Werther*.

Prenatal Venus crossing the place opposite to the position of the Birth Sun, projected to February 7, 1896

When Venus crosses the axis at the Earth Image, we might expect something to do with individual relationships, for this is what concerns the Venus sphere.

On January 22, at the age of thirty-five, Steiner saw Friedrich Nietzsche for the first and only time. We have looked at the Nietzsche affair before, when we saw this overshadowed by the challenge of Pluto atop the Conception Sun. The context of that story is given more fully in the chapter on Steiner's Conception Image, where we see the entire relationship with Nietzsche spelled out. In terms of the Sun-Earth axis, we have here one prenatal anticipation, the actual meeting with Nietzsche himself. By this point, the great man, the proponent of Superman, had gone mad. He lay ill on a couch. Steiner passed through the room, led by Nietzsche's

Friedrich Nietzsche near the end of his life (by Hans Olde)

sister, who had been attempting to persuade Steiner to supervise the organization of Nietzsche's archive.[212] Others who saw Nietzsche at about the same time described him as follows: "The first thing I saw was the forehead, the mighty forehead. There was something Goethean, Jupiter-like in its form, and yet delicate fineness in the temples." Another said: "Immobile, apathetic, and sealed off in a world of his own, he sat there like a robot where someone else's will had set him."[213] Steiner added his own observations: "I saw Nietzsche's soul as if hovering over his head, infinitely beautiful in spirit-light... Lyrically, on Dionysian wings his soul soars aloft in his Zarathustra."[214]

Having successfully shown how he can sort through a mess and extract the gems, Steiner was asked by the sister and guardian of one of the greatest figures of all time to accept the task of finding the gems in his work. Could Steiner permit himself to be locked into that room? Would he too go mad? Could he bring to bear the light of the Sun and bring Nietzsche's madness into the light?

He was tempted and declined. He knew who his elder Star Brother was—Goethe. Later, Steiner understood Nietzsche as "a brilliant, splendid writer" whose "individuality was not in him." Indeed, in Steiner's view, the writer had become a mouthpiece for Ahriman, the Hardener. Nietzsche seemed a "robot," a term used frequently by Steiner to describe human beings under the influence of the Hardener. Thus Steiner had a personal connection with a hardened (ahrimanized) human being, a meeting and life instruction anticipated from his gestation.[215]

Prenatal Saturn crossing the place opposite to the position of the Birth Sun, projected to November 5, 1899

Rarely does Saturn move enough during gestation to interact with a point about which we have some interest, in this case, the Sun-Earth axis of the Solar Cross. As Saturn moves slowly, even one minute (one-sixtieth of a degree) projects into the life in a much longer period of time. Thus the footprint of Saturn at fourteen degrees and thirty-three minutes of Leo spans more time than if the Mercury were there, for example. We can safely look at a few weeks to either side of the November 5 date, and for unique reasons we shall have to do so.

What might we expect from cosmic memory visiting the place of the Birth Sun during the time of gestation, that is, setting a template for the life? A picture of personal destiny, of cosmic memory made available to human awareness. We know that Saturn will oppose the Sun at Steiner's birth. During gestation, it opposes the Birth Sun point for the first time, and then comes back in retrograde motion to oppose the Sun position at the time of Steiner's birth.

Steiner spoke specifically about the importance of Saturn opposed the Sun.

> Going back to the third and fourth millennium prior to the Mystery of Golgotha, we could find that among the teachers, the sages in the mysteries, every individual was judged according to how he had determined his relationship to Saturn by the date of his birth. For these wise men knew quite well that depending upon whether a person was born during one or another of Saturn's celestial positions, he was one who could use his astral body in the physical body in a more or less efficient manner.[216]

Saturn in relation to the Birth Sun during the period of gestation, echoing the birth relation, would then seem important to the life.

There are a few events and themes active at this time. We will warm up to the main one.

Steiner's first marriage. On October 31, 1899, Steiner married Anna Eunicke, for whose children he had acted as tutor for seven years. As we will see, his Eastern Horizon Image concerns marriage directly, and we could say that the encounter with Saturn at this time stimulated his entire Solar Cross. In the chapter on the Eastern Horizon Image we will discuss the meaning of marriage in Steiner's life.

Evolution of consciousness. At the turn of the century, and just into the new century, Rudolf Steiner was completing his *Conceptions of the World and of Life in the Nineteenth Century*. He signed the foreword of the first volume in February of 1900, and was finishing it up over this November date that we have for the Saturn–Birth Sun opposition. The book concerns evolution, and Steiner specifically took Darwin's impulse further, into spiritual sources for human evolution. He emphasized the "objective spiritual impulses—wholly independent of Man—which develop progressively," in other words, spirit resources that change.[217] This does not align with the Oriental thought dear to the Theosophists, in which the spiritual backdrop does not change; nor does it align with modern scientific approaches, where spirit is only superstition overlaying mechanical and chemical processes. Steiner was working with a completely new idea. He gave humankind an extraordinary responsibility—evolutionary change could only occur by cooperative work of *both* humans and gods, working *together*. This was the practical and philosophical fruit of an extraordinary encounter, a Damascus experience.

Damascus experience. Raised in Roman Catholicism, Steiner had rejected the Church and then come to his own experiences of Christianity, first through thinking about it, then through an experience of the Christ. At the very end of the century, he repeats several times that he underwent "severe tests" and that "[I had to] rescue my spiritual world-conception through inner battles."[218] The storms around the Nietzsche affair that we spoke about earlier are still operative here. He writes in a letter to Ludwig Jacobowski: "I'm working myself half to death."[219]

Steiner had endured a time of trial in three areas:[220]

1. His relationship to natural scientific thinking. His training had been in the sciences, and he championed the pro-Darwinian Ernst Haeckel. But he was discovering the limits of science as practiced, how it demeaned the spiritual foundations of the human being.

2. The individual's relationship to his or her life's work. He wrote, "In the I is the being of all things," in German, "Dass im Ich das Wesen aller Dinge." He hadn't yet spoken of the "I AM," though he was getting close. But he understood the problem of rampant individualism, that is, egotism that did not help, but rather paradoxically hindered any kind of pure and helpful connection with one's true "I." How could the "I" lead to triumph? How could the "I" lead to hubris, becoming lost in the world rather than mastering it, and reaping dire consequences for arrogant egotism? Steiner wanted to know the origin of the sense of "I." He wanted to know if the individual could become free enough to know the truth.

3. His relationship to Christianity. He had rejected his Catholic upbringing, and his philosophical works up to this point had made little reference to Christianity or Christ. But something was nagging him.

It all came to a head at the end of 1899. Steiner describes a specific encounter:

During the period when my statements about Christianity seemingly contradict my later ones, a conscious knowledge of true Christianity began to dawn within me. Around the turn of the century this knowledge grew deeper. The inner test described above occurred shortly before the turn of the century. This experience culminated in my standing in the spiritual presence of the Mystery of Golgotha in a most profound and solemn festival of knowledge.[221]

The Mystery of Golgotha—a penetration of what occurred at the crucifixion and resurrection of Christ Jesus. Prokofieff likens this to the lightning revelation to Paul on his way to Damascus, "where the Christ appears as the great Sun spirit and approaches the clairvoyant in the *form* of the Greater Guardian of the Threshold."[222] This experience was not a dream, for Steiner insisted that his spiritual work should be done in clear waking consciousness. It was not a mystical vision, but an experience of spirit-filled or intuitive thinking. It was precise, cool, and clear ... yet overflowing, a "festival"—recall the children in Steiner's Conception Image with their palm fronds and musical instruments. When Steiner says a festival of *knowledge*, he does not mean this in the way that a librarian might speak of encyclopedic knowledge, but as Carlos Castenada might use the word: eminently practical, specific, light-filled, love-filled, and, finally, very powerful. Was this the enlightenment that he foretold? Was this the moment of initiation of the "initiate"? Was this the time that the Sun-Being came to earth and revealed itself to Rudolf Steiner? Not only revealed itself but became this man?

Emil Bock, a Christian Community priest who wrote many books about anthroposophy, concluded in his biography of Steiner that "From one day to the next his entire way of life changed.... This is the moment where, despite all the movement in his work life, a certain kind of breakthrough through a wall to a Christ experience of a new age came about." [223] A "new age"—the New Age? This was a Damascus experience, paralleling Paul's encounter with the being of the Light of Christ on his way to Damascus, an encounter that temporarily blinded him and turned his life around.[224]

When did this event happen? Steiner's life is so well documented. We know what he did on nearly every day in his adult life. At this point he was over thirty-eight years old. We should know what happened, and when. But we don't. Let me lay out the dates that we do know that might qualify:

- August 28: Steiner wrote about what he had pieced together as the secret revelations that made it possible for Goethe to go from his reading of Andreae's *The Chymical Wedding of Christian Rosenkreutz* to his own parable of *The Green Snake and the Beautiful Lily*, upon which Steiner later drew for his mystery plays. Steiner's lecture on this one year later on September 28, 1900, is called "the first anthroposophical lecture." In this precursor in 1899, Steiner spoke on death as sacrifice, quoting Jacob Boehme—"Death is the root of all life"—and Goethe—"So long as you have not known dying and becoming, you are only a gray guest on a dark earth." The green snake sacrifices itself to become a bridge between the spirit world and the sense world.[225]

- October 24: Steiner wrote to Rosa Mayreder, "I'm not sure at this moment where I stand in relationship to my work. German nineteenth-century cultural history must be finished and it will be."[226] He could sense something new coming, in the midst of confusion about his own work.

- October 31: Steiner married Anna Eunicke in a simple ceremony. In our discussion of the Western Horizon Image, we explore the significance of this event occurring in the midst of Steiner's trials and the downpouring of light from the Christ being.

- November 23: Steiner wrote to Ludwig Jacobowski, "I'm working myself half to death."[227]

There are several dates that are suggested by celestial events, but we are looking for something noted in earthly activities.[228]

The period in question is covered by the particular prenatal anticipation that we are looking at, namely November 5, 1899, when the great being of Saturn opposes the Birth Sun position during gestation, sensitizing the being to an experience planned from before birth, that is, planned from spiritual realms. My own intuition, in conjunction with an intuitive friend, suggests that this downpouring of spiritual knowledge occurred over a period of days from November 24 to December 2, ending with the Sun right on top of Antares, the star of the mystery of life and death, the theme that Steiner was working on so diligently during this time. Sacrifice, death, resurrection and true life—these are themes that Christ Jesus modeled in the final days of his earthly life. My intuitive friend further saw in the "festival" a great quantity of liquid golden light coming into Steiner's mouth, from which he was charged and also burned.

Astrological Interlude

Something stands out about the timing of the "festival of knowledge" of Rudolf Steiner. At the moment of his birth, Saturn opposes the Sun, on the axis exactly perpendicular to the Aldebaran-Antares axis. At birth, Uranus sits upon that axis, exactly atop Aldebaran.[229] No wonder Steiner struggled with the unexpected as well as Illusionist temptations all around him (both possible Uranus influences) during his life.

When we have three points of a four-pointed square—Sun in the Water-bearer, Saturn in the Lion, and Uranus at Aldebaran in the Bull—then we become very interested in that final point, the one in the Scorpion directly atop Antares. Empty at birth, that spot receives great attention during this "festival of knowledge." Uranus is on Antares in 1899, exactly, during this entire period of November and December—a Uranus semi-return. The Sun is there in early December; on December 2 it flames right on top of Uranus and Antares. Pluto is not far away from the axis, near Aldebaran, emphasizing the Christ-light transformation aspect of this experience.[230]

At the "festival," Saturn lies nearby, at the beginning of Sagittarius, directly atop the center of our galaxy. Saturn stimulates recollections of cosmic memory with the cosmic message being sent to Rudolf Steiner.[231]

As if to seal the anniversary of this date, just one year later his friend Ludwig Jacobowski died, on December 2, 1900.

I have been very interested in significant world events involving Saturn and the Sun interacting with the Aldebaran-Antares axis. I will mention one. On December 2, 1942, at 3:20 in the afternoon, Leo Szilard and Enrico Fermi triggered a self-sustaining neutron explosion in a block of uranium, in a small laboratory at the University of Chicago. This meant that a bomb was no longer a theory on a blackboard but a feasible idea. Many of those going into this experiment did not know if the runaway fission of neutrons could be stopped. They actually thought that they might be initiating something that would end in an explosion of every atom of the earth. That did not happen, though the nuclear age was born in those minutes. It was the turning point in the development of the atom bomb. Saturn was exactly atop Aldebaran and the Sun atop Antares.[232]

More could be said about the bomb and its first explosions, and their relation to the Aldebaran-Antares axis. In this study of Rudolf Steiner, the point is that much happens in this location. The key demonstration of runaway fission in uranium is a counter-image to Steiner's experience of a "festival of knowledge"—it gives a picture in materialistic worlds of what happened in interior worlds for Rudolf Steiner. As we have said in discussing polarity, all spiritual impulses come in opposites. Steiner and the team of

Fermi, Szilard, and the others were dipping into the same well of Aldebaran and Antares, but their experiences and consequences were completely different. Steiner experienced something inward: his eyes were opened to his spiritual heritage and the destructive power of spiritual energy, what one might call Shiva or Christ in his form of killing off the old personality. Steiner's experience led to great service to humankind. Szilard and Fermi and their team had an external experience, an experience of the power of radioactive decay, a concentration of the forces that have been slowly deconstructing the earth over many thousands of years. From it, they produced a few peaceful medical applications and, more prominently, a bomb that has terrorized human beings ever since. Now we know for the first time that we can, through our own caprice, destroy ourselves.

Steiner had described the working of several sub-earthly forces, among them electricity and electro-magnetism, and one that had not yet been invented in his time, but that would be especially destructive. Did Steiner open this gate to spirit realms at the turn of the century?

Summary of the "Festival" Experience

Steiner spoke often about the Mystery of Golgotha as a euphemism for the revelation of the light of Christ consciousness in a human form. This was his revelation, and he drew upon it frequently. Whenever he mentions it, one has the sense of a great plenum, a fullness, of experience behind it. On occasion he would explain parts of what he knew from his own experience.

How lovely that he speaks of a "festival," just as the children in his Conception Image celebrate a festival—with song, music, and green branches. Did Steiner hear music in this "festival"?

He moved shortly after his revelation from a building with a bland exterior to one that was, unusually for a Berlin apartment building, ornamented in stone with fruits and vines, even showing four goddesses on either side of the doorway, bearing cornucopias and water jars.[233] Does Steiner's choice of this particular building have something to do with the abundant outpouring that he had experienced shortly before?

After this festival he could speak with the authority of personal experience about the core mystery of Christianity. The "festival" was a culmination of his Sun years, marking the integration of his consciousness soul or spirit-soul into his being. In the Eastern traditions, we would call this the date of his "enlightenment."

Thus his book *Conceptions* begins with the words, "Know thyself."

How appropriate to a prenatal Saturn transit, and an opportunity chosen before birth, during the prenatal gestation, to occur at this time of life. From the hysteria that surrounded the turn of the century, Steiner was able to pluck tangible spiritual guidance to take him into the new phases of his life, where his teaching truly began in earnest.

Steiner writes with firmness that he did not betray secrets of ancient wisdom. Why? Because he did not share what he had been told of these secrets by others. Given certain special texts and sworn not to reveal their contents—one goes directly to the Conception Image to see these professors with their secret texts—he did not betray his vow. Instead, he relied upon his own experiences to inform him about the truth. Through personal connection to the sphere of cosmic memory, Saturn, he affirmed certain things to himself. He spoke only from his own knowledge, and thus did not betray what he had been vouchsafed. He could build a chair for a new teaching, both rebuilding what has been known since ancient times and also building something entirely new. This was an active encounter with the being of Saturn, the holder of cosmic memory, the purveyor of destiny, which was set into motion from the moment of conception. Directly from this encounter with Saturn, the anthroposophical movement was formed.[234]

Prenatal Mars crossing the place of the position of the Birth Sun in Aquarius, projected to February 15, 1908

The only time that any planet crosses the actual position of the Birth Sun in Aquarius during gestation occurs in 1860, when Mars crosses this point. One degree of prenatal Mars movement equates to approximately 176 days when projected into the life, so we stay very close to the exact date of crossing when looking at the life.[235]

What would we expect from Mars's interaction with the Sun Image? We would see the pre-earthly intention to find the truth of the life and speak it—expressing either through written word, spoken word, or deed.

Indeed, that is what we find in this time zone. In 1908, Steiner spoke in seven countries of Europe. Indeed, he delivered over 180 lectures in that year on such topics as the Gospel of John, the Apocalypse, Egyptian myths and mysteries, and more. Beginning at this time, and throughout this year, he began to publish his lecture cycles. He inaugurated the Theosophical Society publishing house. He announced that he would begin speaking on advanced themes for those who were prepared. He spoke about higher spiritual beings and the spiritual-physical cosmos; he spoke about world evolution seen esoterically; he spoke about the spiritual processes of the human organism; he spoke in Berlin on exactly this day on the Sun, the Moon, and the stars. Behind the scenes, a good part of *An Outline of Esoteric Science*, what Lindenberg called "the central fundamental book of anthroposophy," was written during this time. Steiner grasped the pre-earthly intention to express significant spiritual truths and outpoured them in this time.[236]

The lectures from this period were not fully recorded, but notes have been saved. He spoke in these days of two gems in the human body, the pineal and pituitary glands. From the pituitary gland, "out of the chaos of emotions, the structuring of the astral body is effected." When the pineal gland has become swathed in golden threads from the pituitary gland, then the astral body can transform into *manas*, and the etheric body into *buddhi*, concepts defined in Chapter 3. Such are the formulas that Steiner imparted during this time.[237]

Though Steiner's later writings are better known, we see here, just before his forty-seventh birthday, a great flowering of his speaking to the stars. Indeed, here Steiner sits in the teacher's chair that has been rebuilt from the ancient mysteries.

We have another detail for this prenatal anticipation that illustrates what we're talking about. In a letter to Marie von Sivers just a week after the exact projection of Mars's crossing of the Sun position projected into the life, Steiner wrote about the people who have been given the same venue for teaching, and how this has been a problem. In terms of our Image, they have been sharing the same teacher's chair. He related that there had been problems with the reception of his lectures "since in the last few days two or three spiritualists had spoken here.... Everyone was asking whether this was going to be another spiritualistic event." He continued, "It is sad that we are lumped together with those pests—for they are pests who are, moreover, stupid."[238] The reputation of the teacher's chair makes a difference for all the teachers who follow. Steiner had to rebuild the chair in order to make it an appropriate platform for his teachings. He did not start out with a stone chair such as the

Areopagus from which Paul spoke to the Greeks in the Acropolis. Steiner had to build and rebuild a proper chair from which to speak.

Real-Time Crossings of the Sun-Earth Axis

During the life, many celestial events occur. Some may relate to the pattern at birth. Though many astrologers look at many possible kinds of angular relationships (what they call "aspects"), we will look only at what actually crossed the axis of the Sun-Earth Images. We will enter into the territory of the outer planets.

Transits to the Sun-Earth Axis

We won't look at the times that Jupiter crosses the Sun-Earth axis, as it does so every six years, thus ten times in Steiner's life. We don't look at Mars's crossings, as they occur approximately every year. We are looking for the rarer interactions, especially of Saturn, the great holder of cosmic memory:

Transiting planet crossing the Sun-Earth axis	Corresponding date in Steiner's life	Steiner's age
Uranus in Aquarius	April 14 and August 21, 1921, and February 4, 1922	60 years, 1 month to 11 months
Saturn in Leo	October 19, 1919, February 29 and July 10, 1920	58 years, 7 months, to 59 years, 4 months
Saturn in Aquarius	March 18, 1906	45 years, 0 months

We will begin our discussion with events from later in the life.

Uranus conjunct Birth Sun (in Aquarius), three passes, April 14 and August 17, 1921, and February 4, 1922, age sixty years, one month, to sixty years, eleven months

Uranus moves slowly, taking eighty-four years to orbit the Earth, so a Uranus conjunction is a rare event. What might we expect in an encounter of Uranus with the position of the Sun at birth? We could look for invasions and innuendoes from the Illusionist. We could look for the unusual, indeed the shocking.

We find in these three passes two main themes: complete newness of material and one of the greatest temptations of Steiner's life.

In the first and second passes of Uranus over this Birth-Sun point, we find Steiner teaching very unorthodox methods of medicine, namely a course for forty medical doctors (from April 11 to 18) and a course on therapeutic and curative eurythmy. Ask a modern Western-trained allopathic doctor to examine the therapeutic suggestions, even the diagnostic techniques, that Steiner advocated, and you will receive a quizzical or even a panicked look. These were, and are, completely new and unusual ideas. Steiner was making good use of his transit with Uranus here. In terms of the Gate Image, we might see that Steiner was finding very unexpected rocks with which to build the teacher's chair, and that it took on a design not seen before.

During this time, Steiner gave his students tours of the Goetheanum, presenting the art there and fending off questions like "What does it mean?" Steiner wrote about his reply: "I said expressly that all 'explanation' of the forms and pictures was very uncongenial, because the artistic is not to be presented through thoughts but should be taken in through direct vision and feeling."[239] Thus Steiner fended off the deceptive powers latent in Uranus.

At the second pass of Uranus, Steiner opened the clinical therapeutic institute called The Coming Day (Die Kommende), complete with ambulatorium and laboratory. Many anthroposophical doctors attended.

At the third pass, we see a bursting of containers—something we could expect from Uranus's influence—in a two-week lecture tour, where thousands came to see him. "The crowd was so great that the traffic police had to control the stream of thousands of persons in the streets leading to the building, all seeking admission and hundreds finding no seats."[240] In this two-week period, Steiner spoke to more than twenty thousand persons. Lecture halls were sold out. Tickets were sold at black market prices.[241] The teacher takes the teacher's chair! At the end of the war, people everywhere, and particularly in Germany, were seeking answers to deep questions. The inflation of currency was beginning to speed up, and people looked everywhere for a philosophy that could make sense of their situation. Even more importantly, they were looking for a charismatic leader to take them by the hand and lead them through the mess out into the light.

This was the temptation, indeed a Luciferic temptation ("Worship me and I will give you kingdoms"[242]). Steiner could have pandered to the audience in order to swell the ranks of anthroposophy. But he did not. He spoke to them soberly and seriously about weighty matters. The titles of the lectures, such as "The Nature of Anthroposophy" and "Anthroposophy and the Riddles of the Soul," were hardly calculated to have a wide appeal. Today, at least, when the term "anthroposophy" is avoided with the general public because the audience cannot pronounce it afterwards, we could not expect such a large turnout using these titles. In that day, the Illusionist delivered thousands of people, and tempted Steiner to take them into his fold. Steiner faced the Illusionist and spoke seriously, to the soul of human beings.[243]

Friedrich Rittelmeyer wrote about one of these sold-out lectures, a crowd of three thousand, with tickets being sold outside the door for outrageously high prices. He had enthusiastically invited friends who, catching the mood of excitement, went along … and then scratched their heads. They didn't understand what was being said. They found it too demanding and never came back. Rittelmeyer was disappointed that his friends could not make the bridge between their expectation of charismatic deliverance and the words being delivered to their souls.[244]

Reading these lectures, we can sympathize with Rittelmeyer's disappointment. In the context of the temptation of Uranus on his Birth-Sun axis, we know what Steiner was doing. As much as to these twenty thousand, he was speaking also to the Illusionist (Lucifer) through Uranus. He was saying to the Illusionist, "I am not the avatar that you tempt me to become. This chair that I help to rebuild is not for me. It is for a greater teacher. I am preparing those who are ready to change." To the people in the halls, he was saying: "I understand your suffering, but I will not invite you into a gaily decorated prison of beliefs about me as your savior. I give you raw gems. These gems that I give out require polishing and cutting, active effort on your part. If you stay with it, you will receive valuable nutrition, but you must work for it."

Saturn (in Leo) opposed to Birth Sun (in Aquarius), three passes, October 19, 1919, February 29 and July 10, 1920, age fifty-eight years, seven months, to fifty-nine years, four months

Saturn passes over the Earth Image position three times in Rudolf Steiner's life, this being the last time. What might we expect when Saturn passes over the position of the Earth Image late in Steiner's life? A cosmic memory of the essence of the Image. At the first pass, Steiner was working on the art of eurythmy for scenes from Goethe's *Faust*.

On October 15, Steiner spoke with others about plans to found a bank. Look at a bank from the point of view of the Earth Image. A prison! When banks are used for ill, they do not serve humanity. Those holding mortgages at high interest may feel imprisoned by their local bank. However, if you use the concept of a bank correctly, then those inside bask in sunlight. I recall a talk given by Bill Mollison, an expert on organic farming and originator of the term "permaculture." The audience came to learn how to enliven their community through application of his principles. All expected a lecture on the superiority of organic farming methods. He began, "The best thing you could do for your community is start your own bank!" He went on from there to describe how the quality of banking in a community shapes that community, by nurturing creative and practical ideas in people to whom one is linked in a matrix of active relationships. Loan officers in modern banks ignore the needs of citizens, looking for the big deals with the big corporations, even going overseas at the expense of those at home. Steiner hoped to bring banking into the midst of anthroposophy. I don't know what happened to that initiative, only that it was talked about on this day, when Saturn vibrated the Image of inmates being let out into the light.[245]

At the second pass, in February, Steiner visited an archive of his lectures in Dornach. What an interesting echo of the time spent in Goethe's archives, and nearly in Nietzsche's archives—the room without light—and to realize that here in Steiner's own archive, there were stored gems for the future.[246] Would the archive become closed or opened to the light?

At the third pass, we see directly the theme of bringing into the sunlight. On July 8, Steiner "led his students ... into the rejuvenating forces." [247] Yes, this seems right out of the Image. What forces were these? The ones that "stream anew with the birth of every human being out of the spiritual world." If seen rightly, every newborn comes with the light of spirit beaming out from her or his face. Steiner took his students further, into the realm of pre-existence, into "spiritual communion" of human being and earth. This he contrasted with the widespread depression and melancholy among children at that time between the ages of seven and ten, meaning those born between 1910 and 1913. Here he was teaching young adults to be ready for these children, that is, to be ready to release the depressed from their prisons of depression.

Saturn in the same position as the Birth Sun (in Aquarius), one pass, March 18, 1906, age forty-five years, zero months

Saturn crosses the Birth Sun position twice, once at age fifteen, about which we don't know enough, and once at age forty-five, in 1906. In the latter crossing, Steiner began to speak about reincarnation and the ancient teacher cultures, making these gems available to humankind.[248]

Some letters that he wrote to those seeking advice have survived, and one is dated very close to this passage of Saturn over the Birth Sun position. In it, he gives advice to a woman in Russia, suggesting how she might work with a client who was very disturbed, and perhaps possessed of a powerful and negative force, something from the Hardener. In preparation for the meeting, he advised that Fräulein Minsloff do the following meditation:

> Think first about your feet, as though the whole of your I-forces were in the foot-soles, then draw this feeling, developed in the foot-soles, up through the whole of your body as far as the heart, thinking the whole time the thought "I"; then think about your finger tips and say to yourself, as though you wanted to send your thoughts into your finger tips: "Through this I shall ward off evil."[249]

Steiner then advised her to use the following formula, one of the most wonderful and practical verses that Steiner left with us, a verse that I work with every morning. It begins,

> In purest outpoured light…

This sets us in the context of the Earth Image. Every day I deepen the imagination of "purest outpoured light." When doubt comes in, permit more light!

> In purest outpoured light shimmers the Divinity of the world.

Not a distant Divinity in heaven somewhere "out there," this Divinity is right here. Everything radiates this purity and intensity of light.

> In purest love for all that lives outpours the Divinity of my soul.

From the "inside" of my "soul," along with the light of all nature, pours out love.

> I rest within the Divinity of the world.

One can see how one can take a seat in the teacher's chair of the Gate Image, which is also the stacked-up minerals of the human body. One need not restlessly push. One rests into the Divinity all around. Activity and effect come naturally, the stacking of stones, the giving out of gems, the releasing of prisoners from their darkness and disease—all into the shimmering light!

> There shall I find myself, within the Divinity of the World.[250]

I might have written "my Self" instead of "myself" to distinguish higher powers from the lesser self, but it doesn't matter. Only one true Self actually exists, and the rest falls away in these streams of light and love.

Eclipses

Three total solar eclipses occurred at the Sun position of the Earth Image. The ones on August 29, 1867, and August 29, 1886, were too early in Steiner's life for us to have much information.

The eclipse on August 30, 1905, comes at a period about which the biographers have little to say.[251] Steiner did write a letter to Mathilde Scholl, with diagrams, that demonstrated the opening up of "present-day clear waking consciousness" into "wakened higher consciousness." He also gave as an exercise the terse gem of a meditation, "I am, It thinks, She feels, He wills," the first to be thought in one's head, the second in the throat, the third in the heart, and the fourth in the solar plexus.[252] Here are gems that need to be soaked and digested in order to be useful.

Recapitulation of Resonant Moments to the Sun-Earth Axis

Let us recall what we've been doing. We have seen how celestial events, both in the womb and in the life, relate to the Images of Steiner's birth, the Gate and Earth Images. The prenatal events we have seen as indications of pre-earthly intentions, as Moon Karma. The actual transits during the life we have seen as opportunities to work with one's destiny, with Sun Karma.

We have also met a group of Steiner's Star Brothers and Star Sisters, as well as some who have been Bodes, leaving behind traces that Steiner had to deal with in his passage into this world.

Meeting the Challenges of the Gate and Earth Images

We can look at a life to see if the person was able to meet the challenge of an Image breathed in at birth. Concerning the Gate Image, the Hardener might have led the person to a mechanical stacking of stones, or a miserly hoarding of gems. Concerning the Earth Image, the Hardener might have led the person to diagnose and affirm the different diseases of the prisoners rather than cure them. About both Images, the Illusionist might have led one to fantastical imaginations about how these magical gems or the single healer would instantly cure all humanity. Steiner found a course that pressed aside the Hardener's cynicism and the Illusionist's fantasies, and successfully realized the potential of these Images.

In the last resonant moment, I shared Steiner's gift of a powerful meditation to a woman challenged by her client. To have given such a meditation to the world, so short and simple and powerful, indicates Steiner's success in facing the challenges and utilizing the gifts of his Gate and Earth Images.

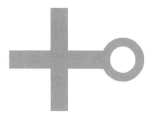

10. THE WESTERN HORIZON IMAGE

A T THE BIRTH of Rudolf Steiner, the Sun lay at 14–15 Aquarius. We imagine our basic stance—Sun shining directly overhead, Earth beneath the feet. To the east we would see 14–15 Taurus, with the great star Aldebaran at its edge, at 15 degrees and 3 minutes of Taurus. To the west, we would see 14–15 Scorpio, with the great star Antares very close at its edge, at 15 degrees and one minute of Scorpio. Together, Aldebaran and Antares create the axis of Royal Persian stars upon which the whole heavens were mapped. At the eastern horizon we have hints about what is rising into the life. At the western horizon, we have hints about what is setting. Future and past.

Here's another way to look at it. Later in his life, Rudolf Steiner created the Foundation Stone Meditation. It includes this repeated phrase:

> This hear the Spiritual Beings in East, West, North, South:
> May human beings hear it.

Steiner emphasized the importance of the four directions, which we see living in all Solar Crosses and implied in the content of his Gate Image. The Foundation Stone Meditation also includes the wonderful phrase:

> Let from the East ignite
> What through the West takes form.

The whole Foundation Stone Meditation reveals the power of the directions, and of the Cross. We take the fire in the east—what for Steiner related to Aldebaran—and let it find form in the west—what for Steiner related to Antares.

Here's how it looks for the human being standing in the center. What shall we see taking form in this Western Horizon? What shall we find setting in this last of the four Birth Images?

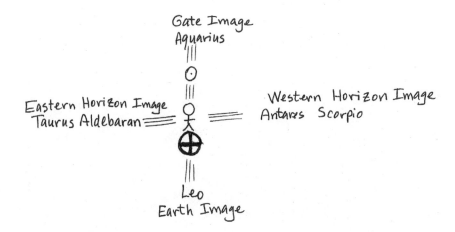

Now prepare to view and map the Image of the West. You are becoming proficient at this now, and you know it is worth taking the time to get your paper and pen ready, turning the page, reading the Image, and then closing the book to create a mind-map of it. You can refer to your mind-map in the subsequent discussions, as you will probably discover aspects that improve the comments made later. Your participation in this connects you to Rudolf Steiner and to the stars—alive then and alive now, too.

Western Horizon Image at Birth

A military town in which three men of zeal were born. The first a religious leader who tormented the people with rigorous and ascetic practices; on this day the people celebrate his death. The second, a rebel against the occupying army who, justified in his righteousness, abused his enemies. The third, an inquisitor who persecuted freethinkers—charged by lightning, he would change from hatred to love, and turn his zeal to the living truth.

Working the Image

Take the time to build a mind-map of this Image. This one can lead off into interesting directions if you let the descriptions of the three men begin to build in your imagination. What did they look like? What did they wear? How did their voices sound? How did they come to command others?

Preliminary Considerations

This Image is all about the right use of the will, the capacity to act, make things happen, and perform deeds—all under the guidance, wise or distorted, of thinking. Ponder the will for a moment. You can extract it, so to speak, from the influence of feeling and thinking, and have a look at it. Walking over a field of boulders, for example, you see how your feet choose which rock to go to next, far more rapidly than your thinking process can keep up with. You observe yourself walking. Picking beans or lettuce leaves in the garden is another activity that reveals the hand working more quickly than the brain. The intellect, which thinks it's in charge, has to bow down to the superior capacity of the quickly moving feet and hands, the will in action.[253]

Actually, the will moves confidently and quietly on its own on many occasions, though usually this is covered over by a thought. The thinking also sets your overall direction through that field of boulders, as a supervisory influence. Moving around your house at night in the dark, too, you can observe with astonishment the body's ability to know where furniture is and where light switches are. Again, the thinking may be setting you on that adventure with some purpose in mind. Typically, thinking, feeling, and willing work harmoniously together. In this Image, we see situations where particular thoughts have urged these men on to extreme behaviors in their will.

Each of these men of zeal—of will—has power to affect others, here measured as the capacity to make others' lives much more difficult. Only the last one finds a way to use his personal power to make lives more sublime. Where does personal power come from? Where do the concepts originate that guide our wills? For what must we use our charisma, our physical strength, our ability to influence others? We shine the light of morality on the use of will. Each of these three men is guided by a dogma that would restrict the freedom of others. We must instead find guidance from a morality based on the mediator of the heart and its medium of feeling.

These men have a system of justification for what they are doing. Each has a story that seems more important than the other lives that are affected. Fighting for one's very survival may seem to justify torture; thus we defend the cruelties that we today call Special Operations against "the enemy," who are, in the end, individuals with families, joys, and sorrows. We might use our striving to be good in the eyes of Divinity to excuse suppressions and ascetic limitations and heavy-handed denials, not only of ourselves but of everyone else, too. In trying to root out all error of thought, we might become inquisitors, interrogating others and punishing dissenters with pain and termination of their life.

Zeal takes the individual will out to others and to the world. The wisdom of the holy men of Israel advises: "When a man frees his heart of all other thoughts that reside in it and seizes upon one thought, then he will undoubtedly be zealous in its execution."[254]

This day has a very strong placement with the star of death, Antares. Beware the power of zeal! It takes you into the realm of death. Perhaps too often the zealot kills too much, kills life itself.

In the Image and in some of the historical personalities, we will come across a parallel term, "ruthless." "Ruth" means compassion, understanding, even the ability to mourn and grieve. Some relate the word to the biblical character Ruth, wife of Boaz and daughter-in-law of Naomi, who knew privation and sorrow and thus could empathize with others.[255] The first two men of zeal do not have ruth, and the third has no ruth until later on in his life, after a transformation. Does everyone from this military town start off like this? What kind of transformation occurred in the third man?

In every instance we see death—death by asceticism from the first man of zeal, death by killing and torture from the military man, and death to the ones who do not conform from the inquisitor. Let us not shrink from this but find out what lies in these death realms. Steiner encouraged us thus: "The new element that must enter into all the different fields of life will be that the human being's content of soul must enable him to regard this having-death-beside-one as something natural.... Human beings will begin to see death all the time."[256] So let us not be afraid of Antares' realm; let us find out what lives positively here.

Let's piece together aspects of the Image.

TOWN OF ONE'S BIRTH

Tourists are attracted to signs that say, "George Washington slept here." Even more, they love to visit the birthplaces. The birth spot has particular importance, as it acts as a door into the realm before birth, to the soul's intentions for the upcoming life. Upon visiting as an adult the place where I spent my first year, I felt the same kind of numinous door open as when I visited the Parthenon and the Sea of Galilee.

This Solar Day, the Teacher visits Gischala, the birthplace of three men of zeal. The first was a man who lived two centuries before, who had founded the ascetic cult known as the Sadducees.[257] The second was John of Gischala, who had started a rebellion in Galilee against Rome and who, in this cause, "committed frightful excesses."

The third was Saul, who later, approximately five years after the Teacher's visit, would travel to Damascus, be struck by lightning, hear the words of the Teacher, and become Paul. Paul was born in the place of this Image, before he moved to Tarsus. As an adult Paul became an energetic inquisitor and persecutor of the followers of the Teacher. After a dramatic experience of insight and visitation by the spirit of the Teacher, he became the major exponent of the Teacher's story, spreading it far and wide into the world.

Standing on that spot, recalling the etheric memory of these men as infants and young boys, opens up lines of communication with their souls. The Teacher, for whom time does not work in a linear fashion, can emanate his blessing to all three.

THE DEATH STAR

Recall that the Royal Star of Persia, Antares, stands at the heart of the Scorpion, at fifteen degrees and one minute. Its effect can be found in nearby degrees and even throughout this entire sign. Antares can be viewed as the

Threshold Star, or the Star of Death and Rebirth. From its region work the beings pictured in the sting of the Scorpion that diminish and kill.[258] In an important way, Antares can bring an encounter with death that embraces the spiritual realities on the other side, a kind of selflessness, as a complement to the self-sense found streaming from Aldebaran, a selflessness that matures into love.

The effect of Antares can appear to us in earthly life as the threat and terror of death and annihilation.

It is no accident that under Antares' gaze, indeed, through the entire sign of Scorpio, the Teacher undergoes the Fire Initiation in the desert, the "forty days in the wilderness." In another year on this same Solar Day, the Teacher travels through the hot sands of the desert toward Egypt, also an activity that occurs throughout the sign of Scorpio.[259]

To the Galaxy and Back Again

A remarkable book by Richard Leviton, *The Galaxy on Earth*, links certain fixed stars in the heavens with special or sacred places on earth.[260] Since we can understand the location of the stars in relation to the Sun's path by drawing perpendiculars from that path into the heavens, we can relate those stars—and the theoretical places with which they are connected—to the Solar Days reported here. Many of the places referred to have little meaning for most people, but the location for this Solar Day has captured the imagination of many. Leviton links the star Antares to Chalice Hill in Glastonbury, England, source of magical and healing waters. How interesting that we will find Glastonbury when speaking of a Star Brother in the opposite sign, John F. Kennedy, and his recreation of Camelot. Whenever the Parzival story comes up, we can think of one of the homes of this far-ranging tale, Chalice Hill.

The man who founded the Chalice Well Trust, Wesley Tudor Poole, initiated a peace meditation during World War II at noon of each day. This had a powerful protective effect for England. After the war, documents were found in Germany saying, "The English have a secret weapon that has made it impossible for our rockets to do as much damage as we planned. We don't know what that weapon is." Perhaps that weapon was the power of massed positive meditation, a kind of zeal, partly emanating from Chalice Hill.

Poole's zeal transformed the aggressive power of war into the power for peace, not as an absence of war, but as a positive force in its own right. We can compare Poole with Paul.

One can test out Leviton's hypothesis by visiting the Chalice Well in Glastonbury, walking through the gardens, and sampling the various waters there. You can compare the White Well and the Red Well. While sitting in one of the several beautiful arbors, or next to the lion-headed waterspout, or at the deep well lined with mossy stone, you can contemplate the Image, the historical personalities, and the life of Rudolf Steiner.

The Aspects of Zeal

Zeal has several aspects, to which I will add very brief connections to Rudolf Steiner:

- Energy becoming power. The zealot seems to accomplish much more than the average human being and cares deeply about his or her work. The energy here has charisma in it, and the power to evoke passion in others. One often hears the term "tireless worker" to describe a zealot. Here is some advice from *The Ways of the Tzaddikim* (holy men) passing through the Gate of Zeal: "Be bold as a leopard, light as an eagle, swift as a deer, and strong as a lion to do the will of your Father in Heaven."[261] Steiner showed a tremendous energy and capacity for pursuing many projects at the same time. For many years he seemed "tireless," sleeping very little. His productivity is still keeping editors busy as even a hundred years later new lectures are being found and published.
- Primacy of concept. Big Ideas, dogmas, and systems of thinking rule the zealot, guiding his or her energy. Perceptions become secondary, and the concept becomes self-fulfilling. When you think someone or some group is evil and treat them poorly, they may very well react in a way that proves your supposition. Note here that even "love," "truth," and "freedom" can become guiding concepts in a way that divorces one from their true living meaning. Each man

of zeal speaks the word "love," but is it a real, vibrant, and living love? Surveying the leaders of initiatives of all kinds, one can see in Steiner some very big ideas, supported by a plethora of concepts. "Freedom," "love," and "truth" guided everything he said. He invited people to experience these as living, and one must ask if these people were able to meet that invitation.

- The "right way." The man of zeal knows one right way, his way. This can mean the use of specialized language whose definition the man of zeal controls. It can mean certain beliefs that are unique to this particular man of zeal. Steiner developed a special language. I can note how useful the language has been to me; however, it remains a special language, and some of the definitions of the terms waffle in relation to various things that Steiner said. People quote Steiner back and forth with different nuances about some of these terms. We can note occasions of intolerance of other views, amidst many examples of broad tolerance for many other points of view. The special views include concepts that, again, I find very useful, but they are ideas that are held by very few other people. A good example is the existence of two Jesus children and two Mother Marys, laid out in Appendix B. Though this can be demonstrated with many good points, it remains a special belief system unique to the anthroposophical movement. Another example is the young Earth, the notion that the present age of the Earth is really only twenty thousand years old or so, at odds with modern geology. Though one can marshal evidence for the younger Earth in the new research showing that the "constants," such as speed of light and radioactive decay, may have been changing, it nonetheless remains a special idea held by this group.

- Antipathy becoming hatred, creating an in-group and an out-group. From *The Ways of the Tzaddikim*: "Let each man put his sword on his side."[262] The opposite of sympathy, antipathy means a distaste for certain others, or indeed, for ascetics, all others. Also from *The Ways of the Tzaddikim*: "Take great care to be extremely zealous to separate yourself from the company of the wicked."[263] Who is wicked? When you set up separations through antipathy, that antipathy develops into hatred and the label of the Other as wicked. Trace hatred back to its source and you find an immense fear of life, change, and difference. There is no warm interest here. The tendency is very strong to polarize and make everything black-and-white.

There are a few occasions where Steiner rejected others, amidst a general tolerant and open acceptance of anyone who came to imbibe anthroposophy. More serious, as is usually the case with strong leaders, are the righteous machinations of the next in command, the ejections of the unworthy from the Anthroposophical Society, for example. When people converse about in-groups, they often ask, mockingly, "Is there a secret handshake?" referring to the several secret brotherhoods who recognize each other with just such a communication device. Actually, anthroposophy does have a handshake, not a special one, but the very fact of a handshake. To get into a Waldorf classroom in the mornings, each student shakes the hand of the teacher, repeating a greeting that Rudolf Steiner himself used. It is a wonderful moment that awakens the child to the day. Notice when reading this if you begin to develop a sense of vigilant judgment, if you have formed an opinion that handshakes are good or bad. This is the operation of antipathy. It can swing into strong sympathy: "I love handshakes!" Or it can swing around to antipathy: "Those people over there use handshakes!" When the handshake has lost its warm interest expressed between human beings, and has become only a symbol for the in-group, then zeal has taken over.

- Willingness to be guided by antipathy. The zealot creates programs and pogroms. Shoot first and ask questions later. Actually, in zeal there is no room for questions. The largest ejection of anthroposophists occurred in 1935, ten years after Steiner's death. There are some who have been named as dangerous and are therefore shunned by others. In general, however, anthroposophy is characterized by inclusion and mutual assistance in the process of personal development.

- Reaction and counterreaction. Zeal in one arouses zeal in others. Conflict results, not only with the opposition but also within the ranks of the righteous, as competition increases. The very existence of a system of philosophy, and of a movement, will arouse in some others a kind of antipathy. Websites that quote Steiner out of context and occasional lawsuits about various matters buzz around the edges of this initiative.

- Followers with a similar character. Truly zealous people have followers who can become more extreme, acting as a kind of police force for the person in charge and his or her ideas.

Zeal for good and zeal for ill are appropriate expressions of Antares' influence. Each of the three men of the Image dispenses death in service of his zeal. Only Paul transforms in the course of his life to love, eagerly and zealously embraced. On this day, the Teacher sees forward in time to transformation of a man of zeal.

Zeal and the Hardener

Another aspect of zeal requires a preface. On a visit to Israel, one day I dropped my wife at a conference center in a Druze village, where she was co-creating the opening of an all-day women's gathering. My hosts had gone to work. I had the car, two errands, and a whole day to myself. In other words, I wasn't in a hurry to be someplace else. I drove away from the conference center on narrow streets, cars parked on one or both sides so that in places there was room for only one car to pass. A car coming the other way stopped in one such narrow place, the driver shouting a conversation with someone in one of the houses next to the street. I didn't see the person in the house, around a little corner. I don't think that person saw me in my car. The driver of the stopped car saw me, glanced quickly in my direction and then away, and continued to converse. I was blocked from movement for four minutes before the driver pulled forward and passed me by, without looking at me.

As I wasn't in a hurry, I could watch my reactions arise and then just as easily let them go. The typical response in that culture would have been to honk the horn, shout, and make gestures that say, "Hey, what's your problem?!" After all, the driver could easily have pulled forward twenty feet and parked, but didn't.

I observed my own reactions and I observed the situation.

The other driver, justified by who knows what reasons, was committing a consciously selfish act that impinged upon another. I watched as the patterning of that act and all her reasons settled in on her being as a fine spray of cement, liquid in the moment but soon setting hard. She hardened. I realized that my life has accumulated so many of these acts as to be overwhelming, so I don't permit myself to see them. Now I had the opportunity to observe just one such act in isolation. In the demeanor of the other driver, I could perceive the puffed-up posture, the stubbornness, the persistence, in other words, the zeal that she took on. Multiply this act many times, and I see how people become hard. The many fine layers of sprayed cement accumulate to make a human being into something hard. Those who have an "ideology" or a "dogma" are particularly susceptible to becoming hard. Every encounter becomes an opportunity to become even harder.

In that brief situation, in a narrow road in a Druze village on Mount Carmel, I could permit myself to observe what operates in me all the time, operates in everyone. Tears came to my eyes for the other driver, as I watched her pull around herself another layer of hardness.

What is Love?

The criterion of superhuman love is the decisive one for Paul, since in the case of miracles (the criterion of superhuman ability) it is a matter of the power of love, and in the case of superhuman wisdom (the criterion of superhuman knowledge) it is a matter of the wisdom of love.

—Valentin Tomberg [264]

How did the transformation occur for the third man of zeal? The Image gives only hints, "from hatred," meaning from antipathy. Zeal has at its core an antipathy, passion against and away from something, rather than toward something. The military commander—and military thinking in general and the whole military town—always has an enemy toward whom hate or antipathy is proper and required. Zeal in the military identifies and repels the bad. Even when the politicians ask the military to defend the good, the military mind's attention focuses specifically and actively on repelling the bad. For the religious leader, ascetic practices can exceed healthy discipline, becoming a hatred of the body, hatred of the self, hatred of this life, and hatred of all life. For the inquisitor, it looks just the same. The good that the inquisitor is supposed to defend pales before the obsession with antipathy for the bad.

To turn hatred into its opposite does not solve the problem, for the "love" that is the opposite of hate can also be obsessive. Sympathy that is opposite to antipathy can obsess, try to possess, energetically intrude. It doesn't go deep, and its life is short.

The true resolution of zealous hate does not source love in a mental concept that directs the will but rather finds the feeling realm in the heart, there finding love as the foundation of creation. True love—what Tomberg calls superhuman love—balances all, and straightens out the knots of the dysfunction that has arisen between willing and thinking, between power and knowledge.

Let us refer to the writings of the Christian apostle Paul, the one who made the transformation in this Image. Probably the one quote most frequently read aloud at marriages comes from Paul's first letter to the Corinthians, chapter 13, beginning:

> If I speak in the tongues of mortals and of angels,

This identifies those who are so attuned and so spacious that words come through them from angels and from advanced human beings. It refers specifically to the time after the downpouring of spirit fire at Pentecost through Mother Mary, then through the students of the Teacher, when they went out, full of the inspiration of this spirit fire, into the streets and were able to speak in the languages—tongues—of many different peoples gathered there for the festival. Everyone understood what was being told them, and they converted to the new religion in droves. Paul continues:

> … but do not have love, I am a noisy gong or a clanging cymbal.

Those who have these powers of tongues but are cold and impersonal do not actually have anything useful for the rest of us. What they miss is love. It is always interesting to see a serious professor of theology speak these lines from Paul, because he drones it out as if the Greek word for love here was *philia*—which is part of the word philosophy, that is, a kind of intellectual warmth and attraction. But that is not Paul's word. He uses *agape*, which means wild, abandoned, fully embodied love. Not thoughtful love, but dynamic love, love that pours forth from the heart and excites the will into loving action. He continues:

> And if I have prophetic powers,

Many would like to master the ability to see into the future, or to see into another person in order to diagnose a medical condition, etc. The three men of zeal are trying by their good works to achieve this state of development.

> … and understand all mysteries and all knowledge

Now we have the greatest of all professors! Indeed, we could say that Faust has nearly reached this state.

> … and I have all faith so as to remove mountains

Now we have a momentous combination. This is a powerful magician, indeed. The faith in the power of divinity is so strong that he or she can command whole mountains to move, and they will do so. Even Faust is left behind here, as he had to team up with the Devil in order to make things happen. We stand firmly in the realm of the superhuman now, and are ready to see what the pinnacle of human development can do. Paul tells us:

> … but do not have love, I am nothing.

From a great buildup, a great letdown. Worldly power is not what it seems. The princes of the world have nothing. Those who seem high and mighty with all their powers won through zeal are actually very low.

So what is this love that he recommends? Let's skip to verse four now.

> Love is patient; love is kind; love is not envious or boastful or arrogant or rude.

When this list is read at a wedding, it goes by too quickly. You have to pause to recall the ways that you are impatient and patient, unkind and kind, envious and un-envious, and so forth. You can only know a virtue if you have experienced its opposite. Such is the power of human experience.

I could go on with Paul's quote, which does go on, and shows in the end of the short chapter that he is speaking in tongues himself, in a kind of *agape*-filled ecstasy! Speak Paul's words aloud, in the way Paul might have spoken them, standing on the Aeropagus, the Speaker's Stone outside of the Parthenon, or on the stage at the great theater of Ephesus, both places where Paul spoke and which you can visit even today. Shout out these words again to know the power that Paul felt in the transformation of hatred to love.

"What Is Truth?"

So spoke the Roman Procurator in his interrogation of the Teacher.[265] The question is not answered, and therein lies a hint. The truth cannot be specified or pinned down. The inquisitors, with their long lists of acceptable and unacceptable answers from the questioned, would prefer that it could be pinned down. Yet the lists don't function properly. Any words that a prisoner gives can be seen as blasphemous, even when he or she quotes the inquisitor's own rule books! The one who harbors antipathy will never be able to soften that antipathy while the thinking realm has ascendance. Only after the feeling in the heart and in the breathing regains its appropriate power can the iron prejudice against the Other—the "Enemy"—dissolve. That's why hatred must first turn to love. The zealous person thinks, "I'm going to rid the world of these bad people," or "I'm going to create a world where everyone agrees on everything," or "I'm going to create utopia here and now, where everyone loves one another," then starts killing all those who disagree. Whole villages are destroyed in order to "save" them. The slogan "Liberty, fraternity, equality!" was shouted by thousands as they slaughtered and maimed thousands of the "others."

The important word in the last phrase of the Image is the verb "turn." After the emotion of hatred "changes" into love, then a physical act can take place, turning, going in a different direction. Rather than full speed ahead toward the goal of utopia, there is a turning away from the mad rush of zeal toward truth. Of course, the zealous claim to be pursuing truth, and generous philosophers speak of many truths. However, a more advanced person knows that truth cannot be specified. Truth, as demonstrated by the Roman Procurator, is a question, an active and dynamic question. It is "living." The very question "what is truth?" directs one toward a warm interest in others, an acceptance of many forms and solutions to life's challenges. Truth itself, as Paul demonstrates, becomes the process of love in movement. Paul says of love:

> It does not insist on its own way; it is not irritable or resentful; it does not rejoice in wrongdoing, but rejoices in the truth.

This "truth" can only be discovered through love, as an effect of love. There is no one truth, but rather a turning to the light, the old certainties cracked wide open. Paul knows that love "bears all things, believes all things, hopes all things, endures all things." We come to realize that the opposite of zeal is not relaxation, nor lethargy, but a dynamic openness. All the energy of zeal remains, "turned" from the goal rabidly pursued to become the servant of love.

Thus Steiner repeatedly gives many "indications" and discoveries that he asks us to verify for ourselves. He recommends the dynamic movement of love that will reveal all. Readers today often have a difficult time finding love in Steiner's intellectual language, but you can only understand what he is saying from a foundation of love.

A truth is larger when the individual, the "I AM," aligns with Divinity. You can tell when people have found this truth because they become compassionate. The larger truth you can call compassionate truth. Those who are unwilling or unable to align with Divinity zealously clutch written laws and regulations that drive them further from their origins and from the soul intentions that live at the place of their birth.

The Image in Relation to Steiner's Life

Steiner was known to have intense energy, and indeed, though some observed him looking sometimes "as pale as death," he worked long hours. His unflagging energy when running from workshop to workshop in the construction of the Goetheanum, his ability to take up hammer and chisel and pound away without stopping for hours, his ability to follow one lecture immediately with another—these were hallmarks of his great vigor. Each afternoon he was known to speak aloud his own translation of the Abwoon Prayer in his office—so forcefully that he could be heard in adjacent rooms.

His asceticism was well known. Andrei Belyi reported, "Steiner's home ... is like that of a cell or commune where no one places any value on comfort." His clothes were simple and subdued, his demands minimal.[266]

Steiner was known to have strong feelings about punctuality. "Everywhere he appeared at the correct time," and he "demanded that people gather in silence some time before the beginning of his lectures." He excluded some students from the School for Spiritual Science because they came late, explaining, "either one wants to come or one doesn't want to come." It was as simple as that.[267]

Steiner was also not immune to antipathy. Here is a fascinating account from a student:

> There are also lightning-quick transitions, or rather no transitions at all, from the charming smile to the loud and clearly uttered pronouncement, in a deep chest-voice: "That is bad, that is very bad." Over such a "That is bad," often tempered again in the same breath, people would weep for many long nights, and their remorse last, not months, but years. [268]

Do those who have zeal realize the effect that they have on people?

Steiner's pronouncements in his lectures sometimes seem extreme, polarized, oversimplified, differentiating the "good people" in the audience from the others "out there." He definitely wrestled with zeal. This became all the more apparent in how others were around him. There was a group of elderly ladies known as the "Tanten" (the "Aunts") who attended lectures and then gossiped, at length taking on a huge power, through rumor and innuendo, to affect the direction and growth of the anthroposophical movement and the development of the science of anthroposophy. Here we can see the Hardener working through zeal.[269]

Often there were others who kept order and made sure people were in their seats on time. One example from a student:

> I had to arrive a day late for the course, and, as I had been absent from Dornach for some months, I waited at the door leading behind the stage to speak to Marie Steiner as she went in. Going up to greet her as she approached, I was dumbfounded when she said, between severity and anxiety, "You should not go into the lectures; people who do not follow the whole course add to Dr. Steiner's burden."[270]

Steiner happened along just then and asked her to come in. For him, seeing an old friend returned from her travels, it was not an issue. The mixture of "severity and anxiety" typifies the zealot, as well as any boundary-maintaining activity of an organization.

On the other side, Steiner had to deal with the Illusionist in his midst. Those who had come to Dornach felt that they had entered heaven. They were the flower children of their time. Their sweetness and floating around the campus even caused Steiner to burst out on one occasion:[271]

It just won't do—to have you running about constantly with such blissful faces and meditating, meditating, meditating! You could at least organize a group to further your education! Or simply sit down together and laugh a little and parody each other!

The man who encouraged meditation had to back off from it because people took him too seriously. Even today there are times at anthroposophical conferences when all the faces are long and serious. To be fair, some have learned to parody each other with delightful and healthy humor. These are all tendencies in relation to zeal that we are observing, not permanent and fatal diseases.

Counterreactions follow the zealous. Steiner was bitterly attacked, especially in the later years. A "poisonous cloud of calumny" was spread, like mustard gas. He was fashioned "a perpetrator of sedition, a wizard with hypnotic powers, a kind of semi-magic, semi-mystic Pied Piper." [272] Critics thought the "Steinerites were a crowd of besotted lunatics enslaved by a confidence trickster." [273] This came from those who did not take the trouble to investigate what Steiner had said or written. Occasionally, one will find an honest reviewer who says, "Though I haven't read anything by him, I know he's dangerous," which reveals the way criticism often works.

A kind of oblivion of the faithful also is common in the realm of zeal: "Opponents covered him with derision and scorn, and anthroposophists let it pass all too easily, and went on enjoying his lectures." [274] That situation is a serious clue to dysfunction. But Steiner the optimist kept on teaching, with the notion perhaps that his audience would eventually discover in freedom that the font of wisdom needed some attention. Protection of the freedom of the individual remained his highest ideal. Steiner felt that he couldn't ask for help. Even the statement of membership in the Anthroposophical Society simply declares that one affirms the right for such an organization to exist. [275] It does not demand that one sign a creed or adhere to a dogma. In this way, Steiner dealt with the Image of zeal into which he was born, by cultivating a devotion to truth in oneself.

Zealous reactions came from inside the movement, too. Some of his followers were so enthusiastic that they began to transcribe his lectures for publication, and then pass these around to those who attended the lectures and those who did not. Steiner called it "spiritual theft," and worried that all would be taken away, leaving his wife, Marie, bereft of income after he had gone.[276]

Could Steiner be zealous? Here's an example of how a eurythmist had put a poem to movement, creating a specific choreography in the pattern for the feet and gestures in the hands, to express the words and lines.

> A certain eurythmist was showing a poem by Albert Steffen. As she fin-
> ished, Dr. Steiner got up and said, "That will not do"; and he went on to say
> that for this poem he had already given a form and this being so, no other
> form should be used. "For any poem there is only one true form"—his
> voice, stern and earnest, remains in my memory.[277]

"There is one right way" is a common trait of the zealous. Insistence on personal freedom at the same time as "there is one right way" can look like "You have the freedom to choose the one right way."

In another example, Steiner had received a complaint that the Berlin drama group had performed his Christmas plays in a modified way. Already we have two aspects of zeal, the sense of spying and anonymous report-ing that continues to this day in a small way in the Society and, secondly, the notion of there being one right way to do things. The Berlin group was called to put on one of the plays for Steiner, so that he could determine that it had not been wrongly modified.[278]

> Without an audience, and with Rudolf Steiner in the front row, we per-
> formed the play that had already been abandoned two months before. I
> noticed how, during the performance, he swung his pince-nez excitedly to
> and fro and moved his leg up and down. At the end he jumped onto the
> stage and shouted: "They are innkeepers and not landladies, and shep-
> herds and not shepherdesses." It thundered out—then dead silence. I
> stepped forward and with the same loud voice declared: "Herr Doctor, it is
> wartime, the men are on the battlefield! We now have to stand in for men!"
> Again, absolute silence. Then he spoke the liberating words one after the
> other: "This-I-can-accept." After that he invited us all to coffee and cake
> and was very warm and jolly.

That's how zeal can work in a healthy way. Had he made his negative pronouncement and then left, everyone would have been diminished by this encounter. As it occurred, the one who spoke up could speak the truth as she saw it, and meet the Master in a true exchange. Some people reading this experience may be put off by the pontification of Steiner. I have directed theatrical productions, and been directed in them, and can state that theater by its nature requires a zealous director.

Three-ness

We have been alerted to look out for numbers in these Images, like the three men of zeal. There are curious occurrences of three in Steiner's life, of which we will mention two. When the first Waldorf School in Stuttgart planned to construct a new building, a parchment of intentions was set into a copper container and lowered into the foundation, then covered with cement. Rudolf Steiner produced a hammer and struck the concrete slab three times. He did this again on behalf of Marie Steiner. Then the founder of the school, all the teachers, and every single child in turn took that hammer and hit the stone slab three times. As the reporter estimated that there were a thousand children in the school, this must have taken a long time. Even though that building was bombed in the Second World War, the concrete foundation was not hurt, and rests today under the re-erected building.[279]

At the important Christmas Foundation Meeting, wherein Steiner imparted the Foundation Stone Meditation, Steiner "opened this event by giving three strong, incisive, measured raps with a gavel upon the speaker's stand, such as those given in the Temple in the Mystery Plays. It was as though the room became thronged with unseen spectators."[280]

We see then the power of the three. One can sometimes find in seemingly inconsequential details important resonance of an Image with the soul gestures of a life.

Historical Personalities

As we consider the various Star Brothers, Star Sisters, and Bodes, we can imagine them meeting one another and beginning to form a group. This is the fellowship of the shared Solar Cross. These are people whose Gate Image lies at the western horizon of Steiner's birth Solar Cross, at Antares.

Composers First: Vincent d'Indy

Start by listening to music composed by Vincent D'Indy, who died into this degree in 1931 and was thus both a Bode and a contemporary of Steiner. You can imagine that he lifted up his life's work into this particular degree in the heavens, to assist those who pass through this way. Because this is his Death Image, concentrate on the music from the latter part of his life, such as *Poème des Rivages* (*Poem of the Shores*—of the Mediterranean, where he lived the latter part of his life), whose fourth movement reveals the stormy emotions that live in this Image. The beginning of his *Jour d'été à la montagne* (Opus 61), called "Aurora" (Dawn), is one of the most beautiful introductions to how truth and love could be born to a person and to the world. You can listen to this while reading the Image or while pondering its meaning, or while reading about the Star Brothers and Star Sisters in this degree.

Star Brother: Edward III, King of England

Very soon after his birth on November 13, 1312, Edward was given lands and titles by his father, King Edward II. At the age of eight he was sent to France to meet his uncle, the French King Charles IV, thus supporting his connection with both crowns. His mother and her lover, Roger Mortimer, forced Edward II to abdicate and put Edward III in his place, crowning him King of England at the age of fifteen but retaining control of the country for themselves. They also arranged his marriage to Philippa of Hainault, whom we met as a Bode in Steiner's Earth Image. She brought a retinue from her homeland in France to attend her. At the age of eighteen, Edward III seized control of the English government, a sort of political coup of the young man over his own monarchy. He had Mortimer arrested and then executed, and exiled his mother from the court.

For young Edward, survival in the royal environment demanded a certain amount of zeal, but one might say he had even more than he needed. When his uncle, King Charles IV of France, died, Edward pressed his own cause to become King of France in addition to being King of England. His claim came through a female line, however, and was opposed by the French nobles. They invoked Salic law, which stipulated that inheritance could only come through the male line. So Edward fought, winning battles and

King Edward III of England

declaring himself King of France on January 26, 1340, commencing a conflict known as the Hundred Years' War. This was the man who started the Hundred Years' War!

In the same time period, Edward III had recurring wars with Scotland; he struggled with the Black Plague that scoured through the country several times; and his sons decided to argue about the succession after Edward III died, a conflict known as the Wars of the Roses.

The Order of the Garter. An important detail that I mention because it has turned up before and will turn up again: Edward III founded the Order of the Garter, an honorary knighthood that began when a woman, while dancing at a court ball, dropped an item of intimate apparel—possibly a sanitary belt, though it was described as made of velvet. Not pausing a moment, the King picked it up and tied it around his own leg, remarking, "Shame upon him who thinks ill of it." Recalling that his predecessors had worn garters into the battles of the Crusades, Edward created a men's club based on honor, chivalry, and high values. The award by the King of a garter and entry into the Order of the Garter became symbols of great status; Edward had started a men's club of the rich and famous. Star Brother Andreae was later linked to the drama of the garter played out with King Frederick's court in Heidelberg. Even Goethe referred to it in *Faust* when Mephistopheles says: "I have no Garter to distinguish me,"[281] meaning that those with power ought to have a garter. Ceremonies of the Order of the Garter are still celebrated in England. They continue to be awarded to high-ranking nobles, and they are embroidered with the words that Edward uttered, "*Honi soit qui mal y pense.*" Andreae linked the Garter to other secret brotherhoods, including the Rosy Cross and even the Red Cross.

How was Steiner related to this stream that appears in the lives of his Star Brothers? One can look at some of Steiner's drawings and find in them parallels, or study the recently released material from the secret groups that Steiner was involved with early on, and find hints, but there is nothing concrete that I have found.

The Burghers of Calais. A scene of zeal from the life of Edward III is depicted in Auguste Rodin's well-known statue *The Burghers of Calais.* In addition to the original in Calais, there are twelve castings of this statue from New York to Seoul to Canberra. In 1346, Edward was expanding England to include France. He could not breach the moats and walls of the key port city of Calais, so laid a siege and waited. The people starved. At one point the townspeople ejected hundreds of children and elderly, so that the adults might have a better opportunity to survive. Edward did not receive the outcasts. These starved to death outside the city walls, wailing to be let back in. On August 1, 1347, after a year under siege, the city lit fires announcing the willingness of the people to surrender. Edward said that he would spare the people if the City Council—the "burghers"—would sacrifice themselves, walking out of the city naked with nooses around their necks, bearing the keys of the city and the castle, and prepared to die. Six men volunteered to go to their deaths in service of their neighbors. Rodin's sculpture depicts this scene, the half-dressed emaciated men, barely able to stand upright, showing what it means to be a pillar of a society, a leader of a citizenry.[282]

In his zeal, Edward was indeed prepared to kill the leaders of Calais. His Queen, Philippa of Hainault, however, had a different motivation. Though her death was twenty years away, its Image was calling to her, the Leo Image of the release of the prisoners into the light. She negotiated for the pardon of the people of the town and the six brave burghers who offered themselves in place of the others.[283]

With politicians and scientists, it becomes much more difficult to sense the soul gesture in the life. We see zeal, we sense righteousness and egotism, but do we sense a transformation that embraces love and truth? The public events that so firmly put us in the right Image for this man obscure what might live behind the scenes.

Given what we do know, we see that Edward's zeal spread too far, to an egotism that led to the deaths of many people in many countries. One could say that Edward did not find the transformation that was promised as possible in his Gate Image.

Star Sister: Louisa May Alcott

Born in 1832, Alcott shared in her family's poverty and Transcendentalist ideals. Those ideals were the basis for Fruitlands, founded by Louisa's father, a utopian community with ideals based on Transcendentalism, that is, a threefold community, one that encouraged development of head, heart, and hand. We will see Count Ludwig Zinzendorf and St. Philip Neri, experimenters with community, living in the Eastern Horizon Image. Fruitlands, however, failed, and the family came onto hard times.

Louisa May Alcott

Louisa became an abolitionist and a feminist. She wrote for the *Atlantic Monthly* and was a nurse at the Union Hospital in Georgetown, District of Columbia, for six weeks in 1862–3, when Rudolf Steiner was very young. In 1868, when Steiner was seven years old, she published the work that she is best known for, *Little Women: Or Meg, Jo, Beth, and Amy.* It recounts the family life during the Civil War of a group of girls, working together to get by and struggling with the questions of growing up. The heart is wrenched by the death of Beth (note that Anne Brontë, at the Eastern Horizon Image, had a sister Beth who died early) and Jo's rejection of young Laurie, who goes away but later woos and marries Amy. And so forth—the human story of how relationships are formed and are negotiated never ends.

This book has been translated into many languages, and the Japanese especially have made several animated versions of it. Different film versions have been made, starring Katherine Hepburn in 1933, Elizabeth Taylor in 1949, Greer Garson in 1978, Susan Sarandon and Winona Ryder in 1994, as well as many others. Who can dislike this piece? It has also become a musical, and even an opera.

Alcott wrote *Little Women* when she was thirty-six years old. Her earlier works were typified by the zeal that is part of this Image. Written under the name "A. M. Barnard," such novels as *A Long Fatal Love Chase* and *Pauline's Passion and Punishment* were known as "potboilers" and "blood-and-thunder tales," which Alcott mentions in *Little Women* as being "dangerous for little minds." The characters are egotistical, ruthless in the pursuit of their own aims, which include revenge on those who have thwarted them. Alcott made a shift in her life, out of this forward thrust, to one of care for others, as shown in *Little Women*. We can see this here because we know about her life, in great part because she wrote about it. We can find out about her inner workings more easily than we can find out about Edward III's, and we have enough information to see how she made the transformation promised in her Gate Image.

Little Women extols the strong heart, that is, the zeal to survive life's tragedies but in an open, feeling way. Emotions flow in the life and work of Louisa May Alcott, and people find their happy ending by enduring.

How interesting to bring in such a contrasting figure to Steiner, who had little to do with the emotion and sentimentality of his elder Star Sister.

Younger Star Brother: Winston Churchill

Churchill was born when Steiner was thirteen years old, and lived a great deal longer than Steiner, to 1965. Even though he is a younger Star Brother, he is so illustrative of this Image that we can learn some things that may be useful.

When asked in a 2002 poll to identify the hundred greatest Britons of all of time, the British still voted Churchill number one.[284] Here certainly is a man of zeal, who appeared in famous photographs of three men of zeal: in Cairo in 1943, with Chiang Kai-shek on the left, Franklin Delano Roosevelt in the center, and Churchill, all in white, on the right, and the more famous meeting at Yalta on the Crimean on February 11, 1945, with Churchill on the left of the picture, Franklin Delano Roosevelt in the center, and Stalin on the right. In each case, three men of zeal. In terms of the Image, which was which?

Three men of zeal (Yalta)

One of the hallmarks of zeal is erratic performance. Men of zeal are rarely well rounded, instead excelling above everyone else in some things, and performing horribly in others. Churchill was this way in school, independent and rebellious, top of his class in mathematics and history, yet refusing to study the classics. He failed several courses but was the fencing champion for his school. He could not be cajoled or threatened to conform to a well-rounded approach to things.

He loved conflict and, after the military college at Sandhurst, went battle-seeking, thrilled to be under fire for the first time on his twenty-first birthday in Cuba. He rushed to fight in the Greco-Turkish War and the Pathan revolt in Northern India, determinedly won an assignment in Kitchener's forces in the Sudan, and was captured in the second Anglo-Boer war, subsequently escaping and traveling three hundred miles overland to a port of safety. He loved the heat of battle for what it brought out in human beings. All this time he wrote magazine columns and books about his adventures. This ability to write culminated in his history of the Second World War, which ran to two million words.

He loved a battle in politics as well. In 1911, as Home Secretary, he took personal charge of a conflict between anarchists and the Scots Guards, joining the gun battle himself. When the building where two of the gang were hiding caught fire, he prevented the fire department from going near, forcing those inside to choose surrender or death.

His outlandish statements showed his passion. He declared that Bolshevism should be "strangled in its cradle." He advocated the use of poison gas and suggested that machine guns be used on striking miners. He considered that the fascism of Benito Mussolini had "rendered a service to the whole world" by undermining Communism. He called Gandhi a "half-naked fakir" who "ought to be laid, bound hand and foot, at the gates of Delhi and then trampled on by an enormous elephant with the new viceroy seated on its back." In his first speech as Prime Minister of England, he declared, "I have nothing to offer but blood, toil, tears, and sweat." A speech given just before the Battle of Britain used his zeal to engage those under his care: "We shall defend our Island, whatever the cost may be, we shall fight on the beaches, we shall fight on the landing grounds, we shall fight in the fields and in the streets, we shall fight in the hills; we shall never surrender." Later he supported the firestorm bombing of Dresden even though it had no military advantage, simply to show the power of the Allies. In 1944, he recommended the mass expulsion of peoples to conform to the new national borders of Poland, Germany, and the Soviet Union, an effort that caused extreme hardship for many: "A clean sweep will be made!" He was the one who described the split between the communist world and the Western world with the famous phrase, "an iron curtain has descended," then blamed others for not acting decisively.[285] He believed in being tough, strong, proactive, even preemptive, for "An appeaser is one who feeds a crocodile—hoping it will eat him last." He saw peacemakers as cowardly and weak. This is the way zealous leaders act and think, for in the zealous action often comes first, and thinking comes later, if at all.

Note your reactions to the statements of this man. Perhaps admiration mixes with horror, sometimes both at once. These are the responses that live around men of zeal.

The National Archives in London recently released some new information about Churchill and his way of thinking. The notes of a cabinet meeting on July 6, 1942, quote Churchill as saying: "If Hitler falls into our hands we shall certainly put him to death like a gangster. This man is the mainspring of evil. Instrument—electric chair." In another meeting in 1945, as the war was coming to an end, he advised telling Britain's allies that show trials would be a "farce," asking for their consent to execute a list of Nazi leaders without trial, and then killing them before the Allies had time to reply.[286]

Among the many awards for his services, Churchill became a Knight of the Garter, the order established by his elder Star Brother, Edward III, and prominent in the background of his alchemist forebear Andreae. There are so many parallels between Edward III and Churchill. We can treat Churchill's sayings as if they had passed from Edward III's lips. In another example, Churchill wrote, "It is said that famous men are usually the product of unhappy childhood. The stern compression of circumstances, the twinges of adversity, the spur of slights and taunts in early years, are needed to evoke that ruthless fixity of purpose and tenacious mother-wit without which great actions are seldom accomplished."[287] These are the hallmarks of the man of zeal.[288]

Churchill's histories of World Wars I and II relied on his inside knowledge of everything that happened. His view is what is called "Whig history," meaning that it ascribes to England a central role in the politics of the world and, indeed, in the evolution of civilization, a view that he shared with his elder Star Brother in Taurus, Henry Thomas Buckle (see Chapter 11). Steiner predicted this: "This is the intention of the Anglo-Saxon world: to completely eradicate the truth of the development of spiritual science in Central Europe, and to set itself in its place."[289] The man of zeal wishes to spread his way of seeing things everywhere.

Churchill saw history as a succession of speeches and battles, rather than the slow progress of economic and social change. Men of zeal look to the world and see men of zeal, principles of zeal, and the networks of people and information they'll need to control if they want to be in command. As Churchill said, "I will leave judgments on this matter to history—but I will be one of the historians." Actually, he sought to become the only historian. He made use of classified information available only to him, both as Secretary of the Navy and Prime Minister. Regarding his history of World War II, Churchill might well have agreed with Thucydides, who wrote, "I have written my work, not as an essay which is to win the applause of the moment, but as a possession for all time."[290] The word "possession" can be turned—the history becomes a sacred possession of the culture, and it also seeks to possess the memory and thus the culture itself. We see in Churchill the desire to write down the truth, but was it his personal truth, giving himself and England a special position in human development, or was it aligned with a greater living truth?

Did Churchill find the transformation promised in his Gate Image? Or was he so bound up with becoming the savior of his age that he never found the path to truth and love?

Younger Star Sister: Shirley Chisholm

Let us look very briefly at a younger Star Sister who barely overlapped Steiner's life—she was born in Brooklyn in 1924—but who illustrates how someone works with this Image successfully.

Chisholm's father worked in a burlap factory and her mother worked as a seamstress and a domestic helper. By age three and a half she was reading, by four she was writing. She won scholarships to Vassar and Oberlin. She earned a master's degree in education from Columbia University and administered the Hamilton-Madison Child Care Center. Then she

Shirley Chisholm

decided to join the public arena. In 1964 she was elected to the New York State Legislature. In 1968 she was elected to the House of Representatives, the first African-American woman in Congress. She cofounded the Congressional Black Caucus in 1969. In 1972, she ran for President. "I ran ... to demonstrate the sheer will and refusal to accept the status quo. The next time a woman runs, or a black or a Jew ... I believe that he or she will be taken seriously.... I ran because somebody had to do it first."[291] This is how zeal speaks!

She tirelessly built coalitions, even directing the anger of the Black Panthers toward community get-out-the-vote drives. Pause for a moment to imagine the zeal required to accomplish that redirection of militant energy. She was almost always alone in her struggles. She received three death threats during her presidential campaign, which deeply affected her. Aloneness is a mark of the zealous person. One can certainly see this in the life of Rudolf Steiner.

Chisholm used the power of her birthright, living in her Gate Image, to take high principles to the arena of public life. When one reads through her speeches, especially on the Equal Rights Amendment that she supported, one gets the sense of someone who knew truth and knew love, and worked to provide it for everyone.

Steiner too worked somewhat in the political realm, and for a time during and after World War I emphasized his solution, the threefold social order. We shall meet his work in this realm in the resonant moments discussed in the next chapter.

Younger Star Brother: C. S. Lewis

The beloved author Clive Staples Lewis was born in Ireland on November 29, 1898. Even as a professor in medieval literature at Oxford, he authored the *Space Trilogy* (*Out of the Silent Planet* in 1938, *Perelandra* in 1943, *That Hideous Strength* in 1945) and the seven novels of *The Chronicles of Narnia* (beginning with *The Lion, the Witch, and the Wardrobe* in 1950 and ending with *The Last Battle* in 1956), all having to do with the struggle between good and evil.

In Chapter 8, we compiled a list of Star Brothers and Star Sisters who were masters of the fairy tale, and C. S. Lewis could certainly be added there. He even wrote a book in the Narnia series called *The Silver Chair* (1953), a perfect counter-image to the kind of chair that Rudolf Steiner and others were building via the Aquarius Image. In Lewis's imagination, the chair is an ornate place of entrapment for Prince Rilian, whose task has been interrupted by an enchanting witch. Every night, while he is sane, he is trapped in the chair. During the day he can roam apparently free but without sanity, in a kind of prison of delusion. The task of the rescuers is to free the Prince from the chair.

However, Lewis's Gate Image is not in the Aquarius-Leo polarity but here in Scorpio. Is there a reason for that? Can we see in his life and work the reason that he would land among the men of zeal? Something that he wrote near the beginning of his literary career (and we are interested in this as this is an Image of birth, not death, for him) was the continually popular *Screwtape Letters* (1942), in which a more experienced Tempter, Screwtape, advises a younger Tempter, Wormwood, about how to lure a young man into such sins that the man's soul would be condemned to Hell forever. Biographers see in Screwtape traces of the zeal of the headmaster of the school that Lewis attended at age ten, which was so violent that the school was actually shut down. One can see Lewis's whole life in the terms of zeal via his encounters with capricious men of power, and how he found his way through their deceptions to a deep and abiding sense of spiritual truth. His story of committed atheism leading, through asking questions and accepting whatever answers came to him, even though "kicking and screaming," to a profound sense of God, reads like a protracted conversion of the inquisitor in the Image. *Mere Christianity* (1952, based on radio talks from 1941 to 1944) takes the person

C. S. Lewis (Burt Glinn/Magnum Photos)

with questions step by step past the Illusionist and the Hardener to an inner certainty based on personal experience. *Surprised by Joy*, Lewis's autobiography of his early life, documents his journey. Lewis's very popular fantasy tales can also be seen in the very serious terms of the Scorpio Image, as battles for love and truth. We can appreciate his life's work in a completely new and deepened way if we see Lewis's life informed by his Gate Image, and also by the leadership of his Star Brother, Rudolf Steiner.[292]

BODES IN SCORPIO

Who died into this degree and left their imprint in that hallway?

The Bode of Alexander Nevsky

The great king of Russia died into this degree on November 14, 1263, in the Julian calendar. At the age of nineteen, he showed his power individually and as a commander when he routed a larger army of Swedes attacking Russia from the northwest. From this encounter at the River Neva he received his surname. He is most famous for his command of a Russian army encountering the Teutonic Knights from Germany, who were attacking Russia to convert it to the Catholic Church. In April of 1242, Nevsky and a band of foot soldiers met the mounted and armored Teutonic Knights on an icy

Bust of Alexander Nevsky

lake. Groups of the foot soldiers surrounded the Knights and lured them out further onto the lake, whereupon the weight of horses, Knights, and armor broke the ice and pitched the Teutons into the lake. When Russia needed to warn its people about the German people's ambitions rising again before World War II, Stalin commissioned Sergei Eisenstein to make the film *Alexander Nevsky* (1938) to retell this story. In the making of this most astonishing film many actors drowned in chilly waters, as if Nevsky's zeal extended even to the Stalinist film producers. Nevsky is portrayed in the way that the Russians saw him seven centuries earlier, as powerful, determined, bigger than life, and loving of his own people. For his patriotic zeal and the power he had in directing the people of Russia, he was made a saint by the Russian Orthodox Church.

We have to ask what effects of a Bode might have been experienced by Rudolf Steiner on his passage to birth. Can we see any of Nevsky's legacy in

Steiner's tenacity, willingness to tackle well-armed opponents, and power to compel followers to feats of daring?

The Bode of Ada Lovelace

Ada Lovelace, by A. E. Chaton

We will meet in Ada's story some fascinating displays of zealous thinking. Her formal name was Augusta Ada King, Countess of Lovelace, and she was the daughter of Lord Byron, taken away from her father at the age of one month. Her doctors bled her to death in 1852 at age thirty-six in an effort to counteract her uterine cancer. Her mother, obsessed with rooting out any of Lord Byron's madness, taught her daughter mathematics to clear her brain. Along the way Ada met Charles Babbage, and between them—it is unclear who did what—they devised the Analytical Engine, which was the first computer. Ada has received recognition as the founder of scientific computing, though it may have been that she wrote about what Babbage had done.

How can we relate this brief tale to the Image? We can think about a calculating method of mind, and see that the power of wealth does not protect one from the imposition of the will of others. Further, Steiner spoke about Lord Byron. He indicated that Byron in an earlier incarnation had been a friend of the individual who reincarnated as Steiner's geometry teacher, a man who had a profound effect on Steiner as a boy. We have then a combination of mathematics, geometry, Byron, and his daughter to contemplate.

The Bode of Oscar Wilde

The great poet and playwright Oscar Fingal O'Flahertie Wills Wilde (remember our discussion of Fingal's Cave for the Leo Image?) was born in 1854, seven years before Steiner, and died in 1900 into this degree in Steiner's Solar Cross. A stickler for the linearity of time would not be concerned on Steiner's behalf about the traces that Wilde's death left in the passageway of this degree. In any case, we will find in Wilde some strong connections with the various Images in this Solar Cross.

Wilde endorsed an anarchistic brand of socialism in *The Soul of Man under Socialism*, continuing the theme of thinking about utopian commu-

nity that we find in Star Sister Louisa May Alcott as well as in Zinzendorf and Neri, whom we will meet in the Eastern Horizon Image. An idealistic approach to the question of how humans should live lies behind anyone related to this Image.

Wilde wrote plays, his most successful and best known being *The Importance of Being Earnest.* This comedy of manners has been called a "masterpiece of pure nonsense," a well-crafted piece of fluff, where nothing is said and all is innuendo as the actors get worked up about ... nothing. Brian Lipson's production of this play in Melbourne bril-

Oscar Wilde

liantly depicted two completely different plays in one—the first being the silly words spoken, and the second the action, a play within a play involving conflicts and games and sexual explorations. Being an Englishman, Lipson understood that what is said and what is done differ widely, and exaggerated the split to the maximum.

Idealism got Wilde in trouble. He ended up in court for "acts of gross indecency with other male persons," in other words, homosexuality. Why, amongst the upper classes of British society, where homosexuality was common, would someone be tried in court and jailed for it? Because the norm was secrecy and Wilde was flamboyant—not about homosexuality but about art, beauty, and what he termed aestheticism, that is, opening the senses. When the prosecutor asked him in court, "What is 'the love that dares not speak its name'?," Wilde replied:[293]

> "The love that dares not speak its name" in this century is such a great affection of an elder for a younger man as there was between David and Jonathan, such as Plato made the very basis of his philosophy, and such as you find in the sonnets of Michelangelo and Shakespeare. It is that deep spiritual affec-

tion that is as pure as it is perfect.... It is beautiful, it is fine, it is the noblest form of affection.... It is intellectual, and it repeatedly exists between an older and a younger man, when the older man has intellect, and the younger man has all the joy, hope and glamour of life before him.

He was sentenced to two years' hard labor in the prison at Reading.

At his release he wrote "The Ballad of Reading Gaol," which describes the prison—a key part of Wilde's Eastern Horizon Image (and Steiner's Earth Image). From this poem by a man who lived through the prison experience in his Solar Cross, we can get an insider's view of the prison, in exactly the terms of Steiner's Earth Image:

> This too I know—and wise it were
> If each could know the same—
> That every prison that men build
> Is built with bricks of shame.
> And bound with bars lest Christ could see
> How men their brothers maim.
>
> . . .
>
> The vilest deeds like poison weeds
> Bloom well in prison-air:
> It is only what is good in Man
> That wastes and withers there:
> Pale anguish keeps the heavy gate
> And the Warder is Despair.

Wilde refers to the stacking of stones of shame, parallel and opposite to the stones mentioned in the Image at Aquarius (Wilde's Western Horizon Image and Steiner's Gate Image). He speaks of stones again:

> For what chills and kills outright
> Is that every stone one lifts by day
> Becomes one's heart by night.

He even includes a specific reference to lepers, deepening what we see in the Leo Image:

> And from all the gaol rose up a wail
> Of impotent despair,
> Like the sound that frightened marshes hear
> From a leper in his lair.

He speaks of the yearning for and also terror of the Sun:

> And, as we prayed, we grew afraid
> Of the Justice of the Sun.

This informs one's picture of what might be going on inside the prison of the Leo Image.[294] A man condemned to death, however, can greet the place to which he will be liberated:

> With open mouth he drank the sun
> As though it had been wine!

The astonishing direction that this poem takes summarizes Steiner's Western Horizon Image at Scorpio. Wilde speaks about the true door, that is, the door of truth and love that the third man of zeal has found, in a completely disarming way:

> And some men curse, and some men weep,
> And some men make no moan;
> But God's eternal Laws are kind
> And break the heart of stone.
> ...
> Ah! Happy they whose hearts can break
> And peace of pardon win!
> How else may man make straight his plan
> And cleanse his soul from Sin?
> How else but through a broken heart
> May Lord Christ enter in?

Here is a man who has suffered through the territory of the first two men of zeal, either as victim or as perpetrator. And he has succeeded, late in his life, heartbroken, to discover the truth and love of the Sun-Being. Thus he lifts up into this degree its completed work, as a confirmation and strengthening of its test.

From the famous aestheticist, creator of the "masterpiece of pure nonsense," this move toward true depth is a hallmark of someone who is working actively with his Birth and Death Images.

A brief endnote to Wilde's life: After his imprisonment, he nicknamed himself "Melmoth" after *Melmoth the Wanderer*, a gothic novel written by Charles Maturin in 1820, which features a scholar who sells his soul to the devil in exchange for a hundred extra years of life. This puts Wilde squarely in accord with Faust from the Leo Image and Calderón's Cyprian from the Taurus Image.

BRIEF MENTIONS

Let's mention a few other historical personalities related to this degree. Alfred Wegener was a Bode who died into this degree in 1930, after Steiner's life. He is the one who proposed the theory of plate tectonics, that is, the notion that the continents of the world fit together at one time in the earth's evolution. We can note the extreme zeal in those who rejected his theory, and went to great lengths to persecute him for holding these views. As a consequence, continental drift, now accepted by science, was obscured for three decades. Historians have commented on the excessive negation that came his way—does this have anything to do with the Image of his death? We will mention him again later on, when we talk about Louis Agassiz.

David Ben Gurion died into this degree in 1973, and though he lived later than Steiner, his zeal illustrates the Image. Ben Gurion pulled together the entire nation of Israel, becoming its first Prime Minister and Minister of Defense. He considered that the establishment of Israel ended the exile of the Jews nearly two thousand years before. His emphasis on military strength and his stronghanded reprisals against those who got in his way made him many enemies.

Aleister Crowley died into this degree in 1947, that is, well after Steiner's life, yet a sense of completion of our presentation of this particular Solar Cross demands that we mention this complicated person. Did his zeal affect others? Yes. He practiced and taught magic, including dark magic, which had an effect on many people. Some people swear by his techniques, literally, as he used curses in his invocations. His books are usually under lock and key in bookstores, and eyebrows are raised when you ask to see them. Why? Because he plumbed the depths of sexual excess as a means to personal power. Relating to Antares, the Death Star, he summoned the spirits and energy of the dead and even turned to necrophilia. Imagine passing through the gateway of your birth, and passing the personality fragment of this one! As we say, he is complicated, and a person with a relationship to this Solar Cross needs to learn about what imprint Crowley may have left in this degree. A brief quote from Crowley summarizes his approach, and places him firmly amongst the zealots of this Image: "Do what thou wilt shall be the whole of the Law."[295] Seen generously, this pronouncement echoes Nietzsche: "...that symbol and motto that was reserved for the highest grade alone, as their secret: *'Nothing is true, everything is permissible!'* ... Truly, that was *freedom* of the spirit."[296] However, in Crowley, personal will for personal ends becomes the highest standard, no matter what the effects on others. Crowley predicted that once one took the oath "to perform the Great Work, which is to obtain knowledge of nature and the powers of my own being," it would "rouse automatically the supreme hostility of every force, internal or external, in his sphere."[297] Resistance can be assigned to the Hardener and the Illusionist, but in Crowley's case also to the natural resistance of a society that cannot permit everyone to pursue and realize only their personal desires.

Crowley agreed with Nietzsche that "everything is permissible." Steiner agreed also, provided that it was used by the "highest grade," in this context meaning those who had trained their own willpower with the strongest discipline of thinking. One can imagine Crowley as attaching to Steiner's work in some way through this choice of a gate of death. Parasite-like, this abuse of the notion of freedom can seek out a true exponent of freedom such as Steiner without hindrance from linear time. We have to be aware of such possibilities when we ponder soul realms and star gates.

Rudolf Steiner's Relationship to the Western Horizon Image

When we look at others whose lives are related to this Image, we can learn some things about the Image itself. We see clearly that zeal requires followers. In the Image, the ascetic does not only discipline himself in some distant cave. He makes everyone suffer. The military commander directs others how to abuse the enemy. The inquisitor does not keep his thoughts to himself, but wants everyone to think in a certain way, demanding punishment for those who don't.

Likewise, the historical personalities exercised power over others in order to get them to do something. Edward III and Churchill commanded armies. In Wilde's case, there were the audiences awaiting his next audacious costume and his next bizarre statement. In Wilde, we have the most personal view. He spoke about the younger men in his life, for whom he was mentor. All of these men of zeal had followers, students, and disciples.

What about the followers, students, audiences, protégés, and mentees of Rudolf Steiner? How did he affect them? We hear that "he burned the candle not only at both ends but also in the middle"[298]—did he demand that of others around him? Did he ask others to join him in shouting out the Abwoon Prayer every afternoon so that the walls shook, or suggest that they do the same? What strongly personal relationships did he have with others? Were there men and women too? What was the quality of his magnetism?

How can we assess the quality of the relationships he had with those around him? We can read accounts such as the following from his personal secretary, Guenther Wachsmuth, about the work on the first Goetheanum:

> Rudolf Steiner worked untiringly with the artists, inspiring, counseling, correcting, supplementing, and most of all taking part himself in the carving and painting with the artists who were bringing his building model to realization.... From early morning till late in the evening, he was at the building place. There the work of all those occupied in the task was concentrated upon carrying out the inexhaustible stimulation which he gave to every one of them. The spiritual greatness, human goodness, and practical ability of Rudolf Steiner imparted the harmony of a common spiritual and artistic direction to all these persons.[299]

Great words, showing that he had indeed the powers that zeal brings, that he worked *with* people rather than against them, and that indeed he was devoted to finding love and truth in action. Therefore, we can say that he succeeded in realizing this Image. Still, reading this account leaves one unsatisfied. It doesn't bring across the passion we would have hoped for. But what else could Guenther Wachsmuth have said to convey this passion to us? It seems to me that no words would have sufficed. This kind of Image, as well as the Image from the Eastern Horizon, must be experienced, up close and personal. The axis of the Horizon Images demands something very intimate and personal. For Steiner, we have to glean this from the accounts that we have about him.

In the embrace of the Threshold Star, Antares, you have to have a relationship with death. You have to understand the limits of your earthly powers. When we see what Steiner put into the Goetheanum, we can ask, as many have, "Wasn't he clairvoyant? Couldn't he see the fire coming? Couldn't he have stopped it?" Indeed, given that Anna Samweber claimed to have warned him from her own clairvoyant powers, why did he not perceive what was happening and stop it?[300] We could discuss the extent of Steiner's clairvoyance, but the main point is this: At some point, you have to understand that you are powerless before the decisions of the gods to determine the length of your life and your works, that, indeed, many things are not vouchsafed for your knowledge. Thus the power that we see exercised in the men of zeal in this Image ultimately finds its edge at powerlessness. That was what happened with the third man of zeal—he found his limit and learned his own fundamental powerlessness in the way he thought he should express it. Then he found a power moving *through* him that was new and actually more powerful than what he had done before, the power of love leading to living truth.

The Issue of Zeal in Rudolf Steiner and Anthroposophy

The power that zeal confers can also be spoken of as charisma, allure, shakti, and magnetism. It asks no questions and entertains no questions—it simply *knows* the right way of thinking and doing things. It can create support for many good initiatives, as well as cults and wars.

Zeal can lead to the feeling that there is one right way of doing things. In anthroposophy, which is a philosophy of balance, this creates some interesting paradoxes. For example, when you hear stated over and over again that people have become "tireless workers" in the cause of an anthroposophical initiative, you can admire the special energy that inflames their abilities, but remember that "tireless" often means constantly exhausted but striving onward—an unhealthy state of being human. Or consider that the concept of freedom has such importance in anthroposophy that anything that a listener does not agree with can become grounds for a charge that the speaker is constraining the listener's freedom: another paradox.

Consider, too, that Steiner spoke often of his observations of spiritual worlds and the evolution of humanity and the cosmos as "absolutely certain facts."[301] A reader of Steiner's books or lectures will recognize phrases that add up to something like this: "Anyone who looks into spirit worlds in the most simple scientific, that is, non-emotional or 'objective,' manner will confirm that these completely new concepts are true, and that conventional science is completely wrong about these things." Steiner does invite others to develop their own capacities to become practitioners of "spiritual science," but many have not been able to do so, and therefore cannot confirm or disconfirm Steiner's "scientific" observations. As "science" has come to mean something that can be observed by others and tested by them, can we call this a science? How can you affirm or deny that the Moon came out of the Earth in Lemurian times, or that humans had a jellyfish-like consistency then? A few can glimpse these as facts from inner experience. Many can't. Those hearing these great ideas from Steiner must face a great choice—"either I take what he says on faith, or I cannot participate in this movement with these fine people." Steiner claimed that every concept he gave came from his personal discoveries in spirit worlds. However, we see many speakers who give out these concepts as a kind of gospel without their own personal experience. That is zeal at work, which is always greater in disciples and students than in the teacher.

Zeal can fuel many good works. It can also lead to dramatic exclusions. Not long after Valentin Tomberg brought his *Anthroposophical Studies of the Old Testament* to the Goetheanum, Marie Steiner said, "Is it permissible that such Studies of the Old Testament by Mr. Tomberg should have *Anthroposophical Studies* as their subtitle? ... Is it conceivable that someone as young as Mr. Tomberg, who has just turned thirty-five years of age, already has the necessary maturity to be an esoteric teacher?"[302] These words illustrate the effect of zeal, whereby Marie Steiner, on account of her closeness to Rudolf Steiner, understandably could not see the possibility of anyone else being an esoteric teacher, let alone the young Valentin Tomberg. But, of course, Tomberg was bringing the results of independent anthroposophic thought, exactly what Steiner would have encouraged.

We have no interest in parading the parochialism of the Anthroposophical Society here. Suffice it to say that the issues of who's in, who's
out, and who decides continue to plague an organization whose founder
had a connection with zeal at his birth. However, it was at his Western
Horizon, the place of setting, and we can also see many people connected
with anthroposophy who have matured to love and living truth, not only
in the warmth of their being but in numerous practical applications in the
world. They have developed a talent for evaluating the new concepts given by
Steiner from their own experience of spirit worlds. May their example serve
to confirm that Rudolf Steiner did indeed overcome the traps that ensnared
the men of zeal, and may all those who follow do the same.

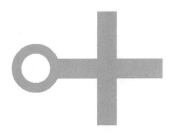

11. THE EASTERN HORIZON IMAGE

WHEN YOU STAND with the Sun above you on your birthday, the Gate Image explodes in warmth and light directly above you, the Earth Image lies directly beneath your feet, the Eastern Horizon Image heralds what is rising in your life, and the Western Horizon Image heralds what is setting.

The Eastern Horizon Image is the final Image of the Solar Cross of Rudolf Steiner's birth. We find it at fourteen degrees and thirty-three minutes of Taurus, at the center of the Bull, indeed near the Eye of the Bull, Aldebaran, the Life Star. Recall the statement from the Foundation Stone Meditation:

> Let from the East ignite
> What through the West takes form.

What comes from the East in Steiner's Solar Cross?

You know the routine. Get (your writing things) ready, get set (to turn the page), go (turn the page, read the Image and make a mind-map).

Eastern Horizon Image at Birth

Miners refine their ore by fire. A marriage is kindled in sensuality and refined by spiritual fire. He who has the bride is the bridegroom. The best man has also sought that bride. Seeing a marriage of spirit fire, the best man rejoices at the union and backs away.

WORKING THE IMAGE

Take the time to create your mind-map and to let the Image work on your Imagination. This Image seems different from the others. The parts don't fit together as neatly. It doesn't tell a simple story as does the Conception Image. It seems more conceptual, more ethereal. This means it will take more time to understand it. Take that time by making another mind-map. Your discoveries will be well worth it as you continue on this quest.

INITIAL IMPRESSIONS

The Earth is mined, and we have a marriage. At the Western Horizon Image, there is certainty. In contrast, at the core of a marriage are questions: "Will you marry me?," and later, "Do you take this person to be your lawful wedded husband?" The questioner may seek a certain answer, but the question is open, leaving the responder to answer in freedom.

Preceding the marriage, a threesome—two men vying for the bride. Jealousy does not erupt; rather, the groom's friend comes away happy for everyone. In human terms, one imagines that there was a time when none of the three knew which man would end up with the woman. Then it all became clear who belonged together.

There is an ore at the center, something that the miner's fire purifies. What is the ore of a relationship? What is the essential substance—an ore— in a twosome? Right away we see a theme so important to Steiner—the difference between the "sensual" and sensory, and what lies beyond it, what Steiner called the "supersensible." Before we apply this to Steiner's life, let's work the Image further.

BACKGROUND

In this earth sign of Taurus, the Teacher speaks to miners about what they know about, earth and ore, noting that ore is refined by fire, just as they must permit themselves also to be refined.

He speaks about marriage, especially to those in mixed marriages, where the two partners have different religious backgrounds, noting that their burden is greater, as they must find a way to become clear, strong, and unified in their religious activity, while not being distracted by sensuality.

John the Water Initiator speaks on this Solar Day the third line of the Image,[303] "He who has the bride is the bridegroom." The parable gives one the sense of a human drama that parallels the divine drama. Two friends court a woman. She chooses one. In a typical storyline for a movie or a television sitcom, this would spell all kinds of trouble. Danger would threaten as sensuality led to passion, unrequited love, miscommunications, jealousy, threats, and danger. In the Image, the second man graciously backs away, stating clearly, "He must increase, but I must decrease."[304] He becomes the best man at the wedding, without jealousy, filled with joy.

This story wouldn't make a movie. Why do we have to make our arts into displays for conflict, miscommunications, and the lowest in life, thus modeling the worst for each other?

The bride is Sophia herself. The groom is Christos, her brother, her consort, and her mate. John the Water Initiator speaks about rejoicing at hearing the groom's voice—in Greek, *phone* (pronounced fohn-EE), also meaning sound, vibration, or word, reminding us of the beginning of John's gospel, "In the beginning was the Word, the Logos, the Sound."

The Hebrew name for Sophia is Shekinah,[305] the elusive feminine presence sought by all the men studying their large tomes of learned works. This is their goal, the one who illumines the Temple, who inhabits with her sensual body the Holy of Holies, who inspires and fills with life force, who protects the sacred places of Israel. When asked how it came to be that Jerusalem was destroyed by the Romans in 70 c.e., the wise men explained, "Oh, that's because Shekinah had left that place already."[306] Behind all politics, the explanation has to do with the lovely and powerful Shekinah.

The Plains Indians of North America have a similar understanding of the much-desired Divine Feminine, as shown in the story of White Buffalo Calf Woman. In brief, she visited to give wisdom, helpful practices, and the way of the pipe to these tribes long ago. Two warriors noticed her first, in the waving grasses of the plains. One was struck by her beauty and resolved to have sex with her, whether she wanted to or not. She accepted him into her cloak, but when she opened her cloak again, a skeleton fell out—unbridled sensuality showing its identification with death forces. The other warrior also saw her beauty and, seeing that she was surrounded by celestial light, bowed to her instead. He became her first student.

There are many other stories about the encounter with the Divine Feminine. Someone with a personal relationship to this Image is charged to find them. In the language of spiritual economics, the decision to honor the feminine constitutes an upgrade from identification with the personality to identification with the soul.

Water Initiation as Marriage

As the Sun approached fourteen degrees and thirty-three minutes of Taurus, John the Water Initiator continued to initiate people at the first site where he worked, at Ainon, near the Sea of Galilee. At the same time, the Teacher moved the water initiation that he offered through his students from the third site (Ono) to the second site (Gilgal). Thus all three sites of initiation were activated along the River Jordan, another appearance of three. The connection between earth and heaven through the ceremony of water initiation sings through most powerfully on this day.

Links to the Galaxy

This Image comes from the same place in the heavens where Aldebaran can be found, which we have described in Part I as the Life Star, the bearer of the "I AM" for humanity.

Richard Leviton's *The Galaxy on Earth* (mentioned in the previous chapter) links the star Aldebaran to the Dome of the Rock in Jerusalem, the place on Mount Moriah where the Temple of Solomon was built. The Romans razed the temple in 70 c.e., and the Western Wall, a holy site where Jews have gone to pray for centuries since, is thought to be the only remains. Higher up on the hill, a mosque also stands upon the site. Finally, one can visit the Dome of the Rock, which shelters a bare rock beneath a very ornate covering. From that rock Muhammad was reputed to have sprung up on his horse to heaven in his Night Journey. On that same rock, Abraham is said to have offered Isaac to God for sacrifice, an act of complete surrender to Divinity. Divinity accepted the offer of Abraham's will forces and turned away the knife from Abraham's son. Aldebaran is about life force. Perhaps

Abraham's intuition about Aldebaran led to the Talmudic tradition that "Abraham had a great astrology in his heart, and all the kings of the east and west arose early at his door."[307]

The rock beneath the dome is reputed to be the first place to harden from the plastic conditions of the Lemurian time, when what we now depend on as solid earth moved easily. Beginning at this point solid ground was provided for the heavenly wedding to take place between the Divine Feminine and the Earth. The doors of the Holy of Holies at the center of the Temple of Solomon were opened at dawn, particularly at the spring equinox, to receive the gift of the Shekinah—the Divine Feminine, the Sophia, the essence of the Mother and of Mary—through the Sun. Fire coming from the East to take form in the West was most honored at that particular place.

Drama Within

Aldebaran works in world history, and it also works within. Life force meets life force; the bridegroom and bride meet as soul. The "best man" as the more superficial worldly personality stands as protector at the door of the sacred soul room. The personality desires this union, too, but it cannot meet the Shekinah. The mature personality becomes fulfilled when it assists, not when it tries to step into the place of the soul. To put the personality in its proper place, we must refine the metal-bearing ore of our being with fire, to separate the bright molten metal of the soul from the rest, what miners poetically call slag.

In this Solar Day, the process of soul gaining the upper hand and the little ego backing away is pictured in its smoothest operation. The best man, sensuality, and John don't disappear. A new balance is struck, and they become servants of a marriage that is a living truth.

SACRED MARRIAGE

This day, this day, this, this
The Royal Wedding is.[308]

So writes Steiner's Star Brother Valentine Andreae in the *Chymical Wedding*.

This Image links the starry heavens with earthly affairs, showing marriage as the intermediary between the cosmic and the sensual in the most positive way: a marriage with the Divine Feminine in which we are all grooms. The words "sacred marriage" have been bandied about by many, but full understanding of the term requires reverence: hushed tones, the lighting of a candle, a private conversation. Sacred marriage is an inherent quality of this Solar Day.

Sacred marriage is kindled by sensuality, but cannot be sustained by it. Sensuality has to be experienced, then mastered and transcended. As the Hierophant speaks in Steiner's mystery play *The Soul's Awakening*,

> The light that weaves the web of spirit-worlds
> can never penetrate into such souls
> where passion spreads a mystic fog between.[309]

However, the Image tells us that sensuality is not absent. It is the kindling. If we have ever tried to start a fire with large logs and no kindling, we know we need the small stuff that lights quickly, flashes with fire, and turns up the heat. Then the larger pieces can begin to burn and we need no more kindling.

As such, this Image balances the masculine with the feminine, the identity of the bull with that of the heifer. Aldebaran as donor of life force and especially of the "I AM" becomes both fierce—the Bull—and also nurturing—the Heifer. Hathor, the heifer-headed Egyptian goddess, has a softness about her that must be added to the sign of the Bull.

HISTORICAL PERSONALITIES

> This day of grace, this day of grace,
> The Royal Wedding shall take place.
> If you by destiny and choice
> Are bidden to the feast, rejoice! …
> No guest this Wedding may endure
> Who keeps not watch and is not pure.
>
> —JOHANN VALENTINE ANDREAE,
> *The Chymical Wedding of Christian Rosenkreutz*[310]

Who are the personalities that accompanied Rudolf Steiner through the Solar Cross of birth into this life in relation specifically to the sacred marriage?

Composers First: Luigi Boccherini and Marcel Dupré

Both of the composers linked to this Image are Bodes, that is, people who united their life's work with this Image. As you ponder this Image, indeed, this entire Solar Cross, listen to the works, especially the works later in life, of Luigi Boccherini, who died in 1805, and Marcel Dupré, the great composer for the organ, who died in 1971.

Shall we consider, in this Image, how Boccherini was called "the wife of Haydn"? Can we enjoy the story of how he handled the refiner's fire when his patron, King Charles III of Spain, ordered him to remove a passage in a new trio that he had written? Boccherini rewrote the piece, doubling the offending passage, and was promptly dismissed. A contemporary said of him: "If God chose to speak to man he would employ the music of Haydn; but if he desired to hear an earthly musician, he would select Boccherini."[311] One is the bridegroom, and one the best man. Listen to the guitar quintets as you ponder this Image, also to the later symphonies, especially the second movement of Symphony no. 26.

Marcel Dupré united his life's work with this degree as a Bode long after Steiner's birth, so we don't imagine Steiner listening to his music as he came through the gate of birth. However, we can use Dupré's music to help us understand this celestial degree better. Listen to the organ music of Dupré, especially the music from the latter part of his life, where he leaves the rousing sounds of his youth and prepares the harvest of his life as an offering to this heavenly degree—the *Choral et Fugue* (opus 57) or the *Annunciation* (opus 56). These sounds can accompany you when you contemplate this Image.

Now let us travel to the sixteenth century.

Star Sister: Marguerite de Valois, "Queen Margot"

Marguerite was born on May 14, 1553, in the Julian calendar. Nicknamed Margot by her brothers, she was the daughter of Henri II and Catherine de Medici. Three of her brothers became Kings of France, as did her husband.

All of this is recorded in her memoirs, a series of twenty-one letters that she wrote about her life: a string of battles (relating to her Earth Image, Steiner's Western Horizon Image), imprisonments, escapes and releases (relating to her Western Horizon Image, Steiner's Earth Image), and marriages (this Image). In the lives of interlinking royalties, very much depended on who was married to whom.

Marguerite de France
by François Clonet,
Musée Condé, Chantilly

The pivotal event of Margot's life was a marriage, her own. Her mother arranged for her to marry Henri de Bourbon, who later became known as Henri de Navarre and finally Henri IV. Henri de Bourbon was a Protestant, a Huguenot, and through this marriage Catherine de Medici wished to knit two warring groups, the Huguenots and the Catholics, together.

Through most of the wedding, young Henri de Bourbon and his eight hundred Protestant men in black waited outside while the flamboyantly dressed Catholics inside went through their lengthy motions. Then he joined the bride at the front of the church. Both bride and groom stared straight ahead, not looking at each other. When the Catholic cardinal asked Margot if she would consent to the marriage, she was mute. Used to a wild lifestyle and many lovers, she resented being used as a political pawn. And she was young, nineteen years old. Her non-response went on for a time, until the King, her brother Charles, pushed her head into a nod.[312]

The wedding occurred on August 18, at a time of unusual heat in Paris, hotter than any summer in anyone's memory. Fancy costumes, created mostly for cold houses in winter, increased the heat. Here is the refiner's fire. What ore came of this fire?

During the wedding festivities, the French King Charles, manipulated by his mother, Catherine de Medici, commanded the French troops to kill all the Protestants. Immediately the fire of the Catholics' hatred for Protestants flamed up, and bands went out in every direction. Some estimate that they killed fifty thousand Huguenots in and around Paris. Margot resisted, giving protection to some, including her new husband. In *La Reine Margot*, she protests to her brothers, "You have killed my wedding guests!" How poignant in terms of the Image into which she was born. A large wedding completed, then one half of the guests kills the other half.[313]

By engaging in the subtleties of intrigue of the court, Margot assured the escape of her husband. First she convinced him to become a Catholic, which he at first resisted. Then she helped him return to Navarre. After many other twists and turns for Margot and Henri, Henri became King, reigning over a unified country from Paris. After a divorce from Margot, he fathered with a second wife the future Louis XIII, whom we have seen before, in the painting by the Star Brother Ingres.

Margot took a place in the palace, helping with her ex-husband's children, supporting the arts and aiding the poor. In her divorce agreement, she had insisted that she retain the title of Queen, so even in the presence of Henri IV's new queen, she was known as Queen Margot.

The refiner's fire in Paris challenged this nineteen-year-old. Petulant and stubborn on her marriage day, she quickly became a force of political power. Imprisoned many times, and released as many, her memoirs go from battle to intrigue to imprisonment to marriage—her own and others'. These were the terms of her Solar Cross, in this Image and in her Western Horizon Image (Steiner's Earth Image), that formed the boundaries of her life.

Now picture to yourself the wise Queen Margot, veteran of many experiences, as Star Sister holding the young Rudolf Steiner's hand, and imagine what that was like.

Star Brother: Johann Valentine Andreae revisited

> Where wedding bells began to ring,
> Where hymns were sung and trumpets blown,
> Where she was Queen and he was King,
> Where both were blessed upon the Throne.
>
> —Johann Valentine Andreae,
> *The Chymical Wedding of Christian Rosenkreutz*[314]

Andreae was born at Steiner's Earth Image, but he had much to say about marriage. He was introduced earlier, but let's get Steiner's summary of Andreae's work on marriage in relation to the present Image:[315]

Many ascetic nuns celebrated mystical marriages.... Valentine Andreae, in *The Chymical Marriage of Christian Rosenkreutz*, meant to express something that was more permeated with reality than the merely mystical marriage of Mechthild of Magdeburg, who was a mystic. The mystical marriage of the nuns only accomplished something for the subjective nature of man; by the chymical marriage a man gave himself to the world. Through this, something was accomplished for the whole world; just as something is accomplished for the whole world by the processes of nature.

A mystical marriage links an individual with Divinity in a personal, intimate, and private way. A sacred marriage links an individual with the whole world.

Star Brother: Count Nikolaus Ludwig von Zinzendorf

Born in 1700, Zinzendorf slowly found his way to the true sacred marriage. He sought a career in theology but rejected the Protestant dogma of the state Lutheran church and the cold rationalism of the culture of the time. Religion for him was a matter of the heart. Even at the age of ten, he had exclaimed, "I have but one passion—'tis He, only He."

Nikolaus Ludwig von Zinzendorf

His family, however, prevailed upon him to study law at Wittenberg. Here is Wittenberg again, the university of Hamlet and Faust, as we noted in the Image where we might have concluded that Wittenberg was a prison! And so it was for Zinzendorf, too, though he finished his studies.

His first love was Theodora, his first cousin, whom he courted most tenderly. Just when he was about to ask her to marry him, he found that his friend, Count Reuss, was also preparing to ask her. Then ensued something straight out of this Image. Zinzendorf proposed to his friend that they visit Theodora together, to see which way the wind blew. Zinzendorf resolved that his love should be purely the desire to do good. He saw that Theodora preferred his friend, and he backed away. He expressed his happiness at the match by composing a cantata for the betrothal ceremony, and in adding a personal prayer for the new couple that apparently brought many to tears.[316]

He married in 1722 and took a government post, apparently treading in the footsteps of his father, a Saxon minister of state of noble descent.

Something shifted when a group of refugees from religious persecution took residence on Zinzendorf's estate. This was the fledgling Moravian Church, known then as the Unitas Fratrum, based on the teachings of Jan Hus, a Bohemian who lived from about 1370 to July 6, 1415. Recall that the Hussites were protected by Rudolf II and by Frederick V. They performed the coronation of Frederick V in Prague. After the defeat of 1620, "that ominous year which weeps so that the skies fall,"[317] they were severely suppressed by the Catholic victors. Later the Unitas Fratrum came to be known as the Church of the Unity of the Brethren or the Moravian Church. They were the first alternative to the Catholic Church. Twenty-five years before Martin Luther's birth, they numbered a quarter million in Eastern Europe. They believed that the morality of the Catholic priesthood should be raised, that the Bible should be written in the common languages of each country, and that all people should be able to receive full communion, at that time reserved only for the priests. They opposed the sale of indulgences by the clergy, which were pieces of paper absolving the purchaser from past—and future—sins. They opposed papal infallibility and favored the primacy of the scriptures in all decisions. Many had been killed in the Thirty Years' War. The Treaty of Westphalia that ended it declared that each nation would follow the religion of its monarch. In unfriendly countries, the Hussites were further suppressed. By the time Zinzendorf met them, they had diminished in numbers but amazingly had not disappeared.

On the Zinzendorf estate, after a particularly powerful communion service on August 13, 1727, the entire community was set afire with religious zeal. They immediately instituted a perpetual prayer meeting, what we would today call 24/7, that lasted a hundred years, sharing what we will see with the first Bode might be called oratories. Perceive this also in the context of the Image: one man and one woman praying together for an hour each day, being replaced by another man and woman praying for the next hour, twenty-four women and twenty-four men in all. Thus they came to be known as "God's Happy People," partly from the realization of a sacred marriage.

Zinzendorf became very involved with this initiative, protecting the community from further persecution and giving them a place to thrive. He came to believe, "There cannot be Christianity without community." In truth the Moravian Church became what Rudolf Steiner would call a three-fold community, with balanced development of the economic, social, and spiritual sides of life. Thus the willing (the economic basis of living), the feeling (the social, political, and festival orientation of a community), and the thinking (the spiritual-artistic illumination of all) were developed in this little community. Zinzendorf developed a pedagogy, or theory of how to educate children. He began to travel to the Netherlands, the Baltics, even to America, where he developed Moravian communities, such as the ones at Nazareth and Bethlehem, Pennsylvania.

Zinzendorf so wished to avoid conflict that he even became an ordained Lutheran priest in order to make bridges between the general Lutheran community and the little church of the Moravians.

When his first wife died in 1756, he married the head of the Single Sisters of the Moravian church, his colleague in missionary work, Anna Nitschmann. He was fifty-six, and she was forty-one. At age fourteen, in recognition of her precocious work on behalf of the community, her name had been put into the lottery box for choice as the presiding elder of the community. The lottery came to her, and she became the overseer of the women of the community. Zinzendorf tried to dissuade her. The young peasant girl stood tall before the twenty-nine-year-old nobleman and landlord, reminding him that the system of lots meant that Divinity had chosen her for this job. After she had been further refined by the fire of communal living—for twenty-seven years—they married.

Opposition to the small sect rose and fell. At one point Zinzendorf was banished from his home; later he was accepted back again. He was able to earn an official government recognition of the Church of the Unity of the Brethren both in Germany and England. Opponents pointed out that the Church had a passionate, even erotic involvement with the wounds of Christ. Perhaps this indicates something of the sacred marriage that Zinzendorf had been seeking.

Zinzendorf told his people that each had to prepare for a sacred marriage. Speaking from the parable about a wedding feast where the King finds one man without a wedding garment, he found in that one man "all haughty people, all conceited people, all self-righteous people, all sanctimonious people."[318] A sacred wedding such as he experienced with Divinity required the kind of humility that we see in his Gate Image. Zinzendorf would have agreed with the warning from the *Chymical Wedding*, "No guest this Wedding may endure who keeps not watch and is not pure."

Certainly this Star Brother was interested in the same sorts of things as Steiner, and pioneered various initiatives that would have been dear to Steiner, two and a half centuries before. One can easily imagine how Steiner's soul may have benefited from this elder brother going on ahead. One of the things he learned, and copied, was the form of marriage, which we shall discuss at the end of this chapter.

Star Brother: Louis Agassiz

The biographies of the Swiss scientist Louis Agassiz, born in 1807, emphasize the famous people he knew, the scientific expeditions he undertook, the many books he wrote, and the Museum of Comparative Zoology at Harvard University, which he began. Perhaps one could say that he had such a strong internal fire that he had to live on top of a glacier for some years, studying its movements. Indeed, he courted the cold and was the first scientist to propose a glaciation of the world some thousands of years ago. This came at a time when Darwinists were assuming that things didn't change

Louis Agassiz

much—what was called uniformitarianism—in order to explain parts of the theory of natural selection. Agassiz opposed the Darwinian theory of evolution until the end of his life.

But what about the theme of marriage? You have to look very closely, as the biographers are more interested in the books and lecture tours. As a young man, Agassiz married, and his wife became ill. Seeking to make a living, he left for America in 1846, five years before Steiner's birth. He had the idea of coming back for his wife, or sending for her, but they never saw each other again before she worsened and died. Then he married another woman, who kept the house and raised the children from the first marriage. Our domestic reporting on Agassiz is limited mainly to "professor's wife" stories, for example: The new wife of the professor goes to put on her shoes, and in one there is coiled a poisonous snake. Through her screams, he explains that he has brought home five of these, and wonders aloud where the other four may be.

This example helps us understand that finding the soul gesture of a Solar Cross Image can be challenging, even more so when the person is famous and well published. We know that all of our Star Brothers and Star Sisters can be studied in greater detail in order to get a sense of the soul gesture of an Image, and this presses the point home. What was the quality of Agassiz' relationship to marriage, to a sacred marriage, to the sacred? The sacred marriage combines heavenly matters and earthly matters, so that we see the earthly paralleling or affected by the heavenly. This brings up the question—what was Steiner's relationship to women like? What of his early marriage, about which we hear so little? Indeed, what about his later marriage to Marie—what was it actually like? Agassiz' life raises these questions.

The Bode of Alfred Wegener appeared only briefly in the Western Horizon Image, since Wegener died into that degree in 1930, after Steiner's life. Wegener had proposed the idea of one vast continent, Pangaea ("All-earth") surrounded by the vast waters of Panthalassa ("All-sea"), a sacred union that split apart into the continents as we know them today. Agassiz and Wegener belong together in relation to Steiner because both of these Star Brothers understood the earth as moving, changing, transforming. Steiner's ideas included great changes of the nature of substance itself since relatively recent times, from the Atlantean period on. He understood the earth itself to be in constant change, looking back to the period of warmth (a period that he called Old Saturn), followed by the addition of light and air (Old Sun), then the addition of water (Old Moon), then the concretization of all these in the Earth itself.[319] If we see these plastic unions and separations in terms of fire and sacred marriage, it gives the theories of each of these scientists a feeling tone that lights up the theories themselves. Within the present Image of refiner's fire, the ore of the whole Earth and our whole beings within the Earth begin to have life. Anticipating James Lovelock's recent concepts of Earth as a living being (the Gaia hypothesis), Steiner said: "The earth is an organism with soul permeated by spirit, and ... the human being, as he lives as physical Man on the earth, is a member within this organism."[320]

Younger Star Brother: John F. Kennedy

John F. Kennedy

Sometimes we have to include a younger Star Brother or Sister, someone who may have been led by Rudolf Steiner's hand as he or she came to birth. Or, if we hold time loosely, we don't have to say that one came first and the other one later. We can simply see how they both show the resonance of the Image at work.

The birth of John Fitzgerald Kennedy into this Image shapes the way that we see him. We can perhaps recall what people most remember about his life: first, the way he died by assassination, which naturally connects more to his Death Image, second, his marriage to Jacqueline Bouvier, third, his politics that seemed so wonderful and ideal, and yet led the United States into wars in Cuba and Southeast Asia.

Everyone had watched this golden boy rise in fame and attainments, through his own efforts and those of his parents, Rose and Joseph Kennedy. He had gone through Harvard, then served in World War II, then become a Senator. On September 12, 1953, he married Jacqueline Lee Bouvier in the marriage of the century. There were 750 guests in the church with a Catholic cardinal presiding (note that Queen Margot's marriage also rated a cardinal's presence). Outside, they passed through three thousand well-wishers to a reception for 1,200 people. The first dance, for the bride and groom alone, was "I Married an Angel." The ice cream was sculpted to resemble roses. After fifty years, these details are still talked about. This was the marriage that adorned the covers of the main magazines of the time. This was the marriage that typified the mystique of this man, and eventually earned his whole world the name of Camelot. In the book *JFK and Jackie*, Kennedy's entire life has been written from the point of view of his marriage.[321]

What is Camelot all about? In part, it is about the Round Table of King Arthur, a symbol of the equality and diversity that we see in other Star Brothers and Sisters of the Horizon Images. The court of Camelot was inspired by a purpose, to find the Holy Grail. Conquest and conflict—and the zeal of Kennedy's Earth Image—served the goal. The means served the end. But let's look more deeply at that end. The Holy Grail symbolizes and confers a sacred marriage between the true bride and the true groom, a marriage in heaven brought to earth. We think of Camelot's flower-bedecked festivals, laughing children, knights in shining armor, great beasts that threaten the realm met by the courage of men who wear an ornament or a token of clothing from their lady (such as the garter referred to above), and after the adventure celebrations in large feasts under brightly colored banners where stories were told about the seeking of the sacred marriage. The public loved the sense of adventure with a romance at its center, even though the histories had been mixed together, Holy Grail, the President's Catholicism, and a sacred and sexy marriage.

The sacred marriage with spirit in the form of the Holy Grail has an underside. King Arthur struggles with his marriage. He's torn between Guinevere and Morgana, personalities that have been depicted in many different ways in books and films. Is Morgana a great magician or a nasty witch? Is Guinevere pretty and weak, or a mate that matches Arthur? The radiance of Camelot conceals a problem with Kennedy's Gate Image, marriage.

Fifty years later, we know more about Kennedy and the sacred marriage. He had the sensuality and the fire. He had the perfect picture-book marriage to Jackie. But he was unable to accept this. "No other president of the United States can have contrived to invent a life as recklessly promiscuous as his had become by the autumn of 1963,"[322] writes Peter Evans. Now many of his affairs are known.

Let's look elsewhere in Kennedy's life. As a young man, he became involved in World War II. However, he had had severe back problems and was rejected from the regular armed forces. He ended up with the Coast Guard, where the PT boat he commanded was rammed by a Japanese destroyer, throwing everyone overboard. Kennedy swam three miles to shore with others in tow, earning him an award for heroism. Because of the pain, he blanked out several times during this rescue. This was how the man acted under the refiner's fire. From the ore refined in such experiences came Kennedy's book, *Profiles in Courage* (1954–1955), which earned him the Pulitzer Prize for biography in 1957. Though his marriage suffered, he had the zeal of his Earth Image when needed—most of the time. There were a few situations where his zeal was aberrant, the two most serious involving Cuba.

In the invasion of Cuba at the Bay of Pigs, Kennedy had to confront the zeal in his Earth Image (Scorpio). He had become convinced by his advisors that the Cubans would welcome an attacking force and join it to overcome Fidel Castro's dictatorship. Zeal has a way of convincing you that the world is a certain way, in this case, that others will rise up in zeal to join your cause. The attack failed miserably, partly because Kennedy withdrew support by the Air Force and Marines that would have made it a full-scale invasion. Instead, there were botched attempts to make it look like an attack by Cuba on the United States.

The Cuban Missile Crisis in 1962 put the world as close as it has come to nuclear war. A hair's breadth away from a war to end all wars, Kennedy and his administration would not back down. It was Khrushchev who backed down, showing himself as less a zealot than Kennedy.[323] Had Khrushchev not budged, and had Kennedy kept up his stubborn refusal to negotiate, the world might have a very different landscape today. While the Bay of Pigs invasion showed a lack of zeal at important junctures, the Cuban Missile Crisis showed dangerously excessive zeal.

So much information came out about Kennedy's life after it was abruptly ended, about uncontrolled eroticism, extramarital affairs, addiction to drugs for the pain in his back, and so on. During his life, he'd been able to avoid scandal—partly through the influence of his potent supporters, but there was something else as well. Kennedy had what would be called "the right stuff" in the same era when that criterion was used to choose the first astronauts—and what we might call the "ore" at the core of his Gate Image. In his marriage, he failed to realize the potential of his Gate Image, but in the image that he portrayed to the citizens of the United States and to the world, there was a confidence and a charisma that inspired many.

THE BODES OF THE EASTERN HORIZON IMAGE

Who put their life's harvest into this degree, fragments of which might bode ill or well for one passing through into birth?

The Bode of Saint Philip Neri

Neri died into this Image in 1595. Let us note one interesting detail before going into his contribution to this degree. In 1593, in his seventy-eighth year, he persuaded Pope Clement VIII to withdraw the excommunication and anathema of Henry IV of France, who was, as we may recall, Queen Margot's ex-husband and father of Louis XIII, whom we mentioned at the Gate Image in discussions of Ingres.

Saint Philip Neri

Neri founded the Oratories, communities of secular priests, what some have called "a residential clerical club." We could add, "a *men's* club." Adult males over thirty-six years old were given simple rooms, but they had to pay their own expenses. A monthly fee was put into the communal account for food expenses, and all clothing, books, furniture, and medicines had to be purchased by the individual. Everyone, including the superior, helped out with the various tasks around the place, including waiting on tables.

By 1760 there were fifty-eight such Oratories in France and Italy.

The work of the Oratory involved "spiritual exercises" set to music—prayers, hymns, readings from Christian Scriptures, from the various Christian fathers and the Martyrology—all religious but not part of the formal liturgy or regular services. These were followed by a lecture or discussion of some religious question. The musical works illustrating scenes from biblical history were called *oratorios*. From their beginning under Neri's supervision, they evolved into a major musical form, developed to great heights of artistry by Handel, Vivaldi, Bach, Haydn, and modern composers. The best-known oratorio is Handel's *Messiah* (1742).

Neri was known for the excessive heat that his body poured out, requiring him to open the windows of his room and his shirt even in winter, and for the radiance of his face that poured forth to all. In 1544, while praying with devotion to the Holy Spirit, who had saved his life as a boy, a globe of fire entered his mouth and pressed itself into his heart. The fire of love became so intense that he stripped off his shirt and threw himself onto the cold stones to try to cool it. When he stood up, he found that his chest had expanded by the size of a fist, which caused him no pain. However, from his heart would come violent agitations. Those around him would describe these as "being like the blows of a hammer," shaking the chair in which Neri sat. At his death, medical examination of Neri's body revealed that he had broken two of his ribs, an injury attributed to the expansion of his heart while praying in the catacombs years earlier. He was beatified in 1600 and canonized in 1622.[324]

What was this internal and external fire all about? It was a spiritual marriage with the Madonna. Once, during an illness a year before his death (and thus also related to his Death Image), his friends quit his room, believing him dead. When they heard him shouting to the Madonna—"Ah, my most holy Madonna, my beautiful Madonna, my blessed Madonna!"—they rushed back in to find him prone and levitating a foot off the bed, in the ecstasy of his relationship to the Divine Feminine. This direct experience led to his cure from that particular disease.[325]

Neri's story shows just how passionate he was about the one to whom he was married—the Sophia imbued with Christ Light. This Bode would be very helpful in assisting someone birthing into this Solar Cross.

Neri's heart was made large by the visitation of the refiner's fire. What would an autopsy of Rudolf Steiner's heart have revealed? This is the kind of question that a historical personality can raise for one related to him or her. Just what was the quality, size, and power of Rudolf Steiner's heart?

The Bode of Pedro Calderón de la Barca

This Spanish dramatist and poet, born in 1600 and passing in 1681, paralleled Zinzendorf in his career choices. From an education at a Jesuit college, and the assumption that he would join the Jesuits, he dramatically switched and studied law, then served extensively in the military and wrote plays—seventy plays in twenty years. He joined the priesthood at the age of fifty-one but continued to write plays, specializing in *autos sacramentales*, short dramatic allegories to be performed during the feast of Corpus Christi, the Body of Christ. In all, he wrote 120 plays, eighty *autos sacramentales*, and twenty shorter comedies that he called *entremeses*. The themes of the development of masculine sexuality, and of love as a force of salvation run throughout his works.[326]

Perhaps Steiner received from the Bode of Calderón the gift of prolific output. Strikingly, in a lecture of February 18, 1922,[327] Steiner spoke about Calderón's play *El mágico prodigioso* (The Great Mage or The Wonder-Working Magician) in exactly the terms of the Image. Steiner compared Calderón's magician, Cyprian, with Faust, both accomplished in the worlds of philosophy, science, and law. Both feel empty. In both cases, a woman enters the scene: an ideal, a perfect woman. In Calderón's play, her name is Justina. "The drama depicts

Pedro Calderón de la Barca

her quite simply as a woman, but to see her solely as a female human being is not to see the whole of her."[328] She is a woman of beauty; she is the principle of Justice; and she is the Divine Sophia herself. Thus immediately we learn that Calderón wrote in the terms of the Image, at least according to Steiner's reading. Aligning further with the Image, Calderón depicts the learned magician feeling a passion for Justina, wanting her so badly that he employs the services of Satan, just as Faust did to win Gretchen. Justina wants nothing to do with Satan's allurements. To fulfill his promise to deliver Justina to Cyprian's bed, Satan can bring only a shadow form of her that, after he embraces it as the consummation of his lust, turns into a skeleton that speaks: "Cyprian, such are all the glories / Of the world that you so covet."[329] The dissatisfaction with the shadow form drives Cyprian mad. Because of Satan's manipulations, Justina is thrown into prison and condemned to death. In contrition for his deeds, Cyprian demands that he die also. The two meet at the beheading platform, and a great serpent flies through the air declaring that they are both saved, through Justina's continued virtue and Cyprian's transformation. They both rise up into heaven.

Where *Faust* could be said to focus on the theme of prison and release from prison, *El mágico prodigioso* focuses more on sex, lust, and coupling, just as we might expect from the different Images to which these authors are most related. We still get sex for Faust and prison for Cyprian, but the emphases accord with the Images to which the two authors are related. Calderón gives us two other threesomes, just as in the Image. Two men, servants of Cyprian, covet the servant maid of Justina. They solve the rivalry by agreeing to alternate days in her presence—a stalemate, literally, for there is no mating consummated. A bit more refined are the governor's son and his friend, who covet Justina. They begin with a duel for her hand, even though neither has told her about it. They each presume that the winner of the duel will simply walk up to her and say, "We both loved you, now he's dead, and you're mine." Many men do think this way, and are surprised when Sophia does not respond as expected. These men are very susceptible to deception by the Illusionist, who toys with them. They are sent to jail (Steiner's Earth Image) by the governor to cool off.[330] Again, a stalemate, a non-resolution of the Image.

All throughout the play, we hear about smokes and sulphurous fumes from fires that are not burning hotly or cleanly. We hear about fires from passion, volcanoes, and hell. Only in Cyprian do we see the refiner's fire turned up to a heat that causes transformation.

We look at this tale, realize that it relates intimately to the terms of the Image, and then wonder where to take it. Steiner gives us a hint: "The whole of the Christian struggle of the Middle Ages is contained in this drama."[331] An astonishing statement, lifting us quickly out of the petty level of this Image, about who gets the girl. The girl is powerful! The Demon sends all his forces against her:

> Abyss of hell prepare!
> Thyself the region of thine own despair.
> From out each dungeon's dark recess
> Let loose the spirits of voluptuousness,
> To rain and o'erthrow
> Justina's virgin fabric pure as snow.
> A thousand filthy phantoms . . .[332]

Justina is able to withstand the Illusionist's temptations. As in the Image, she is strong, as Sophia. The main drama lies in Cyprian, for he is the one who changes. He is the one who desires with volcanic fire the woman to possess for himself, and learns over time that she is meant for a heavenly partner. He assigns his soul to the Demon, signing the contract in blood, and realizes in the end that his soul is identical to the holy being of Justina herself. This realization liberates him from his bargain with the Demon.

Steiner says in reference to the play: "Christ came down to earth because human beings could no longer see what in earlier times they had seen in their middle, rhythmic system [the pulses of heart and lungs], which was [in ages past] trained by the breathing systems of yoga."[333] So we are dealing with the core of feeling, and taking into one's heart the certainty of the light of Christ consciousness. Steiner does not recommend the breathing systems of yoga, finding them outdated and even dangerous for modern times. Between the thinking of the head and the outward movement of the limbs, he recommends movement and speaking to develop this middle area of the human being—not to transcend the earth plane, but to find the truth here on earth.

The true marriage with the spirit of Christ-consciousness occurs for Cyprian and Justina at the moment of death. At that moment, the woman and the archetype of Justina, as well as the man and the archetype of Cyprian, are married with each other and with Divinity.

Pedro Calderón de la Barca was a good Bode for Rudolf Steiner. Both Goethe and Calderón imagine the apotheosis, loss, and redemption of the "I AM" in this Aldebaran-Antares axis, expressing the essence of that anchoring polarity.

Steiner would recommend the very same process of development, loss, and redemption, but on earth, not in a martyr's death with eyes upturned to heaven. Though Cyprian concludes that "human glories are but ashes / Dust, smoke, wind, delusive, empty,"[334] just before he soars into the glories of heaven (as Faust also does in Goethe's imagination), Steiner would suggest that Cyprian find his way to spiritual realization on the earth, for "Christ came down. Because they no longer have him in their memory of the time between death and a new birth, human beings must find him here on earth."[335]

The Bode of Anne Brontë

Anne was born in 1820, the last of six siblings, and her mother died a year after her birth. Her two eldest siblings died of tuberculosis when she was very young, two others died when Anne was twenty-eight, and Anne herself died at the age of twenty-nine. Her poetry was first published in 1846, in a volume with the poems of her sisters Charlotte and Emily. Her first novel, *Agnes Grey*, was published the next year, two years before her death. It examined the life of a governess to the rich, following a young woman "with no good prospects" through the lives of the wealthy and their

Anne Brontë
(sketch by Charlotte Brontë)

spoiled children, ending with the governess starting a school and finding happiness with a man who loves her for herself. Thus marriage is the final goal toward which everything else seems like an obstacle on the twisting and turning way.

Anne published a second novel in the year before her death. *The Tenant of Wildfell Hall* has come to be known as one of the first feminist novels. It follows a woman who leaves her abusive and degraded husband to support herself and her child. One critic at the time pronounced it "utterly unfit to be put into the hands of girls." Steiner would have liked that show of courage, especially given the constraints on the lives of women in this time.

Anne passed into this degree on May 28, 1849, just over eleven years before Steiner was born into this Solar Cross.

To illustrate the values Anne held in accord with the Image in Taurus, we give selections from the first page of *Agnes Grey*:

> My mother, who married [my father] against the wishes of her friends, was a squire's daughter, and a woman of spirit. In vain it was represented to her, that if she became the poor parson's wife, she must relinquish her carriage and her lady's-maid, and all the luxuries and elegancies of affluence, which to her were little less than the necessaries of life.... Finding arguments to no avail, her father at length told the lovers they might marry if they pleased, but, in so doing, his daughter would forfeit every fraction of her fortune.

Note this repetition of the choice made between a marriage based on class, convenience, and the maintenance of wealth, and a marriage based on the fire of love. Anne Brontë takes this further, speaking of her grandfather's attempt to suppress her mother's true love:

> He expected this would cool the ardour of both; but he was mistaken. My father knew too well my mother's superior worth, not to be sensible that she was a valuable fortune in herself ... while she, on her part, would rather

labour with her own hands than be divided from the man she loved, whose happiness it would be her joy to make, and who was already one with her in heart and soul.... You might search all England through, and fail to find a happier couple.

The one who has the bride is the groom. Though other men may not be happy, the "best" man can be happy at others' happiness.

The Bode of Henry Thomas Buckle

Can we feel an impression from someone passing the threshold in a place where we have particular sensitivity, that is, in our birth Solar Cross, even after we have passed through that hallway in our birth?

Henry Thomas Buckle passed over the threshold on May 29, 1862, when Rudolf Steiner was fifteen months old. Buckle is interesting because he tried, like Steiner, to create a theory of everything. Buckle looked at all of history and planned a multivolume *History of Civilization*, but completed only an introduction to the part on England and Europe before he died of fever in Damascus.

Steiner too took on the history of civilization, understanding the progress of cultures from Old India to Old Persia to Old Egypt, then the classical civilizations of Greece and Rome, and the present European Age. Steiner took this even into the future, with the forthcoming Slavic Age, followed by the seventh and last age, the American Age. In *An Outline of Esoteric Science*, Steiner went out into the cosmos, showing the history not only of civilization but of all creation.

Buckle's introduction shows the conclusions that he never got around to demonstrating in the actual text of his planned work. Can Buckle's ambition, and what he did accomplish, at least in its projected scope, be seen as affecting Steiner's interests?

Toward the end of his life, Buckle wrote an argument for immortality based on the yearning of the individual's affections to regain communion with the beloved dead. Thus the severance of a marriage is only temporary, as the groom will find the bride again in time. He is also known to have said, "Acts of virtue must far outnumber acts of vice or humanity would long ago have perished," a sentiment that Steiner would echo.

Honorable Mentions

We could mention just a few others who were Bodes in this degree. Pope Sylvester II (d. 1003), originally known as Gerbert of Aurillac, gained the reputation of *Stupor Mundi* (Wonder of the World) for his advanced learning. English anthroposophist Daniel Dunlop died here in 1935, as did the author Boris Pasternak in 1960.

Goethe Revisited: His Western Horizon Image

Johann Wolfgang von Goethe is a Star Brother of Steiner's, and this is Goethe's Western Horizon Image. When we looked at Steiner's Earth Image, we spoke about Goethe and his great work, *Faust*, which gave us hints about how Goethe related to the Image of his birth. Goethe also had something to say about fire and marriage. He might have been Philip Neri when he said, "My heart is burning within my breast,"[336] adding that

> I search through the world with all my senses,
> ... I reach out for the most exalted words
> And call this fire that burns inside me
> Infinite, eternal—yes, eternal![337]

> For what does the fire burn?
> He [Mephistopheles] fans within my breast a savage fire
> For that bewitching image of a woman;
> So from desire I stagger to enjoyment
> And then, enjoying, languish for desire.[338]

The climax of Part One, with Gretchen in jail, tells us something about the real wedding. "It would have been my wedding day,"[339] she exclaims, and we cringe, knowing that dawn marks her execution day. Jail, wedding, and death commingle. Only later do we find her soul in heaven and know that, indeed, it was her wedding day, a wedding with the divine.

In *The Fairy Tale of the Green Snake and the Beautiful Lily*, Goethe develops the theme of marriage further. The Young Man is destined to marry the Beautiful Lily, but when he crosses over into her realm, he is lamed, then dies. As Steiner explained, "One who approaches the ruler of the supersensory kingdom without being inwardly ready will suffer harm in life, as does the Young Man."[340] But the Snake then sacrifices herself by becoming a bridge from the earthly sensory realm of necessity to the heavenly supersensory realm of freedom. The sacrifice may be seen as the ultimate in "conversation," recommended by the Snake as grander than gold or light itself, a conversation between the earthly and the spiritual. From this sacrifice—the refiner's fire—the Young Man is resurrected and then can marry the Lily. As Steiner summarized, "The two become one"—two characters, two realms, two realities, becoming one.[341] This reinterprets Steiner's Eastern Horizon Image to mean that the best man, in the end, after a death and a sacrifice, consummates the marriage that he had passed over. He becomes that which he had seen in his more deserving friend.

Rudolf Steiner and the Sacred Marriage

When we ponder this Image, its background, and the historical personalities related to it, then hold before ourselves the life of Rudolf Steiner, some impressions arise. First and foremost, how is it that anthroposophists know so little about Rudolf Steiner's married life? First there was Anna Eunicke. Working on the Goethe archive in Weimar in the 1890s, Steiner joined her household to tutor her daughters. She followed him when he moved to Berlin in 1897, and they married on October 31, 1899. Recall that Steiner's "enlightenment" experience occurred very close to this marriage. How do we comprehend that juxtaposition? What was the quality of the marriage? How did it happen that Steiner moved out in 1903, and labeled Anna his "estranged wife" in 1907?[342] What occurred between their wedding day and Anna's death in 1911?

"My life with the Eunicke family," Steiner wrote, "afforded me the opportunity of a quiet basis for a life that was both inwardly and outwardly extremely eventful. For the rest, a person's private life does not belong to the public. It is of no concern to the public."[343]

Yes, we can respect a desire for privacy. Yet Steiner's autobiography is full of much lengthier accounts about his women friends and many other private matters. We would not have noticed the absence of details about marriage, perhaps, had we not been given this particular Eastern Horizon Image.

We are told of a woman in Dornach who had the Theodora part in one of Steiner's mystery plays, decided that she was fated to be Steiner's soul mate, and pursued him relentlessly. Steiner had to take the whole issue public, to make it clear that he was not "available" for this sort of thing. Were the woman's feelings sexual? Were they spiritual-sexual? Or was "sexual infatuation" an easy label that diverted attention from something more at the core of Steiner's relationship with everyone in the Society? How refined by fire were his relationships? An entire book is devoted to the details of this particular case.[344] It's one of those incidents where rumors fly, everyone has an opinion, and no one knows what's really going on, including those most closely involved. Steiner's lectures to the Society to cajole them into banishing the offending parties seem from a distance very poorly handled. The realm of the Eastern Horizon Image is Steiner's cutting edge of growing.

The power of sexuality truly affects every human relationship. No "spiritual" relationship is without it, for sex is passion for life; it is Dionysos; it is freedom in expression. It need not be acted upon in the physical body, but only a slight increase in perceptual capabilities will show that it takes place between astral bodies in all sorts of situations. Certainly a kind of sexual energy runs between spiritual teachers and their students. You may call it shakti or prana or whatever you wish, but this primal life-force energy is what makes the world go round. It attracts students to teachers as much as it attracts males to females, and vice versa in both cases. If you wish to find the sacred marriage with divinity, to link yourself truly with Sophia or Christ or whatever divinity you relate to, then you had better become familiar with that sexual energy, and then refine it in fire, rendering the ore and the fire itself purer and purer. The Image suggests a kind of split there—the "best man" understands that the true marriage takes place with a kind of refined energy that he does not have. He is the one who will seek the more earthly sexuality. Even if the Image contrasts earthly sexuality between physical bodies, and heavenly sexuality between souls, sexuality flows in both relationships. Anthroposophists sometimes frown on sexuality, but they are cutting themselves off from the divine marriage. As the poet Bode Baudelaire cautioned, "A man unfamiliar with the arts of love is like a monkey playing a Stradivarius."

Some say Steiner married Marie von Sivers, whose Russian name was Mariya Yakovlevna, whom he had known for many years, to make himself "unavailable" for others who might pursue him. Their wedding was not a John Kennedy and Jacqueline Bouvier affair, where fashions and the food were talked over and remembered ever afterward. It was more of a Count Zinzendorf and Anna Nitschmann situation: a marriage between professional spiritual coworkers, forged in a fire of strong karmic connection. Marie was secretary, traveling companion, confidante, "constant translator" of many languages (Steiner only ever mastered German), master of ceremonies for all the many meetings, keeper of manuscripts, editor of the first publication company, keeper of the typewriters and manager of the transcriptionists, tapping away as fast as possible to keep up with Steiner's speaking and correspondence. She attended Steiner's early lectures in 1904, where an observer described her as having "golden hair ... blooming and delicate complexion ... unbelievable eyes, fiery blue, like sapphires ... a mouth, delicate but firm ... a well-formed chin."[345] They were married in December 1914, after a long acquaintance—or perhaps the slow burn of a very refined fire? Steiner said, "Marie von Sivers herself will always be with me, our union remains indissoluble."[346] This sounds very like a sacred marriage.

Was it true, as some claimed, that Marie Steiner was a reincarnation of the librarian of the Greek Lyceum and the secretary of Aristotle? And that Steiner as the reincarnated Aristotle joined with her again? Recalling that the great philosopher was pressed into service to educate the new Macedonian conqueror, Alexander, was there an Alexander to Steiner's Aristotle? A most interesting study by Margarete and Erich Kirchner-Bockholt names Ita Wegman as the reincarnated Alexander. Indeed, it lays out evidence that Steiner was Thomas Aquinas and Dr. Wegman was Aquinas's companion and nurse in old age, Reginald of Piperno. Steiner wrote to Wegman, "You once separated from me to lead a life of widely influential deeds. Before then, with far-reaching consequences, we had unveiled before our consciousness a vista of mighty impulses."[347] "Consciousness" is singular, shared between them. Steiner also sent her a verse:

> The power of an old bond lives for me in thee
> And when thou bringest me love
> It becomes for me the bearer of the Spirit,
> Every clear signal of thy soul
> Is a messenger to me from realms of spirit.[348]

Was Steiner's relationship with Ita Wegman sexual? Let's take the cue from another of Steiner's confidantes, the feminist writer Rosa Mayreder.

> There are two ways in which the freedom of the personality may be saved from the oppression of the sexual instincts: by asceticism, the mortifying of the flesh ... or by that reconciliation of the two conflicting sides of man's nature which is brought about by love.... For love permits of the sexual relation being transfused with a content of personality.[349]

We can expect that Steiner took the latter route, though this did not stop a jealousy arising within Marie Steiner, shown after Steiner's death with Wegman's expulsion from the Anthroposophical Society.

∞

It's important to realize that we don't know about personal and intimate aspects of Steiner's life, including sexuality and the quality of his human marriages. Indeed, he opposed conventional marriage. As his student Andrei Belyi put it, "It was whispered that he destroyed marriages. This criticism, like any distortion, was not altogether unfounded."[350]

Steiner had no patience for the economic or sexual arrangements that typified the normal middle-class marriage. "Every true marriage he greeted with enthusiasm."[351] Only those who had gone through the refiner's fire, and surpassed economic and sexual arrangements, could have a true marriage.

How did love—the stated accomplishment of the Western Horizon Image and the unstated underlying force of the entire Eastern Horizon Image—appear in Steiner? We just can't get a sense of it from reading lectures. Andrei Belyi again fills in for us: "He never said, 'I love, I feel.'"[352] That puts him out of the New Age movement immediately. Was he then stuck back in his Conception Image as the dry and unbending philosopher? Belyi denies this:

> He made love visible indirectly, a faintly noticeable glowing sun-warmth around his mouth, around his eyes, that outlasted years and bore fruit in moments of despondency. He had, as it were, a therapeutic smile; his countenance blossomed in the abundance of perfect love into a barely discernible rose-exuding fragrance.[353]

This passage is well worth reading again, referring as it does first to the Sun, then back to one's personal moments of despair, then to "perfect love" and then to a sensory experience of the flowers blossoming on the Rosy Cross. Belyi speaks about Steiner's smile with frustration because he says that not one of Steiner's photographs showed it. He speaks about Steiner's love with frustration, because none of the printed works revealed its true extent.

Belyi was able to describe the most astonishing transformations in the presence of "this atmosphere of glowing warmth that purified me from my sins and my pain."[354] Is not this the description of a sacred marriage?

Another sort of sacred marriage in Steiner's life was observed by Anna Samweber on the evening of the burning of the first Goetheanum:[355]

> From below, the colours of the metal organ pipes glowed in the flames and I heard a sound but, at the same time, a shrill cry. When I looked to the other side, to the de Jaagers house, I saw Rudolf Steiner surrounded by a huge white aura of light.... I knew something was happening between the Doctor and the burning building. My companions did not notice this and the picture vanished.

Could Steiner be said to have been married to his building? More likely to the work of hundreds of artists, and to a spiritual ideal. Steiner had said that the burning of the Temple of Artemis at Ephesus seared its genius into spiritual realms. By tradition, this occurred on the night of Alexander's birth. As we bring together Alexander, Ephesus, Artemis, Sophia, Goetheanum, Aristotle, Steiner, and Wegman, we can take guidance from Steiner's *Philosophy of Freedom*: "Through thinking we join together into one everything that we separated through perceiving."[356] Linking everything together in a kind of marriage-with-all, we see Steiner standing near the burning building as the best man assisting a sacred wedding, via the refiner's fire, between his students who had built the place and spiritual realms.

When Anna Samweber asked Steiner if they would meet again, he replied, "If you ponder on who I am with love and enthusiasm, we shall meet again."[357] Indeed, many anthroposophists claim to experience Steiner's presence here and now, a feeling of his supervision and guidance lighting their way from unseen realms. These are spiritual marriages with those who knew him, as well as with those who have "found anthroposophy" since then.

∞

The absence of ready knowledge about Steiner's earthly marriages causes us to ask about Steiner's spiritual marriages in the refiner's fire of his inner being. Musicians, poets, and painters give us their inner lives in their art, and we can look to Steiner's art to understand more than we might learn from words. When we see a pure and powerful gesture in eurythmy that in that moment opens the entire heavens to our feeling life, we realize that we have experienced in some part a legacy of Rudolf Steiner. When we admire the glass windows of the new Goetheanum, we may realize that here lies an imprint of Steiner's inner fire. Even artwork that was created under his direction, or squarely within the anthroposophic work that he inflamed in others, offers hints about his inner life.

There is a story about Steiner's great sculpture in wood, *The Representative of Humanity*. This towering piece, over thirty feet high, depicts the Christ-Being in the center holding at bay the Illusionist above and the Hardener below. We will speak more about it later, but will say here that the power of this piece warrants a long visit at its location in the second Goetheanum in Dornach. As the story goes, had Steiner created this piece in the way that he wished, it would have been too difficult for humanity to bear. That arouses one's curiosity! What would it have shown? There's a warning that there is a refiner's fire at work, that power is in play, that zeal is here, that a marriage is possible though not ensured, certainly not for the unprepared. To the East, we feel the seat of Aldebaran, the Life Star. To the West, we feel the power of Antares, the Star of Death and Life. Recall some of the Star Brothers, Star Sisters, and Bodes, and you see how power plays out in the world and in relationships in these Horizon Images of Rudolf Steiner:

Queen Margot		Alexander Nevsky
St. Philip Neri		Edward III
Zinzendorf	+	Oscar Wilde
Anne Brontë		Winston Churchill
John F. Kennedy		Aleister Crowley
		Shirley Chisholm

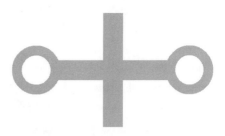

12. RESONANT MOMENTS IN THE EAST-WEST HORIZON IMAGES

As we did in chapter 9, we will look at the celestial events during the time of gestation as well as a few events during the life.

PRENATAL ANTICIPATIONS IN RELATION TO EAST-WEST HORIZON IMAGES

PRENATAL PLANET CROSSING THE EAST-WEST HORIZON OF THE BIRTH SUN	CORRESPONDING DATE IN STEINER'S LIFE	STEINER'S AGE
Mercury in Taurus	June 22, 1861	4 months
Mercury in Scorpio	July 12, 1901	40 years, 4 months
Mercury in Scorpio (Rx, retrograde)	October 22, 1906	45 years, 7 months
Sun in Scorpio	May 5. 1907	46 years, 2 months
Mercury in Scorpio	October 11, 1912	51 years, 7 months
Venus in Scorpio	June 5, 1915	54 years, 3 months

How different from Steiner's Conception Sun position, which showed little activity during the prenatal period!

We see that during Steiner's gestation Venus and the Sun crossed the axis of the East-West Horizon Images once, and Mercury four times. In astrological language, we would say that this axis and these points were "square" to the Birth Sun position. In our view, the choice of these points for stimulation was made in spirit realms. In other words, pre-earthly intentions were impressed into the developing fetus and can be mapped out onto the life in dates ranging from near birth to the age of fifty-four.

The first crossing, Mercury at the Eastern Horizon Image in Taurus, takes place at such an early age that we don't know what occurred in the life. Then comes a long gap of four decades where these Images are not stimulated.

The next earthly event from this axis comes in Steiner's fortieth year, which begins a Mercury "loop," that is, Mercury apparently crossing a point, then going backward (retrograde) over that point, then forward again. A Mercury loop calls attention to the time of our life when relationships have particular importance for our destiny. That's easy to say about a period that covers ages forty to fifty-one! Who doesn't have important relationships between forty and fifty-one? However, let's watch out for this theme in the three times that Mercury crosses the Western Horizon of the Birth Sun.

What might we expect of Mercury and Venus during the prenatal period? We might expect to see places where Steiner met individuals and groups that were significant in a karmic way, related to the destiny patterns of his soul. Technically, the soul, upon crossing the threshold, passes first into the Moon sphere. Then it expands to the Venus sphere, which has to do with a review of relationships with individuals in one's life. The soul then expands to the Mercury sphere, which stimulates a review of one's relationships to groups, that is, destiny groups, research circles, nationality groups, language groups, esoteric groups, and what one might call one's *karass*.[358] Then one passes into the Sun sphere, which relates to one's sense of individuality *per se*, that is, the soul's experience of many lives, not just this one. As there is a confusion about which comes first, the astronomical Mercury or the astronomical Venus—indeed a confusion about the possibility that these names have been switched since ancient times—we don't differentiate too rigidly between the personal and group realms of relationship.[359]

Prenatal Mercury crossing the Western Horizon of the Birth Sun, in Scorpio, projected to July 12, 1901, age forty years, four months

Sometimes we have mountains of information about a particular time. Sometimes, as here, we have only a few tidbits, but those tidbits can reveal a great deal. We have on July 3 Steiner's eulogy for Hermann Grimm, who had died on June 16. Here Steiner strengthens a connection to an individual and a group that were important to him. He spoke about Grimm as someone could easily have spoken about Steiner himself: "He was for us a living bridge to the age of Goethe. Those whom Hermann Grimm knew personally experienced him as though Goethe himself were speaking to them."[360]

In his autobiography, Steiner described his coworkers at the Goethe and Schiller Archives in Weimar, all of whom strove to resurrect the contributions of these great poets of German civilization. Steiner renders each character colorfully, to the point of caricature—bringing to mind the talent of his Star Brother Honoré Daumier. In Steiner's descriptions, we see that quirks of character in and of themselves become a direction of the will, in other words a kind of zeal. Thus, while Steiner could describe Grimm as "a sort of spiritual descendent of Goethe," he could also recall a luncheon meeting with Grimm in 1891: "I had before me a man whose spiritual vision reached as far as the creative spiritual, but who would not lay hold upon the actual life of the spiritual, but remained in the region where the spiritual expresses its life in man in the form of fantasy."[361]

Steiner noticed that Grimm detested details, attaching firmly only to vague eulogies of Goethe. Thus even a fantasist, one prone to the shifting rosy clouds of the Illusionist, has developed a kind of rigidity—a kind of zeal—that we find in the Western Horizon Image, in this case a zeal for the vague and rosy.

Elsewhere, Steiner related the following story about Hermann Grimm:

> Hermann Grimm's only response to such mention of the spiritual was to make a warding-off gesture with his hand, indicating that this was a realm he was not willing to enter. A supremely true utterance, consisting of a gesture of the hand, was made at that moment.... He made a parrying gesture because he had no notion of how to *think* about the spirit.[362]

This alerts us to watch for the gestures through which zeal moves, and for other gestures of will—those of eurythmy—noting how these express the foundations of the truth and light indicated in the Western Horizon Image.

The turning over into forty years of age was of great significance to Steiner. In private correspondence he said: "I had reached the age of forty, an age before which no one in the sense of a master may openly appear as a teacher of occultism. Everywhere where someone teaches earlier than this there is an error."[363]

Prenatal Mercury, moving retrograde, crossing the Western Horizon of the Birth Sun, in Scorpio, projected to October 22, 1906, age forty-five years, seven months

The two lectures Steiner gave on October 13 and 19 seem more related to the Gate-Earth Axis. "The Relation of Precious Stones to the Human Senses" brings in the notion of stones in the Gate Image, and "The Relation of the Human Senses to the Surrounding World" relates to the release of the prisoners into the light of the world that we find in the Earth Image. Based on the insights expressed in this period, a School for the Art of Jewelry—the precious gems from the Gate Image—was established in Dornach.

Exactly on the projection of this Mercury crossing, on October 21, the General Meeting of the German Section of the Theosophical Society took place. Steiner gave the first report, noting the resistance and obstruction in the world to the work of the Society. In other words, he spoke about the zeal of opponents. Steiner said: "Let us do positive work without polemics—even polemics against our attackers.... Everything can be judged by its fruits. We shall do positive work leading to the higher realms; fighting does not solve problems." In this he spoke directly to the men of zeal from his Western Horizon Image.

In writing about this time of Steiner's life, Wachsmuth notes: "He refused on principle to consider reading from manuscript as has become widely customary nowadays, and maintained, therefore, always a living contact with his audiences." Again, surrounded by the "right way" of doing things, that is, zeal, Steiner chose to align himself with life force.[364]

This meeting laid the ground for the separation from the Theosophical Society, which occurred a few years later, interestingly in the next prenatal event of the East-West Horizon Axis.

On this day, Steiner delivered a lecture to a group of his most serious students. There was no shorthand copy of the lecture made. Notes from a member of the audience record, "Sublime, exquisite, there are no words to describe what we received. The Masters of Wisdom ... were surely in our midst. The strength that issued from our Teacher was great. In the end I saw him beaming and youthfully transfigured." Something special came through on this day, aided by the perturbation of Mercury on the Western Horizon Image.[365]

Prenatal Sun crossing the Western Horizon of the Birth Sun, in Scorpio, projected to May 5, 1907, age forty-six years, two months

Sun conjunct Antares means, of course, Sun opposed Aldebaran, for these two stars lie exactly opposite each other in the zodiac. The Sun never conjuncted Aldebaran in utero. However, the Aldebaran-Antares axis was encountered here and activated. As we have seen, this is the axis of Life and Death, where the Life pole comes primarily from Aldebaran, and the Death pole from Antares. Together they give us the possibility of resurrection.

Eleusis. How interesting that just at this time Rudolf Steiner became a theater director for *The Sacred Drama of Eleusis* by Edouard Schuré, to be performed at the summer conference of the Theosophical Society. Eleusis was the mystery center outside of Athens where for centuries hundreds of people would come annually to the "lesser mysteries" and a smaller number to the "greater mysteries." The initiates would prepare for a year with little ceremonies, daily exercises, and prayers. Then they would march the twenty miles from Athens to the ritual center, singing and dancing. Once there, they stood in complete darkness, in turns chanting or in silence, and occasionally a window would open to let a shaft of light illuminate tableaux of the secret teachings. To reveal these teachings outside the circle was punishable by death. The dominant theme was death—the inevitable death of human beings—then resurrection, as the soul enjoyed the miracle of birth from a woman. All this was overseen by the goddess Demeter. The core teaching was summarized in a stalk of grain, the grain that gave its life to feed humanity, the grain that fell from the stalk as if dead and then miraculously sprouted into new life, just as a human being would apparently die but then reincarnate in a new form.[366]

The Sacred Drama of Eleusis, rewritten by Steiner for this occasion, with his wife-to-be, Marie von Sivers, playing Persephone—the beautiful young woman who is abducted by Pluto into the underworld—took Steiner's attention during this time, preparing a performance for the great conference of Munich that began on May 18, 1907.

Presidency of the Theosophical Society. The Founder-President Colonel Olcott had just died on February 17. On his deathbed, in conversation with two unseen "ascended masters," he had nominated Annie Besant to suc-ceed him. Some people thought Olcott—that is to say, the Masters advising Olcott—should have chosen Steiner. True to the power of a predestined event, the Sun during Steiner's gestation did not shine on Steiner as Presi-dent of the Theosophical Society. Had Steiner been named, there might never have been an Anthroposophical Society or movement. Sun on Sun: the (prenatal moving) Sun working on the (Western Horizon of the Birth) Sun wanted something absolutely fresh and new from the heavens.

On exactly these days, we can see from Steiner's writings the struggle with issues of the Western Horizon Image. The topic is the upcoming elec-tion, and the apparent nod of the unnamed Masters toward Annie Besant—Besant's Masters as well as Olcott's. We have a copy of an article that Steiner wrote in *Lucifer-Gnosis*, the newsletter of the German Section of the Theo-sophical Society, as well as a letter he wrote to the Executive Committee of the German Section, and another to all the members of the German Sec-tion, all dated within a few days of the prenatal crossing of Sun over the Earth Image position.[367] Certain ways of speaking in these letters makes it clear that zeal is in the air. "I now wish to be as far removed as possible from influencing anyone in the very slightest." However, Steiner is too deeply involved, and everything he says has the hint of influence in it. Later in the same document he confesses, "I do not therefore make a secret of the fact that I also have great misgivings." He cautions that he cannot reveal what he knows—"I am not allowed to speak about these revelations"—but few could miss what he intends. He begins the process of separating out his followers from others: "Once more I emphasize: Whoever has no faith in me, in these matters should pay no attention to me," implying that the ones who have faith should pay a lot of attention.[368]

The whole system of Masters, advanced human beings hidden to all but a chosen few, and some Masters more evolved than others, evokes imagina-tions of what the three men of zeal listened to. Where do zealots get their directives? From higher powers. Of course, some of these powers may be cor-rect, and some may not be. How do we tell? In the end Steiner sees the whole thing as an inappropriate mixing of politics with the most intimate spiritual matters. In a letter marked "Private and confidential!" Steiner confides to a friend, "It may be that the Masters will no longer bother themselves about a society that assigns to them a role such as the one presently upheld by Adyar [the central office of the Theosophical Society]," namely the appointment of a bureaucratic head of the Theosophical Society.[369] What hurts Steiner the most is the misuse of power that can be wielded by the mention of Masters. "The Masters made me do it" is the Hardener speaking.

A letter from Steiner to Marie von Sivers shows how the Society was struggling with who should hold office, how to change the statutes of the organization, whether to boycott a vote, that is, how the Sun at Antares reconciles issues of organizational life that has ceased to serve human life, and how to bring about a death and resurrection of that organization.[370]

This encounter with who should shine forth as the President of a mighty initiative was forecast in the movement of the Sun over the position of the Western Horizon Image. The flurry of activity increased in intensity, then everything changed direction. We could certainly label this a meeting with destiny.

The Munich Conference. The conference took place at Pentecost in 1907, and in that event we find also the themes of life, death, resurrection, and ascension.

The curtains of the hall of the conference were red, as were the carpets. A large red pillar stood at the front of the room, marked with a "J," for Joachim. Another pillar, blue, on the other side, was marked "B," for Boaz. The seven seals of John's Revelation decorated the room.[371] All of these flowerings of spiritual art were in active preparation during this period, activated by the Sun during Steiner's gestation. One can think of this in terms of the Eastern Horizon Image—all is prepared as for a great marriage, the sacred marriage of each person to his or her "I AM," to the soul.

The German theosophists under Steiner's direction were becoming independent of the leaders of the Theosophical Society. Then as now, the actual practice of "theosophy" meant the dedicated study of the works of Blavatsky and a few others. Clearly Steiner had unleashed a flood of creativity, stimulated in our view by the power in the life-death axis of Aldebaran-Antares, in turn stimulated by the prenatal Sun. As Steiner recounted later,

> Thus it was that, outwardly, my smaller circle had the appearance in the earlier years of being a section of Mrs. Besant's esoteric school. Inwardly it was anything but this; and, in 1907, when Mrs. Besant was among us at the Theosophical Congress in Munich, any outward connection was also

brought to an end as a result of an agreement made between Mrs. Besant and myself.[372]

From death comes a new energy, Antares as the phoenix.

During this time Steiner interacted with the women of his life. He competed with Annie Besant for the direction of the Theosophical Society. He celebrated the anniversary of the death on May 8 of Helena Petrovna Blavatsky. He worked actively with Marie von Sivers, casting her as Persephone, directing with her on the direction of the play of Eleusis, and working with her in the direction of the organization of theosophy. In the background was his wife, Anna Eunicke; in the foreground his future wife, Marie von Sivers.[373]

Thus we see that this turning point in Steiner's career was set into motion when he was a fetus in the womb sensitively registering celestial events.

A Sacred Marriage

> Theosophy can be built. One can build it architecturally.
> —RUDOLF STEINER, 1907[374]

During the 1907 conference a model for what would become the first Goetheanum was revealed.[375] Its two hemispheres atop two cylinders intersecting look like a very crude depiction of marriage:

Frances Yates tells us that the two large towers of the castle at Heidelberg housed the sacred dramas during the brief golden age of Frederick V, in which Andreae played such an important part.[376] In Steiner's models the two towers have been brought together and partially merged. From above it would look like a form that we viewed in relation to the interacting spheres of Aldebaran and Antares:

The lens of the human eye has a similar shape to the overlapping area.

However, there was an important difference between the overlapping circles that we have been viewing and the design of the first Goetheanum. These cylinders were not the same size. Their proportions were 3:4: if the smaller one on the left in the photograph had a radius of three units, then the larger one had a radius of four units.[377] The geometer Frank Chester relates this ratio to the Egyptian 3-4-5 triangle, also known as the Pythagorean triangle. Chester relates the tradition of 3-4-5 to Moon, Earth, and Sun. In this proportion, then, the building relates to the meeting and marriage of Moon and Earth.[378] The center section then has two different arcs and more closely resembles the profile of the human eye.

During this prenatal stimulation of the Sun upon the Western Horizon of the Birth Sun position, the notion of a polarity between the earthly and the heavenly was brought into form. Steiner imagined that the place in the middle, where the two spheres of heaven and earth overlap, was the place where revelation could be delivered and where it could be heard. He had intended that the *Representative of Humanity* statue be placed at the far end of the spiritual side, and that the earthly side be adorned with paintings of the progress of evolution of human consciousness. The in-between place, where the etheric enlivens physical substance, would be where Divinity touched human beings, through their souls. Steiner planned that speakers would stand in this middle area, receiving from Divinity, and delivering to human beings, gems of truth (from the Aquarius Image).

This depicts the marriage of the Taurus Image. Steiner consummated his sacred marriage architecturally.

Prenatal Mercury crossing the Western Horizon of the Birth Sun, in Scorpio, projected to October 11, 1912, age fifty-four years, three months

Several kinds of events occurred in this last crossing of Mercury, all important for the destiny of the movement that Steiner was activating.[379]

Theosophical Society. A student noted from a talk given at this time: "It is understandable that esotericists think their esoteric life is now threatened by all that is presently happening in the exoteric theosophical movement."[380] Given that the decision to separate from the Theosophical Society was presented on January 13, 1913, we can imagine that at this time Steiner was formulating the details of the final announcement. In this divorce of what had seemed a perfect marriage he determined a new and different course for the group that was following his teachings. Here we have Steiner ostensibly managing groups, but behind it we must see him managing souls, the ones who have sought in service of their soul development to study esoteric teachings. He guides those under his care, teaching them, in the terms of the Conception Image, to invoke and receive the Sun-Being. In the end, he sees this separation as fated at his birth: "At the point of departure of my present incarnation it came strongly and symbolically to me that we in Central Europe have the task of freeing ourselves from the special interests of theosophy."[381]

Steiner also speaks to his students about the efforts of the Illusionist to make them susceptible to men of zeal. From the notes of a student, "There are sluggish souls who do not want to learn; of these the luciferic powers [Illusionist] take control and suggest to them that, instead of studying, instead of seeking the direct path ... they would rather wait for a world leader who will give to them with both hands, so that they do not have to exert themselves."[382]

Final Mystery Drama. We learn from the chroniclers that Steiner was preparing his final mystery drama during this time for production in the next summer. We can find in *The Soul's Awakening* various themes that relate to his Images, and here note one that relates to the Eastern Horizon Image theme of marriage via the Western Horizon connection with Antares and death. In Scene viii of that play, we see the protagonist, Johannes, incarnated as a woman in ancient Egyptian times, mourning the loss of her lover, who is this day being initiated into the temple:

> This is the hour in which he dedicates himself
> to serve the ancient, holy mysteries,
> which tear him evermore away from me.
> From out these heights of light to which his soul
> has turned, the ray of death descends on mine.—
> Without him—there remain for me
> but sorrow on the earth—
> renunciation—suffering—and death.[383]

We see, however, that the tearing apart is not "evermore," for Johannes and Maria continue their sacred marriage for lifetimes. Indeed, this whole series of mystery dramas can be seen as a love story of the soul.

Journey to Italy. Exactly on the day of the conjunction, October 11, Steiner left for Florence and Assisi, visiting the places of activity of Saint Francis, who we can all agree was an extraordinary man of zeal, indeed a man, like Paul, who lived at the edge that joined ascetic rejection of the world and the realization of love in one's own being.

One can also see this trip as a replay of Goethe's formative trip to Italy, in which he played through all the Images of this Solar Cross. Goethe was thirty-seven when he embarked on his trip, Steiner fifty-four.

Steiner visited the house of Giotto. He admired the works of Michelangelo. Especially mentioned is his visit to the Medici Chapel, where in Michelangelo's tomb for Lorenzo and Giuliano Medici he saw how the artist had mastered in three-dimensional form the divine elements of the human being. Two seated figures represent the two dukes. Lorenzo (grandfather to Steiner's Star Sister Marguerite de Valois), with face shaded by a helmet, personifies reflectivity. Giuliano holds the baton of an army commander, showing us activity. Below them recline the figures of "Night," a female giant, writhing in uneasy slumber, "Day," a muscular male, looking over his shoulder with exaggerated awakeness to the point of wrath, the male "Dusk," and the female "Dawn." A Madonna and Child can also be found, along with various saints.[384] What did Steiner learn from this statue that he might have translated into his grand *Representative of Humanity*, for which he began models less than two years later?

As Lorenzo was the one to whom Machiavelli addressed his tract *The Prince*, a work completely at odds with Steiner's vision of a balanced three-fold social order, one wonders if Steiner pondered these questions during his visit to this shrine.

New View of Gospels Suppressed. At the end of September Steiner finished the lectures on the four gospels begun in 1902, ending with the gospel of Mark, the lion. During these lectures he received a telegram from Holland, from the Order of the Star of the East, the local branch of the Theosophical Society. It stated clearly that what he was speaking about could not be made public. The subject matter was to be "forbidden or suppressed" (*verboten oder abgesagt*). Thus Steiner confronted the zeal of others. This obviously had a large impact on the decision to separate the two groups, the monument of the Theosophical Society and the fledgling Anthroposophical Society.

The Sacred Site at Dornach. During his lectures on the gospel of Mark, Steiner visited nearby Dornach and climbed the red clay hill "with which both destiny and free spiritual decision lastingly united him in the following year," in the siting of the Goetheanum. About the profound moment of this first visit to the future site of his greatest physical work, Wachsmuth adds: "This constituted a decisive turning point in karma."[385] Whose karma? Steiner's, surely, but also that of all those who would, through Steiner's assistance, recall their connection to the adventures of Parzival in the ninth century. For here was where much of the drama occurred—Trevrizent's cave nearby, the Grail Castle nearby, the whole area holding a geographical memory of the successful search for the Holy Grail. On this day, Steiner united himself, and those who followed, more intimately with the Grail Stream, that is, the entire myth and reality of the San-Graal, the Sang-Real, the cup and the blood of the sacrifice of Christ, and the growth in human souls that resulted from that. Recall our mention of John F. Kennedy and his association with Camelot. Steiner's visit to this place, set as a destiny moment in his own gestation period, reignited for many the importance of that tale for human development.

Indeed, this tale of Parzival covers the map of the East-West Horizon axis. It tells of carnal love and spiritual love; of battles, imprisonment, and people so headstrong (zealous) that they fight the wrong person or have to be defeated to get their thinking turned around.[386]

New View of Life after Death. Just after this transit from Mercury, Steiner began a series of lectures on the realities of life after death, mapping out the process in very clear terms, including how the soul prepares for a future birth. Wachsmuth declares: "Never before in the history of mankind had these questions been expounded in such a way as to include the details of actual events between death and reincarnation."[387] While one may find other references in the writings of the highly intellectual philosophical schools of Vedic and Buddhist thought, for the West, Wachsmuth's statement holds true.

What is the most profound effect of this kind of knowledge? To connect one with one's soul purpose, and, in the realms of Mercury and Venus, with one's destined relationships with individuals and groups. When did this important initiative take place in Steiner's own biography? When Mercury crossed the site of the Western Horizon of the Birth Sun, very near the star Antares, Threshold Star, Star of Death and Rebirth.

The Year of Michael's Ascendancy. Steiner declared that Michael had become regent of the Earth in 1879. Normally, we would think of this as the year that Steiner himself turned eighteen. But there is a curious feature in one of Steiner's publications that suggests otherwise. In a calendar that Steiner made for 1912–1913 (from Easter to Easter), not repeated in any subsequent year, with new artistic depictions of the twelve signs of the zodiac and the spiritual biographies of people associated with each day, he counts the years from the crucifixion and resurrection of the Christ being.[388] Thus 1912 becomes the year 1879. On the front cover of Steiner's calendar for 1912 appears the number 1879! As Michael's Day is September 29, we can see the actual introduction of Michael's regency as September 29, 1912, within the zone of influence of this prenatal transit of Mercury. This gives an entirely new dimension to the notion that Steiner first walked on the hill of Dornach on September 29, 1912. Did he meet Michael there?

All of these events were laid down at conception, destiny meetings that would reveal themselves when Mercury strummed the string set up at the time of spirit entering matter.

Origin of Eurythmy. The entire discipline of eurythmy was born from a single question: a mother asked if there might be a new and more spiritual form of dance that her daughter could learn. Steiner replied that he had been awaiting the question, and his answer blossomed into an entire approach to movement and gesture.[389] So much hinged on that question, as Steiner said that he would not come forth with new material until asked. Working with the daughter, the seventeen-year old Lory Smits, Steiner began to create the discipline that is now taught and practiced around the world.

Prenatal Venus crossing the Western Horizon of the Birth Sun, in Scorpio, projected to June 5, 1915, age fifty-four years, three months

I have spoken above about the pursuit of Steiner by an infatuated woman, beginning in the autumn of 1914 and addressed directly by Steiner in lectures from August through September 1915.[390] We can imagine that upheavals were occurring in the Society in June—though we don't know what specifically occurred during early June in relation to this drama, Steiner mentions the extent of the gossip in his lectures. This is in line with Venus's task of posing questions about relationship issues, and with the Image's exploration of the quality of relationship between people.

Exactly during this time, Steiner was working on another drama, a rendition of the Ariel scene from Part 2 of Goethe's *Faust*.

Theater in its best form employs the sacred word, the power of human speech in its primal and highest power. In this scene, Faust experiences the being of the Spirit of the Earth awakening to the music of the spheres at sunrise. One could say that the awakening at dawn stimulates world powers to repeat and reaffirm the foundations of true speech.[391]

Let's look into this short scene a little more deeply. Imagine Steiner as the director:

> Any one who took part in [these] rehearsals … could observe Rudolf Steiner completely immersed in his element as creative molder.… At the beginning of the rehearsals one stood helpless and clumsy on the stage; the movements were often terribly awkward, the speech too affected or intellectual for popular types of persons—in short there was every sort of blunder of the beginner. Dr. Steiner sat in the hall observing; now he sprang up, came on the stage and played every single role himself.[392]

Eurythmy was added too—and we see here how Steiner's notion of speech included gesture—"speech made visible." He was truly the "creative molder."

What about this Ariel scene? It begins with Ariel just before dawn, to the music of Aeolian harps, speaking over the reclining Faust:

> When the vernal blossom showers
> Sink down to embrace the earth,
> When green fields, alive with flowers,
> Fill all human hearts with mirth,
> Then great spirits, looking lowly,
> Rush to help those whom they can;
> Whether wicked, whether holy,
> They would heal the wretched man.[393]

This defines the task of true speech, to "heal the wretched man." What is "wretched" about the man, Dr. Faust? His separation from his own divine origins, that is, his forgetting. Thus Ariel sets herself the task of reminding the "wretched man" of his true origins, his karmic streams, exactly what we would expect from a connection with the realm of Venus.

We could go on with this little scene, imagining the gestures that accompanied this artful outpouring, and sensing Steiner's participation in the uplifting of human speech into the realm of cosmic word. Indeed, hear what Ariel says next, instructing the airy spirits around Faust's sleeping body, and hear it as the lifting up into the cosmic realm of word as nascent action. "Watch" is a naval term meaning a two-hour term of staying awake and vigilant; "Lethe" is the goddess of forgetting, who accomplishes her task with water.

> You who surround his head in airy beauty,
> Prepare to do the elfins' noblest duty:
> Relieve the bitter conflict in his heart,
> Remove the burning arrows of remorse,
> And cleanse his mind of memories that smart.
> Four watches mark the nightly course,
> Without delay fill them with friendly art.
> First let his head recline on a cool pillow,
> Then bathe him in the dew of Lethe's spray;
> The limbs, stiffened by cramps, grow lithe as willow,
> When rest has made him strong to meet the day.
> Perform the elfins' fairest rite:
> Restore him to the holy light![394]

In this way we see pictured the work of helping spirits around all of our sleeping bodies as dawn grows near.

During this time, on May 29, 1915, Steiner received a set of questions from an experienced student of theosophy, and wrote back about the twelve masters or bodhisattvas at any time in existence, seven of whom are always in incarnation. This is a rare insight into Steiner's teaching of the sources to humanity of the spirit fire of the Eastern Horizon Image, and the truth and love of the Western Horizon Image.[395]

On June 10, Steiner spoke about "The Problem of Mephistopheles," Faust's guide, tempter, and imprisoner.

During this time, beginning on June 10 and going until July 6, Steiner spoke about the great wooden statue he had recently begun, *The Representative of Humanity*. Today the statue stands—still unfinished—in a special room at the grand Goetheanum in Dornach. It rises over thirty feet into the air, the central figure—thought by most to represent the Christ being in human form, and by extension the potential of everyone—holding at bay the Hardener below and the Illusionist above. Thus *The Representative of Humanity* gives a picture of the three-ness that underlies all of life, with two faces of evil—of zeal, if you will—that we must all encounter. With left arm upraised, the flying Illusionist (Lucifer) is not merely banished but actively grasped, and drawn into service to humankind. With right arm strongly pointed downward, the Hardener (Ahriman) is likewise confined to his proper realm. The power of the central figure actually transforms these beings.

> Christ is the one who stretches his hand out because he must do this by reason of his inner being. He does not break the wings of Lucifer; but Lucifer, there above, cannot endure what streams out from this hand, and he himself breaks his wings.... This is self-knowledge in Lucifer, the experience of himself.[396]

In parallel to the axis that we are viewing, Wachsmuth says that this statue, and the lectures of this period, concerned the balance of East and West. Further, I believe that the revelation of its significance to others comes through at a time that was determined by a prenatal event, Venus passing over the position of the Western Horizon Image. [397]

The Group, or The Representative of Humanity
by Rudolf Steiner and Edith Maryon

Real-Time Crossings Square to the Birth Sun Position, in the East-West Horizon Axis

During the life, many celestial events occur. Some may relate to the pattern at birth. Though many astrologers look at many possible kinds of relationship (what they call "aspects"), we will look only at what actually crossed the axis of the East-West Horizon, that is, planets that were "conjunct" the East-West axis and thus "square" to the Gate-Earth axis. Please recall the introductory material from Chapter 3 about the outer planets.

What were the transits to the East-West Images? As before, we shall begin nearer to the end of the life, viewing only the major transits to this axis.

Transiting planet crossing the Eastern-Western horizon axis	Corresponding date in Steiner's life	Steiner's age
Saturn in Taurus (Eastern)	June 2, 1913	52 years, 3 months
Uranus in Scorpio (Western)	February 22, March 31, and November 24, 1899	38 years, 0 to 9 months
Sun in Scorpio (Western), with Biela's Comet	November 27, 1872	11 years, 9 months

Saturn at the same position as the Eastern Horizon Image (Taurus), one pass, June 2, 1913, age fifty-two years, three months

On June 4, Saturn lay exactly at the place of the Eastern Horizon Image at Antares, at the same time that the moving Sun lay on the position Aldebaran, exactly opposite Saturn. This opposition of Sun and Saturn across the axis of Aldebaran and Antares occurs no more frequently than every fifteen years, and sometimes waits thirty years. One such time was in 1942, on December 2, when Leo Szilard and Enrico Fermi were able for the first time to create a runaway nuclear reaction at the University of Chicago, the key experiment that led to the development of the atomic bomb. "Miners refine their ore by fire!" The beginning of June lies six months away from December 2, so the Sun and Saturn were in opposite positions to the ones we're discussing now.[398]

On this day, Steiner spoke to the freedom of the soul. He spoke about the *Bhagavad Gita*, the core of the Mahabharata or Great Story that underlies all of Hindu culture. Herein the divine Krishna teaches Arjuna, the great warrior and archer, the truths of life. Krishna teaches about the role of dharma or duty, therefore the occasional rightness and necessity of war. He teaches about the foundations of existence and consciousness. On June 2, 1913, Steiner revealed that Krishna reincarnated as the Nathan Jesus, the one who was transformed on the cross, who was refined by fire and became the being of cosmic light![399]

The "best man" of the Taurus Image is really Arjuna. He has sought the bride of truth and backs away, letting Krishna go forward as the Sun-Being who bears the "I AM" for humanity.

Steiner explains how the "quarrelsome" Paul—the third man of zeal from the Scorpio Image—had been a learned scribe and sage who then lost the balance inherent in the harmonious wisdom cultures of India. Paul had to confront his weakness and create a relationship to the Christ-illumined heart. Paul realized, like Arjuna, that a marriage was taking place, and he was privileged to be present. He became the "best man."[400]

Uranus at the same position as the Western Horizon Image (Scorpio), three passes, February 22, March 31, and November 24, 1899, age thirty-eight years, zero months, to thirty-eight years, nine months

What would we expect of Uranus stimulating the Image at Scorpio? We might expect a challenge from denizens of the Illusionist seeking to put Steiner off the track of his spiritual work, sending him into one of the paths of the first two men of zeal, creating a challenge that had to be faced and overcome. We might also expect something revolutionary, surprising, even shocking. Let's see what the evidence suggests.

There is such an astonishing connection with the third date that we will concentrate on it. Indeed, we have seen this event before in Chapter 9, when prenatal Saturn in Leo opposite to the Birth Sun's position in Aquarius projected out to this time of Steiner's life. From prenatal Saturn, we would expect to find a destiny event (Saturn) set by spirit as Moon Karma (prenatal), determined from before birth. From transiting Uranus, we would expect to see a shock to the life system (Uranus) as Sun Karma (transiting), where a meeting occurs and one can respond or not. The event at the very end of 1899 was the "festival of knowledge," which now we can see both in terms of the cosmic memory guide of Saturn and the revolutionary influence of Uranus. We will go over the same territory with material appropriate to this different focus.

Leading up to this time, Steiner spoke about working himself to death, a consideration that arises whenever we speak of Antares, the Death Star. At this point Steiner was concerned, even distraught, about the one-sidedness of individualism, about the individualism of the personality becoming egotism that overpowers the true self, as well as overpowers others. He is quoted as saying, "The human being at a decisive turning point comes to a karmic crisis. He makes a decision that could lead to his death. This leads him to an abyss without knowing it. Then he hears a voice—stop!—and must stop without knowing why—only knowing that the voice comes from the spiritual world."[401]

Steiner too found himself at an abyss. How did help arrive? Friedrich Rittelmeyer reports that Steiner spoke about his teachers, extraordinary individuals who would come to meet him at the right moment to help him, in order to recognize and develop his capacities and to help awaken him, especially the one whose voice he heard at this time.[402]

Steiner met the one whom he termed the Master when he was twenty-one years old. At the very end of 1899, Steiner describes a specific encounter with the one whose voice came from spiritual worlds: "This experience culminated in my standing in the spiritual presence of the Mystery of Golgotha in a most profound and solemn festival of knowledge"[403] (see also chapter 9). After this experience he could speak with the authority of personal experience about the core mystery of Christianity.

As Emil Bock says, from one day to the next Steiner's whole way of life changed. In the same way Paul did not repeat the mistakes of the other men of zeal related to this day, but found his way to love. It all changed for Paul on his way to Damascus, in one experience on one day.

The call at the abyss gifts us with a higher freedom, a freedom from which love naturally emanates. Two zealots of the three fall into the abyss; only one survives in light.

One can see how this leads up to Steiner's first esoteric lecture on September 29, 1900, which he titled, "Goethe's Secret Revelation: A Rosicrucian Mystery." The Christ being had come to him, either as Christian Rosenkreutz or as Christ Risen. Steiner had experienced the sacred marriage spoken of in the Taurus Image. Anything that was zealous in a misguided way—the Scorpio Image—was turned around, and Steiner set on a new path.

Less Is More

An astrologer is happy to consider many more points in his or her investigation by adding transits between planets and different sorts of angles between planets, as well as wider orbs. For real-time transits, we have used very close orbs. For prenatal conjunctions we have used extremely tight orbs. Here less is more, and a researcher can always come back to add in more resonant moments.

A Special Event: Biela's Comet on November 27, 1872, with Sun at Western Horizon Image Sun position (Scorpio), age eleven years, nine months

> Something quite new and different enters the progression of the human race on earth through the appearance of a comet.
>
> —RUDOLF STEINER[404]

In 1773, Joseph Jérome de Lalande, a professor of astronomy and director of the Paris Observatory, was to give a public lecture on comets. When his lecture was cancelled due to a problem with scheduling, a rumor arose that he had been expected to predict a collision between a comet and the earth that year, and that the police had stopped him from making this public. A great panic erupted. Despite Lalande's public statements that the rumors were untrue, people rioted in fear of the end of the world.

A similar situation existed in Steiner's lifetime. Named after the astronomer who described its trajectory and period of return, Biela's Comet had made a dazzling show in previous decades. General opinion held that the comet was coming closer to the earth on every return. Conditions made it difficult to observe the comet in the 1860s. It was expected to return in 1872, when Steiner was only eleven years old. Steiner later recalled that leaflets were distributed saying that the comet would collide with the earth and the world would come to an end. Anxiety ran very high. Instead of the comet, however, there appeared on this day a "most wonderful, beautiful meteor shower, as though a fire were falling to the earth from the night sky in myriads of tiny fading sparks."[405] As Steiner mentioned that "Satan lies in wait for every comet that turns up ... with the intention of changing the whole planetary system"—what we might see as appropriate for the center of the Scorpion—it was important that Biela's Comet "chose the path of becoming absorbed by the earth."[406] Indeed, in 1879, "the regency of Michael came down in that shower of golden light."[407] These days we can experience the diminishing myriads of sparks of Biela's Comet as the Andromedid meteor showers in November.

Though the transiting Sun in the sky moves past the Western Horizon Sun position in Scorpio once every year, the presence of Biela's Comet makes that ordinary crossing extraordinarily important. Panic about the end of the world relates to the notion of zeal, and finding this transformed into a "myriad of sparks" under the regency of archangel Michael shows how the powers of the Death and Rebirth Star Antares can likewise be transformed. Recall how the meeting with Michael was set up by Mercury crossing this axis during Steiner's gestation period. In Biela's Comet, young Steiner received confirmation that Michael was moving in the physical spaces of the heavens. Later he had interactions with Michael that were the outcome of pre-earthly intentions, as, for example, his first visit to Dornach hill when the prenatal Mercury crossed the Western Horizon Image at Antares.

ECLIPSES

Two solar eclipses occurred at exactly the degree of the Eastern Horizon Image. We don't have much information about Steiner's life at the first, May 28, 1900. The second, May 29, 1919, occurred one day before all those who had been planning what became Waldorf education first visited the potential site of the new school, in Stuttgart. The party included not only Rudolf Steiner and Marie Steiner, but also Herbert Hahn and E. A. K. Stockmeyer, both important teachers in the first school, as well as the funder, Emil Molt, of the Waldorf-Astoria cigarette company. From this first visit, the new building venture was approved and the mother school of the Waldorf movement was purchased.[408]

What's interesting here is the occurrence of this visit at an eclipse of the Sun on one of the birth Solar Cross Images of the inspirer of this curriculum. Eclipses of the Sun have to do with relations to the whole of the Earth and even with the cosmos, far beyond the human being's individual dramas. We see then that Steiner's biography intertwines with a celestial event in order to speak to an earthly situation.

The actual founding of the School took place on September 7, 1919, just over three months after the eclipse. Steiner called the founding a "Festival Act in the History of Mankind."[409] With the solar eclipse in mind, we might see the "festival" as a celebratory aftermath of that first visit to the site that set the stage for this gift to the Earth.

Summary from Steiner

Steiner summarized the connection between marriage (Taurus Image) and imprisonment (Leo Image) by giving us the following practical gem (Aquarius Image). In this passage, he refers to the intellectual soul. This comes from an understanding of the evolution of soul powers in the human being, beginning with sentient soul, the ability to really feel things with the senses in a most alive and non-mechanical way, then developing to the intellectual or mind soul, the thinking soul that mentally grasps one's experiences, and moving further to the consciousness or spiritual soul, the ability to sense one's relation to the entire cosmos through experiences on earth.

> When we recall the impressions of the day, it seems as though the subtle etheric forms behind ordinary reality were changed into stiff figures. Things during the day appear to us as though they were bewitched, with their real nature held prisoner within them. Wherever a plant or being appears bewitched, it has happened like this: We see the substance of a wise being behind the physical appearance and we remember, "Yes, by day that is only a plant; it is separated from my intellectual soul so that I cannot really reach it during the day." When we feel this estrangement between the objects of the day and what is behind them, for example the perception of the lily in the daytime and the form behind it related to our own intellectual soul, we will perceive that our intellectual soul has a strong kind of longing to unite with what is behind the object or the lily; it would be a "marriage," a union of the night-form with the day-form. [410]

One's path to find the hidden truth—the "bride"—spans day and night. This dynamic of darkness and light takes us back to themes that we discovered in the first axis, the Gate-Earth axis. This passage comes from a lecture on fairy tales. Steiner concluded that the best way to unite the night-forms and day-forms was through fairy tales!

Meeting the Challenges of the Eastern and Western Horizon Images

Did Steiner meet the challenges and realize the potentials of his Eastern and Western Horizon Images? Examine the progeny in human beings and initiatives of this great representative of humanity, and answer. One can through this process begin to understand the identity of the "ore" that is refined by spiritual fire, the actual stuff that forms and will form through wisdom (*sophia*) the true and becoming human being (*anthropos*).

Steiner struggled with issues of zeal—zeal for freedom in combat with zeal for the one right way. In zeal the other disappears except as an object to be used. Steiner found a way to encounter a goodly number of people, but not all, with heart.

In sacred marriage, the other becomes both human and divine. Relationship is the foundation and key. Steiner struggled with right relationships to sexuality, physical and spiritual. Certainly he improved upon Thomas Aquinas's misogyny.[411] He sought to bring others to what he had experienced in 1899 and continued to experience, to a "festival" that was a sacred marriage with the most divine.

We could revisit each of Steiner's Star Brothers, Star Sisters, Bodes, and Resonant Moments to compare successes and failures. You can refer to your mind-maps of these Images to see what additional insights you had about Steiner's navigation of these Images. Most simply we can conclude here that the Horizon Images pressed Rudolf Steiner to his growing edge.

We can hope that over the course of Steiner's life the issues of rigidity and dogmatism lay more and more behind Steiner, and that the Anthroposophical Society he left behind will continue to elude those traps. We can hope those who study Steiner will find their way to personal transformations in spiritual fire, to a sacred marriage with spirit that refines the ore of their entire being, down to their deepest physical nature.

13. THE GATE IMAGE AT CROSSING THE THRESHOLD

To many people, the word "death" signifies finality, an ending. In contrast, the term "crossing the threshold" suggests a significant moment in a process. Crossing a threshold can be understood as a change in the life-stream of an individual rather than a termination. One can imagine a continuity of awakeness as one moves from primary attention to the made-world to primary attention to the spirit world. Indeed, many accounts of those who have passed and come back to our consensual made-world show that awakeness, that is, continued consciousness, is possible.

At birth we imagine the newborn activating the astral body with the first breath. All the bodies are growing, except the soul, which begins to contract in order to relate to the single location of the human body. The infant's body receives a gift as an imprint from the cosmos that the person either does or does not realize during the course of a life. At crossing the threshold, the gesture differs. Here, as the physical body shrinks in vitality, the person offers up the harvest of his or her life into a specific place in the heavens, as an impulse of alignment and as an impulse of change. An impulse of alignment means, "My spirit perceives this passageway into the great being of the zodiac, for which I have been preparing—I give my life's harvest into this being."

What does an impulse of change mean in this context? Over great spans of time, the zodiac is intended to become humanized, to change from a line of mostly animals to one that has a human face in every direction. *This will come about because of the gifts made by human beings who, through struggles in earthly life, will add the content and face of wisdom to the cosmos.*

As you have five times before, get ready to view this last Image, get set, and now go.

Death Image

Wild winds on the lake. An intense storm. Many in danger. A virgin in the heavens, her right foot resting on the moon, a rainbow about her. A child is born who brings wisdom of earth and stars. Wise kings watch from afar as, swirled about by gusts and water spray, the child, smiling, luminous in the wild storm, secures the helm of the threatened boat. All are safe.

WORKING THE IMAGE

As before, it is best to let this Image work in your own imagination for a short while before going on. Read it again, and let it begin to expand for you. Get the picture as accurately as possible, and then let it amplify. Make a mind-map, and perhaps another. We hold the Death Image of this great man in our imagination. Treat it with respect and see what your own Imagination will tell you before we give you other hints. Take the time to do this now.

EARLY IMPRESSIONS

A storm—where did it come from? What was it like? Wind and rain, surely. *Wild* wind! Darkness also? Lightning? In the story of Jonah, the prophet attempts to escape his responsibilities by hurrying onto a boat and sailing in the other direction from Nineveh, the city to which he is supposed to preach. Divinity raises a storm. The sailors fret, asking, "Who has sinned against Divinity that we should have such a storm?!" They query each other and can find no fault. They finally ask Jonah. He confesses and asks them to throw him overboard. When they do so, the storm subsides. In this Image, are there any escapees on the lake, in the boats, who have not listened to Divinity?

Goethe describes such a scene:

> Branches are quaking and breaking,
> Tree trunks are mightily groaning,
> Roots are straining and moaning!
> Tree upon tree is falling,
> In a tangled mass they are littered
> And through the gorge's wreckage
> The winds are hissing and howling.[412]

We learn from Steiner's Star Brother something else of importance about the storm. This upheaval of nature comes from witches and devils. Do we see the unleashing of destructive powers in this Image?

Likewise, in one of his mystery plays, Steiner gives words to the Lesser
Guardian of the threshold between earth and spirit worlds that relate the
storm to more than a local weather pattern. The Guardian observes human
beings with unpurified emotional bodies coming toward its realm, as one
might peer into a storm:

> What violent desires are here resounding!
> So rage men's souls, that are approaching me
> before achieving full serenity.
> Such beings are impelled by strong desires....
> The souls which show themselves in such a way
> I must send back to earth,
> for in the spirit regions they provoke
> confusion only, and disturb the deeds
> which cosmic powers wisely preordain.
> To their own being also they do damage.
> They breed destructive urges in themselves,
> which they mistake then for creative power.[413]

Such is Steiner's understanding of the storm that exists between earthly
realms and spiritual realms.

When death comes near, can people find the second phrase of the Rosicrucian formula? The first phrase is "Ex Deo nascimur"—from Divinity we
are born. We can see Divinity shine from the faces of the children at Steiner's Conception Image. We can see Steiner's recognition of the Divinity that
we are born with in his Gate Image, rebuilding the chairs of those who will
teach us how to recognize Divinity. The teachers proclaim to all: "From
Divinity we have our birth, we have everything!"

The second phrase of the Rosicrucian formula is "In Christo morimur"—
in the light of Christ consciousness, we die. Or when we die, we do so into
the being of Christ-light. Are the people on the boats ready for this kind of
death? Are we always ready for this, no matter what storms we encounter in
our lives? Can we see our death and the Christ-light coming over the waters?
Does the calmness at the end signify that we have been returned to life on
earth, or does it mean that we have been returned to life in spirit realms?

There is a promise in the third phrase, *"Per Spiritum Sanctum revivis-
cimus"*—through the Sacred Spirit or Holy Spirit, we are revived, we are

resurrected. But you may not come to this third phrase unless you have gone through the second, death or the willingness to die into truth and into love.[414]

Who is the child? What does the child look like? Is the child male or female? Does the child speak? Do we hear in sound or inside ourselves the following words given by Steiner about how the Christ Light speaks?

> I am not now the one who walks about in the physical world; I am the one in whom the god who has descended is living; I am the One whose name comprises all the sounds of speech, the One who was in the beginning, who is in the middle and who shall be at the end. I am the Alpha and the Omega.[415]

If we heard these words, either in the air or in our inner hearing, what would we do? How would we act? What new responsibility would we know that we now had?

BACKGROUND TO THE IMAGE

A tempest had come on the previous day, and abated, then come again with greater strength. Now many are in danger. The Christ individuality—the Teacher—prays again and is found at the helms of the threatened boats.

In an earlier year on this Solar Day, the human being who carries the soul of the great Zarathustra is born, the one we call the Solomon Jesus, the one who later sacrifices his own being to the bearer of innocent love. For this one, birth and sacrifice are closely linked, for sacrifice comes at an early age. For a more complete story about the Solomon Jesus, consult Appendix B. It tells of the two Jesus children, the one who bears the Krishna stream—the Nathan Jesus—and the one who bears the Zarathustra stream—the Solomon Jesus. In this Image, we follow the Zarathustra stream to the birth of the Solomon Jesus, the fourteenth incarnation in that line.[416]

Zarathustra had lived ages before, in each of seven lives mastering the seven major religions of the ancient world. He taught Hermes Trismegistus, who took Zarathustra's teachings to found the ancient civilization of Egypt. Zarathustra incarnated again as Zoroaster, the priest-king and teacher in Babylon. In that life he trained Pythagoras, the prophet Daniel, King Cyrus of Persia, and others, including the stargazing priest-kings who see in the stars on the very night of this Image signs of the rebirth of their founder, Zarathustra, whom they have expected for five hundred years.

When Zarathustra was born previously he smiled immediately. A King tried to kill him but when the King raised his sword to kill the infant, the arm was paralyzed, so the King sent the baby to be devoured by wild beasts. All these storms Zarathustra survived, just as all survive the storms of this Solar Day.[417]

The carrier of Zarathustra brings an advanced wisdom of the world and of the stars. He is the one who would say, "There are three that give testimony: the water, the stars, and the blood, and these three are one."[418] On this Solar Day we find the waters turbulent and then stilled; we find the starry witnesses, sources of creation; and we find the blood of kings born this day.

The Kings awaiting their teacher's birth for five hundred years see in the sky of this night a virgin with her foot resting on the moon, crowned by a rainbow, a precursor to the woman clothed with the Sun, with the Moon under her feet, crowned by twelve stars.[419] The physical body that will carry Zarathustra is the fruit of this virgin, come to rescue those caught in the tempests of earthly life. Steiner knew about this deed of the three Kings (or magi): "The three Magi from the East … drew upon their knowledge in order to understand the phenomena of the heavens; by so doing they could become aware of a significant event taking place on earth, one that far transcended the ordinary."[420]

When the Sun lies in the constellation of Pisces, at midnight we indeed see the Virgin directly above us, just as the Kings did long ago. We can look again in that vicinity, without creating connect-the-dots images, but with an open heart to the pictures given to us out of the heavens. Gaze into the vicinity of the Virgin with Spica at its end and permit pictures to come to you, too. Don't be in a hurry. The magi noticed many things but gazed for five hundred years before seeing the rebirth of their teacher.

Rudolf Steiner has given us another very interesting idea about this individuality. The Solomon Jesus descended from Abraham in forty-two generations, which is the time it takes to fully realize the attainments that Abraham made, all the way to the physical body. Then the Solomon Jesus gave this perfection as a gift to the Nathan Jesus.[421] In this Solar Day we receive the perfection of Abraham.

Crossing the Threshold
in Relation to Steiner's Life

Let us see a detail from the funeral in light of this Threshold Image. Friedrich Rittelmeyer performed the funeral ceremony for Steiner. He reports that, during this ritual,

> A drop of the sprinkled water fell in the center of the forehead and shone there through the whole service like a sparkling diamond. The light of many candles was reflected in this glittering star—even as the revelations of light from higher worlds had been reflected in his spirit.[422]

This is the Solar Day of Rudolf Steiner's passing over the threshold, to unite with the origin place of the Solomon Jesus, the bearer of Zarathustra. Steiner brings the harvest of his life to unite with his teacher—Zarathustra—and to deepen this place in the zodiac, the center of the mutable sign, Pisces. He had been attracted earlier in his life to one who claimed to be Zarathustra—Friedrich Nietzsche—but found this brilliance to be not the pure and original brilliance of the ancient teacher whom he sought. Much of what Nietzsche said lured Steiner to him, but he was disappointed in the end.

What then was Rudolf Steiner's relationship to Zarathustra? What part of this great being found a home in the bodies—physical, etheric, astral, or soul—of Rudolf Steiner? Was Rudolf Steiner an incarnation of Zarathustra? The anthroposophists who suggested this connection affirm its truth: "Yes, absolutely!" Others have shrunk from such a pronouncement: "But Steiner never said that he was Zarathustra!" Their reaction is understandable, as people can look for and find a quote in Steiner's work on every topic. It would take more than a lifetime to read and digest everything that Steiner said. But you need not look for such a statement. Steiner would never have proclaimed his kinship to Zarathustra; this would have been spiritually inappropriate. To answer such a question requires active and new research on the part of those who are left behind, without reliance on any quotes or directives from the man himself.

Perhaps in the Image of his death Steiner affirmed his association with Zarathustra and the circle of the highly developed beings, the bodhisattvas, who watch over and guide the affairs of the earth. For "who one was" in a past lifetime matters less than "who one works with" over lifetimes. In *Spiritual Economy*, Steiner speaks about the etheric body of the original Zarathustra going to Moses and the astral body going to Hermes Trismegistus.[423] These are statements that we can hardly grasp as concepts, let alone begin to determine what energy went from one individuality to another. In the end it doesn't matter. It's who you work with, whom you speak with in your quiet moments, who assists you from more advanced realms, how deeply you have penetrated the mystery—that matters.[424] From this point of view, Rudolf Steiner had a very intimate connection with the great teacher Zarathustra.

Steiner prefigured this encounter with the Christ being in various ways in his speaking:

> Only at the moment of death ... [do we experience] that the entire secret connected with human consciousness is drawn together.... Death is also that moment when we too may hope to attain an intensified comprehension of Christ.... For it was life, that is, consciousness, which rose out of death: a living consciousness. [425]

We shall add this to our understanding of this Image: "living consciousness" imbues the scene. Elsewhere Steiner added:

> Christ Himself brings the message that when space is overcome and one has learned to recognize the Sun as the creator of space, when one feels oneself placed through Christ into the Sun, lifted into the living Sun, then the earthly and physical vanishes and only the etheric and the astral are there.... The stars no longer twinkle down upon us but gently touch us with their loving influence.[426]

Finally, in his fourth mystery play, he characterizes one of his heroes who has recently died as "Sun-mature—thou wilt as spirit-star illumine now thy friends."[427] Together these statements paint a potent picture. Steiner fulfills his predicted meeting in his Death Image, through the Sun into the akashic zone or zero-point field, to become a star for others.

Does this mean that the people on the boat die, or do they live? Both are true. When you embrace "In Christo morimur"—in the Christ-light we die—then you realize that both are true, indeed, all the time. Steiner's Star

Brother Goethe realized this too: "Death is nature's device to create more life,"[428] and this process occurs again and again, indeed, continuously.

This Image confirms Steiner as one of the mightiest defenders of the human soul. It is akin to Michael in the twelfth chapter of the Revelation to John, combating and beating down the dragon that would devour the woman and the child. As Andrei Belyi spoke of Steiner: "From the dimension of storms he threw lightning bolts."[429] Belyi understood that Steiner knew of the realm of storms—a whole dimension!—so we can guess that Steiner was quite comfortable going through the storms in his death passageway, on his way to the luminous child.

Near the end of his life, Steiner spoke directly to what would become his Death Image. He spoke about the imagination of kingly students of Zarathustra who observed in the heavens: "In those times the initiates ... really saw the woman clothed with the sun, with the dragon beneath her feet, and giving birth to a male child. Those who saw and understood such a thing said: For the heavens that is the birth of Christ, for us it is the birth of our 'I.'"[430]

Steiner also helps us with the quality of what the light-edged child brings—safety, yes, and more, much more—wisdom, as a means of love. Let us hear Steiner on this, keeping the repetitions that were in his lecture, as they affirm and reaffirm the power of this statement:

> If, in the realms into which the luciferic [the Illusionist] constantly streams and into which the ahrimanic [the Hardener] constantly streams, we look towards the divine that holds balance, we find there pure love as the fundamental force of everything that streams continuously, forming the human being outwardly, and giving him soul and spirit inwardly. This fundamental force is pure love. In its substance and in its being, and in so far as it is the cosmos of the human being, the universe consists of pure love, it is nothing other than pure love. In the part of the divine that is associated with the human being we find nothing except pure love.[431]

How does this love appear in the world? How does the little luminous child bring love and grace into the storms of regular living? "The ground of the world is the being of inward love appearing outwardly as light.... The outer appearance of [spiritual] beings is love, and the outer appearance of love is light."[432] Love and light; radiant light and penetrating love. Steiner himself burned very brightly in his last years, finding somehow more and more energy to deliver his wisdom. Toward the end, before his collapse, he delivered four to five lectures a day, on different topics, to different groups assembled to hear him. Accounts express the delight of the audience at this outpouring of love and light, trying to keep up with this extraordinary being, burning bright, slowly lifting up his arms to deliver himself to the embrace of the luminous child.

The child smiles. Rudolf Steiner "had the gift of 'the smile' ... and the faculty for direct expression from the heart.... Many knew his sunny smile; we spoke of it."[433]

At Steiner's cremation, the final refiner's fire, there suddenly appeared a flock of white birds that rose in spirals with the smoke and disappeared high up into the blue.[434]

Historical Personalities

We will not look at historical personalities here, for this is the place into which Steiner gifted the fruits of his life, and stands as Bode. Those born later into this degree will be able to enjoy those fruits as they pass the imprint that he has left in this gate of the heavens.

Other Images

We likewise will not look at the Earth and Horizon Images in the Solar Cross of Steiner's death. Naturally, it is tempting to do so, because we have seen how those who died into Steiner's birth Solar Cross are linked to other wings of that Solar Cross. However, one can only absorb so many Images. Thus we will discipline ourselves to concentrate on this Image only as the place into which Steiner lifted up the harvest of his life, and stand as Bode for the future.

14. RESONANT MOMENTS IN CROSSING THE THRESHOLD

All on a sudden ariseth so horrible a Tempest, that I imagined no other
but that through its mighty force, the Hill whereon my little House was
founded would flye in pieces.

—JOHANN VALENTINE ANDREAE,
The Chymical Wedding of Christian Rosenkreutz [435]

And struggling through the gloom,
Facing the storm, a mighty ship seeks room
On the open sea, whose rage it seems to court,
Flying the dangerous pity of the port,
The noise, the terror, and that fearful cry,
Give fatal augury
Of the impending stroke. Death hesitates,
For each already dies who death awaits.
—PEDRO CALDERÓN DE LA BARCA,
The Wonder-Working Magician [436]

THE SUN AT Steiner's death lay at 15 Pisces 26 (fifteen degrees and twenty-
six minutes). We can look at how the planets between conception and
birth interacted with that position, and we can look at how the planets in his
lifetime interacted with that position.

Prenatal Anticipations
and the Sun at Crossing the Threshold

Prenatal planet crossing Death Sun position	Corresponding date in Steiner's life	Steiner's age
Mercury (in Virgo) opposed to Death Sun position	April 24, 1891	30 years, 2 months
Sun (in Virgo) opposed to Death Sun position	April 1, 1892	31 years, 1 month
Venus (in Virgo) opposed to Death Sun position	January 15, 1903	41 years, 10 months
Mars (in Pisces) conjunct the Death Sun position	November 19, 1919	58 years, 8 months

Prenatal Mercury crossing the place opposite to the position of the Death Sun, projected to 24 April 1891, age thirty years, two months

Something was happening with Steiner's connection with theater in this time period. On April 24, he wrote a long letter about his fascination with Henrik Ibsen's work. In early May he attended an eight-day theater festival.

Having joined the Goethe-Schiller archives the previous autumn (September 30, 1890), he wrote of a longing of the butterfly of his own spirit to emerge. He felt an inner tempest and felt the desire to unfold his own wings.

Also in this time, Steiner began his work on *The Philosophy of Freedom*, which would later be titled *Intuitive Thinking as a Spiritual Path*. Listen to one of Steiner's students, one of the two who stayed up in an all-night vigil at Steiner's deathbed before the funeral. In describing the contribution that Steiner made through *The Philosophy of Freedom*, he speaks about what it is like to make thinking into something free and independent of the bodily instrument:

> One feels like a man who has pushed off from the shore and who must strive with might and main to maintain himself in the raging sea. The sheer power of cosmic thought is such that at first one loses one's identity. And perhaps one would lose it for good, if it were not for the fact which now emerges from the hidden mysteries of Christianity. One does not

finally lose one's identity because He Himself has walked the waves and extended a helping hand to Peter who ventured out prematurely. Generally the waves seem to calm down, and a condition ensues which Steiner expresses in a wonderful phrase: "Thinking itself becomes a body which draws into itself as its soul the Spirit of the Universe."[437]

Thus we work with the Image, finding exact parallels that deepen the Image and our understanding of Steiner's legacy.

Prenatal Sun crossing the place opposite to the position of the Death Sun, projected to April 1, 1892, age thirty-one years, one month

On April 2, Steiner gave out an article that he had written on "Nietzscheism," in which he detailed the process that had led Nietzsche to madness. He characterized Nietzsche's nerves and thinking as becoming gradually elastic, overreacting to things, becoming "an electric nerve-machine." He described how, on encountering objects, Nietzsche would create an actual electric spark. Nietzsche's perceptions heightened to such a degree that he became mad. The description of Nietzsche parallels the one we find in the Image, the electrically sparking luminous child. What happened to Nietzsche came from the outside and overpowered him. The child's electricity comes from its own nature.

Steiner further explained that Nietzsche had been unable to find the true being of the Christ, which, you may recall, Steiner was himself able to encounter at the very end of 1899, seven and a half years from this date.

Somewhat later, on May 19, Steiner's Ph.D. thesis, *Truth and Science*, was published.[438]

Prenatal Venus crossing the place opposite to the position of the Death Sun, projected to January 15, 1903, age forty-one years, ten months

In the sphere of Venus, we would expect to see negotiations, so to speak, with one's relationships with individuals and with groups. In relation to the Death Sun position, we might expect to see relations with groups that needed resolution before passing out of the earth-life, where so much can be accomplished in these relationships before entering the spiritual world.

In this time, Steiner gave lectures at the Theosophical Library on theosophy. On January 3, he spoke on "Evolutionary History of the Human

Being: The World-View from the Oldest Oriental Times to the Present: Or Anthroposophy." At the end of the talk, an expert in theosophy asked, "But what you have been saying is by no means in agreement with Mrs. Besant's teaching." In other words, he was called onto the carpet for saying something not in accord with the content and style of the Theosophical Society. Rudolf Steiner replied: "Then it is, no doubt, as you say."[439] This was the beginning of a split with the Theosophical Society and the inauguration of the term "anthroposophy."

How curious that the name of the Society, movement, and guiding angel—Anthroposophia—should be identified in a celestial event in relation to the Death Sun position! You can see how the magnetism of the death degree begins its work back into the life.

At this time Steiner also began to receive letters containing questions on esoteric matters, asking for advice and exercises adapted for the individual questioner.[440]

Also founded at this time was the magazine *Lucifer*, which became an important vehicle for Steiner's writing and transcripts of his talks. The title was changed in 1904, and Steiner formulated a very different opinion of the being of Lucifer, whom I have called the Illusionist.

Prenatal Mars crossing the place of the position of the Death Sun, projected to 19 November 1919, age fifty-eight years, eight months

What might we expect from Mars in relation to the Death Sun position? Cosmic speech, holy word, in relation to the crossing of the threshold. Though Steiner had talked some about the archangel Michael in 1913, on November 21 he began a "foundation-laying" series of lectures on the Michael Impulse under the title "The Mission of Michael, the Revelation of the Real Mysteries of Man's Being." Herein he spoke of the one who is "pathbreaker for the spiritual comprehension of the Being of Christ."[441]

Bring the Image to mind when Steiner speaks about Michael thus: "We must move forward to meet the revelation of Michael; we must prepare ourselves in such a way that He sends into us the strongest forces so that we become conscious of the supersensible in the immediate environment of the earth."[442] Prepare for the luminous child. Prepare for the kind of miracles that the Image sets forth for us.

These lectures on Michael formed the foundation for the ensuing courses in natural science, astronomy, pedagogy, medicine, and theology that took place in the following year. Cosmic speech, empowered by the connection with the Death Sun position, established Steiner's relation to Michael, which further emboldened him to speak out on many other topics. The smiling luminous child not only calms the storm; he inspires further practical work in the world.

Tracing Saturn Back through the Life

Before we look at how the planets passed the position of the Death Sun, we will use a different technique, special to astrosophy. One can trace the touch of Saturn back through the life, noting when the Great Memory was last at the place where the planets lay at the time of death. When Saturn was there, no one knew that it was an important place, because no one knew when the death might be. However, we can look back to see how the life was played out. In the larger study of Steiner's astrological biography, we go into how Saturn interacted with the death positions of each planetary sphere. From the point of view of the Solar Crosses, we concentrate on the Sun, for we restrict our interest to the stimulation of the Death Image.

Saturn passes the threshold Sun for the last three times—June 13 and August 31, 1908, and February 28, 1909, age forty-seven to forty-eight years

What is the purpose of a life? Can it be prefigured even long before its completion? Here we look at three passes, beginning June 13, 1908, then August 31, 1908, and ending on February 28, 1909. In the three passes of Saturn over the death-position of the Sun, we find significant statements about the importance of the light of Christ. For the man thought of as the John of the modern age, that is, the forerunner of the Christ, it seems significant that he delivered the lectures on the Gospel of John at this time, first in Hamburg in May, then in Nuremburg and Christiania, Denmark, in June. He said, "It will come to be understood that Christianity is only at the beginning of its influence, and will fulfill its real mission only when it is understood in its true form," to which he directs the rest of his life. What is its true form? "Spiritual."[443]

Steiner also spoke at the beginning of these transits of Saturn on the topic of Whitsun or Pentecost, a rare subject in his lectures. Pentecost was a Jewish ceremony for fifty days after Passover. The tradition was to pray all night long. At the original Christian Pentecost the disciples gathered in a circle, the main eleven ringed by the dozens behind. Mother Mary sat at their center. In the early hours of the morning spiritual fire began to pour down from heaven, first through Mary, then into each and every one. During the Saturn transit to Steiner's Death position, Steiner asked what was the source of this downpouring of spiritual fire into human beings. He answered: The Sun itself. This is Steiner at his best when Saturn triggers his Death Sun position:

> The soul will, at death, overcome death. *Ex Deo Nascimur. In Christo Morimur.* But Christ Himself brings the message that when space is over-come and one has learned to recognize the Sun as the creator of space, when one feels oneself placed through Christ into the Sun, lifted into the living Sun, then the earthly and physical vanishes and only the etheric and the astral are there.... The stars no longer twinkle down upon us but gently touch us with their loving influence.[444]

This statement could be understood as a foundation of Solar Cross work, our connection through the Sun to the cosmos. It applies specifically to Steiner's relation to the Christ being coming from his Death Sun position.

At the second pass of Saturn, he said: "The deepest thought is connected with the figure of Christ, with the historical, the external."[445]

And at the third and final pass, in February 1909:

> Just as far removed in conduct as mankind seems today from being perme-ated with the Christ Spirit on the physical plane, just so near to human souls is the Christ, who is coming, if only they will open themselves to Him. And the seer is even able to indicate how, since about the year 1909, in a distinctly recognizable way, that which is to come has been in course of preparation: that, since the year 1909, we live inwardly in a very special time.[446]

Look for the luminous child, he said, as the themes of his Death Image were resonating under the influence of Saturn.

At the last passing of Saturn, in February 1909, he also spoke about the principle of spiritual economy. He explained how it could happen that the etheric, astral, and soul bodies of Christ Jesus could be duplicated in divine worlds and could be woven into bodies of St. Francis and the German mystics. He thus explains how the very soul of Jesus could be woven into the "I AM" of human individuals. This is a Sun Mystery and opens the door to understanding the spiritual capacities of Rudolf Steiner himself. The soul of Christ-inspired Jesus lies outside of any religious order or doctrine. It follows spirit, not organization, and is available to all human beings.

This teaching releases Christianity from its institutional form in our time into the hands of the human being striving to become a true individual. Without the assistance of Christ-light in this way, we could not reawaken to our higher spiritual nature.[447]

RESONANT MOMENTS DURING THE LIFE— PLANETS AT THE DEATH SUN POSITION

TRANSITING PLANET CROSSING THE DEATH SUN POSITION	CORRESPONDING DATE IN STEINER'S LIFE	STEINER'S AGE
Pluto square Death Sun	Five times from July 28, 1921, to April 5, 1923	60 years, 5 months, to 62 years, 2 months
Saturn on Death Sun	September 21, 1922	61 years, 5 months

PLUTO'S CHALLENGE

The rape of Persephone has been brought about by soul-forces which lie deep in the subconscious, forces which in outer Nature are represented by Pluto. —RUDOLF STEINER[448]

We can look at when planets crossed the Death Sun position, or entered into some kind of powerful relationship with it. First off, we notice that Pluto squared the Death Sun position five times before the death, from July 28, 1921 to April 5, 1923. As Pluto moves very slowly, any relation to the positions of conception, birth, or death is noteworthy. We haven't looked at squares or right angles yet in this study, although we noted that the horizontal arms of the birth Solar Cross are square to the vertical arms. So we have been working with squares already. As Pluto moves so slowly, we will look at its square, an "aspect" or geometrical relationship that can be characterized as struggle and tension, more so than with an opposition.

Under pressure from Pluto we could say that this entire period of time from the middle of 1921 to the middle of 1923 involved the trials of opposition to Steiner and to anthroposophy, including black magic and other occult attacks. Hecklers interrupted his lectures. In May of 1922, Steiner was physically attacked in a hotel, and was protected by his friends; he had to escape through a back door. Trevor Ravenscroft learned from an informant who worked with the Nazi Party that Steiner had barely escaped having shotguns being fired into his face.[449]

Toward the end of this period, on December 31, 1922, the Goetheanum was burned to the ground. In line with the ongoing attacks on Steiner's work, everyone assumed the fire had been started by an arsonist, though the fact that the fire began inside the walls, and the walls had to be chopped through in order to get to the fire, posed the question of how the arsonist got in there. Both arson and electrical malfunction can be laid at the feet of Pluto's disturbance. Through the hole chopped by the ax through the wall, one student "espied bluish flames which shot forth with tremendous speed like serpents."[450] A whole life's work went up in smoke.

On the earlier side of this period, on June 27, 1921, the finances of the Goetheanum were in critical condition, and continued in crisis for many months.[451] Toward the end of this period, Steiner suffered energetic assaults from unseen forces. Certain people close to him were assigned to be on guard at all times against these attacks. A brief lapse in this protective cocoon has been given as an explanation for how Steiner suddenly became ill and began to deteriorate. He met this attack with an increased activity, especially in the autumn of 1924, until he finally had to retire to his bed, where he deteriorated further until his death at the end of March 1925.

Listen to Steiner's theme when Pluto first encounters the Death Sun position (July 28, 1921). In early August, Steiner said:

> We gradually learn to see that death, when it confronts us upon the cessation of life, is really only something like a summation, a totality I mean to

say, of single processes which are going on always within the human being from birth on. Fundamentally considered, we are dying all the time; but we die in extremely small fractions.... That which simply lives, which is simply vital, takes away our consciousness, it makes us unconscious, and the processes of death within us, the dying processes, those which destroy the vital, and which are always occurring in us fractionally—it is these which bestow consciousness upon us, which make us thinking, rational human beings.[452]

Thus Pluto in relation to the Death Sun position stimulated Steiner to think about death.

Toward the end of the Pluto period, Steiner wrote his wife that the hearings in the local council about the fire at the Goetheanum had stimulated a "fierce debate," in which "anthroposophy was heavily attacked by the clerics." The term "witch hunt" was used. Even amongst the supporters, there were "many dissatisfied people with all kinds of criticism."[453]

SATURN'S PASSING

In the middle of the long period of Pluto's challenge, with five passes of the Death Sun position, we see Saturn pass through quickly, to oppose the Death Sun position, on September 21, 1922. What do we have there? Just five days away, that is, very close by and within a very tight orb, on September 16, we have the founding of the Movement for Religious Renewal, otherwise known as the Christian Community, and the first celebration of the Act of Consecration of Man (the *Menschenweihehandlung*)—what I call elsewhere the Act of Consecration of the Human Being, but here I wish to emphasize the *manas* or imaginative thinking at the base of the term Man. The course for theologians ended on September 22, 1922, one day from the exact transit.[454] Forty-two priests attended, both men and women, the number echoing the previous citation in this chapter of forty-two generations in descent from Abraham to the Solomon Jesus.

Let me explain how important this timing is. In the midst of the Plutonian attacks against anthroposophy, indeed against the divine being that stands behind it, against Anthroposophia herself, at this time, we have an event that Saturn brings in from the vast reaches of cosmic memory which goes forward as well as backward—from the connection with Rudolf Steiner's death uniting with the wisdom of Zarathustra. This may sound complicated, so let's put it together more thoroughly.

Two years after the event with the Movement for Religious Renewal occurred, in September 1924, near the end of his public appearances, Steiner spoke about the significance of this first Act of Consecration of Man, in his lecture course to the priests of the Christian Community, which has only recently been released from the protection of that group and published as *The Book of Revelation and the Work of the Priest*.[455] Steiner gave a kind of report for the event that had occurred two years previously, that is, during the transit that we are examining.[456] He put this event in the context of the Plutonian challenge on either side of this visitation from Saturn: "comprehending apocalypse profoundly and fully was only possible when one was standing entirely within the act of consecration of Man."[457] Pluto surrounded him with the destructive power of apocalypse. Up through the smoke and broken world came the Christ-in-us that makes all things new, the renaissance of apocalypse. As he said, "What I experienced in the small White Room of the southern wing of the Goetheanum, I considered to be among the most festive moments of my life."[458]

"The act of consecration of Man, which brings the divine, spiritual life directly down to the earth" was reinstituted in this transit with Saturn, renewed in order to open a direct experience of apocalypse, or revelation, in both its destruction of the old and vivification of the new.[459] The young Emil Bock relates: "The time was right and our hearts were open so he could bring down from heavenly heights that which is united with Christ and the reigning spiritual powers, a gift of blessing for future humanity."[460] Again and again, Steiner spoke of this renewed rite in terms that come directly from the Image—as sun-radiance coming down from the spiritual world. He took the role of the saving child, exhorting the priests of the Community to have strength, courage, and perseverance to receive the spiritual downpouring. He equated consecration with Transubstantiation, that is, revelation of the spiritual archetypes in all matter, in other words, the revelation of the radiant gem-like essence within all things. All was bathed in light. Though Albert Steffen said publicly that he could not speak about this sacred experience, his notebooks from that day, opened after his death, reveal his experiences: "I may say that Christ was there. . . . It was the first time that I saw the Christ as a being before me. The arms were stretched out and the head was surrounded with light, and I experienced that he healed and blessed. He was there and is there."[461] Light streaming for the forty-two.

Other Images of Steiner's four Birth Images arise at this consecration. We hear Steiner refer to the sounds needed for the rite, sounds that have been imprisoned. "Humanity has treated the sounds of speech like the police treat criminals, giving each sound a number, just as criminals are numbered when they are shut up in their cells. By losing their names and gaining numbers instead, the sounds of speech have lost their inner nature."[462] To effect the rite properly, one must liberate these sounds from their prison, just as the Sun-Being liberated those from the prison in the Earth Image. Then the sounds become a "magical Word," a true gem, so that one could say, "As I speak, the god is speaking in me."[463]

In his introduction to the *Revelation* lectures, Johannes Werner Klein related the beginning of the group of the new religious impulse in terms that strongly evoke the Death Image:[464]

> We feel like a little band of travelers clinging together in a boat tossed by the stormy waves of our time, constantly faced with the danger of drowning and unable to turn either to any representative of external culture of the spirit in these times. We cannot but feel blessed by being able to come to you, and grateful that you have called us and will speak to us here.

The only difference from the exact Death Image is that Steiner has actually come to them in their boat, rather than they to him, though they don't seem to realize this. We may seem to travel to a teacher, but spiritually speaking the teacher comes to us. Steiner speaks in the lecture immediately following this introduction: "When the cultus brought the supersensibly powerful gods to be there amid the celebrants."[465] In other words, when the ancient Mystery traditions empowered the scene such that the priests could receive the blessing of Divinity, "this was when something was attained in the ancient Mysteries that has always given meaning to an act of consecration of Man, namely the Transubstantiation." The celebrants felt that the divine light in themselves and everything around them was revealed, and was perceived and known as the light and love of Christ consciousness. The substance of matter became divine. Thus the light-limned child works to rescue the "little band of travelers" from the storm.

Listen to Steiner once more, speaking as the luminous child, the bearer of the wisdom of Zarathustra, to those who yearn for spirit on the storm-tossed boat. First he speaks of the fact that the first renewed Act of Consecration of Man occurred in the very room where the fire was lit that burned down the Goetheanum, mixing sweetness with sorrow:

> We may regard the initiation which took place here, in the hall over there which was then devoured by fire, as being lit by the light that shines out when heaven is opened and the white horse appears with the One who is seated upon it, whose name only he himself knows and who must be embodied in us if this name is to mean anything to us.[466]

We may find it easy to say, "Steiner means the Christ, for whom he acts as messenger." However, this passage warns us that, even if we are correct, we do not yet know the true meaning of that name, for our sounds may still be imprisoned. We can correctly conclude that Steiner understands the purpose of his life, and realizes fully the potential of the Death Image. What is the name of the luminous child? Are Steiner and that child one and the same?

The first public Act of Consecration of the Human Being, led by Friedrich Rittelmeyer, with Emil Bock assisting, took place with the Sun exactly at Steiner's Eastern Horizon Image. Because they had no church, it was held in the showroom of a music store, the large windows curtained off and the instruments pushed aside. Bock and one of the women priests brought a temporary altar on a wagon.[467]

ECLIPSES

Only one eclipse occurred during Steiner's life at this degree, on October 1, 1921. This date occurs in the middle of the theology course that formed the foundation of the creation of the Christian Community a year later, which we have been discussing. As a solar eclipse indicates a macrocosmic relation rather than an issue of the personal drama of a human being, we can see Steiner setting forward his agenda for a renewal of religious-spiritual activity for human beings. He dealt with this eclipse upon his Death Sun position in the most positive manner.[468]

STEINER AS THE CHILD

In the commentaries on the Conception Image, we asked if Steiner was bending down to the child, or if Steiner was the child being bent down to. In the Death Image, we see the child coming down to the human beings in danger. A "child" always implies that growth is happening, and that maturity beckons and is coming. The presence of a child implies the future. Listen to one of Steiner's students with this in mind:[469]

> Each time that Dr. Steiner greeted one of us, and we met his affirmative glance, it was as though this moment was anticipated out of the future. We had the feeling: the one whom Dr. Steiner is greeting there, who is permitted to greet him, is in fact not yet fully present. But each one of us answered with the solemn promise that someday he would be present with his whole being.... We knew that this prodigious life had gone through death. The love which one met in this glance was akin to death.

Love and death. To become a lover, to become worthy of divine love, one must die to the past. The future lived in the present at these moments. A student feels always as a child growing into himself or herself, urged on by "this countenance woven out of light."[470]

GOING UP OR COMING DOWN?

How important that a student recalls Steiner's gaze as "akin to death." In his birth Solar Cross, Steiner lived in the polarity between Aldebaran and Antares, Life Star and Death Star. The death that spiritual beings brought to humanity meant that we could learn from our life—each life in a series of lives. The force of death brings us to consciousness. To those attentive to it, the death process occurs all the time. *"In Christo morimur."* Did Steiner at his death "go up" with the luminous child, into the arms of the abundant and loving Sophia? Faust did that with Gretchen. Cyprian did that with Justina. No, Steiner stays on earth and remembers the spirit-brightness of the Earth. "I tried to show that nothing *unknowable* lies *behind* the sense-world, but that within it is the spiritual world."[471] The Conception and Death Images combine. Steiner is the bright-eyed child again, hearing from a luminous child, "The Sun-Being is already on Earth, in your very own nature."

STEINER AS BODE

What would it mean to have Steiner as a Bode in your birth Solar Cross? How could you work with the gifts that he developed in his life and left in this hallway as aids to those who pass?

PART III
SOLVING THE PUZZLE OF A LIFE

A T THE EXPLORATORIUM in San Francisco, and at many science museums that have built exhibits whose designs were pioneered at the Exploratorium, you can find a particular demonstration of a resonant field. A square metal plate twelve inches on a side and a quarter of an inch thick is mounted horizontally, attached in its center to a vertical pipe. You spread fine sand on the plate in a smooth layer. Then you take a violin bow and run it along an edge of the plate at an even pressure, setting up a vibration, a fine hum. The plate vibrates, some parts more vigorously than others. The sand moves around, hopping away from the vigorous places and collecting in the less vigorous places. From a homogeneity of sand emerges a pattern that might look like the title page of Part III. If you apply the bow with a different pressure, or try a different bow, the pattern changes. If you change the size, shape, or thickness of the metal plate, the pattern changes.

Such is the way that we might view a life, a puzzle that does not have pieces to fit together, but rather a resonant pattern that becomes increasingly clear as we work with it. We have gathered episodes of a life rather than a timeline dutifully followed over a thousand pages of thorough biography. We have what may look like a collection of pieces, yet each apparent piece or detail is actually not a separate "thing," but a hologram, meaning that each has a picture of the whole within it. In the terms of this study, each Image, each resonant moment, each Star Brother, each Star Sister, and each Bode carries a sympathetic vibration to the whole of Rudolf Steiner's life.

Do we look for puzzle pieces?

Or do we look for a bit of a resonant pattern of the whole?

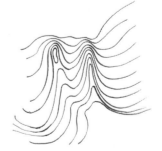

A hologram is a special piece of film through which you project light to see an image. You can cut a hologram into pieces, but each piece, when light is projected through it, gives the same picture as the larger hologram, the difference being that the smaller pieces show this wholeness with less focus and less accuracy. The wholeness gets very fuzzy the smaller the piece we look through. However, a resonant whole exists, even if fuzzy. Perhaps that is the most astonishing confirmation of these imaginings of Rudolf Steiner—to see demonstrated a comprehensive resonant whole in earthly events, heavenly events, and relations to other human biographies.

Let us review our various techniques, listening, of course, to the music of Luigi Boccherini, Vincent D'Indy, Tomás Luis de Victoria, and Marcel Dupré.

REVIEW: IMAGES OF THE SOLAR CROSS

Our primary technique of biography involved the Images of conception, birth, and death. We chose the main Image of the conception and death, and all four Images of the birth Solar Cross. This gave us six rich Images to work with. We could have brought in the three additional Images of the Solar Crosses of conception and the three additional Images of death for more accuracy. This has been tempting as, indeed, some people important in Rudolf Steiner's actual life have a strong relationship to these unrevealed Images. Ita Wegman, for example, the soul sister of Steiner in life, the medical doctor who co-created anthroposophical medicine, died into the Solar Cross of Steiner's conception. Likewise, Emil Bock, the Christian Community priest, biographer of Steiner, and author of many weighty tomes about anthroposophy and the esoteric understanding of the Cosmic Christ, died into the Solar Cross of Steiner's conception.[1] As we saw Steiner die into the Solar Cross of the birth of the Solomon Jesus, the reincarnation of Zarathustra, we take these connections very seriously.

A further connection is the death in 1935 of Daniel Dunlop, a key anthroposophist in England, into the Eastern Horizon Image.

However, a study of this nature, introducing new ways of looking at things, must show some restraint and not examine absolutely everything that could possibly be related. Ideally one gets a taste that then stimulates the appetite for more. Otherwise, one could be overwhelmed and run away from the whole thing. We have to take our own advice about limiting the intake of images in this world.

Lawful Images

Recall that I spoke in Part I about taking a fast from unlawful images. My emphasis here has been to find *lawful* images, images that speak to the soul, perhaps feed the soul, and certainly engage the soul to speak back, that is, to begin a process of transformation in relation to the celestial Images. This reinstates a timeless law of intercourse between humanity, the heavens, and the Earth, a law that we can often forget and that has often been intentionally abused. What sort of images do we find in our daily lives? Do they feed the soul? Do they promote dialogue with the stars and with the mother of the Earth? If not, then we may wish to have less and less to do with these unlawful images. Once the soul gets the taste for something better, once we find—in the terms of the Gate Image—the true nutrition that cures the starvation of the soul, then we may never wish to ingest false foods again.

"True imaginations" are those that offer security and safety as they lead one on a path of development. They do not lead one down an alleyway, as do the ubiquitous images of the Illusionist. One might say that the true role of Christ consciousness is to rescue the imagination so that we might develop it on the road to developing spiritual intuition. Steiner's verses constitute secure and safe images that one can ponder without fear of intrusion or detour.

The Lesson from Sleeping Beauty

Recall the tale of Sleeping Beauty recounted in Part I. Twelve great beings surround the infant human being, bestowing their blessings, mimicking exactly the operation of the twelve great beings of the zodiac. The thirteenth fairy was not invited because there is really no place for her; she is Time itself, the one that shakes awake the human being so that he or she may mature enough to make manifest the great blessings.

Whenever we look at a Solar Cross Image for birth, we can concentrate on the exact degree and the sign in which the Sun lies, and the Earth Image below, and the Horizon Images to the sides. We can also look at all the signs at that same degree, in Steiner's example, all twelve signs at 14 degrees and 33 minutes, thus, 14 Aries 33, 14 Taurus 33, 14 Gemini 33, and so on. This sets up twelve particular Images surrounding us at our birth.

Within the signs of birth and death, the position of the Sun at Steiner's death (15–16 degrees) is one degree different from his birth (14–15). We can note that the twelve-fold unfolding of Steiner's birth and death would include the point of the mystery of crucifixion (14–15 Aries), the point of John the Water Initiator's death (14–15 Capricorn), and the point of resurrection (15–16 Aries), as well as other Images that might be included in a comprehensive understanding of his place in the heavens.

Looking at a twelve-fold Solar Cross is an advanced technique for someone able to comprehend and integrate many imaginations at the same time. One enters into conversation with the twelve great beings around the spirit spark of a human being, the thirteenth being Time, through which the spirit manifests in actual events in the actual world. If we work constructively with Time, rather than try to deny her, the original twelve divine beings present at our birth awaken in our consciousness.

Review: Historical Personalities

We looked at historical personalities who shared Steiner's birth Solar Cross, through the lens of the shared Images. Often an event or a person has something to teach us about Rudolf Steiner or about the Image itself. Sometimes we don't see the connection and can only report it, wondering if perhaps a deeper biographical understanding of both individualities would show how they are related.

We see in the studies of these individuals such different cultural contexts, such different careers and proficiencies, and yet we can find that the soul gestures to which the Image alerts us have many similarities.

Historical personalities related to one's Solar Cross form a karmic group, differentiating between, on the one hand, Star Brothers and Star Sisters, and on the other hand, the Bodes, those who have died into the portal of one's birth and whose personality fragments remain there.

Of course, there are many others than the ones we have chosen. What about Mary Magdalene or Saint John of the Cross or Milarepa or many others, noble or criminal, with whom we are related by our gate to the heavens? The absence of these beings from our Solar Cross does not mean that they are not there. Since we don't know the dates of their birth or death, they may indeed be there. Our roster of historical personalities is a partial list. Perhaps the native of a degree would intuitively know who else connects with that degree.

To find one's own karmic groups can further a process of self-knowledge. We realize that we do not stand alone on Earth but have relationships in our entry from out of spirit realms. This seems particularly important with extraordinary pioneers such as Rudolf Steiner because his followers tend to separate him off from the rest of humanity, making him special and isolated. The exercises with historical personalities impress us with the obviousness of our relation with many other human beings, including those who have gone before and those who have come after. For anthroposophists, the presence of Goethe and Montessori and Andreae in Steiner's Solar Cross will seem to confirm the usefulness of the concept. However, there is a danger here of crowing about the famous people to whom one is related, not too different from the many people who confidently feel that they are, in fact, the true reincarnation of Cleopatra. The desire to have great people in one's Solar Cross should yield to the notion of having the *karmically right* people in one's Solar Cross. That is, one needs to get to know the historical personalities to whom one is related because they are the ones that share this connection with a particular gate in the heavens.

We each have karmic groups to which we are related during our life, that is, the groups of people to whom we are attracted. Then we have karmic groups to which we relate by affiliation, for example, few people alive have met Rudolf Steiner, but many may feel that he is part of their karmic group, and they experience this through a pursuit of anthroposophy. Some people feel an affinity with King Arthur, and find their modern connection through esoteric Grail mythology, or through visiting Glastonbury or Tintagel. Some feel a lasting connection with Buddha, and find their way to this group through meditation. The Solar Cross work introduces you to a karmic group to whom you are related because of your connection with a particular portal in the heavens, the one you took at birth. When you begin to study the historical personalities to whom you are related, you may have the same kind of experience of "aha" as we've seen here with Rudolf Steiner.

REVIEW: RESONANT MOMENTS

We also looked at resonant moments to which celestial events pointed us, one set of events from prenatal anticipations formed in the period of gestation and another set from transits of planets during the life. In the longer astrobiography, more and different events are examined. Here we restricted ourselves to events related to the Sun positions of conception, birth, and death, and restricted ourselves in many other ways. Normally, astrologers and astrosophers examine many more events in an analysis.

When we see a prenatal anticipation, we assume that, at the point of the spirit's entry into the time-space density of the earth realm, an intention has been set into motion that will be found projected into the life. This fulfills a pre-earthly intention of the soul. When we find a celestial event occurring in the life, that is, a real-time transit of a planet over a particular point of sensitivity, then we see that this is an opportunity given by destiny, to which the individual could respond or not, depending on the inclination of the moment.

To summarize in the words of Steiner's Star Brother, Goethe:

> For, what purpose would those countless suns and planets and moons serve, those stars and milky ways, comets and nebulae, those created and evolving worlds, if a happy human being did not ultimately emerge to enjoy existence?[2]

After all the resonances have sounded, we know that the summary effect has been to awaken us into greater awareness—and enjoyment.

We can think of an Image as a taut string, and the conjunctions to it by celestial bodies as a strumming of that string. When the string is strummed, what pops up in the life? The strumming of Steiner's Death Image at the position of the Sun at death gives us important events related to the formation of religious renewal through the Christian Community. The strumming of the Western Horizon Image gives us a connection with the first visit to the hill at Dornach. And so on.

Does it matter whether the strumming comes form Mercury or Saturn or an eclipse? Sometimes we simply see events related to the Image; that is, the string vibrating is the Image brought into activity in relation to the life.

Sometimes we see a signature of the body that strummed the string. Saturn strumming the Conception Image string, for example, gives us a picture of commencement of work on the Saturn capital of the Saturn pillar of the first Goetheanum.

True Biography

This approach makes possible a new kind of biography. Steiner once said that an anthroposophical biography was not possible at the present time because the biographers described only what happened when the person was awake, what could be seen in the events of the day. They ignored what occurs in the sleep world, in the activity of the soul.[3] The Solar Cross Images take us into the backstage of the life, so to speak, so that we can perceive what moves behind the scenes, in the realm of the soul. In this way, an individual's story becomes a gateway for all of us to the stars.

Building Themes

When you study the Images over time, the themes within them begin to emerge more clearly. You can continue to construct mind-maps of the Images, and you will notice that they begin to transform. True Images should transform. If they are indeed hints of soul gestures and keys into a divine realm, then they live and change. If you observe them transform in your own being, then you know that you have tapped into something living.

The Images themselves can be seen as mere words, as dehydrated food awaiting the awakening of water. We add water and bring these words alive through the details of the historical personalities, the details of the resonant moments, and, most importantly, your attention. Then you can learn something about the stars, about Rudolf Steiner, and about yourself. Were the central figure of the study different, if it were another person whose life we were interested in, and even with the same birthday, the study would take a new direction, in subtly different colors and flavors.

Notice how the Gate-Earth axis emphasized the issues of spirituality and health—Goethe, Tomberg, Andreae. The East-West Horizon axis emphasized the concerns of politics and power—Churchill, Edward III, Kennedy. Many men, few women, though those women were powerful in their own right. Think of Queen Margot in relation to the political power axis! The Conception Image emphasized the brightness of children's faces receiving; the Death Image emphasized the brightness of a child giving.

It had amazed me for many years why Steiner so vehemently opposed the connection between the Movement for Religious Renewal (what is called now the Christian Community) and the Anthroposophical Society, even though he had given inspiration to both of them.[4] Some anthroposophists have explained to me that a true anthroposophist has already completed the work that the Christian Community is engaged in. That seems like a dismissal, but within it lies an important point. Steiner had explained that the Movement for Religious Renewal, as with all religions, relies on a "cultus," by which he meant a receptive container in the body of the priest through which pure bright spirit could funnel down to those waiting on the Earth. He contrasted this to the "reverse cultus" wherein the fully lived lives of spiritually awake human beings would bring light back to divine realms. In other words, in religion, the stars speak to Man, and in true anthroposophy, Man speaks to the stars.

Noting how Steiner's Death Image, as it appeared in his life, relates so closely to the formation of the Movement for Religious Renewal, especially in the Act of Consecration, we can learn something more from Steiner's life. Steiner insisted that the Movement for Religious Renewal was utterly divorced from the anthroposophic movement. We can hypothesize the reason for this. The first emanated from the celestial influence of his death, and the second from the celestial influence of his birth. They actually combine in the Conception Image, the wise philosopher bending down and the children looking up. But for Steiner, they are separate focuses, separate directions, separate initiatives—the vortex of death and the vortex of birth. This may be why he emphasized over and over again that they were separate.

The Death Image shows us the power of the luminous child, the Solomon Jesus, come to Earth. This is Steiner's lineage, that of Zarathustra through Solomon Jesus, through the King Stream, through enlightened philosophy, through Christian Rosenkreutz.[5] From this vantage, he admires the other luminous child, the Nathan Jesus, who warms the heart of the Kings, the philosophers. From this warmth taken inward, with head and heart combined, a truly good work with the hands can take place on earth. This then is lifted up to the stars—the "reverse cultus." Then one builds structures of stone (Gate Image) wherein human beings are given this light and warmth. Then one liberates the sick of mind and body from the prisons of their beliefs and of their senses (Earth Image). One finds the energy of zeal and, through struggles and conflicts, directs that death-dealing energy to life forces (Western Horizon Image). One becomes refined in fire and becomes eligible for the sacred marriage of one's soul with spirit, with the blessing and with the continued friendship and support of the earthly part, the personality (Eastern Horizon Image). These all affirm the through-line of the human opportunity, with all its difficulties and trials, the prickly road turned into the golden road to the realization of Divinity within the self.

Events That Were Absent

How interesting, also, to know of other important events in the life of Rudolf Steiner that did *not* relate to the celestial events we've examined here. Of course, we could "capture" these events within the star biography by opening up our strict criteria. We could look at the movements of planets in relation to other planets instead of only looking at Sun positions. We could look at different aspects between planets—add in squares, trines, quintiles, and so forth. We could expand our orbs which have been fractions of a single degree to the more standard four degrees, six degrees, or more. But holding back in this way, that is, holding up a smaller net, gives us a good picture of the difference between fate and choice. Some events in Steiner's life were fated—and some were undertaken simply as a free deed of a free individual. He did not depend on the stars to give him the push, but rose up as an individuality to create.

What about those events that seemed fated? Does their occurrence limit our understanding of free choice? We will speak a little more about predestination below. Please understand that celestial events may point to the possibility of an earthly event without guaranteeing its occurrence. We always have the freedom to relate to an urge of destiny or not.

Those who have studied Steiner's life find certain events particularly resonant. They must ponder how these events may have been set into his life's destined unfolding at conception or at birth—or perhaps were free deeds not related to the stars. Let's take some examples.

- Steiner's life-changing meeting with the Master on his twenty-first birthday.[6] There are other celestial connections that influence that meeting, but not the fundamental celestial patterns of the Conception, Birth, or Death Sun, to which we have restricted our view here.
- The laying of the Foundation Stone in the foundation of the first Goetheanum on September 20, 1913.
- The exact day of the burning of the first Goetheanum building, the fruit of years of labor.
- The giving of the Foundation Stone Meditation, commencing at ten in the morning, December 24, 1923, and ending on January 1, 1924. Whole books have been written about those seven days, in which a great verse was given and, in the style of the Teacher, many hours put into the background for each phrase. Steiner called it a "Cosmic Turning Point of Time Beginning."[7]

These events don't relate to the Solar Cross Images, that is, to the Sun locations of conception, birth, or death. This means that an individual creates an initiative that is not foreordained. An individual creates out of complete freedom. Recall the verse from Chapter 3—"The stars once spoke to humanity." In instances of events not related to the fundamental engines coming through the Sun, the individuality speaks to the stars. We can feel a thrill when we show up for a meeting foreordained by our soul and set into motion at our conception. We can also feel a thrill of adventure when we create something powerful for our own soul, and for the world, that does not stand on a particular celestial event, but rather stands upon all of the heavens and all of the earth combined.

Life's Purpose

This study has several purposes: to make you aware of the Oracle of Solar Crosses and of Rudolf Steiner's fascinating biography (both human and star biography), and to arouse your imaginative powers so that you can recapture your own pre-earthly resolves, what you intended for this life. You begin to understand that different people have different purposes. Now you can become aware of the hidden architecture that links life to life across time. In a world focused on winning things and winning outcomes, on beating out the other guy, you may begin to realize that the *process* of bringing heaven to earth is what has value, not specific results. Note the many times that something apparently inconsequential occurred in Steiner's life (or the lives of his Star Brothers or Star Sisters), something that would have gone unnoticed in any life less well chronicled. We saw how it was revealed as related to soul purpose.

We are not here to deify Rudolf Steiner, or to glorify ourselves because we know a lot about this famous man, this "initiate." Nor are we are here to minimize our own lives in the face of a greater life. We are here to open doorways of perception of our own soul-inspired star-studded lives, to reawaken the sense of sacredness of each and every human being, and to comprehend the arc of our lives in relation to others, some who will lead us and teach us, some who will make our passage more difficult, and some who will follow in our example. For we must remember that we are the elder Star Brothers and Star Sisters to set an example for others yet to come, and we will be the Bodes for still others someday.

Predetermination and Free Will

Regarding length of life we would vow to abide by God's will.
—Fifth vow of the Knight of the Golden Stone,
from *The Chymical Wedding of Christian Rosenkreutz* [8]

Modern human beings, treasuring their individuality, nurture the belief that nothing is really determined—everything is open to possibilities unknowable and immeasurable. We may think that random fluctuations govern everything around us. This is a version of "freedom" at its height. In this view, only the individual can exercise will, make a choice, and create an intentional vector that moves through the surrounding chaos. An accidental relationship is chosen, an accidental circumstance is grasped, and so one moves through the accidental world. The key word becomes "random," and within a world of random occurrences, one makes one's way through the chaos of chance calamities as best as possible.

Even those who begin to hedge this complete "freedom" with notions of fated relationships or karma or past lives still adhere to the sense that the moment of death is an accident, determined by a host of mostly unknown factors, including planned and unexpected interventions, close calls, readiness in the will to let go, and unpredictable spontaneous remissions. Thus individuality speaks.

Let us ease into another point of view. Some say that, when you die, you become a star in the heavens. Steiner suggested that we each have a star that is not only our home, but is also the same as ourselves. Some freethinking individualists like this idea, and see in it the traditions of great beings projected by divinities into constellations in the heavens, such as Hercules, Pollux, Castor, and Andromeda. It means that the first hierarchy—the thrones, cherubim, and seraphim—remember the deeds of becoming a divine human being and acknowledge these deeds; that at the point of death, as well as throughout our life, we are beheld and known by the divine. An aboriginal saying goes, "Everything that happens is seen and known by the water, the stars, and the blood."

We are beheld and known by many spirits. They surround us and interpenetrate us even at this moment. Yet we have been granted a space wherein we have the privilege of holding the thought of independence. Thus, even as we thrive within a comprehensive matrix totally dependent upon the creating and holding power of spirits, as individuals we feel responsible for our lives. However, we cannot achieve true independence without admitting the power of these beings that have created a place for us to stand. Thus we see a frailty of the consciousness soul that we are developing: this insistence on independence in all things, including the choice of our time of passing. As Steiner said about the claims of the individualist to freedom, "This freedom is not real; it is but the illusion of freedom."[9]

These spirits hold us in the embrace of space, and also in the embrace of time. They know the timing of our entrance, and also the timing of our exit. We have to begin to entertain these ideas in order to earn the right to work *with* these spirits, rather than endlessly argue about whether they exist or not.

We must remember that we are not human beings seeking a spiritual experience but rather spirits seeking a human experience. We swim in spirit, the personality that we identify with only a tiny part of our true nature. We must ask again, "What is the source of my innermost being?" Not the personality, but the I AM—which comes from beyond the zodiac. This becomes more than the single individual. We are all part of the tapestry of the cosmic weaving of the heavens.

In the larger picture held by spirits, death is not an aberration that has to be postponed as long as possible. Death is an ending of a chapter, and an opening to another chapter. The personality finds death a great inconvenience, and very much a threat, for we cannot fit the personality through the eye of the needle of death. Knowing I will die, what do I do with the opportunity between birth and death? That is the question, not how can I cheat death, a fantasy that has lived strongly in human stories since stories have been told.

Three questions can help us further:

1. Who am I? Engaging this question opens thinking and connects us with the Holy Spirit.
2. What do I love? Engaging this question opens feeling and connects us with the Son/Daughter.
3. Knowing I will die, what must I do? Engaging this question opens the sense of purpose-directed will and connects us with the Father/Mother.

The Illusionist holds us in a fantasy of immortality, and so we do not address these questions, and come—yet again—ill prepared when crossing the threshold of death.

Several analyses of Rudolf Steiner's life reveal the timeliness of his passing. We can look at the Image into which he died, linking him intimately with the spirit and being of Zarathustra. One looks at the prenatal anticipations, which were not so clear. Then one can trace Saturn back through the positions of the planets at his death, which in Solar Cross work restricts us to the passage of Saturn over the Death Sun position. Finally, Saturn crosses Steiner's Death Sun position in the first Act of Consecration of Man.[10]

Did Steiner die by foul play? Did he die by choice or was life prematurely stolen from him? All these questions pale when we understand that far greater beings hold the threads of our life force, within the context of a much larger picture. Look at the Conception Image: calling forth the Sun-brilliance to come to Earth. Look at the Death Image: the arrival of the Sun-brilliance on Earth.

Can we begin to understand that the Father/Mother knows the time of our death?

We prepare for our death this very day, not knowing when it will come about, nor by what means. Death is the best-kept secret of the Hardener because he knows that death is a rebirth into spirit. His goal is to conceal from us the true countenance of death, which is the loving Father/Mother out of whom we have been born. He creates fear that we will lose our personality, our sense of self, and guides us away from living our lives fully into a perpetual spasm of fear about death. The Christ nature reminds us that our spiritual essence grows and prospers through each death and rebirth, through each threshold that we find the courage to walk through. Christ as our prototype demonstrates to us that the gods of our origin demand we become gods also, that we become fully divine. For human beings to become fully divine, we must evolve in our consciousness, confident that death is rebirth in the spirit and comes when greater spirits deem it appropriate. We may not control the time of our entrance and exit, but within those constraints, we strive to live fully. We then desist from forcing our way against death, either by postponing it from fear or by hurrying it through anxious martyrdom. We exercise active will and also openness to what spirit beings have chosen for us to confront and accomplish.

Could Steiner have died in a later year into the same Image? Yes. Are there other Images that would have been brilliant places with which to unite his life's harvest? Yes. One must ponder the question about the time of death on one's own, asking most importantly what are the consequences of various beliefs on this issue. On the Earth side, we can agree that a birth occurs and that a death occurs. Astrology has been used for centuries to help us understand the truth and rightness of birth. Perhaps it will begin to do this for death also. We can await verification when we have crossed over to the Spirit side.

The Power of an Image

We began this book with the picture of Raphael, setting up his deathbed so that the painting of the Transfiguration stood behind his head, showing the Christ-light floating in the incandescent clouds, with Moses and Elijah near him, the apostles in the middle, and in the bottom darkness the mad boy and the townspeople. Likewise, Steiner's deathbed was set up at the foot of his grand sculpture, The Representative of Man, with the Christ-being—that power of light in all of us, that presence of love manifest on Earth—in the center with outstretched arms holding the Illusionist and the Hardener at bay. This representative for all of us prevents these two forces from harming human beings, and presses them into service of humanity. The Illusionist is flying above, wings broken but still floating. The Hardener grovels in the bowels of the earth.[11]

Raphael and Steiner pulled images into their proximity in their dying. Both knew the power of images they had forged themselves to relay them into the realms of spirit.

APPENDIX A
HOW THE SOLAR CROSS
IMAGES CAME TO BE

A Cautionary Note for Christians and Non-Christians

In my work at the StarHouse in Boulder, Colorado, I deal with many different faiths and have found it important to create bridges. I often work with people who have been hurt by Christianity and want very little to do with it. I work also with those who think they know everything about Christianity, and they are more challenging. One person, questioning the analysis of a Greek word, said, holding a Bible in his hands, "If English is good enough for Jesus, then it's good enough for me." At those times patience is needed. These sacred documents were originally written in metaphoric languages where each word has to be wrestled with. Wrestled? Even the word Israel, which an angel gave to Jacob, means "The one who wrestles with Divinity." In other cultures, whole schools have arisen where people learn to wrestle with the Divinity in the many nuances of meaning of the original words. Let's not forget that in this process of the Solar Crosses. Thus we wrestle with Divinity and acknowledge the continuity of divine revelation from many sources. Every tradition, religion, and system has something to offer.

Doctrinal arguments do not interest me—who's right, who's wrong, and what terrible deed was done in the name of a particular religion. One's relationship to the stars stands taller than this. The cruel misdeeds of the few should not veil the beauty of a particular tradition or knowledge. I have made every attempt to put this material in terms that are universal and thus accessible for everyone.

Perhaps this is enough to ease people into speaking about Jesus Christ. It was through a book by Robert Powell, *Chronicle of the Living Christ*,[1] that we were able to see what lay in the zodiac and find our way to the Images in this book.

The word *Jesus* is absent from the Images and rare in the commentaries. We speak instead of Jesus's role as Teacher, Healer, or Sacrificer, paralleling his functions in the realms of thinking, feeling, and willing (cognition, emotion, and action). The Teacher came to the Earth to model a way of being, not to get people to join an organization. He came to model holy energy, for which I use the old Sanskrit word *shakti*, which sounds like what it is— lightning-filled energy. He came to receive the anointing of the Christ-light shakti, to model the truest love and acceptance of the "I AM" or divine spirit spark within each human being. Jesus did not intend that he be singled out as the only individual who could act as he did. Rather he intended that we follow, learn, and surpass him—that we all become Christ-lighted divine beings on Earth. He is a Teacher of a way of living, as we have had and will have other great teachers. In the same way, Jesus is a Healer as we have had healers in the past and into the future. The intuitive Anne Catherine Emmerich, about whom more will be said later, mentions, for example, that the healings performed by the Teacher's students surpassed those of their Teacher in drama and miraculous cure. Finally, rarely overt yet underlying everything that the Teacher did, he acted as Sacrificer, showing how one can lose a life and win a soul. Thus thinking was purified by the Teacher, feeling purified by the Healer, and willing purified by the Sacrificer.

Though we have used dates for other advanced beings when we know them, we have concentrated on this Christ-on-Earth. Here the Sun-Being has come to work through a human being, and we are very interested in what the Sun-Being does on this Earth.

Jesus is not meant to be isolated from humanity but rather linked to humanity. Thus these Solar Crosses are appropriate for those in Christian churches as well as those outside them.

As the great Catholic theologian Thomas Aquinas, said in the fourteenth century, "One may never have heard the sacred word Christ but be closer to God than a priest or nun."[2] That from the core philosopher of the Catholic Church! Having spent time amongst followers of other religions, I have come to realize that this work will be understood best if we see the Teacher as an extraordinary human being, permeated by Divinity—a teacher among other teachers. In this one who brought new life forces to the Earth, planting seeds of a new Sun on Earth and awakening all beings to their Sun nature, we see a forerunner of possible human development. Following Aquinas here, it doesn't matter if you name this Teacher as the one who walked as Jesus, but it does matter that you find some route to this experience. Religions threaten those who leave their ranks with social and spiritual excommunication, not just ostracism but condemnation, and sometimes death. There is no need to abandon the ceremonies of one's religion, which knit together a community in observance of natural cycles. However, the true spiritual understanding of the Divine Light of Consciousness must penetrate beyond the forms of religions in order to determine one's personal relationship to Divinity.

I invite a completely fresh and new look at this history, which may surprise you in its richness. I ask that a person from any religion simply understand the foundations here, which are meant as an offering to all people. In other words, persevere for a bit, and you will see how it all fits together.

Let's begin to put the pieces of the story into place.

Anne Catherine Emmerich

Between 1820 and 1824 a German nun named Anne Catherine Emmerich began to have clairvoyant visions. Though she had had visions from her youth, she began to have very specific pictures of the daily life of Jesus Christ, beginning with the Baptism in the Jordan River and ending with the Resurrection and Ascension, events that I rename the Water-Initiation and the Light-Body Substantiation, to encourage us to new ways of thinking about them.

Anne Catherine Emmerich's highly specific visions spanned over three years. An Italian author, Clemens Brentano, heard of her gift, visited her, and sat at her bedside for most of this time, with some gaps when he had to attend to personal business, or Anne Catherine was too ill to speak. Every day he recorded what she said, then read over to her what she had said the previous day, to make sure he had got it right. These visions as recorded by Brentano comprise four volumes in English and some more material in German manuscripts. They are a goldmine of stories and imagery in comparison to which the four gospels appear as summaries.[3]

Clairvoyance varies widely as to its accuracy and validity. Why would we believe anything that Anne Catherine Emmerich said, no matter how lovely? Various tests of her veracity have been performed. For example, Anne Catherine described the place where she intuitively saw Mother Mary spend the last years of her life and the house where Mary died. Following her descriptions, Lazarite monks found this place in the hills above Ephesus, Turkey, renamed Selcuk. The house was exactly as she described it—though she could not have seen it with her physical eyes, never having traveled more than twenty miles from where she was born. Though the walls had fallen down, the room plan was clear. Archaeologists followed, and now two Roman Catholic popes have visited to affirm this as Mary's house. This holy spot is also special because Muslims and Christians alike come to pay homage, as the Koran accepts Mary as the most divine of all women.

Anne Catherine reported on the modes of dress and ceremonial practices of the Romans and Jews during that time, which have been later corroborated by archaeological research. She described aspects of the life and relationships between the main characters of this story that were corroborated in part by later findings, such as the Nag Hammadi texts written in the second century, discovered in Egypt in 1945. In contrast to her rich accounts of events and people, the regular gospels appear as summaries.

Some of her visions were marred by her prejudices and lack of experience. She did her best as a reporter. For example, she saw in a vision young men around a deep pool of water with a narrow opening, lined with stone, inside a building. The men go in and out of the water in a reverential mood. She had no idea that she was observing the *mikvah*, a common Jewish practice then and now for ritual purification through water. Anne Catherine had no experience of this in her Catholic town in Germany; hence at times one has to know more than she did about the history of the time to understand what she's describing.

Of course, we always must ask what powers the Illusionist—the powers of deception that would lure us away from the truth—exerted over her. That's a fair question to hold when examining her visions or anyone's visions. As with every human realization, they are indications and lights on a path, but not the end of the path. They point in a direction that we must take. As pointers, they are very helpful.

Little has been done with this resource except Mel Gibson's popular movie *The Passion of the Christ*, which was based on her descriptions. People are eager to learn the "truth" about what happened, and the movie has sold many millions of copies. Unfortunately, the film emphasizes the harsh details of what Anne Catherine added to the Gospels while underplaying the resplendent and positive. However, it is the most visible outward sign of the acceptance of Anne Catherine's visions.

Robert Powell

In the late 1980s, Robert Powell, an English mathematician, astrologer, and Ph.D. from the Polish Academy of Sciences, was moved by Anne Catherine's account. From his intimate understanding of the Roman and Jewish calendars from two thousand years ago, he could locate in time Anne Catherine's references to Sabbaths and to festivals, both Roman and Jewish. He put actual dates to the events that she described. He published this as *Chronicle of the Living Christ* in 1996.[4] Here we find brief summaries of the daily activities of Christ Jesus for the last three and a half years of his ministry, as well as very careful working out of the birth and death dates of the major actors in this great drama.

This book included dating of echoes of the daily events, mapped from the years 29 to 33 onto the years 1996 to 1999 as the sixtieth repetition of the life events. Astrologers would understand this as a parallel to a Saturn return. When Saturn returns to the same place that it had at our birth, then we feel that we can revisit and renegotiate the issues that Saturn imprinted into our being when we took our first breath. Likewise, if we can see in the life of Christ Jesus a perfect unit of thirty-three and one-third years, then we can relive the daily events mapped out onto present time. Robert Schiappacasse, William Bento, and I went over and over this material, the first time from February of 1996 to September of 1999, matching day for day the activities described.

When you have actual dates for events you can make astrological charts, though you need a special astrological program to go back two thousand years. My colleagues and I looked at the planetary configurations for many of the events in the life of Christ Jesus.

Rudolf Steiner

To the material from Anne Catherine Emmerich, Robert Powell added the insights of another clairvoyant, Rudolf Steiner. Powell integrated these insights into what he saw in Anne Catherine's visions.

One of Steiner's great contributions was to alert us to the idea that the Christian story is more complicated than previously expected. You can find out more about this in the next appendix.

The Sun and the Planets

After years of the study of Anne Catherine Emmerich as enlightened by Rudolf Steiner's spiritual observations, I was overwhelmed by the complexity spinning around each event. When you read an astrological chart, there is so much going on, so many interrelationships between starry worlds and planets! I had to step back. I decided to look only at the Sun. When you are born and take your first breath, into your being comes an impulse from the Sun. From the planets come various conditionings and qualities. The Sun, however, brings pure impulse from the cosmos. Thus I left planets to the side, and concentrated on the Sun as the laser-focused light coming from an exact position in the zodiac.

After working with Powell's dating of Emmerich's observations, and including Steiner's insights, I asked what was common in Christ Jesus's work on each day that the Sun was in one place, that is, on one Solar Day. For example, what happened every time the Sun lay at five degrees of Taurus, no matter what the year? I put together the daily activities of the same day for every year—the years 29, 30, 31, 32, and 33—for which I had information. There were gaps for some stretches of days when Anne Catherine was too ill or too blissed to speak.

When I put the same days together from different years, I found astounding similarities in theme and also in geographical place. What was taught was often the same. The geographical location of the Teacher was often the same. The Teacher traveled widely, and visited many places important to the spiritual history of humanity. I have termed this *spiritual geographical memory*, meaning the use of place to access what has happened there and the people who acted there. For most people the reactivation of spiritual geographical memory is called pilgrimage, and they visit a place to receive its essence and vibration into their own being. The Teacher took other steps: Before receiving, he activated the place, activated its memory. Then he built it up through his own words and activity and sent it as a message into the cosmos, imprinting it there to be accessed again by humans in the future.

The Teacher traveled a zigzag path through the lands of the Middle East, visiting many places of historical importance. I treat this as an activation of that place and the people involved and what happened there, as if the events of the past were fresh to the moment of the visit, sometimes hundreds of years later. In the last year before the Sacrifice, the visits to the land of Egypt (activating the previous cultural epoch) and Persia (activating the cultural epoch previous to that) take on special importance from this point of view. Steiner explains, "The paths of Jesus in Palestine were the paths of the Sun-force that had come down to the Earth."[5] Valentin Tomberg adds, "[Archangels] are Space-spirits in the sense that they endow space with moral quality. True spiritual geography consists in the knowledge of the activities of Archangels, and the boundaries in space of these activities. The spiritual map of the Earth is quite different from the political or national map."[6] Hence the attention placed in the Oracle of the Solar Cross on *spiritual geographical memory* and *place*.

The many correspondences over different years in the same Solar Day justified for me the combination of the material from different years. Thus, all the days that the Sun lay at the sixth degree of Pisces, for example, were placed together, and all the days that the Sun lay at the sixth degree of Virgo were placed together. For some Solar Days we have information for two years, sometimes three, and on a few occasions four years.

I laid before myself everything that Anne Catherine Emmerich saw on a particular day in each of the years for which I had material from her. For example, the activities of every day that the Sun lay before the tenth degree of Gemini, no matter what the year, were put on the table. Then, if she said that the Teacher spoke from Isaiah, chapter 56, I laid those verses on the table. If she said that the Teacher spoke about Joseph, son of Jacob, I brought in everything known about Joseph in the Hebrew Bible as well as in Rudolf Steiner's writings, in Biblical commentaries, in the Jewish *midrashim*, in mythology, and so forth. If the Teacher came to a certain geographical place, all the history and legendary activities of that place were added to the material of that day. I brought in etymology of the Greek, Hebrew, and Aramaic words spoken. I brought in *gematria*, the science of sacred numbers formed from the number values of the letters of the Hebrew words. If Anne Catherine told a story from another century in the context of that day, I added the content of that story as part of the day, with the assumption that she was resonating with the shakti of that Solar Day. Only once did she speak about the birth of Moses, for example. I considered the possibility that, through resonance, she intuited a connection of this particular day with the birth of Moses. Thus I brought in the whole story of Moses's birth, including all the commentaries about what "really" happened, and who Moses "really" was. Anne Catherine often spoke about Roman festivals and celebrations in some detail. She spoke about the lives and lifestyle of the Three Kings of Babylon in great detail. All these were added.

Over the years that I have been working with this material, I have developed the distinct impression that the Teacher went deliberately to certain places on this earth and said certain things out loud so that these would impress themselves through the Sun into the akashic record. If the activities reported primarily involved others close to the Teacher, such as John the Water Initiator or Mary Magdalene or Mother Mary, I concentrated on what they were sending forth. I speculated that they entrusted their legacy to be discovered by someone who could see and hear from the akashic record itself. Often, they would come to a place of great importance for one day only, as if to impress a relationship between a particular location in the heavens and a particular location on the Earth.

Of course, everything known about Mary Magdalene, the Essenes, the Egyptians, the newest archaeological discoveries such as John the Water Initiator's cave, and so forth—all this was added in. The main references are given at the end of this book, and many more, mentioned in the text, were used only once or twice.

Furthermore, the insights of Rudolf Steiner into many stories in the Christian gospels, as well as his insights even into the ancient Kings of Persia such as Djemschid, and so forth—all this was added to the table.

I also began to add in other events known from history. I added to the table some of the great deeds of extraordinary human beings from all religions, those who had attained a high level of development. I added all artistic renderings from museums around the world of the events of the day or the events referred to prominently on that day. Thus what was laid on the table for a single degree, one degree of 360, included all traditions: Christian, Hebrew, Egyptian, Persian, ancient Indian, including Sanskrit and Shaivism, pagan (Roman, Greek, and Celtic), Trans-Himalayan Wisdom teaching, the Perennial Wisdom, Theosophy, Anthroposophy, and others. Though the core reporter was a Catholic Christian nun, all these traditions have found a place in this Oracle.

The Secrets of the Heavens

Meanwhile, in our work with Star Wisdom, we had become interested in Sabian symbols,[7] a set of 360 word images corresponding to the 360 degrees of the zodiac that Marc Edmund Jones elicited from an intuitive seer in 1925. They include phrases and short sentences that stimulate the imagination and awaken the soul. Reading such phrases as *A Chinese woman nursing a baby with a message* (for 12 Cancer) and *Indians rowing a canoe and dancing a war dance* (for 5 Capricorn) made us want to know more. Even with Jones's explanations, we knew more lived in the mansions of the degrees of the heavens, and we did not find what we were seeking in the Sabian system. (Besides, the Sabian symbols were based on a tropical or seasonal calendar, and did not relate to the actual zodiacal signs, even though they used that terminology.)

Now, however, with all the materials I had collected from widespread sources—adding up to several dozen pages, sometimes a hundred, for each Solar Day—I pondered each Image in turn, an hour or a day or whatever it took. Through meditation and patience, invariably a single unified Image would arise, as a *punctum*, declaring itself from this material as the essence of the day as stored in the zodiac. Let me explain the *punctum*.

Roland Barthes

In his writings as an art critic, Roland Barthes developed the idea of the *studium* and the *punctum*, particularly relevant in viewing photographs. When you look at a picture, perhaps you notice what the picture is supposed to be about. We see a family posed for a portrait, for example. The *studium*, the studied or formal purpose, is a record of the family, meant for the family album, to remind everyone that they existed, that they smiled, proving that they were happy and enjoyed their life together. However, Barthes said that always in a photograph something will jump out at you, regardless of the *studium*—something compelling and interesting, something not intended, hitting you like a dart: the *punctum*. You notice, for example, the long, delicate, white fingers of the young boy in front of a family of simple farmers, whose hands are stubby and dark. Or you notice the particular tilt in the head of a new wife, a subtle gesture that says she's asking herself about her decision to marry. A friend once took a photo of his girlfriend after a hike in the mountains, with the mountains in the background, meant to record the fact that he had been there with his fiancé, and that she was happy. Later on he found in the photo the head of a mountain lion peering out from behind a nearby tree. The *studium*—the smiling girlfriend on an outing, meant for the family album—had no notion of this! The *punctum* revealed what was living more deeply in the story. Viewing the image of the photograph, the *punctum* darts out at you. It is the underlying and perhaps truer story behind the studied purpose of the photo.

Watch for the *punctum*—that's where the soul speaks past the conscious and planned intentions, past the stage set that most photographers attempt. The *punctum* speaks straight to you from soul to soul. The *studium* is always a little dead, predetermined, the party line. The *punctum* shouts out, always alive and changing as our interpretation changes, led by the *punctum* to the deeper meanings living behind the images.

By this method we redirect our attention from the studied casual to the unstudied causal. The *studium* tends toward the conceptual—as in someone putting on a smile for the documentation of the moment, when you know he or she is actually struggling with a job or marriage. Where is the truth? What can take you past the veneer and give you something real to hold on to, to grasp? The *punctum* gives you something to ponder and ruminate, something that, like a mountain lion behind you, wakes you up to the story behind the story.

I laid out all the material for this one degree of 360, this one slice of zodiacal time. I did not bring in at this point the births and deaths of historical personalities, kings and queens and artists, and so forth. I was interested in how the stars were speaking into the earth, as revealed by actions in the world by powerful people whom we might call "tuned in" to the cosmos. Sometimes this took days to arise. I would read and reread the material, expand upon it if necessary, bring in more and more. Then I would patiently meditate on this, and ask for a single Image to reveal itself. Invariably it did so, with some taking longer than others.

In the commentaries to the Images I explain many of the words and phrases of the Image, their historical, archaeological, and mythological origins. But the Image is a compression of the truths lying in that zodiacal degree, which can be used as a key to open up far vaster treasures that live there. The best people to use this key are those who have been born into this degree, for they have an intrinsic memory of its wonders—and its great challenges.

What Is the Truth?

After I have given this explanation, some people ask, "But where did the Images come from?" I thought I had already told them. I have come to realize that the subtext of their question is: "What ancient and holy scripture that I didn't know about have you discovered and now are quoting?" To reiterate, then, I'm not quoting anything. The ancient and holy scriptures have helped as a foundation but are not the source. They have helped me find the source. Aided by the many resources that I have named, I have wrestled and I have formed these words out of my own self. It has been an experience closely akin to what Rudolf Steiner calls *spiritual science*. There is research and study—the *studium*—and there is the light-filled sense of the *punctum*. What comes as a result are light-filled words as gems, each one polished to reveal a sparkle of a magnificent being of the heavens.

Is there a danger of arrogance in this kind of work? Of illusion? Of distortion because of my specific life experiences? Yes, certainly. Let us address this more specifically, beginning with the concept of validity.

Validity—Internal and External

Trained in statistics and experimental design, I have been very aware of the question, "How can you prove any of this?" This is a fair question. There are two forms of validity of a new system or a new measure of something: internal validity and external validity.

The internal validity ascertains how all the data coordinates inside the system, how all the parts agree with each other. As I said before, I was quite surprised by the number of times that, at the same zodiacal degree, the Teacher was in the same geographical place, literally the same spot on earth, sometimes two or three years apart, yet on the same Solar Day. Or that the same theme would be spoken about on that Solar Day in different years. This encouraged me to continue with this approach. Also, in the four positions of the cross, for example, nine degrees of all the fixed signs (Taurus, Scorpio, Leo, and Aquarius), I often found similar connections between geographical locations and themes.

Of course, we would neither expect nor desire that every time that we came to nine degrees of Taurus that the Teacher would be in the same place, like clockwork. It might please an experimental designer, but it would not please the soul of a human being, which needs its freedom. However, this happened enough times to convince me that one of the Teacher's activities included spiritual geographical memory—relating certain places on the Earth with a thin slice of the heavens, what lay behind the Sun in the zodiac on that Solar Day—and thematic issues that, I hypothesized, lay behind the Sun in the being that dwells in that degree.

External validity means that the system works in the big world, with historical personalities, with modern individuals, and with clients. As we are working actively with about three thousand people for whom we have good biographies, and looking at both their births and their deaths, this will take time to work through completely. I have given readings to many people at this point, for whom I have brought out the historical personalities related to them. Over and over again, revealing the historical personality of someone related to the person's Gate Image, Earth Image, or Horizon Images has brought out an "Aha! I knew it!" and a reflective look from the client. The whole face becomes soft, and I know that an elder Star Brother or elder Star Sister has been affirmed. The person knows the connection already, in the bones. The Solar Cross work confirms it and encourages him or her to investigate more thoroughly.

Likewise, the Images, when they work, go deeply into the client, and are worked with actively. How do you "prove" something that speaks stars-to-soul? Using modern methods of statistical demonstration, requiring double-blind studies and random assignment, you don't. Yet to dismiss it as unscientific, at most an "art," would be unfair. This study should not encourage a relaxing of acuity, but rather requires the same kind of lucid discernment as does standard science, as well as an openness to the nuances of an alive and active feeling life.

Ways of Knowing

We have been trained in our "age of science" to seek only the objective—the great verities—suspecting the bias of the subjective and personal. Modern philosophers, including philosopher-scientists such as Werner Heisenberg, have taken pains to demonstrate that objectivity without subjectivity is not possible or even desirable. Asking for the objective without the subjective asks for spirit without personality—and without soul. The "I AM" of the soul commingles the impressions of the senses conditioned by upbringing, that is, the personality, with the "ALL IS" of the spirit.

Too often people quote a pithy passage of "objective truth" and you wonder, "So what?" In this squeaky clean rejection of anything personal and messy, you find that soul is lost and there hasn't been any learning.

I recommend the process whereby these Images were created as a process wherein you can make these your own. The mind-mapping exercises are intended to allow your soul to transform this material.

A risk has been taken in publishing these Images as words. Overwhelmed by printed media, people skim, trying to get the information or the stimulation quickly. An Image that relates to the foundations of your life's purpose should not be skimmed. Every attempt has been made in this book to move slowly, to take the Images of Rudolf Steiner's life seriously, and to permit them to transform in your own soul life.

Historical Personalities and Events

After the Images were set, I began to look at historical personalities to find out how the Images played out in another person's life. These can be very helpful to illustrate how an Image is breathed with a person's first breath and often becomes a major theme of his or her life. At death, one unites one's life-harvest with a Solar Degree, and one can see how the fruits of a life can be taken up in a theme consonant with that life. Work with historical personalities has depended upon the very fine work done by Robert Powell in researching dates for births and deaths of known personalities.[8] I have also used the thirty thousand records of the AstroDataBase, begun by Lois Rodden. Unfortunately, they do not value records of death very highly, while we value them very much.

I have doubled Powell's database, adding many artists, poets, composers, and characters from different cultures. I have also added many historical events, under the theory that potent events imprint themselves back through the Sun into a zodiacal degree. What lives in a zodiacal degree into which you were born can thus condition your birth (or your conception, if this can be determined).[9] From breakthrough inventions to calamities, these can be helpful to know about.

In all of these additions, it is the Image that focuses one's attention on what meaning an event can have. A prominent person's birth or death, a great invention, a huge natural disaster—these can all be understood and made sense of in terms of the Image.

Some people have asked what the criterion is for choosing a historical personality, and why we can't have some simple people. Why Winston Churchill and not Jane Smith? When we know that a good biography exists about the details of someone's life, so that we and the client can learn about how they dealt with the same Gate Image, for example, then we are happy to include people who are less well known. Without the biography, or some way of knowing about them, we can't bring that person's example to bear on the client's life.

It's interesting when clients are certain that a particular person will be related to their birth Solar Cross. Sometimes this happens, but often there is another kind of relationship, often exposed through an astrological analysis.

The pioneer of astrosophy Willi Sucher worked with historical personalities, which he called "similars," matching up not only the Sun but the other planets also. He had worked out many charts by hand, and felt that these relationships constituted the core of a soul-based astrology.[10]

When you lay out all the Star Brothers, Star Sisters, and Bodes, often the client nods knowingly at some and finds others a complete surprise. In the process of a reading we let speak beyond the circumstances of the lives, to discover a common soul gesture.

⟳

As with all works of scriptures and spiritual commentary, these Images have to be taken as hypotheses, something to be tested in one's own experience. I offer these insights as routes to the heavens, and you will have to try them out for yourself, which means making them your own, to test their verity.

APPENDIX B
THE STORY OF THE HOLY FAMILY

H ERE IS A story from Rudolf Steiner that you may need to know to understand some of the commentaries to the Solar Cross Images. It is a beautiful story, brilliant, shocking to some, revealing to others. In this book, it becomes particularly important at the Death Image.

Every effort has been made to extract the wisdom of the events of the Teacher so that the Images can be met without doctrine, dogma, or sectarian reactions. One need not join one of the myriad of Christian churches in order to appreciate this story, which presents a very different way of understanding the being of Christ Jesus, and those around him, than churches tend to offer. Indeed, when you apprehend this story and begin to find it useful, it may become more difficult to join one of the Christian denominations. Here we enter the dangerous territory of "spirit and nature, dancing together."

Shall we simply jump in? How is it that two very different accounts occur in the gospels of Matthew and Luke about the birth of the Teacher? One is born in a house, one in a cave or manger. One is visited by kings, the other by shepherds. One has brothers; the other is an only child. Even the genealogies are different. Does this all come from confusion or sloppy reporting? Couldn't they get their stories straight? The philosopher and clairvoyant Rudolf Steiner penetrated spiritually into the facts, and announced that there were two Jesuses, indeed two Marys and two Josephs too. This upsets most people at the beginning but becomes very interesting to investigate more closely.

For a much more thorough demonstration and proof of this hypothesis, I refer you to the wonderful introduction and summary by Robert McDermott to Rudolf Steiner's lecture cycle *According to Luke*, as well as to the lectures themselves, also to Edward Reaugh Smith's books, especially *The Burning Bush*, and Robert Powell's *Chronicle of the Living Christ*.[11] I leave the demonstrations and proofs to them and simply tell you the story. If the references to spirits and reincarnation streams seem fantastical, this is because modern human beings have lost their clairvoyance, their ability to see into spirit realms readily. Materialism has stunted these supersensible capacities. "Just the facts, ma'am," means only the grossest physical substances are accepted as real. We all know that there is more to life than that, but distrust anything unseen because it might be illusion. The caution is fair, and I am asking that you consider these ideas as a hypothesis, and see how that hypothesis plays out in this study (and in your particular Solar Cross).

First the story from the Gospel of Matthew, with additional features from our other sources, including actual dates. In 6 B.C.E., a wealthy couple named Joseph and Mary gave birth to a special child whom they named Jesus, pronounced Yeshua, a common name, the same as Joshua.[12] The parents had other children too who would later become students of the Teacher. The parents had prepared diligently, especially in a training of their thoughts and emotions, that is, the astral body. The birth was "virginal," meaning that the mother was pure in her astral body. Indeed, Mary had been born in the same way, from a mother who was virginal. From this point of view, sexual relations between partners who have purified astral bodies are sacred. As the Matthew gospel traces the ancestors of Jesus to King Solomon, son of David, we call these characters the Solomon Mary and the Solomon Jesus.

The stargazing priest-kings in the desert, near the old cities of Babylon and Ur, had observed in the heavens the coming of the Solomon Mary and later the coming of her son. They could see pictures in the stars that told them of these events. Then they traveled two months through the deserts to visit this extraordinary infant. They brought gold, myrrh, and frankincense as well as many other gifts. Why did they travel this far to see a baby? Because the heavens had revealed to them that the great teacher of their lineage, Zarathustra, had been reborn, as he had promised five hundred years previously. Zarathustra, which means golden star, had, in distant ancient times thousands of years ago, mastered in seven lives the seven major spiritual traditions.[13] He then inaugurated the ancient Persian civilization, imparting his wisdom to Hermes Trismegistus, who took this wisdom as the seed of the next civilization, the Egyptian. Zarathustra had then incarnated in Babylon, where he taught Pythagoras, the prophet Daniel, Cyrus the Great, king of Persia at that time, and others, in the arts of astronomy and astrology. He said he would return in five hundred years. Generation after generation, the stargazing priest-kings watched for signs of his return.

Here again was their founder, their master, the wisest human being on earth—the Solomon Jesus.

The three magi traveled across the desert to Jerusalem, stopping to consult King Herod about the exact location of the newborn King. Sensing their excitement and impressed by their wealth, King Herod feared for the future of his kingship, and ordered that all the infants of the realm be killed. But, guided by a dream, the Solomon Joseph had already led the Solomon Mary and the Solomon Jesus away from the land, to Egypt, where they would stay for some years, until they returned to Judea.

Then at a particular Passover celebration in Jerusalem, the Solomon Jesus, at age seventeen, gifted his entire Zarathustra nature to another, and soon after that died. Who was this other? It was the Nathan Jesus, the one described in the Gospel of Luke in very different terms.

The Nathan Jesus was born to very poor parents, in simple circumstances, according to Anne Catherine Emmerich, in a cave that had also been used to shelter farm animals from the winter cold, thus what came to be known as the manger. Here too we see two individuals with purified astral bodies creating a human child. Shepherds were awakened by angels proclaiming the victory of this Sun-Being coming to earth. The Luke Gospel traces his earthly genealogy to Nathan, the prophet, also son of David. In the Nathan Jesus was born the simplicity of what is called the sister soul of Adam, that is, the part of Adam, the primal human, that had not yet incarnated.[14] In the Nathan Jesus could be found the profound love and power of Krishna, overseen by the spiritual body of the Buddha. All these spirits may be confusing to some, and I mention them to introduce you to what esotericists talk about and work to understand. It brings up a question—what spirits are in the atmosphere around you right now?

At the age of twelve, this very simple, wide-eyed, and loving Nathan Jesus, a true nature boy, visited the Temple in Jerusalem for the Passover ceremony. There the somewhat older Solomon Jesus passed his essential wisdom, indeed his entire being, to the innocent Nathan Jesus, who thereupon mounted the teacher's chair in the Temple, the highest pulpit in the land, and began to dispute with the learned lawyers and theologians, astounding them with his knowledge and penetrating insight. Of course, this was a complete turnaround for the simple child, and thus it was remarked in the Luke Gospel. Thus the essence of Zarathustra had gone from the Solomon Jesus to join the essence of Krishna and Adam in the Nathan Jesus.

Now for some changes, summarized rapidly. The Solomon Jesus died, leaving his brilliance in the Nathan Jesus. The Solomon Joseph died, as did the Nathan Mary. The Solomon Mary then married the Nathan Joseph, who himself died some months before the Water Initiation (or Baptism) of the Nathan Jesus. The one we call Mother Mary is the Solomon Mary, who was not the biological mother of the Nathan Jesus, but had adopted the young Nathan Jesus and accompanied him through his ministry and trials.

At the Water Initiation (or Baptism), the Krishna, Adam, and Zara-thustra natures of the Teacher stepped aside so that the Nathan Jesus was empty, ready to receive the divine Christos, the Sun-Being, into his human body. This explains why some people distinguish between Jesus and Christ. Jesus was the prepared vessel, the container and reception, for the light of Christ. When people say Christ consciousness, they refer not to a human being, but to the divine brilliance of what entered the vessel of Jesus, hence Rudolf Steiner's lecture series *From Jesus to Christ*. Also at the Water Initia-tion, and again at the Sacrifice, the Nathan Mary united with the Solomon Mary, and both united with the great Sophia, divinity of wisdom. There is a great story of the women, including Mary Magdalene, that has not been told. Many more hints than can be found in the Bible come out in the Solar Crosses.

If you are confused, you might make a chart for yourself. The point is that two streams came into the being of Jesus, assisted by two sons, two mothers, and two fathers. Each had a role to play. Each had a birth and a death, all of which are important in the Solar Crosses. We don't know the birth and death dates for the Josephs, so these aren't included, but Powell has worked out the birth and death dates for the Marys and Jesuses. Indeed, he has worked out the conception dates too, based on the Rule of Hermes.

Here's an easy way to remember much of this. You can connect the Mat-thew Gospel with the Solomon Jesus, who is the carrier of Zarathustra, the King Stream. You can connect the Luke Gospel with the Nathan Jesus, who is the carrier of Adam and Krishna, the Shepherd Stream. The individu-ality whom we follow after the Water Initiation combines qualities of all these, organized by the powerful light-radiating crown and fiery heart of the

Christ. Christ consciousness, Light of Christ, Heart of Christ—all of these refer to this ineffable and unnameable divine reality that showed itself in a human body most completely, though not exclusively, in this story.

These are people who live in human bodies, meet the daily challenges of bodily cares, and have networks of relationships with other people. They are human beings in a more intimate connection with divine realities. Their deeds, feelings, and thoughts have been imprinted into the akashic record and are then available as a resource to us. Knowing the stories helps us resonate with the specific gifts left for us long ago.

Appendix C
Availability of Solar Crosses and Ongoing Research

We originally published the Solar Cross work as two compact discs (CDs), one with introductory material, and one with the spoken Images and commentaries related to that degree. This method was chosen because the best transfer for imaginal content is listening, as one would hear stories around a campfire. This is the healthiest way for the imagination to grow. Reading engages a different part of the brain, and a film definitely defeats the point, as it often overwhelms the senses. Listening, the old style of learning, comes back again. The client becomes the audience—from *audio*, meaning hearing—of one.

In the recorded versions of the Solar Crosses, we also encourage people to take the Images further with mind-mapping. When the Images appear in print, it's even more important to use a technique such as mind-mapping to loosen up the written words. Now Readers in Star Wisdom have been trained who work with clients on their Solar Cross Images. We speak the Images, a few times, to the client, who can then take them in slowly. As the Readers in Star Wisdom are trained in the Oracle of the Solar Cross, and can work through all the details with the client, this is the best way to encounter this content. Then historical personalities, which took up too much room to fit onto the spoken CDs, can be brought in. We can also address resonant moments in the life. The process can take four separate meetings, in person or over the telephone. Four consultations cannot encompass the depth that appears in this book, but it can make for a very good start.

The best preparation for an inquiry of this nature is to begin to write your own biography, that is, note the important events of your life. Begin to form the skeleton of what happened when, and perhaps even to flesh out some of the details. Into this matrix, a Star Brother or Star Sister can be received with welcome.

Ongoing research into Star Wisdom can be found at www.starwisdom. org. One can order a Solar Cross reading from this resource center as well.

APPENDIX D
THE BIRTHDAY OF RUDOLF STEINER

THE BIRTHDAY OF Rudolf Steiner is often reported as February 27, 1861. Robert Powell has done significant research to show that this is the day of his christening in the Catholic Church, and not his birth, which happened two days earlier. Apparently one can still see the records of the little church in Kraljevic that shows this date as the date of christening.

We also have documents in Rudolf Steiner's own handwriting, stating, "My birth took place on February 25, 1861. I was baptized two days later."[15] Steiner celebrated his birthday on the twenty-seventh—his day of christening—and few knew that the real birthday was the twenty-fifth. A letter cited in the same source, by a student, Eugenie von Bredow, shows that she knew this:

> My reverend Master: Today, on the day which is actually the day of birth of your Individuality in this incarnation (whilst hitherto we always held to be February 27), I would like to express to you in true commemoration my warmest good wishes for your well-being....

Her letter is dated February 25, 1921.

Marie von Sivers, later Rudolf Steiner's wife, told the theosophical astrologer, Alan Leo, that Steiner was born at 11:15 P.M. Leo, however, applied this to February 27. The Dutch astrologer Jan Kampherbeek finally published the corrected horoscope, for February 25, 1861, at 11:15 P.M.

The hermetic rule states that the conception moment is determined by interchanging the rising sign (point of the horizon) and the Moon position with those positions in the birth chart, which takes us back ten lunar months—in Steiner's case to June 1, 1860. The application of this rule often leads to a small modification in the birth time, in this case to 11:26 P.M.[16]

Reference Works
Used Frequently

MANY OTHER WORKS have been consulted, and are not mentioned here if used fewer than four times in the bulk of this study. I give here the abbreviations that we use in this book.

ACE: An abbreviation for Anne Catherine Emmerich, specifically references the four volumes of *The Life of Jesus Christ and Biblical Revelations: From the Visions of the Venerable Anne Catherine Emmerich as Recorded in the Journals of Clemens Brentano* (Rockford, IL: Tan Books, 1986, reissued 2004).

Allen *Rosenkreutz* — *A Christian Rosenkreutz Anthology*, compiled and edited by Paul Marshall Allen (Blauvelt, New York: Rudolf Steiner Publications, 1974, second edition).

Allen *Time* — *The Time Is at Hand!, The Rosicrucian Nature of Goethe's Fairy Tale of the Green Snake and the Beautiful Lily and the Mystery Dramas of Rudolf Steiner*, by Paul Marshall Allen and Joan deRis Allen (Hudson, NY: Anthroposophic Press, 1995).

ASNT — *Anthroposophical Studies of the New Testament*, by Valentin Tomberg (Spring Valley, NY, second edition, 1985).

ASOT — *Anthroposophical Studies of the Old Testament*, by Valentin Tomberg (Spring Valley, NY, second edition, 1985).

Autobiography –*Rudolf Steiner: An Autobiography*, by Rudolf Steiner (New York: SteinerBooks, second edition, 1980, trans. by Rita Stebbing).

Belyi *Meetings* — "The Man, Rudolf Steiner," in *Meeting Rudolf Steiner: Classics from the Journal for Anthroposophy*, edited by Joan Almon; series editor Robert McDermott (Ann Arbor, MI: Anthroposophical Society in America), 32–89. Also in Belyi *Reminiscences*.

Belyi *Reminiscences* — *Reminiscences of Rudolf Steiner*, by Andrei Belyi, Assaya Turgenieff, and Margarita Voloschin (Ghent, NY: Adonis Press, 1987). There is a great deal of overlap of material here with *Meeting Rudolf Steiner* (Anthroposophical Society in America, 2005).

Book with Fourteen Seals — *The Book with Fourteen Seals: The Prophet Zarathustra and the Christ-Revelation*, by Andrew Welburn (Sussex: Rudolf Steiner Press, 1991).

Calderón *Magician* — *The Wonder-Working Magician (El mágico prodigioso)*, by Pedro Calderon de la Barca (www.kessinger.net reprints). Denis Florence MacCarthy's translation uses the meter of the original, written in Spanish in 1637.

Christmas Conference — *The Christmas Conference for the Foundation of the General Anthroposophical Society, 1923/1924*, by Rudolf Steiner (Hudson, NY:

Anthroposophic Press, 1990). Though the author name is given to Rudolf Steiner, many contributors have created this work that traces the hourly activities of the week from December 24, 1923 to January 1, 1924, and beyond.

Chronicle — *Chronicle of the Living Christ: The Life and Ministry of Jesus Christ: Foundations of Cosmic Christianity*, by Robert Powell (Hudson, NY: Anthroposophic Press, 1996).

Correspondence — *Correspondence and Documents: 1901–1925*, by Rudolf Steiner and Marie Steiner-Von Sivers (Hudson, NY: Anthroposophic Press, 1988).

Faust/Jarrell — *Faust*, by Johann Wolfgang von Goethe (New York: Farrar, Strauss and Giroux, 2000, translated by Randall Jarrell).

Grosse Christmas Foundation — *The Christmas Foundation: Beginning of a New Cosmic Age*, by Rudolf Grosse (North Vancouver, Canada: Steiner Book Centre, 1984, originally 1976).

Lawlor Voices — *Voices of the First Day: Aboriginal Dreamtime* (Rochester, VT: Inner Traditions International, 1991).

Leading Thoughts — *Anthroposophical Leading Thoughts: Anthroposophy as a Path of Knowledge: The Michael Mystery*, by Rudolf Steiner (London: Rudolf Steiner Press, 1973).

Lindenberg — *Rudolf Steiner: Eine Chronik: 1861–1925*, by Christoph Lindenberg (Stuttgart: Verlag Freies Geistesleben, 1988). Translations of the German in Lindenberg's books are by Robert Schiappacasse.

Lindenberg Biography – *Rudolf Steiner: Eine Biographie*, by Christoph Lindenberg (Stuttgart: Verlag Freies Geistesleben, 1997, two volumes with continuous pagination). Translations of the German in Lindenberg's books are by Robert Schiappacasse.

Lowe Goethe and Palladio — *Goethe and Palladio: Goethe's Study of the Relationship between Art and Nature, Leading through Architecture to the Discovery of the Metamorphosis of Plants*, by David Lowe and Simon Sharp (Great Barrington, MA: Lindisfarne Press, 2005).

Man Before Others — *A Man Before Others: Rudolf Steiner Remembered* (Bristol: Rudolf Steiner Press, 1993).

Marvels Miracles — *Mysteries Marvels Miracles in the Lives of the Saints*, by Joan Carroll Cruz (Rockford, IL: Tan Books and Publishers, 1997).

Meeting Steiner — *Meeting Rudolf Steiner: Classics from the Journal for Anthroposophy*, edited by Joan Almon; series editor Robert McDermott (Ann Arbor, Michigan: Anthroposophical Society in America, 2005).

Our Heritage — *The Book of Our Heritage: The Jewish Year and Its Days of Significance*, three volumes, by Eliyahu Kitov (New York and Jerusalem: Feldheim, revised and expanded edition, 1997).

Prayers of the Cosmos — *Prayers of the Cosmos: Meditations on the Aramaic Words of Jesus*, by Neil Douglas-Klotz (New York: Harper, 1990).

Prokofieff Encounter — *The Encounter with Evil, and Its Overcoming through Spiritual Science, with Essays on The Foundation Stone*, by Sergei O. Prokofieff (London: Temple Lodge, 1999).

Prokofieff Steiner New Mysteries — *Rudolf Steiner and the Founding of the New Mysteries* by Sergei O. Prokofieff (London: Temple Lodge, second edition, 1994).

Ramsbotham — *Who Wrote Bacon? William Shakespeare, Francis Bacon, and James I: A Mystery for the Twenty-first Century*, by Richard Ramsbotham (Forest Row: Temple Lodge, 2004).

Rittelmeyer — *Rudolf Steiner Enters My Life*, by Friedrich Rittelmeyer (London: The Christian Community Bookshop, 1940, translated by D. S. Osmond).

Samweber — *Memories of Rudolf Steiner and Marie Steiner-von Sivers*, by Anna Samweber (London: Rudolf Steiner Press, 1991).

Seasons of Our Joy — *Seasons of Our Joy: A Modern Guide to the Jewish Holidays*, by Arthur Waskow (Boston: Beacon, 1982).

Sefer Yetzirah — *Sefer Yetzirah: The Book of Creation*, edited by Aryeh Kaplan (Boston: Weiser Books, 1997).

Signs in the Heavens — *Signs in the Heavens: A Message for Our Time*, by William Bento, Robert Schiappacasse, and David Tresemer (Hygiene, CO: Sunshine Press, 2000, now available from www.StarWisdom.org).

Steffen Meetings — *Meetings with Rudolf Steiner*, by Albert Steffen (Dornach, Switzerland: Verlag für Schöne Wissenschaften, 1961).

Steiner Fairy Tales — *The Poetry and Meaning of Fairy Tales: Two Lectures by Rudolf Steiner* (Spring Valley, NY: Mercury Press, 1989, lectures of February 6, 1913 and December 26, 1908).

Steiner First Esoteric School — *From the History and Contents of the First Section of the Esoteric School, 1904–1914, Letters, Documents, and Lectures*, by Rudolf Steiner and others (edited by Hella Wiesberger, Hudson, NY: Anthroposophic Press, 1998).

Steiner John — *The Gospel of St. John*, by Rudolf Steiner (Spring Valley, NY: Anthroposophic Press, 1962, original lectures 1908 in Hamburg).

Steiner Luke — *According to Luke: The Gospel of Compassion and Love Revealed*, by Rudolf Steiner (Great Barrington, MA: Anthroposophic Press, 2001, original lectures 1909). This edition has much to recommend it, including the fine material by Robert McDermott both before and after the lectures.

Steiner Mark — *Background to the Gospel of St. Mark*, by Rudolf Steiner (London: Rudolf Steiner Press and Hudson, NY: Anthroposophic Press, 1968, original lectures 1910–1911).

Steiner Matthew — *Gospel of St. Matthew*, by Rudolf Steiner (London and New York: Rudolf Steiner Publishing and Anthroposophic Press, 1946, original lectures 1910). As this edition has been superseded by others, references are made to lecture numbers rather than page numbers.

Steiner Nietzsche — *Friedrich Nietzsche: Fighter for Freedom*, by Rudolf Steiner, with introduction by Paul Marshall Allen (Englewood, NJ: Rudolf Steiner Publications, 1960). This includes the original book from May of 1895 as well as two papers and a memorial address from 1900.

Steiner Revelation — *The Book of Revelation and the Work of the Priest*, by Rudolf Steiner (London: Rudolf Steiner Press, 1998). Eighteen lectures from September 5 to 20, 1924.

Steiner Secret Stream — *The Secret Stream: Christian Rosenkreutz and Rosicrucianism* by Rudolf Steiner (Hudson, NY: Anthroposophic Press, 2000). Excellent introduction and notes by the editor, Christopher Bamford.

Tarnas — *Cosmos and Psyche: Intimations of a New World View*, by Richard Tarnas (New York: Viking, 2006).

Turgeniev — *Reminiscences of Rudolf Steiner and Work on the First Goetheanum*, by Assya Turgeniev (Forest Row, East Sussex: Temple Lodge, 2003).

Wachsmuth — *The Life and Work of Rudolf Steiner: From the Turn of the Century to His Death*, by Guenther Wachsmuth (Blauvelt, NY: Spiritual Science Library, second edition, 1989, trans. by Olin D. Wannamaker and Reginald Raab).

Wilson *Steiner* — *Rudolf Steiner: The Man and His Vision*, by Colin Wilson (London: Aeon, 2005, originally from Aquarian Press, 1985).

Yates — *The Rosicrucian Enlightenment*, by Frances Yates (New York: Barnes and Noble Books, 1972).

Other Steiner references can be found at the Rudolf Steiner Library (www.rslibrary.elib.com) and the Rudolf Steiner archive website (www.rsarchive.org).

Biblical references

For references to Amos, Revelation, Zechariah, Matthew, and so forth, refer to "books" of the Hebrew Bible (Old Testament) and the Christian Bible (New Testament).

References that have assisted this research include: *The Harper Collins Study Bible: New Revised Standard Version: A New Annotated Edition by the Society of Biblical Literature* (New York: HarperCollins, 1989); *The New Oxford Annotated Bible* (Oxford: University Press, 2001, third edition); *Zondervan Handbook to the Bible* (Grand Rapids, MI: Zondervan Publishing, third edition, 1999); *The Nag Hammadi Library*, edited by James M. Robinson (San Francisco: HarperCollins, 1988); *Dictionary of Biblical Imagery*, edited by Leland Ryken and others (Downers Grove, IL: InterVarsity Press, 1998); *The Interlinear Hebrew-English Old Testament*, three volumes, edited by Jay P. Green (Lafayette, IN: Sovereign Grace, 2000); *Strong's Exhaustive Concordance of the Bible*, by James Strong (New York: Abingdon, 1890).

Notes & References

Part 1: Preparing to Use Star Wisdom

1   Alice Bailey, *The Rays and the Initiations* (New York: Lucis Publishing, 1950).

2   Steiner's birthdate is often given as February 27, but that is the date of recorded baptism. An explanation for the February 25 date is given in Appendix D.

3   Wilson *Steiner*, 29.

4   The original German title was *Die Philosophie der Freiheit*. Joel Kobran ("An Introduction to *The Philosophy of Spiritual Activity*," *Journal for Anthroposophy*, #71, 2000, 38–51) relates that Steiner insisted on the English translation being "*The Philosophy of Spiritual Activity*." The German word *Freiheit* is fairly clear – it means freedom, liberty, detachment, ease, liberty, or privilege. We will stay with "freedom," noting Kobran's insistence that "spiritual activity" is a dimension of freedom.

5   A modern example might be the community that sprouted up at the sacred architectural marvel of Damanhur, in Italy. Various accounts are available of this, for example, Silvia Buffagni et al., *Damanhur: Temples of Humankind* (Berkeley, CA: North Atlantic Books, 2006).

6   See citations in the bibliography at the end of the book.

7   Calderón *Magician*, Act 1, Scene iii.

8   Calderón *Magician*, Act 1, Scene iii. Another passage from the Illusionist (Act 3, Scene ii): "Though my mighty power/ Cannot enslave free will even for an hour,/ It may present / The outward show of rapture and content, / Suggesting thoughts impure: / If force I cannot use, at least I lure." Calderón even names this Demon "Lucifer" in Act 3, Scene xv.

9   There are many technicalities about the different aspects of each of the named attributes of the soul. In anthroposophy, the main soul functions are thought to be in the higher astral body, and are sometimes differentiated from the "I AM" from the spirit. Alice Bailey's esoteric psychology draws the line in different places. It's most useful to see a continuum from heavenly spirit to physical substance, with strong concentrations of consciousness at certain places along that continuum.

10 Rudolf Steiner, *Michaelmas and the Soul-Forces of Man* (Spring Valley, NY: Anthroposophic Press, 1946, lectures of 1923). I changed "man" to "human being."

11 The basic resources existing at this time are featured at www.starwisdom. org, including Robert Powell, *Hermetic Astrology*, Volumes 1–3 (Kinsau, Germany: Hermetika, 1987–1991), and the works of Willi Sucher and Elizabeth Vreede. Works in progress include a more formal study of the birth and death charts of Rudolf Steiner, as well as other works of the new Star Wisdom.

12 I have put "humanity" in place of "Man," as the latter is often misunderstood as male only. This verse can be found in Rudolf Steiner, *Verses and Meditations* (Bristol: Rudolf Steiner Press, 1993), 97. It was given to his

wife, Marie Steiner, at Christmas 1922 (*Correspondence*, 169).

13   John Michell, *The Temple at Jerusalem: A Revelation* (Glastonbury: Gothic Image, 2000).

14   Revelation 22:2, also Ezekiel 47:12 and 1 Enoch 10:19.

15   Steiner *Mark*, 75.

16   Anthroposophists may be interested to know that Steiner used sidereal astrology and not tropical, and used equally sized houses. This is demonstrated in several publications by Robert Powell, from *Hermetic Astrology* (Kinsau: Hermetika, Volumes 1–3, 1987–1991) to the *Christian Star Calendar* (from www.SophiaFoundation.org).

17   Additional adjustments have to be made for other calendrical systems. The Julian calendar was updated to the Gregorian calendar in the German Catholic states by 1583, in England by 1752, but not in the Soviet Union until 1918. In the later years, the errors of the Julian calendar had increased to about 13 days' difference from the reliable Gregorian calendar still in use today.

18   Robert Powell's *Hermetic Astrology* describes this original system of Zarathustra, as does his recent doctoral thesis, *The Definition of the Babylonian Zodiac and the Influence of Babylonian Astronomy on the Subsequent Defining of the Zodiac* (Warsaw: Polish Academy of Sciences, 2005).

19   Rudolf Steiner, *The Spiritual Hierarchies and Their Reflection in the Physical World* (Hudson, NY: Anthroposophic Press, 1983), 107 and passim.

20   Ibid., 104 and passim.

21   Revelation, 4:9. Also Ezekiel 1:5–25, 10:1–22, and Exodus 25:17–22. The work in progress on the astrobiography of Rudolf Steiner's life goes into these fiery beings of heaven in much greater detail.

22   Rudolf Steiner, *The Astronomy Course*, from Rudolf Steiner Library, Ghent, NY.

23   On the Sun as transmitter: "Rather than refer to the sun in general terms, it is preferable to describe the effect of the sun from one of the twelve constellations of the zodiac." Steiner *Fairy Tales*, 16.

24   *Awakening Osiris: The Egyptian Book of the Dead*, translation by Normandi Ellis (Grand Rapids, Michigan: Phanes, 1988), 47–48. Ellis points out that the Egyptian Book of the Dead was collected between 3000 BCE and CE 300.

25   Gudrun Burkhard, *Taking Charge: Your Life Patterns and Their Meaning* (Edinburgh: Floris Books, 1997, original 1992); Betty Staley, *Tapestries: Weaving Life's Journey* (Stroud, Gloucestershire: Hawthorn Press, 1997).

26   Adapted from Burkhard, Ibid., 20.

27   The time of conception is often termed the "epoch," a term that we don't use here. The mapping of celestial events during the gestation onto the life after birth we here call "prenatal anticipations;" others refer to this as the "astrological biography," a term that we use in a more general way in this study. Though Willi Sucher computed the Rule of Hermes by hand, the Astrofire computer program by Peter Treadgold does this computation for us, which is helpful as many choices have to be made in this analysis.

28   Rudolf Steiner, *Human Questions and Cosmic Answers* (lecture of June 25, 1922, translated by Robert Powell).

29   At the meeting of the IAU at Prague, August 24, 2006.

30   Leonard George, speaking at the Roots of Western Esotericism conference (Weimar, September 2006) about the fourth century philosopher's response to the question put by Porphyry. See

also Leonard George, "The Teachings of Iamblichus: Between Eros and Anteros," *Lapis*, 13, 61–68.

31 Redrawn from a diagram in Mary Settegast, *When Zarathustra Spoke: The Reformation of Neolithic Culture and Religion* (Costa Mesa, California: Mazda Publishers, 2005), 43. Many plates and bowls with similar cross designs were discovered, and adorn Settegast's book. What were they used for? None were used for cooking, but perhaps were intended to hold "*haoma* twigs, grain or bread, milk, during the *yasna* ceremony" (private communication from Mary Settegast). The combination of circle and cross had the tradition of "unity in Zoroastrian theology, [in which] the earth is said to be motionless, with the sun standing overhead, as at high noon" (Settegast, 75).

32 In the northern hemisphere, the Sun is usually a bit to the south. When you face it and raise your arms to the horizons, your left hand will point to the east and your right hand to the west. In the southern hemisphere, your right hand will point to the east and your left hand to the west.

33 ASOT, 60.

34 ACE II 135.

35 Marc Edmund Jones, *The Sabian Symbols in Astrology* (Santa Fe, NM: Aurora, 1993, revised edition), 137. More on the Sabian Symbols is given in Appendix A.

36 From Numbers 12:8. I noted a new translation of this passage by Rebbe Nachman of Breslov, and went back to the original Hebrew to check it out, making my own version of this. See David Sears, *The Tree That Stands Beyond Space: Rebbe Nachman of Breslov on the Mystical Experience* (Jerusalem: Breslov Research Institute, 2002), 32.

37 1 Samuel 16:7.

38 Book of Enoch, XCIX, 165.

39 Lynne McTaggart, *The Field: The Quest for the Secret Force of the Universe* (New York: Harper, 2001). Of many references to Akasha in Rudolf Steiner's works, Steiner *Luke*, 27, is a good place to start.

40 Lawlor *Voices*, passim.

41 Steiner *Nietzsche*, 110, quoting from Nietzsche's *Case of Wagner*.

42 From a lecture given on December 31, 1915, titled "The Year's Course as a Symbol for the Great Cosmic Year," translated in *Anthroposophic News Sheet* of the General Anthroposophic Society, Dornach, December 24, 1944.

43 Steiner *Revelation*, 176, 235.

44 This very helpful concept comes from Dennis Klocek at the School of Goethean Studies, Rudolf Steiner College, Fair Oaks, California.

45 Julia Cameron, *The Artist's Way* (New York: Tarcher/Putnam, 1992), 87; Natalie Goldberg, *Writing Down the Bones* (Boston: Shamballa, 1986).

Part ii: Star Wisdom in the Life of Rudolf Steiner

1 To determine this location, we used the Hermetic Rule described in Part I, and the birthday calculations shown in Appendix D. Note that Steiner's parents were married on 16 May 1860, two weeks before conception.

2 *Leading Thoughts*, 49.

3 Steiner *Revelation*, 109.

4 Appendix A explains why we use the words Teacher and Healer for the activities of Christ Jesus as perceived by Anne Catherine Emmerich. This makes these activities more accessible to all.

5 Douglas-Klotz, *Prayers of the Cosmos*.

6 Other possible translations are given in *Prayers of the Cosmos*, 19.

7 The Revealing is a new name for the Transfiguration that we saw in

the painting at Raphael's deathbed. The Sacrifice is a new name for the Crucifixion.

8 Calderón *Magician*, Act 1, Scene iii. The Demon in the play shows attributes both of the Hardener and the Illusionist.

9 Andrei Belyi, "The Man, Rudolf Steiner," in *Meeting Steiner*, 54. Note that this use of "instinct" varies fundamentally from Steiner's use of it when speaking about Nietzsche. Belyi uses it in the crudest and least conscious sense.

10 Steiner *Revelation*, 109.

11 Rudolf Steiner, *Verses and Meditations*, op. cit., 129. This translation by George and Mary Adams, even with some of its odd words, has the very best meter of all the translations. Also in *Christmas Conference*, 291.

12 Andrei Belyi, "The Man, Rudolf Steiner," in *Meeting Steiner*, 57.

13 Steiner *First Esoteric School*, 21.

14 Nine months' gestation goes through three-fourths of a year, though we seldom find that the conception and birth occur in exactly the same Solar Cross.

15 "Hark! The whirlwind is in the wood! A low murmur in the vale! It is the mighty army of the dead returning from the air." From MacPherson's poem *Fingal*, in John Matthews (ed.), *From Isles of Dream: Visionary Stories and Poems of the Celtic Renaissance* (Hudson, New York: Lindisfarne, 1993), 25. We meet Fingal later in the Birth Images.

16 Lindenberg, 393–394; Wachsmuth, 335–342.

17 Steiner *First Esoteric School*, 265–267.

18 Edouard Schuré, cited in Wachsmuth, 78.

19 Wachsmuth, 80.

20 Lindenberg, 245; Wachsmuth, 76–80.

21 Lindenberg, 336; Wachsmuth, 205.

22 Rudolf Steiner, "The Soul's Awakening," from *Four Mystery Dramas* (London:

Rudolf Steiner Press, 1997, translated by Ruth and Hans Pusch), 108–111.

23 Rudolf Steiner, *Eurythmy: Its Birth and Development* (Weobley, England: Anastasi, 2002), 50.

24 Lynne McTaggart, *The Field: The Quest for the Secret Force of the Universe* (New York: Harper, 2001).

25 Lindenberg, 344–345; Wachsmuth, 217.

26 The events occurred in the ninth century, and were written by Wolfram von Eschenbach in the thirteenth century in *Parzival* (New York: Vintage Books, 1961, translation and introduction by Helen Mustard and Charles Passage).

27 Lindenberg, 344–345; Wachsmuth, 217–221.

28 Reminiscences of Nathalie Turgenieff-Pozzo, sister-in-law of Andrei Belyi. In "Glimpses of the Building of the First Goetheanum and the Start of the World War," by Sonia Tomara Clark and Jeannette Eaton, in *Meeting Steiner*, 91.

29 Cited in John Fletcher, *Art Inspired by Rudolf Steiner* (Mercury Arts Publications, 1987), 78.

30 Steffen *Meetings*, 93.

31 Steffen *Meetings*, 79.

32 The crossings by Pluto of the conception Sun position take place between August 5, 1894, and May 14, 1896. In astrology, an "orb" is allowed of a degree or two in either direction to take into account the response of a heavenly-earthly interface to the vibrations of a connection. That is, there may be delayed responses after the last crossing in the physical plane, as well as anticipatory reactions before the first crossing. Thus the first letters between Elisabeth Förster-Nietzsche and Steiner begin on May 28, 1894. The final falling out takes place in December 1896. Lindenberg, 128–142.

33 Steiner cited in Steiner *Nietzsche*, 31. Steiner devotes Chapter 18 of his

Autobiography to his experience of Nietzsche.

34   Rittelmeyer, 82.

35   Steiner *Nietzsche*, 48.

36   Rudolf Steiner, *Christianity as Mystical Fact*, Chapters 4 and 5. Much more is also said in the latter lectures of Rudolf Steiner, *Wonders of the World, Ordeals of the Soul, Revelations of the Spirit* (London: Rudolf Steiner Press, 1963, lectures of 1911).

37   Rittelmeyer, 29.

38   Steiner *Nietzsche*, 43. *Thus Spake Zarathustra* was written in 1883, when Steiner was twenty-two.

39   Ibid., 47.

40   Ibid., 83, 168.

41   This was actually not cited by Steiner, but comes from a citation in Tarnas, 347.

42   Steiner *Nietzsche*, 57, 132.

43   Ibid., 91.

44   Steiner *Nietzsche*, 54.

45   Ibid., 72, quoting Nietzsche.

46   Ibid., 133.

47   Nietzsche cited in Tarnas, 347.

48   Lindenberg, 128–142. In his *Autobiography*, Steiner mentions "accusations" (p. 222), implying that she directed her manipulations and ire at him.

49   *Autobiography*, 220.

50   Steiner *Nietzsche*, 173. Steiner's main papers on Nietzsche's "psychopathology" were written the year of Nietzsche's death (August 25, 1900), and are included in the Steiner *Nietzsche* volume.

51   Ibid., 104.

52   From "Thus Spake Zarathustra," in Kaufmann, *Nietzsche*, op. cit., 282–283.

53   Curtis Cate, *Friedrich Nietzsche* (Woodstock, NY: Overlook Press, 2002), 548–551.

54   Steiner *Nietzsche*, 166, 169. Only later could Steiner look back and see some of Nietzsche's nastier attitudes, for example, Nietzsche's "first tenet": "As

first tenet of *our* love for mankind, the weak and misformed shall be destroyed. And one should even assist them in this." Ibid., 187. Did he include himself in his last decade in this prescription?

55   Steiner *Revelation*, 156; *Autobiography*, Chapter 18. See also Rudolf Steiner's *Karmic Relationships*, Volume 3 (lecture of August 8, 1924) and Volume 4 (lecture of July 20, 1924). In a recent play, Richard Foreman has the mad philosopher say, "Nobody likes being chained to the wall by somebody else's imagination. Please! Wipe me out!" Richard Foreman, *Bad Boy Nietzsche! And Other Plays* (New York: Theater Communications Group, 2005), page 5 of rehearsal script.

56   Steiner *Nietzsche*, 117.

57   Ibid., 65.

58   Rudolf Steiner, *Christianity as Mystical Fact*, op. cit. Chapters 4 and 5.

59   Marie Steiner, introduction to Rudolf Steiner, *The Christ Impulse and the Development of the Ego-Consciousness*, cited in Wachsmuth, 125. Further connections here: Annie Besant was born on October 1, 1847, fourteen years before Steiner's birth, putting her into the Solar Cross of his death, to the very degree, Steiner at Pisces and Besant opposite at Virgo.

60   Lindenberg, 282; Wachsmuth, 123–125.

61   Lisa Dreher Monges, "A Student's Memories of Rudolf Steiner," in *Meeting Steiner*, 94.

62   Arvia MacKaye Ege, "Impressions of a Young American Student," in *Meeting Steiner*, 108.

63   Monges, op. cit., *Meeting Steiner*, 95.

64   op. cit., 96.

65   Rittelmeyer, 18, 29.

66   Ibid., 25.

67   For example, Ilona Schubert, in *Man before Others*, 218.

68   Andrei Belyi, "The Man, Rudolf

Steiner," in *Meeting Steiner*, 51, 76, 87, 88.

69 See Appendix B for an explanation of these terms.

70 Belyi, op, cit., 83.

71 Arvia MacKaye Ege, "The Christmas Foundation Meeting," in *Meeting Steiner*, 118.

72 The moment of birth, fourteen degrees and thirty-three minutes of Aquarius, is explained in Appendix D.

73 Goethe writing Schiller, cited in Steiner's 1899 article on Goethe, "The Character of Goethe's Spirit," cited in Allen *Time*, 160.

74 Steiner *Revelation*, 19.

75 Ibid., 79. The Vernal Point is shown at the position of the Sun at the spring equinox sunrise.

76 *Prayers of the Cosmos*, 47.

77 From Matthew 5:3–12 and 6:9–13. Neil Douglas Klotz's *Prayers of the Cosmos* explores the original Aramaic for these formulas, finding a much broader interpretation. Klotz gives other possibilities for this (p. 12) and all the lines.

78 John 6:55, and connecting to "true words," John 6:68.

79 The Sophia Foundation of North America (www.SophiaFoundation.org) has study courses on each of the lines of the Lord's (Abwoon) Prayer and the Beatitudes that spreads them out and makes them accessible.

80 *Sepher Yetzira*, 190.

81 Rittelmeyer, 48 and 43.

82 Rudolf Steiner, *Verses and Meditations*, op. cit., 65.

83 Emil Bock, in *Man before Others*, 97–98.

84 Rittelmeyer, 19–20.

85 You may wish to ponder on the observation by Steiner that the spirits of the cycles of time (the Archai), which are the astral body of the earth, work together with the spirits of the elementals, the etheric body of the earth. The sphere of their

activity stands at a certain angle to the sun at 3:00 P.M. that makes it more available. Friedrich Benesch, *The Hemispheres: The Celebration of the Christian Festivals on the Southern and on the Northern Earth*, private publication of three lectures, 1980, 3. In summer, adjust for Daylight Savings Time by observing and participating at 4 P.M.

86 Steffen *Meetings*, 169.

87 Wachsmuth, 507–509.

88 Recollection of Steiner's words by a student, Andrei Belyi, in "The Man, Rudolf Steiner," *Meeting Steiner*, 81.

89 Sonia Tomara Clark and Jeannette Eaton, "Glimpses of the Building of the First Goetheanum and the Start of the World War," in *Meeting Steiner*, 92.

90 "He regarded the future temple of mankind as lost if it were built upon medieval foundations." Rittelmeyer, 77.

91 Andrei Belyi, *op. cit., Meeting Steiner*, 64.

92 Ibid., 69.

93 Steiner *Secret Stream*, writing between 1917 and 1918, 186. Adding from the anthroposophist, Friedrich Benesch, op. cit., 6: "The earth as a whole has a consciousness and this consciousness is located in the mineral elements."

94 Ibid., 86; Revelation 2:17.

95 Friedrich Hiebel, in *Man before Others*, 211.

96 Belyi *Meetings*, 79.

97 Wilson *Steiner*, 137.

98 Jean Adhémar, writing in *Encyclopedia Britannica*.

99 From *Les Épaves* (Scraps), 1866, translated by Roy Campbell, *Poems of Baudelaire* (New York: Pantheon Books, 1952).

100 Raymond Cogniat, "Renoir, Pierre-Auguste." *Encyclopedia Britannica*.

101 Padraic Collum, Introduction to *The Complete Grimm's Fairy Tales* (London: Routledge & Kegan Paul, 1975), pages vii to viii. This edition also has a fine commentary by Joseph Campbell.

102 Steiner *Fairy Tales*, lectures of
February 6, 1913 and December 26,
1908, passim. He speaks very favorably
of the Grimm Brothers in these
lectures.

103 Bruno Bettelheim, *The Uses of
Enchantment: The Meaning and
Importance of Fairy Tales* (New York:
Vintage, 1989).

104 *Complete Grimm's Fairy Tales*, op. cit.,
xiv.

105 Ludwig Denecke, "Grimm, Jacob
Ludwig Carl and Wilhelm Carl."
Encyclopedia Britannica. Viewed
October 16, 2005.

106 Though Wilhelm is mentioned as
second author, this was his bow to
alphabetical order. He put much more
time than his brother into the fairy
tale collections.

107 Born February 14, 1900 (in the Julian
calendar, which equates with this
day in the Gregorian calendar), died
February 24, 1973 (11–12 Aquarius),
both in the sign of the Water Bearer.

108 Sergei O. Prokofieff, *The Case of
Valentin Tomberg: Anthroposophy or
Jesuitism?* (London: Temple Lodge,
1997), critiques Tomberg's move
from anthroposophy to the Roman
Catholic Church. In the template of
the Solar Crosses, one can see a shift
from influence of the Gate Image, and
its relation to the Star Brother Rudolf
Steiner, to the influence later in life
of the Death Image. Some of the
critiques are harsh and exaggerated,
which led to Irina Gordienko's
rebuttal: *Sergei O. Prokofieff: Myth and
Reality* (Basel: Moskau-Basel-Verlag,
2001). In addition to the rebuttal,
Gordienko offers one of the most
provocative and thorough expositions
of the foundations of anthroposophy
for the serious student—detailing
what the demands are for one
who would develop capacities for
receiving Sophia-wisdom. More
recently, Prokofieff has written

*Valentin Tomberg and Anthroposophy:
A Problematic Relationship* (Forest
Row: Temple Lodge, 2005, original
2003), which concentrates on a letter
that Tomberg wrote but never sent
just before the end of his life. The
letter is a very interesting testament
of someone pulled by a Death Image,
and does not relate to Tomberg's Birth
Solar Cross, which connects him to
Rudolf Steiner as Star Brother.

109 ASOT 123.

110 Luke 15:1–10.

111 From *ASOT*, 19, 153, and from *ASNT*,
48.

112 We give the capitalizations as they
appear in materials of the Sophia
Foundation of North America, from
whom this meditation and extensive
commentaries and meditations can be
had (www.sophiafoundation.org).

113 Lady Jane Grey, executed Feb. 12, 1554.

114 Romans 8:22–23.

115 Leviticus 13:45. Leprosy classically
does not mean Hansen's disease, in
which the cartilage and bones of the
body disintegrate.

116 Scalia, dissenting in Hamdi
v. Rumsfeld (03-6696) 542 U.S.
507 (2004), citing W. Blackstone,
Commentaries on the Laws of England,
132–133 (1765).

117 2 Kings 5:7. The incurability
of leprosy is also shown by the
demonstration of Divinity to Moses
in Exodus 4:6–7: "Again, Divinity
said to him, 'Put your hand inside
your cloak.' He put his hand into his
cloak; and when he took it out, his
hand was leprous, as white as snow.
Then Divinity said, 'Put your hand
back into your cloak' – so he put his
hand back into his cloak, and when
he took it out, it was restored like the
rest of his body." Divinity gives Moses
this experience as a sign that Moses
working with Divinity could cure (and
create) leprosy, something that mere
humans could not do.

118 This is not showing off on the Teacher's part but is a step of the official process of determining whether a person has been cured, as set forth in great detail in Leviticus 13 and 14.

119 Gladys Mayer, in *Man before Others*, 88.

120 *Four Mystery Plays* (London: Rudolf Steiner Press, 1973), 5. Mixed with a translation from Allen *Time*, 103.

121 Samweber, 11. She wore her badge for many years afterward, under her outer clothing.

122 One reference that becomes important to our investigation later on: From *The Balance in the World and Man, Lucifer and Ahriman* (November 20, 1914, Lecture 1): "Owing to this imprisonment of wisdom in the nerve process, the premonition arose at the dawn of the Fifth Post-Atlantean epoch [the European Age following upon the age of Greece and Rome] that Mephistopheles is shackled to the human being, stands at his side."

123 *The Spiritual Hierarchies*, Lecture 2, April 12, 1909.

124 Andrei Belyi, "The Man, Rudolf Steiner," in *Meeting Steiner*, 35, 55. Samweber, 25.

125 Gladys Mayer, *Man before Others*, 87.

126 Rittelmeyer, 68, 130.

127 Steiner *Revelation*, 110.

128 Arvia MacKaye Ege, "Impressions of a Young American Student," *Meeting Steiner*, 106.

129 Rittelmeyer, 36.

130 Emil Bock, *Man before Others*, 89, 91.

131 Rittelmeyer, 147.

132 Samweber, 13.

133 Andrei Belyi, passim, *Meeting Steiner*, 32–89.

134 Samweber, 37.

135 Steiner's *Autobiography*, cited in Wilson *Steiner*, 81, where Wilson also describes his experiences with this point of view (also pages 161–171).

136 Frances Yates, speaking about the philosophy of Johann Valentine

Andreae, in Frances Yates, *The Rosicrucian Enlightenment* (New York: Barnes and Noble, 1972), 178.

137 How interesting that we have seen another Friederich and Elizabeth pair in this study—Nietzsche and his sister.

138 Martin Luther died in 1546, and John Calvin in 1564. The Council of Trent (1545–1563) began reforms in the Catholic Church. By the beginning of the seventeenth century, the uneasy truce between Catholic and Protestant was holding, and made all of these developments possible. Much of this information comes from Frances A. Yates, *The Rosicrucian Enlightenment* (New York: Barnes and Noble Books, 1972—elsewhere referred to as "Yates"). Other sources are R. J. W. Evans, *Rudolf II and His World* (London: Thames and Hudson, 1997), Ralph White, editor, *The Rosicrucian Enlightenment Revisited* (Hudson, NY: Lindisfarne, 1999), Christopher McIntosh, *The Rosicrucians: The History, Mythology, and Rituals of an Esoteric Order* (Boston: Weiser Books, 1997), Susanna Akerman, *Rose Cross over the Baltic: The Spread of Rosicrucianism in Northern Europe* (Leiden: Brill, 1998), Steiner *Secret Stream*, Ramsbotham, and Allen *Rosenkreutz*.

139 "Proposition of the Archdukes of Vienna," writing in 1606, in Evans, *Rudolf II and His World, Ibid.*, 196.

140 *Confessio Fraternitatis*, 1615, cited in Ralph White (ed.), *The Rosicrucian Enlightenment Revisited*, op. cit., 20.

141 Yates, 207.

142 Ramsbotham, 57. Steiner *Secret Stream*, introduction, 13. Yates, passim.

143 Yates, 66.

144 From *The Chymical Wedding of Christian Rosenkreutz: A Modern Poetic Version*, by Jon Valentine (Spring Valley, NY: St. George, 1981), 16.

145 Allen *Rosenkreutz* brings all these resources together in one place, except

the beautiful "poetic vision" of Jon Valentine (Ibid.).

146 Rudolf Steiner, *Karmic Relationships*, Volume 1, Chapter 12. Also, Chapter 10 in Steiner *Secret Stream*, written for the alchemist Alexander Bernus in 1917–1918.

147 Another example: "They [the facts of cosmogony] were, one can say, discovered *for* me and I wrote them down in *Occult Science*." Steiner *Fairy Tales*, 13. Italics added.

148 Cited in the introduction to Steiner *Secret Stream*, 18.

149 Yates, 148.

150 Goethe wrote of his birth, "On the 28th of August of 1749, as the midday bell struck twelve, I was born into Frankfurt by the Main" (from *Poetry and Truth*, cited by the tourism brochure for Frankfurt). This puts Goethe's Birth Sun at just one half of one degree from exactly opposite to Steiner's Birth Sun. He continues, with my comments: "My horoscope was propitious: the Sun stood in the sign of the Virgin [he was using the tropical system popular in his day], and had culminated [reached its zenith] for the day; Jupiter and Venus looked on him with a friendly eye [they were opposite to each other at 5 degrees Pisces and 5 degrees Virgo, thus in dynamic relationship], and Mercury not adversely [indeed, conjunct Regulus in Leo, the King Star]; while Saturn and Mars kept themselves indifferent; the moon alone [at 21 Aquarius], just full, exerted the power of her reflection all the more, as she had then reached her planetary hour. She opposed herself, therefore, to my birth, which could not be accomplished until this hour [of the full moon eleven hours previously at around one in the morning] was passed."

151 Rudolf Steiner, "The Nature and Significance of Goethe's Writings on Organic Development," in *Goethean Science* (Spring Valley, New York: Mercury Press, 1988), 76, cited in Ramsbotham, 66.

152 John Barnes, *Goethe and the Power of Rhythm* (Ghent, New York: Adonis Press, 1999), 13. The shape of the music stand is the top part of an octahedron.

153 Goethe's *Italian Journey*, letter of September 11, cited in Lowe *Goethe and Palladio*, 53 and 9.

154 Ibid., letter of October 12, cited in Lowe *Goethe and Palladio*, 77.

155 Goethe's *Flight to Italy*, letter of October 19, cited in Lowe *Goethe and Palladio*, 78.

156 The edition of Goethe's *Metamorphosis of Plants* with Rudolf Steiner's introduction was published by the Bio-Dynamic Farming and Gardening Association in 1974.

157 Lowe *Goethe and Palladio*, 15–16.

158 Steiner *Fairy Tales*, 2.

159 The most brilliant and accessible way to experience this story is through the work of actor/storytellers Glen Williamson and Laurie Portocarrero.

160 Goethe's tale in Allen *Time*, 128. Allen uses "speech" rather than "conversation," though others tell the story as I've written it, noting that "The Fairy Tale of the Green Snake and the Beautiful Lily" occurs as one of the tales in Goethe's *Conversations of German Immigrants*.

161 Wolfram von Eschenbach, *Parzival* (New York: Vintage Books, 1961, translation and introduction by Helen Mustard and Charles Passage). Old German and its translations from various scholars of that period.

162 Shakespeare, *Hamlet*, Act II, scene ii.

163 Rudolf Steiner, *Old and New Methods of Initiation* (London: Rudolf Steiner Press, 1991, original lecture February 24, 1922), 129ff, quote on p. 131.

164 Ibid., 116.

165 *Faust*/Jarrell, Scene v, 124. The

modern translation by Jarrell has much more accessible language than other translations.

166 Ibid., Scene i, 25.

167 Ibid., Scene iv, 81.

168 Ibid., Scene iv, 89.

169 Ibid., Scene xiv, 201, and xix, 221.

170 Ibid., Scene xxv, 284.

171 Ibid., Scene ii, 50.

172 From Steiner's 1899 article "The Character of Goethe's Spirit," in Allen Time, 166–167.

173 *Faust*/Jarrell, Scene xxiii, 271.

174 Rudolf Steiner, *Four Mystery Dramas* (London: Rudolf Steiner Press, 1997), *The Portal of Initiation*, Scene ii, 57. I have presented this scene on several occasions, and find it the most emotionally powerful and accessible to the modern audience of any of the dramatic scenes in these plays.

175 *Faust*/Jarrell, Scene xxv, 278, 280, 286.

176 *Goethe's Faust*, translated by Walter Kaufmann (New York: Doubleday, 1961), lines 12069–12075 and 12092–12095.

177 John Barnes, *Goethe and the Power of Rhythm*, op. cit., 59.

178 Steiner's 1899 article "The Character of Goethe's Spirit," included in Allen Time, 161.

179 Ibid., 62, translation by Barnes. Steiner (in Allen Time, 171) notes that Goethe wrote this on August 29, 1795. On this day the Sun lay on the Leo Image (fourteen degrees Leo, seven minutes), with Uranus close by at twelve degrees Leo.

180 Heinrich Proskauer, *The Rediscovery of Color* (Hudson, NY: Steiner Books, 1986), has many demonstrations with black-and-white cards and a prism that demonstrate the complexity and beauty of light.

181 L. Gordon Plummer, *By the Holy Tetraktys!, Symbol and Reality in Man and Universe* (Buena Park, California: Stockton Trade Press, Point Loma Publications no. 9, 1982). Steiner speaks in the most penetrating terms of the fourfold nature of the human being destined to be become twofold, then threefold, before returning to unity, in *Foundations of Esotericism*, lectures 3 and 4, September 28 and 29, 1905 (from www.rsarchive.org).

182 The Sun inspiration at the root of the Sphinx experience is hinted at by Ingres's Star Brother Steiner: "When persons who have remained standing at a certain stage of evolution, among the peasants perhaps, rest in the fields at midday in the hot glow of the summer sun, and fall asleep, they may have what could be called a latent sun-stroke. Through such an impact on the physical body, the astral and etheric are loosened from a part of the physical. Then such persons are translated to the astral plane and they see this last decadent offspring of the Sphinx." From Rudolf Steiner, *Egyptian Myths and Mysteries: The Ancient Egyptian Doctrine of Evolution: The Cosmic View of the Organs and their Coarsening in Modern Times*, Lecture 11, September 13, 1908 (from www.rsarchive.org).

183 Steiner *John*, Lecture VIII (from www.rsarchive.org).

184 *The Balance in the World and Man, Lucifer and Ahriman*, Lecture 1, November 20, 1903 (www.rsarchive.org).

185 From James MacPherson's *Fingal*, part of the *Songs of Ossian*, in John Matthews (ed.), *From Isles of Dream: Visionary Stories and Poems of the Celtic Renaissance* (Hudson, NY: Lindisfarne, 1993), 26.

186 James MacPherson, born October 27, 1736 and died February 17, 1796. *The Poems of Ossian* can be had in many editions, including one from www.kessinger.net. More about MacPherson and the poets that he inspired in John Matthews (ed.), *From Isles of Dream*, op. cit., 13f, 22f. *Fingal* was first published in 1762, then later

as *The Songs of Ossian* in 1846.

187 Paul Marshall Allen and Joan deRis Allen, *Fingal's Cave, the Poems of Ossian, and Celtic Christianity* (New York: Continuum, 1999). Steiner's lecture in Berlin on March 3, 1911, was very close to his birthday. Three planets formed a T-square on that evening in the latter degrees of the mutable signs, Mars, Moon, and Neptune, the T-square pointing to its resolution point at the star Spica, the fifth Royal Star of Persia that focalizes the divine feminine. Thus we can consider that Steiner's concerns about Fingal and Ossian point to the same underlying foundation, the Divine Sophia.

188 Felix Mendelssohn's Death Saturn conjuncted Steiner's Birth Sun and opposed Steiner's Birth Saturn. Thus this day when the Sun lay atop Steiner's Birth Sun (and atop Mendelssohn's Death Saturn) had power in it.

189 Steiner as quoted in Allen and Allen, *Fingal's Cave*, op. cit., 145.

190 Steiner quoting Macpherson, in Allen and Allen, *Fingal's Cave*, op. cit., 191–2.

191 Ibid.

192 *Songs of Ossian*, cited in Allen and Allen, *Fingal's Cave*, 111.

193 Further connections here: Louis XIII was born into the Solar Cross of Steiner's death, Steiner at Pisces and Louis at Virgo.

194 Edited by Raphael Brown, *The Little Flowers of St. Francis* (Garden City, NY: Image Books, 1971), 131–133; *Marvels Miracles*, 489–490.

195 Part II, Chapter VI, *Modern Idealistic World Conceptions*.

196 February 6, 1913, in Steiner *Fairy Tales*, 13.

197 Seven types from *The Psychology of Peoples* (*Völkerpsychologie*, 10 volumes, Leipzig, between 1900 and 1920), cited in the Preface to second edition of V. Propp, *Morphology of the Folktale*

(Austin: University of Texas Press, 1968).

198 From *Les Épaves*, "Femmes Damnés."

199 From Edna St. Vincent Millay's translation of *Flowers of Evil* (New York: Harper and Brothers, 1936).

200 Lowe *Goethe and Palladio*, 15–16.

201 Allen *Time*, 110.

202 Steiner *Fairy Tales*, 8, 10.

203 Steiner *Nietzsche*, 102, quoting from Nietzsche's *Thus Spake Zarathustra*, First Part, About War and People of War.

204 A point made in "The Recovery of the Living Source of Speech," lecture of April 13, 1923 in Dornach, and attributed to Hermann Grimm, about whom more will be said later.

205 Joseph Campbell, Commentary to *The Complete Grimm's Fairy Tales, op. cit.*, 864.

206 *Complete Grimm's Fairy Tales, op. cit.*, 17.

207 Rudolf Steiner *Fairy Tales*, 35. I added these beginnings and endings to "The Queen Bee" story.

208 Samweber, 32.

209 "When it seemed justified in spiritual terms, Rudolf Steiner could also sharply admonish people. This is what happened to a desk clerk in Vienna when Rudolf Steiner, upon arriving by train in the morning, found the rooms he had reserved not yet ready. The desk clerk of this first-class hotel may have been a snob who imitated the airs of the hotel guests (formerly aristocrats, now the *nouveaux riches*). When Steiner was asked why he had been so indignant – a moment later he was again utterly calm – he said that one had to yell at demons." Friedrich Hiebel, in *Man before Others*, 211.

210 Lindenberg, 69, *Autobiography*, 103–4.

211 Lindenberg, 78, *Autobiography*, 108.

212 Lindenberg, 137.

213 From Sander Gilman (ed.),

Conversations with Nietzsche: A Life in the Words of his Contemporaries (New York: Oxford University Press, 1987), 254, 237. Peter Gast, the first writer, also said that Nietzsche did not make this Jupiter-like impression in his healthy days. Astrologically, at Nietzsche's conception, Jupiter lay at four degrees Aquarius, just opposite the King and Queen Star, Regulus, in Leo. At his conception, Jupiter lay close to Neptune, and at his birth to Uranus, so we can see the possible influence of the Hardener and the Illusionist.

214 *Autobiography*, 223, 225–226.

215 Steiner *Revelation*, 156; *Autobiography*, Chapter 18; see also lectures in *Karmic Relationships*, vol. 3 (August 8, 1924) and vol. 4 (July 20, 1924).

216 Rudolf Steiner, *Materialism and the Task of Anthroposophy* (Hudson, NY: Anthroposophic Press, 1987), Lecture 13 (May 5, 1921), 246.

217 Wachsmuth, 6.

218 Autobiography, 317, 318.

219 Lindenberg, 172, letter of 23 November.

220 Lindenberg *Biography*, 291.

221 *Autobiography*, 319. One can read the details of what Steiner experienced and then held out to others as possibility at the end of Chapter 5 of *Outline of Esoteric Science*.

222 Prokofieff *Steiner New Mysteries*, 58.

223 Emil Bock, *Rudolf Steiner: Studien zu seinem Lebensganz und Lebenswerk* (Stuttgart: Verlag Freies Geistesleben, 1967), 164. Also cited in Lindenberg *Biography*, 296.

224 Some have said that this encounter was with Christian Rosenkreutz as representative of the Christ, about which Steiner spoke on September 27, 1911: "Those who are affected by [the etheric body of Christian Rosenkreutz] will be granted Paul's experience on the road to Damascus." Steiner *Secret Stream*, 136.

225 Lindenberg *Biography*, 296–297. The full article, "The Character of Goethe's Spirit as Shown in the Fairy Tale of *The Green Snake and the Beautiful Lily*," appears in Allen *Time*, 158–171.

226 Lindenberg, 171.

227 Lindenberg, 172.

228 Robert Powell (*The Christ Mystery*, Fair Oaks, California: Rudolf Steiner Press, 1999, 26, 27, 87) suggests September 10, 1899, because Jupiter, from the point of view of the Sun (heliocentrically) enters the sign of Leo. November 5, 1899, is suggested by the prenatal anticipation at which we are looking, prenatal Saturn exactly opposing the Birth Sun. December 1, 1899, is suggested by the simple fact of the Sun conjunct the position of the Persian Royal Star, Antares, the potent star ruling the threshold between life and death. December 5, 1899, is suggested by the opposition of transiting Uranus to the Birth Uranus position, which is square to both Sun and Saturn at the birth. December 30, 1899, is suggested by transiting Uranus and transiting Moon both conjunct Antares. From this point of view, the birth position of Uranus is the front-line and representative of the powerful fixed star, Antares, and therefore the closer to the source we are, the more powerful. These many relations to Uranus suggest both the Illusionist and the working of unexpected revolutionary events. Certainly December 30 qualifies as "around the turn of the century." See text for other possibilities that also relate to Antares.

229 Uranus at 15 Taurus 15 minutes, Aldebaran at 15 Taurus 3, Birth Sun at 14 Aquarius 33, and Birth Saturn at 13 Leo 14.

230 Antares at 15 Scorpio 1 minute, Uranus at 15 Scorpio 3, Sun at 16 Scorpio 45, Pluto at 22 Taurus 28.

231 Saturn at 0 Sagittarius 54. About the

history and importance of the Galactic Center, see Paul LaViolette, *Earth on Fire* (Schenectady, New York: Starlane, 1997).

232 Saturn at 15 Taurus 1, Sun at 16 Scorpio 5, with Venus and Mercury very close by. About the first fission, see an article by Robert Schiappacasse and myself for *New View* magazine in London, April 2002.

233 The address presently is 95 Bundesallee, previously named Kaiserallee and renamed when the Germans had had enough to do with Kaisers. Steiner and his wife, Anna Eunicke, lived there with her children from 1900 to 1903. They had moved from Habsburgerstrasse 11.

234 Wachsmuth confirms that it was at the beginning of 1900 that the movement was formed, pages 13–14.

235 This is a true approximation for this time period. As Mars increases and decreases in speed, this projection can become greater or smaller. The point here is that the smallest orb in Mars's movements prenatally affects a large number of days in the life.

236 Lindenberg, 430–438, Wachsmuth, 107. One can still feel this kind of rousing content in the building in which Steiner lived during this time. From 1903 until the end of his life he kept rooms, along with the publishing company, at Motzstrasse 30 (previously numbered 17), adjacent to which now there is a very complete esoteric bookstore, as if continuing to resonate with the energy of the thoughts that once lived there.

237 Steiner *First Esoteric School*, 186–189.

238 *Correspondence*, 105–106, letter of February 23, 1908.

239 Wachsmuth, 406.

240 Wachsmuth, 432.

241 Samweber, 32.

242 Luke 4:5–8.

243 Recall that we are trying out the association of Uranus with the Illusionist. It works very powerfully in this instance, and can help us understand the dynamics in the heavens simultaneous to the interpersonal dynamics on earth. However, we cannot assume that Uranus will always act in this way, or that the Illusionist acts exclusively through perturbations of Uranus.

244 Rittelmeyer, 115–6.

245 Lindenberg, 422; Wachsmuth, 366.

246 Lindenberg, 426; Wachsmuth, 378.

247 Wachsmuth, 385.

248 Lindenberg, 244; Wachsmuth, 75.

249 Steiner *First Esoteric School*, 106–108.

250 Steiner, *First Esoteric School*, 108. I use a translation a little different from the one given in 1906. The background and accompanying meditations to this one can be found in Rudolf Steiner, *Guidance in Esoteric Training* (Hudson, NY: Anthroposophic Press, 1994), 35. The study of light can be supplemented by a study of the most extraordinary modern teacher, Sai Maa Lakshmi Devi, *Petals of Grace* (Crestone, Colorado: HIU Press, 2005).

251 Lindenberg, 233; Wachsmuth, 70–71.

252 Steiner, *First Esoteric School*, 98–101. This also is explained in more detail in Steiner, *Guidance in Esoteric Training*.

253 Andrei Belyi paraphrases Rudolf Steiner: "When an inspiration becomes active within us, our muscles pull us all on their own to the right spot where destiny awaits us." From "The Man, Rudolf Steiner," *Meeting Steiner*, 38.

254 "The Gate of Zeal," from Orchot Tzaddikim, *The Ways of the Tzaddikim* (Jerusalem: Feldheim, 1995, edited by Rabbi Gavriel Zaloshinsky), 283.

255 Ruth has her own book in the Hebrew Bible that tells her story.

256 Steiner *Revelation*, 75.

257 This has strong similarity in name, technique, and zeal to the Hindu cult of ascetics, the Sadhus.

258 Rudolf Steiner, *The Spiritual*

Hierarchies and Their Reflection in the Physical World (Hudson, NY: Anthroposophic Press, 1983), 104 and passim.

259 It is very interesting that the account of the day where the Teacher visits Gischala mentions that the rabbi of that town had been sent by the people to Egypt, a rare mention of that place amongst Hebrews. The people wished to have a tolerant and well-educated person rather than a religious tyrant as their leader.

260 Richard Leviton, *The Galaxy on Earth: A Traveler's Guide to the Planet's Visionary Geography* (Charlottesville, Virginia: Hampton Roads, 2002).

261 *Ways of the Tzaddikim*, op. cit., 291.

262 Ibid.

263 Ibid.

264 Valentin Tomberg, *Covenant of the Heart: Meditations of a Christian Hermeticist on the Mysteries of Tradition* (Rockport, MA: Element, 1992), 8–9 (new edition, *Lazarus, Come Forth!*).

265 John 18:38.

266 Andrei Belyi, "The Man, Rudolf Steiner," in *Meeting Steiner*, 44.

267 Ibid., 41.

268 Ibid., 48.

269 Ibid., 49.

270 Juliet Compton-Burnett in *Man before Others*, 190.

271 Andrei Belyi, "The Man, Rudolf Steiner," in *Meeting Steiner*, 54.

272 Rittelmeyer, 10, 76, 61.

273 Wilson *Steiner*, 137.

274 Rittelmeyer, 127.

275 Ibid., 70.

276 Samweber, 19, 23.

277 Juliet Compton-Burnett, in *Man before Others*, 190–191.

278 Samweber, 12–13.

279 Lisa Dreher Monges, "A Student's Memories of Rudolf Steiner," *Meeting Steiner*, 97.

280 Arvia MacKaye Ege, "The Christmas Foundation Meeting," *Meeting Steiner*, 117.

281 *Faust*/Jarrell, Scene xxi, 247.

282 The position of the Sun at Rodin's birth and death has nothing to do with the Solar Cross that we are investigating, but at his death Mars was exactly at the Leo pole of this Solar Cross and Jupiter exactly at the Taurus pole.

283 At the end of the siege of Calais, when the drama with the burghers took place, the Moon stood at fourteen degrees and fifty-three minutes of Taurus, directly opposite Edward's Birth Sun. Queen Philippa played the part of the Moon, opposing his instinct to kill his enemies.

284 BBC poll in 2002.

285 "It could have been prevented in my belief without the firing of a single shot ... but no one would listen." In Barbara Leaming, *Jack Kennedy* (New York: Norton, 2006). The "iron curtain" remark was made on March 5, 1946, at Westminster College, Fulton, Missouri.

286 Citations from *Encyclopedia Britannica* and current newspaper articles. See also John West, *Churchill and Roosevelt: Icons or Massacre Perpetrators* (Bundaberg, Queensland: Veritas Press), 1976.

287 Jon Meacham, *Franklin and Winston: An Intimate Portrait of an Epic Friendship* (New York: Random House, 2003), 313–314.

288 Another observation from his friend Lord Moran: "I used to watch him as he went to his room with swift paces, the head thrust forward, scowling at the ground, the somber countenance clouded, the features set and resolute." Meacham, Ibid., 139.

289 Rudolf Steiner, "The Spiritual Origins of the First World War," March 12, 1916, cited in Ramsbotham, 69.

290 *History of the Peloponnesian War*, I.22

291 From Gloria Steinem, "Shirley Chisholm: Front-Runner," *New York Magazine*, January 17, 2005.

292 At his birth, Lewis had a "stellium" or congregation of planets at this midpoint of Scorpio, including Uranus at 11 degrees Scorpio, Sun between 14 and 15 Scorpio, Venus at 17 Scorpio, and Saturn at 20 Scorpio. When planets gather like this, their effects can be seen to commingle.

293 Richard Ellman, *Oscar Wilde* (London: Penguin, 1988), 435.

294 Another statement that Wilde made illuminates the prison in the Leo Image from the inside. On his death bed, he said, "My wallpaper and I are fighting a duel to the death. One or the other of us has to go." Comical, and poignant from the inside of the prison. Richard Ellman, *Oscar Wilde*, op. cit., 546.

295 Quote from *Liber Legis*, AL I:40, and in Colin Wilson, *Aleister Crowley: The Nature of the Beast* (London: Aquarian, 1987), 73. To learn about this figure, begin with the balanced portrayal in Colin Wilson's biography. Beware of the influence of the Illusionist when going into his main work, because his promises of powerful magic can appear very attractive–his books are often under lock and key in bookstores—but is actually very dangerous.

296 Friedrich Nietzsche, *Genealogy of Morals*, cited by Steiner *Nietzsche*, 53.

297 Crowley, cited in Colin Wilson, *Aleister Crowley, op. cit.*, 89.

298 Alfred Heidenreich, in the introduction to *Christianity as Mystical Fact* (1961).

299 Wachsmuth, 226.

300 Samweber, 29.

301 Steiner *Fairy Tales*, 38, as one of numerous examples.

302 Marie Steiner, *Briefe und Dokumente* ("Letters and Documents") (Dornach, Switzerland: Rudolf Steiner Nachlassverwaltung, 1981).

303 John 3: 29, from the full passage 22–36.

304 John 3:30.

305 Most Westerners pronounce this Sheh-KEEN-ah. More accurately, it is pronounced with little emphasis on vowels: Shk-een-AH. The important first consonant is Sheen, the fire letter.

306 Rabbi Yehoshua ben Levi, in Elie Wiesel *Wise Men and Their Tales: Portraits of Biblical, Talmudic, and Hasidic Masters* (New York: Schocken Books, 2003), 230.

307 Cited in *Sefer Yetzirah*, xiii.

308 Allen *Rosenkreutz*, 69.

309 "The Soul's Awakening," in Rudolf Steiner, *Four Mystery Dramas* (London: Rudolf Steiner Press, 1997), 99.

310 Version by Jon Valentine, *op. cit.*, 13. The invitation and announcement ends with the loveliest line, "Signed: Bride and Bridegroom."

311 Norman Lebrecht, *Book of Musical Anecdotes* (New York: Free Press, 1985), 53.

312 This scene and others from Margot's life can be seen in the excellent film *La Reine Margot* (1994, directed by Patrice Chéreau, Margot played by Isabelle Adjani), based on Alexander Dumas's novel of this name.

313 Marguerite's *Memoirs*, especially Letters IV and V, speak about these events, though not with the fanfare of Dumas. The Massacre of St. Bartholomew took place on August 24, 1572.

314 Version by Jon Valentine, op. cit., 70.

315 Lecture 4, "Morality as a Germinating Force," from the lecture series, *Cosmic and Human Metamorphoses*, Berlin, February 27, 1917.

316 J. E. Hutton, *History of the Moravian Church* (London: Moravian Publication Office, second edition, 1909), also at http://www.npmc.org/hutton/ii1.htm, chapter on Zinzendorf's youth.

317 Mylius, a student of Michael Maier, cited in Yates, 89.

318 The Christian Bible passage: Matthew 22:11–14. From the third

sermon, at the Reformed Church in Germantown, February 4, 1742. In *A Collection of Sermons from Zinzendorf's Pennsylvania Journey*, edited by Craig Atwood (Bethlehem, PA: Moravian Church of America, 2001, trans. Julie Weber).

319 Rudolf Steiner, *An Outline of Esoteric Science* (Hudson, NY: Anthroposophic Press, 1997), especially Chapter 4.

320 Wachsmuth, 337.

321 Tim Hill, *JFK and Jackie: Unseen Archives* (New York: Barnes and Noble, 2004).

322 Peter Evans, *Nemesis: Aristotle Onassis, Jacki O, and the Love Triangle That Brought Down the Kennedys* (New York: Regan/HarperCollins, 2004), 109, a summary of the many details brought out in recent research.

323 Nikita Krushchev did not have his Birth Sun at the Scorpio Image. He did, however, have many birth planets—Pluto, Neptune, and Jupiter—right at Kennedy's Birth Sun at Taurus. Krushchev was thus very concerned with issues of the Life Star, and this Image.

324 V. I. Matthews, *St. Philip Neri: Apostle of Rome and Founder of the Congregation of the Oratory* (Rockford, IL: TAN Books, 1984), cited in *Marvels Miracles*, 77–8, 164–5, 177.

325 *Ibid.*, 35.

326 Thomas Austin O'Connor, *Myth and Mythology in the Theater of Pedro Calderón de la Barca* (San Antonio, TX: Trinity University Press, 1988), Chapters 5 and 8. Pedro Calderón de la Barca's best-known play is *Life's a Dream* (Boulder, CO: University Press of Colorado:, 2004, trans. and ed. Michael Kidd).

327 Rudolf Steiner, *Old and New Methods of Initiation* (London: Rudolf Steiner Press, 1991), lecture 9, 103–7. How interesting that Calderón and Goethe, the authors of these two versions of *Faust*, relate to the same Solar Cross. I

wondered about the other main author of the Faust theme, Christopher Marlowe, and find his Birth Sun at eight degrees Aquarius, close enough for most astrology, but not for the stringent orbs we use here. However, Marlowe's birth Moon position lies exactly on Antares, and his birth Neptune exactly on Aldebaran. The story of Faust relates intimately to the Aldebaran-Antares axis. Marlowe (born 1564) and Calderón (born 1600) both precede Goethe (born 1749). If we see C. S. Lewis (Birth Sun at Antares in Scorpio, 1898) as another author of the Faust theme, in his *Screwtape Letters*, we get a sense that connection to this position of the zodiac encourages one to imagine in the terms of the Faust story.

328 *Ibid.*, 103.

329 Calderón *Magician*, Act 3, Scene xiii. Calderón took his inspiration from the account of Saint Justina in Jacobus de Voragine, *The Golden Legend* (Princeton, NJ: Princeton University Press, 1993, two volumes, original around 1260), II, 192–195, which has other twists interesting to the Faust parallels developed here.

330 Calderón's best known play is *Life Is a Dream*, wherein people are taken in and out of the prison of their lives (the prison Image being Calderón's Eastern Horizon Image), leading to the conclusion: "What is life? A frenzy. What is life? An illusion, a shadow, a fiction, and the greatest good is very little because all life is a dream and dreams are only dreams" (lines 2182–87, spoken by Segismundo, in *Life's a Dream*, op. cit., 132).

331 Rudolf Steiner, *Old and New Methods of Initiation*, op. cit., 105.

332 Calderón *Magician*, Act 3, Scene iv.

333 Rudolf Steiner, *Old and New Methods of Initiation*, op. cit., 105.

334 Calderón *Magician*, Act 3, Scene xxi.

335 Rudolf Steiner, *Old and New Methods*

of Initiation, op. cit., 105.

336 *Faust*/Jarrell, Scene vi, 138.

337 Ibid., Scene xi, 180.

338 Ibid., Scene xiv, 196.

339 Ibid., Scene xxv, 286.

340 Steiner's 1899 article on "The Character of Goethe's Spirit," in Allen *Time*, 166.

341 Ibid., 170. In notes at the end of his article (Allen *Time*, 171), Steiner notes that the first time that he ever spoke about the *Fairy Tale* was on November 27, 1891. I note with interest that during that period, Pluto and Neptune were exactly conjunct this position in the middle of Taurus, Pluto at 14 Taurus 41 and Neptune at 14 Taurus 30. Jupiter lay exactly square (at 15 Aquarius 52), with the Sun close to a square also (at 11 Scorpio 43). In other words, the Solar Cross of Steiner's birth was very activated.

342 *Correspondence*, 101.

343 Steiner's *Autobiography*, cited by Wilson *Steiner*, 69.

344 The basic situation is presented in Rudolf Steiner, *Community Life, Inner Development, Sexuality and the Spiritual Teacher: Ethical and Spiritual Dimensions of the Crisis of the Anthroposophical Society, Dornach, 1915* (Hudson, New York: Anthroposophic Press, 1991, with introduction by Christopher Schaefer). The controversy about what "really happened" in the Heinrich Goesch and Alice Sprengel case can be found in an article by Catherine MacCoun, "Work on What Has Been Spoiled" (at http://members.aol.com/kitmac/workon.htm). Responses to MacCoun's penetrating critique can be found at http://ipwebdev.com/hermit/rebuttal.html and at http://uncletaz.com/at/febmar04/.mccounpamph.html.

345 Margarita Voloschin, "Life Memories: Meeting," in Belyi *Reminiscences*, 111.

346 Samweber, 19.

347 Margarete and Erich Kirchner-Bockholt, *Rudolf Steiner's Mission and Ita Wegman* (London: Rudolf Steiner Press, 1977), 50. Permission to quote from this rare book was given specifically by the Rudolf Steiner Press in London. The Bockholts trace the incarnational stream back further with this pair.

348 Ibid., 87.

349 Rosa Mayreder, *A Survey of the Woman Problem* (Westport, CT: Hyperion, 1983, original 1913, trans. Herman Scheffauer), 117.

350 Andrei Belyi, "The Man: Rudolf Steiner," *Meeting Steiner*, 42.

351 Ibid.

352 Ibid., 34–35. Of course, after reading such a statement, one begins to notice all the times that Steiner said just these words. But the general sentiment rings true.

353 Ibid.

354 Ibid., 36.

355 Samweber, 30.

356 Rudolf Steiner, *Intuitive Thinking as a Spiritual Path* (Hudson, NY: Anthroposophic Press, 1995), Chapter 5, paragraph 26, page 89.

357 Samweber, 27.

358 "Karass" was coined by Kurt Vonegut to mean those to whom one is related for reasons of karma or soul connection.

359 Examination of the switch of names and roles of Venus and Mercury is found in the more detailed astrobiography of Rudolf Steiner.

360 Lindenberg, 189.

361 *Autobiography*, Chapter 14.

362 Rudolf Steiner, "Spiritual Emptiness and Social Life," lecture of April 13, 1919.

363 From a letter quoted in Prokofieff *Steiner New Mysteries*, 26. This may very well be the reason that Marie Steiner rejected Valentin Tomberg at age thirty-five.

364 Wachsmuth, 82–84.

365 Amalie Wagner, cited in Steiner, *First Esoteric School*, 205–207.

366 Karl Kerenyi, *Eleusis: Archetypal Image of Mother and Daughter* (Princeton, NJ: Princeton University Press, 1991).

367 Steiner, *First Esoteric School*, 289–303.

368 Ibid., 292, 294, 299.

369 Ibid., 286.

370 *Correspondence*, 101, letter of April 29, 1907.

371 *Autobiography*, 404, 536; also Wachsmuth with other details, 91–96.

372 Steiner quoted in Wachsmuth, 95.

373 Lindenberg *Biography*, 256–257.

374 Cited in Lindenberg, 251.

375 Lindenberg *Biography*, 527–529.

376 Yates, 68, and plate after 24.

377 Frank Chester revealed this to me from his years of study of the Goetheanum in relation to other buildings constructed on principles of sacred architecture.

378 Chester relates this to the study by John Michell, *Dimensions of Paradise: The Proportions and Symbolic Numbers of Ancient Cosmology* (San Francisco: Harper and Row, 1988), 69.

379 Lindenberg, 320–321; Wachsmuth, 181.

380 Notes by Mathilde Scholl, in Steiner, *First Esoteric School*, 315.

381 Prokofieff *Steiner New Mysteries*, referencing a retrospective comment made in 1912, 29.

382 Notes by Mathilde Scholl, in Steiner, *First Esoteric School*, 318.

383 Beginning of Scene viii, 102, in *The Soul's Awakening*, in *Four Mystery Dramas* (London: Rudolf Steiner Press, 1973).

384 Michelangelo worked on this sculpture from 1520 to 1534, and it was finished by his students. The whole piece was commissioned by the Pope, also a Medici, just after Lorenzo's death in 1518, just before the birth of his daughter, Catherine, who was Marguerite's mother.

385 Wachsmuth, 181, also 178. This visit was probably on Michelmas, that is, September 29. About the color, we hear from one of the artists who built the Goetheanum: "All these people wander happily through the soft red clay which engulfs our rubber boots beyond retrieving." Sonia Tomara Clark and Jeannette Eaton, "Glimpses of the First Goetheanum and the Start of the World War," in *Meeting Steiner*, 90.

386 Robert J. Kelder has brought together the researches of Werner Greub on the locations of the Grail sites, adding his own commentaries. One such resource is Werner Greub, *Wolfram's Grail Astronomy* (Amsterdam: Willehalm Institute for Grail Research, 1999), available from www.StarWisdom.org.

387 Wachsmuth, 181.

388 Rudolf Steiner, *Calendar 1912–1913* (Great Barrington, MA: SteinerBooks, 2003, edited and introduced by Christopher Bamford).

389 Wachsmuth, 179.

390 Rudolf Steiner, *Community Life, Inner Development, Sexuality, and the Spiritual Teacher*, op. cit.

391 Wachsmuth, 266.

392 Wachsmuth, 284–285.

393 *Goethe's Faust*, translated by Walter Kaufmann (New York: Doubleday, 1961), 422–423. Kaufmann kept the meter of the German original, so you can feel the meter accurately in this passage.

394 Ibid., 422–425.

395 Steiner, *First Esoteric School*, 191–195.

396 Wachsmuth, 267.

397 The fact that Venus lies at this same place at the Water-Initiation (Baptism) of Christ Jesus, that is, atop the star Antares is the kind of additional insight that we explore much more fully in the forthcoming book on Rudolf Steiner's astro-biography.

398 See an article that Robert Schiappacasse and I wrote about this

for *New View* magazine in London,
April 2002.

399 Lindenberg, 335–336; Wachsmuth,
203–205. To understand the meaning
of Nathan Jesus, please consult the
longer account in Appendix B. There
are two streams: the Nathan Jesus
stream, that brings us the life force
of Krishna, and the Solomon Jesus
stream, which brings us the legacy of
Zarathustra.

400 Partly from comments by Andrei Belyi,
who attended this lecture. What the
words of a lecture say and what those
who recall what they heard can differ.
The latter is most valuable because
it shows what came through most
strongly in the lecture. Andrei Belyi,
"The Man, Rudolf Steiner," in *Meeting
Steiner*, 87.

401 Lindenberg *Biography*, 295–298.

402 Rittelmeyer recalls Steiner saying,
"Unforgettable for me is especially one
of these spiritual individualities—*that
was a very important individual!*"
Rittelmeyer says, "In this moment [of
speaking about him] there was a kind
of reverence for this great knower of
humanity." Lindenberg *Biography*, 295–
298; Wachsmuth, 13–14. Rittelmeyer
and Bock cited in Lindenberg
Biography.

403 *Autobiography*, 319. The specification
of the exact day is discussed amongst
the prenatal anticipations relating to
the Sun-Earth Images, in Chapter 9.

404 Rudolf Steiner, *The Christ Impulse and
the Development of Ego Consciousness*
(Spring Valley, NY: Anthroposophic
Press, 1976), 108, lecture of March 9,
1910.

405 Steiner *Revelation*, 227–228. We
are interested in this celestial
phenomenon because Steiner
mentioned it in his lectures, and
because it occurred with the Sun right
at Steiner's Earth Image, that is, in
the middle of Scorpio. Actually, the
orb for this event is a bit wider than

what we have been using in this entire
study. In the rest of the study, we have
limited ourselves to a half-degree
orb from fourteen degrees and thirty-
three minutes, which is very "tight,"
that is, very demanding. The Sun at
the 1872 return of Biela's Comet was
at thirteen degrees Scorpio and two
minutes, so it is a slightly wider orb,
though also very close when compared
to other astrological practice.

406 Ibid., 159 and 228. Comments also in
Rudolf Steiner, *The Christ Impulse and
the Development of Ego-Consciousness*,
op. cit., 109.

407 Ibid., 232.

408 Lindenberg, 410–411; Wachsmuth,
360.

409 Lisa Dreher Monges, "A Student's
Memories of Rudolf Steiner," in
Meeting Steiner, 94, 95.

410 Steiner *Fairy Tales*, 33 (lecture of
December 26, 1908). "Bride" reference
is at 37.

411 Thomas Aquinas "abhorred the sight
of women." Marie-Louise Von Franz
(editor and commentator), *Aurora
Consurgens: A Document Attributed
to Thomas Aquinas on the Problem of
Opposites in Alchemy* (Toronto: Inner
City Books, 2000), 70.

412 *Faust*/Jarrell, Scene xxi, 241.

413 *The Guardian of the Threshold*, in *Four
Mystery Plays* (London: Rudolf Steiner
Press, 1973), beginning of Scene vii, 87.

414 Source of the Rosicrucian formula
or mantram is the *Fama* cited earlier,
one of the two works that preceded
Johann Valentin Andreae's *Chymical
Wedding* (cited in Yates, 248, and in
Ralph White, editor, *The Rosicrucian
Enlightenment Revisited*, op. cit., 12).
Steiner's own rendition of the three
phrases comes from the mouth of
Theodora in his fourth mystery play,
The Souls' Awakening: "From God
arose the Soul of Man; it can plunge
down at death to depths of Being;
and it will free from death at last the

Spirit." (*Four Mystery Plays*, London: Rudolf Steiner Press, 1973, 444).

415 Steiner *Revelation*, 27–8.

416 Book with Fourteen Seals, passim.

417 Steiner *Mark*, pages 88–91.

418 Anne Catherine Emmerich (ACE), Volume 2, 328. ACE hears "spirit" instead of "stars," but given the context of speaking to astrologers about star events, this seems to be what the Teacher means. David Mowaljarlai, in *Yorro Yorro : Everything Standing Up Alive* (Broome, Western Australia: 2001, also an edition by Inner Traditions International), agrees with these three testimonies to the Divine, completely in accord with the original understanding of aboriginal Australia.

419 Steiner *Revelation* 12.

420 Rudolf Steiner, *The Festivals and Their Meaning* (London: Rudolf Steiner Press, 1996), 78, lecture, January 1, 1921.

421 Steiner *Matthew*, lectures 3 and 4, referring to the genealogy given in the Gospel of Matthew, chapter 1. This story is told with a bit more detail in Appendix B.

422 Rittelmeyer, 130–131.

423 *The Principle of Spiritual Economy in Connection with Questions of Reincarnation: An Aspect of the Spiritual Guidance of Man* (Hudson, NY: Steiner Books, 1986).

424 In relation to the question "In whose company are you keeping?" Jesus said, "I'm about my Father's business," Luke 2:49; also John 4:34.

425 Lecture of August 28, 1917, in *The Karma of Materialism* (Spring Valley: Anthroposophic Press, 1985), 81–82.

426 Rudolf Steiner, *The Festivals and Their Meaning* (Forest Row: Rudolf Steiner Press, 1996), 311, lecture of June 7, 1908.

427 *Four Mystery Plays* (London: Rudolf Steiner Press, 1973), 502.

428 Goethe, "Nature" in *Scientific Studies*, Volume 12, 4, cited in John Barnes,

Goethe and the Power of Rhythm (Ghent, New York: Adonis Press, 1999), 76.

429 Belyi *Meeting*, 39.

430 Steiner *Revelation*, 171–172.

431 Ibid., 210.

432 Ibid., 210–211.

433 Belyi *Meetings*, 35.

434 Lisa Dreher Monges, "A Student's Memories of Rudolf Steiner," *Meetings*, 103.

435 Allen *Rosenkreutz*, 68. Andreae did not share the Solar Cross of Steiner's death, but these words from this Star Brother of his birth do serve to illustrate the encounter that Steiner had at that crossing of the threshold.

436 Calderón *Magician*, 82. Star Brother Calderón did not share the Solar Cross of Steiner's death, but created an artistic rendering of what Steiner encountered there.

437 Alfred Heidenreich, in the introduction to 1961 edition of *Christianity as Mystical Fact* (Great Barrington, MA: SteinerBooks, 1997).

438 Lindenberg, 112–113. In Steiner *Revelation*, 156, Steiner explains that, when Nietzsche was writing *The Antichrist* and *Ecce Homo*, the Nietzsche individuality was not in the man.

439 Though Wachsmuth, 25–26, suggests that this happened at the end of 1902, Lindenberg, 206, suggests that it happened just into the new year of 1903.

440 Letter from Mathilde Scholl, the first such letter, given in Steiner, *First Esoteric School*, 46–47.

441 Wachsmuth, 366 and 367; also Lindenberg, 423.

442 Wachsmuth, 368, quoting Steiner.

443 Wachsmuth, 109, generally 107–111. He had delivered the first set of lectures on the Gospel of John in Basel at the very end of 1907.

444 Rudolf Steiner, *The Festivals and Their Meaning* (Forest Row: Rudolf Steiner

Press, 1996), 311, lecture of June 7, 1908.

445 Wachsmuth, 109.

446 Wachsmuth, 119.

447 Wachsmuth, 122. Also Lindenberg, on the year 1909. Rudolf Steiner, *The Principle of Spiritual Economy in Connection with Questions of Reincarnation* (Hudson, NY: Steiner Books, 1986), 135 and passim.

448 Rudolf Steiner, *Wonders of the World, Ordeals of the Soul, Revelations of the Spirit* (London: Rudolf Steiner Press, 1983), lecture of August 19, 1911, 30. In this we combine a mythological reference with the name of a "dwarf planet," given in 1930 by an astronomer. We are fortunate that the name of the "dwarf planet" Pluto corresponds with the quality of Pluto's behavior. The name was derived intuitively, and the intuition was correct. Naming of planet-like objects has since become much more impish, and we can't depend on the name to tell us about the quality.

449 Trevor Ravenscroft (*The Spear of Destiny*, York Beach, Maine: Samuel Weiser, 1973), 170, 264. This would have been very early for the Nazi Party, though certainly Steiner and his work had made enemies by that point. According to Christopher Schaefer, despite its inaccuracies, Ravenscroft's book has been responsible for more people finding their way to anthroposophy than any other.

450 Colin Wilson assumes the fire came from faulty electricity. Ravenscroft (ibid.) insists that it was arson, initiated by the Nazi party. Assya Turgeniev (Turgeniev, 125) reported that, after the fire was discovered, the fuse boxes were examined and found in proper order.

451 Wachsmuth 447f., 491f., 499.

452 Wachsmuth, 417–418.

453 *Correspondence*, 171–172, letter of March 15, 1923.

454 Lindenberg, 494; Wachsmuth, 462–466. "Man" refers to both genders,

male and female. The German use of "Mensch" makes this clear.

455 Steiner *Revelation*, from lectures September 5 to 22, 1924.

456 Steiner *Revelation*, 13, 21, 33, 104, 163, 175, 214, and 219.

457 Ibid., 15.

458 Steiner cited in Lindenberg *Biography*, 760.

459 Steiner *Revelation*, 31.

460 Bock cited in Lindenberg *Biography*, 760.

461 Steffen, Lindenberg *Biography*, 761. Also Bock, *A Man before Others*, 97.

462 Steiner *Revelation*, 40.

463 Ibid., 30–31.

464 Ibid., 9.

465 Ibid., 16.

466 Ibid., 146.

467 Sun at Antares in the center of Scorpio, at Steiner's Western Horizon Image, on December 2, 1923. Story from Christiane Marks's review in *The Rudolf Steiner Library Newsletter* (January 2006, #38), of *Friedrich Rittelmeyer: Sein Leben—Religiöse Erneuerung als Bruückenschlag*, by Gerhard Wehr (Urachlaus, 1998).

468 Lindenberg, 469–470; Wachsmuth, 422–425.

469 Margarita Voloschin, "A Painter's Conversations with Rudolf Steiner," in Belyi *Reminiscences*, 137.

470 Ibid.

471 Cited in Wilson *Steiner*, 81.

PART III: SOLVING THE PUZZLE OF A LIFE

1 Ita Wegman's death Sun occurred at 18–19 Aquarius. Bock's death Sun occurred just a few minutes over the line from 18–19 Scorpio into the next degree, exactly one degree from square to Steiner's conception Sun. As we have traced the birth and death dates of only a fraction of anthroposophists,

there may well be others who are related. In previous footnotes, we have also linked the theosophist, Annie Besant, with the Solar Cross of Steiner's death.

2   Goethe, *Essays on Art*, cited in Lowe *Goethe and Palladio*, 83.

3   Steffen *Meetings*, 165.

4   The lecture of 30 December, 1922, "The Spiritual Communion of Mankind," which can be found in *Man and the World of the Stars* (1963) states over and over again that these two initiatives are separate.

5   Further hints as to Steiner's personal relation to this stream, and how much he stood next to it, and how much stood within it, can be found in many places, notably a lecture from 27 September 1911, "Who was Christian Rosenkreutz?," Steiner *Secret Stream*, Chapter 7.

6   Described in great detail in our forthcoming book on Steiner's astro-biography.

7   The German words *Welten-Zeitenwende-Anfang* are in this order, which is more interesting than the more grammatically correct "Beginning of a Cosmic Turning Point of Time". Grosse *Christmas Foundation*, 12. This event appears in the forthcoming astro-biography of Steiner.

8   Jon Valentine version, op. cit., 126.

9   *Leading Thoughts*, 164. This was written during Saturn's last crossing of the death-Saturn position.

10 Another method for evaluating the time of death of Steiner, explored in the forthcoming astro-biography, concerns a detailed exploration of the positions of the planets at death in relation to the conception and birth.

11 The death picture of Steiner from one who attended the all-night vigil between his death and his funeral, Alfred Heidenreich, in the introduction to *Christianity as Mystical Fact* (1961 edition, op. cit.).

APPENDICES

1   Robert Powell, *Chronicle of the Living Christ: The Life and Ministry of Jesus Christ: Foundations of Cosmic Christianity* (Hudson, NY: Anthroposophic Press, 1996).

2   From Daniel Landinsky (editor and translator), *Love Poems from God* (New York: Penguin, 2002), 125.

3   For example, according to Anne Catherine Emmerich, many of the parables and stories mentioned only once in the gospels happened frequently. See Anne Catherine Emmerich, *The Life of Jesus Christ and Biblical Revelations* (four volumes, Rockford, Illinois: Tan Books, 1986, reissued 2004), Volume 4, 22.

4   op. cit.

5   Steiner *Mark*, 197.

6   ASOT, 61.

7   Marc Edmund Jones, *The Sabian Symbols in Astrology* (Santa Fe: Aurora, 1993, revised edition).

8   Powell's database on historical figures can be found in Peter Treadgold's *Astrofire* program, which also offers many good techniques for working with these data.

9   Thanks to the careful work of Megan Walrod in helping to create this database.

10 Works by Willi Sucher are available from the Astrosophy Research Center, P.O. Box 13, Meadow Vista, California 95722.

11 Two recent books from Temple Lodge discuss the two Jesus children in detail. Bernard Nesfield-Cookson, *The Mystery of the Two Jesus Children: And the Descent of the Spirit of the Sun* (Forest Row, England: Temple Lodge, 2005) and Gilbert Childs, *Secrets of Esoteric Christianity: The Two Marys, the Two Families of Jesus, and the Incarnation of Christ* (Forest Row, England: Temple Lodge, 2005). Also, Charles Tidball (with Robert Powell),

Jesus, Lazarus, and the Messiah (Great
Barrington, MA: SteinerBooks, 2005),
and Edward Reaugh Smith, *The
Incredible Births of Jesus* (Hudson, NY:
Anthroposophic Press, 1998). Edward
Reaugh Smith's longer exposition
comes in the exquisite *The Burning
Bush* (Hudson, NY: Anthroposophic
Press, 1997).

12 The same name has caused at least
one researcher to assume that Jesus
was Joshua, who lived many centuries
previously. However, the name Yeshua/
Joshua was not rare.

13 In *The Book with Fourteen Seals*, by
Andrew Welburn (Sussex: Rudolf
Steiner Press, 1991), Zarathustra
had thirteen incarnations to come
as Zoroaster, the fourteenth being as
Solomon Jesus.

14 Confirmed by ACE I 368.

15 *Beiträge zur Rudolf Steiner
Gesamtausgabe 49/50* (Dornach,
Easter, 1975), pp. 5 and 6, and Robert
Powell in *Hermetic Astrology* (Kinsau,
Germany: Hermetika, 1987), Volume
1, 288.

16 More about this process of rectification
of Steiner's birth chart can be read in
Powell's *Hermetic Astrology*, Volume 1,
288–292.